Tête-à-Tête

ALSO BY HAZEL ROWLEY

Richard Wright: The Life and Times

Christina Stead: A Biography

Tête-à-Tête

Simone de Beauvoir
and
Jean-Paul Sartre

HAZEL ROWLEY

HarperCollins*Publishers*

2231260

FIRST EDITION

Designed by Joseph Rutt

Printed on acid-free paper

Library of Congress Cataloging-in-Publication Data

Rowley, Hazel.
Tête-à-tête: Simone de Beauvoir and Jean-Paul Sartre / Hazel Rowley.—1st ed.
p. cm.
Includes bibliographical references and index.
ISBN-10 0-06-052059-0
ISBN-13 978-0-06-052059-5
1. Beauvoir, Simone de, 2. Sartre, Jean Paul 3. Authors, French—20th century—
Biography. 4. Philosophers—France—Biography. I. Title.
PQ2603.E362Z873 2005
840.9′00914—dc22
[B]   2005040232
05 06 07 08 09 NMSG/RRD 10 9 8 7 6 5 4 3 2 1

To my father, Derrick Rowley
(1922–2004)

CONTENTS

Preface   ix

ONE   Nineteen Twenty-Nine   I

TWO   The Pact   26
October 1929 – September 1932

THREE   Olga Kosakiewicz   48
October 1932 – April 1937

FOUR   The Prospect of War   71
May 1937 – September 1939

FIVE   War   96
September 1939 – March 1941

SIX   Occupied Paris   123
March 1941 – September 1944

SEVEN   Fame   147
November 1944 – January 1947

EIGHT   Wabansia Avenue, Jazz, and the Golden Zazou   173
January 1947 – Summer 1950

NINE   Crystal Blue Eyes   205
January 1951 – December 1954

TEN Exiles at Home 235
August 1955 – February 1962

ELEVEN White Nights, Vodka, and Tears 263
June 1962 – November 1966

TWELVE Tragic Endings, New Beginnings 296
November 1966 – May 1971

THIRTEEN The Farewell Ceremony 323
May 1971 – April 1986

Notes 355

Selected Bibliography 383

A Note on Sources 391

Acknowledgments 395

Index 399

Permissions 413

PREFACE

Like Abélard and Héloïse, they are buried in a joint grave, their names linked for eternity. They're one of the world's legendary couples. We can't think of one without thinking of the other: Simone de Beauvoir and Jean-Paul Sartre.

At the end of World War II, Sartre and Beauvoir quickly gained iconic stature as freethinking and engaged intellectuals. They wrote in a remarkable range of genres: plays, novels, philosophical essays, travel narratives, autobiography, memoir, biography, journalism. Sartre's first novel, *Nausea,* was a landmark in French contemporary fiction; his ten plays were the talk of the Paris theater season; his philosophical essays, *Being and Nothingness* and *The Critique of Dialectical Reason,* made an impact, and his massive biographical essays *Saint Genet* and *The Family Idiot: Gustave Flaubert, 1821–1857* were considered major works, but he is probably best remembered for his autobiographical narrative, *Words,* which won him the Nobel Prize. Beauvoir will always be associated with her groundbreaking feminist essay, *The Second Sex,* her novel *The Mandarins,* which so brilliantly evokes the postwar atmosphere in Europe, and her memoirs.

She would become one of the most famous memoirists of all time. Most of Beauvoir's writing in some way reflects her own life. In addition to four volumes of memoirs, she wrote a book about her travels in the United States (*America Day by Day*), a book about her trip to China (*The Long March*), a narrative about her mother's dying (*A Very Easy Death*), another about Sartre's final years (*Adieux: A Farewell to Sartre*), and two autobiographical novels, *She Came to Stay* and *The Mandarins.* In a sense, Beauvoir was not only Sartre's companion; she was also his biographer, his Boswell. In writing about her life, she also wrote about his. Sartre encouraged her. As existentialists, they believed that individuals are no more or less than the sum total of their actions, and offered themselves up willingly to the judgment of posterity.

They shared a thirst for the absolute. "Naturally one doesn't succeed in everything," Sartre said, "but one must want everything." Beauvoir's favorite of the 1968 student slogans was "Live with no time out." Both were lifelong rebels. As students, they could not have performed more brilliantly in the French educational system, and yet they turned their backs on academic rigidity and bourgeois niceties, and scorned anything that had the slightest whiff of staid conventionality.

We think of Sartre and Beauvoir and we think of freedom. "Man is constrained to be free," Sartre said. His philosophy of freedom was not ivory-tower theorizing. It was meant to be applied to life. As existentialists, he and Beauvoir refused any notion of "human nature." As philosophers, they challenged all social conventions. Nobody was going to tell them how to live their lives, not even their love life. They were conscious of "inventing" their relationship as they went along.

They rejected marriage. They never lived together. They openly had other lovers. They were often friends with each other's lovers; on occasion they shared them. Their original agreement (not conveyed to the third parties involved) was that whereas their other loves would be "secondary," theirs would be "absolute."

Sartre and Beauvoir spent their lives grappling with questions of ethics and morality. How were they to make the best use of their liberty? At first they were preoccupied with individual freedom. Later they were highly critical of this rather prolonged early period, which they looked back upon as their irresponsible youth. The Second World War made them conscious of history. In 1945, they established *Les Temps modernes*, a journal that would have a major impact on intellectual life in France, Europe, and even the third world. From that time on, they became public intellectuals who wrote "committed literature" and embraced political *engagement*.

They never forgot that they had choices to make, and that freedom comes with responsibility. They discussed these questions constantly.

Which of the possible actions before them would be most responsible? What would be the consequences of acting in this way rather
than that way? Sartre, in particular, a passionate advocate of world
peace and socialism, grappled with the big question of the day: communism. In the 1950s and 1960s, both took courageous stands
against the Algerian and Vietnam wars. Sartre's writings on colonialism and racism made him a spokesman for the anticolonial struggle.
With *The Second Sex,* Beauvoir wrote what is generally regarded as the
founding text of the modern women's movement.

Never for a second did Sartre and Beauvoir, in their relationship
with each other, stop living as writers. It was a total commitment,
every moment of the day. They promised to tell each other "everything," down to the smallest detail. Turning life into narrative was
perhaps their most voluptuous pleasure. As Roquentin reflects in
Sartre's novel *Nausea:* "For the most banal event to become an adventure, you must . . . begin to recount it." It was impossible to say which
was the more satisfying for Sartre and Beauvoir: the voyeuristic thrill
of hearing about each other's life or the cozy enjoyment of narrating
their own.

Both were heavily imbued with what Sartre called "the biographical illusion"—the idea that "a lived life can resemble a recounted life."
Already in their adolescence they dreamed of their future lives as if
through the eyes of posterity. "I . . . was extremely conscious of being
the young Sartre, in the same way that people speak of the young
Berlioz or the young Goethe," Sartre writes. Beauvoir imagined people poring over the narrative of her life, as she did with the lives of
Emily Brontë, George Eliot, and Katherine Mansfield. "I wanted
people to read my biography and find it touching and strange."

Along with their mythmaking impulse went a passionate belief in
truth-telling. To them, the notion of privacy was a relic of bourgeois
hypocrisy. Why keep secrets? As they saw it, their task as intellectuals
was to probe beneath the surfaces, plumb the depths of experience,
debunk myths, and communicate unvarnished truths to their readers.

They often said they would like the public to know the truth about
their personal lives. "It wouldn't occur to me to get rid of letters and
documents concerning my private life," Sartre said. "So much the better if this means I will be . . . transparent to posterity. . . . I think that

transparency should always be substituted for secrecy." Both remarked in interviews that they would have liked to have been more open about their own sexuality, and the only thing that held them back was that other people were involved.

When Beauvoir was seventy, the German feminist Alice Schwarzer asked her if there was anything she had not written in her memoirs that she would say now if she could write them again. "Yes," Beauvoir replied. "I would have liked to have given a frank and balanced account of my own sexuality. A truly sincere one, from a feminist point of view. I would like to tell women about my life in terms of my own sexuality because it is not just a personal matter but a political one too. I did not write about it at the time because I did not appreciate the importance of this question, nor the need for personal honesty. And I am very unlikely to write about it now because this kind of confession would not just affect me, it would also affect certain people who are very close to me."

There were omissions in Beauvoir's memoirs, but there was also a lot that she said—enough to excite generations of readers. From the time they started teaching, in the early 1930s, Sartre and Beauvoir were extremely conscious of being a model to young people. They liked teaching, and enjoyed influencing youthful minds. Their enduring friendships were always with much younger people. Both readily inspired "acolytes," as Sartre called them. This phenomenon hugely gained in momentum when Beauvoir's memoirs began to appear in 1958. In the sixties and seventies, those years of heady social experimentation, innumerable young people took Sartre and Beauvoir's open relationship as their model.

I did too. When I read Beauvoir's memoirs in the late sixties, I was exhilarated—intoxicated, one might say. She made the impossible seem possible. Didn't we all want an intellectual partner with whom we could share our work, ideas, and slightest thoughts? Didn't everyone want to write in Paris cafés amid the clatter of coffee cups and the hubbub of voices, and spend their summers in Rome in complicated but apparently harmonious foursomes? Who wanted monogamy when one could have freedom *and* stability, love affairs *and* commitment?

Everyone knew—Sartre said so in interviews, and Beauvoir said so in her memoirs—that their relationship with each other was superior to all the other relationships in their lives. Young women dreamed of having Beauvoir's audacity, courage, and liberty. When Geneviève Idt interviewed Sartre in 1974, she asked him if he was conscious of being "macho" in his relationships with women. There was a long pause, and his answer was considered: "I do not believe I was with the Beaver." (For him, Beauvoir was always "the Beaver.")

In November 1976, I interviewed Simone de Beauvoir in her apartment in the Rue Schoelcher, opposite the Montparnasse cemetery. I was a graduate student, writing a doctorate on "Simone de Beauvoir and Existentialist Autobiography," and deeply involved in the women's movement. Beauvoir had changed my life, and I worshipped her. I asked burning questions about her relationship with Sartre— about truth-telling, jealousy, third parties, and double standards for men and women. Beauvoir insisted there had been no jealousy between them, and as for double standards, she thought relationships between the sexes easier for women than for men because, given women's secondary status, men tended to feel guilty when they left them. She answered my questions as if by rote, without the slightest reflection or hesitation. By the time she ushered me out the door, I could see, and it saddened me, that she herself could not disentangle the reality of her life from the myth.

Already then existentialism had an old-fashioned ring to it. We had entered the postmodern era. It was modish to scorn the notion of individual responsibility. Now that the whole sordid truth about Stalin's crimes had emerged, the French "New Philosophers," as they were called, viewed Sartre's sympathy for communism during the cold war as the foolishness of a deluded Stalinist. And the so-called "radical feminists" were impatient with what they saw as Beauvoir's "male" values, and in particular her indulgence of that execrable male chauvinist Jean-Paul Sartre.

Sartre died in 1980; Beauvoir in 1986. They did not destroy their letters or journals, and they made it clear that they intended them to be published at some point after their deaths. The bulk of their correspondence to each other was published a few years later. Readers were left reeling with shock. It turned out that these two advocates of truth-telling constantly told lies to an array of emotionally unstable young girls. (Sartre called them "little fibs," "half-truths," and "total lies.") And here was Beauvoir, who throughout her life had publicly denied ever having had an affair with a woman, telling Sartre about her pleasurable nights making love with young women! We wondered, how could Sartre write so coldly and clinically about taking his latest girlfriend's virginity? And why were they both so disparaging about the young women they went to bed with? At the same time, they were more vulnerable than we had imagined. And their passion for sharing the tiniest details of their daily lives—the smell of the rain, the color of headlamps in the dark, a humorous conversation they overheard in a train—was frankly endearing.

In recent years, Sartre and Beauvoir have continued to divulge their tangled secrets from beyond their graves. Beauvoir's love letters to Nelson Algren, published in 1997, astonished readers. Her correspondence with Jacques-Laurent Bost, published in 2004, surprised people all over again. Was this feverish, ardent, sensuous woman the Simone de Beauvoir they thought they knew? If so, why on earth did she stick with Sartre? "How could she live with that bespectacled fellow, with his metallic procurer's voice, his creased blue suit, his obsession with crabs, homosexuals, tree roots, the slime of being, and the whole Heideggerian marmalade," one critic puzzled, "when she had such vitality, fire, wit, and freshness? What a mystery."[1]

Today the wheel has come full circle. After several decades in which Sartre and Beauvoir aroused little interest, particularly in France, there is a new recognition that they had the courage and daring to flout convention, they tried to live according to an ethic of freedom and responsibility, and they opened many doors. Maybe they strained at times against their own philosophy, but whatever their failures, few people have lived life more intensely. Who would have imagined that Bernard-Henri Lévy, France's most famous New Philosopher, would write a book, tantamount to a love letter, called *Sartre: The Philosopher of the Twentieth Century,* and that in it, he would defend Sartre's relationship with Beauvoir as one of the great love stories of all time?

I, too, felt a need to return to this past terrain. Like many others, I was once personally invested in the success or failure of the Sartre-Beauvoir relationship. Michel Contat, the well-known Sartre scholar, who writes that his personal life was much influenced by his existentialist mentors, describes the stakes Sartre-Beauvoir enthusiasts once faced: "If Beauvoir and Sartre succeeded, we were not wrong, and if we failed we could only blame our own deficiencies. But if they failed and hid their failure, they were fakers and imposters."[2]

With the distance of time, I am no longer concerned with Sartre and Beauvoir's success or failure. I am interested in the truth, and truth does not fit into categories. What we know about this relationship comes mostly from Beauvoir. I have always wondered: What did Sartre feel about it? How about their lovers and friends?

This is not a biography of Sartre and Beauvoir. I leave it to others to pay justice to their writing, politics, and the intricate details of their enormously rich lives. This is the story of a relationship. I wanted to portray these two people close up, in their most intimate moments. Whether or not we think it is one of the great love stories of all time, it is certainly a great *story*. Exactly what Sartre and Beauvoir always wanted their lives to be.

ONE

NINETEEN TWENTY-NINE

Jean-Paul Sartre had been interested in her for months. At twenty-one, she was the youngest of the Sorbonne students preparing that year for the *agrégation* in philosophy, the competitive national teacher's examination. She had given a talk in class on Leibniz, and Sartre was struck by her beauty and brilliance, her husky voice, and her rapid-fire speech.

His friend René Maheu had been courting her since the spring. Maheu was married, but he and Simone de Beauvoir seemed very taken with each other. They both went to the Bibliothèque Nationale, the National Library, to prepare for their exams, sat beside each other to work, and often had lunch together. Sartre had been hoping for an introduction, but Maheu guarded her fiercely. One afternoon, the two men had been strolling together in the Luxembourg Gardens when they saw Mademoiselle de Beauvoir across the pond. She was by herself, and it was obvious she had seen them, but Maheu chose to ignore her rather than present her to Sartre.

Early in May, she disappeared. A week or so later, Sartre and Maheu were sitting on a windowsill outside the lecture theater in one of the long, labyrinthine corridors of the Sorbonne when she appeared, wearing a black dress and little black hat swathed in crepe. Maheu went up to her, grasped her hand warmly, and asked why she was in mourning, but he did not introduce her to his friend.

Then Sartre took the initiative. During dull lectures, he and his friends entertained themselves by drawing humorous sketches in which they none too delicately expressed what they thought of certain philosophers and their philosophies. He picked out a particularly irreverent one, wrote on it, "To Mademoiselle Simone de Beauvoir, in memory of an explication of Leibniz," and asked Maheu to give it to her, which he did.

Sartre then made a suggestion to his two friends René Maheu and Paul Nizan. They were planning to prepare for the oral exams together. Simone de Beauvoir knew her Leibniz well and was clearly very bright; suppose they asked her to join them?

By mid-June, the written exams were over and there was only a month before the orals. Maheu was off to join his wife in Normandy for ten days. Sartre told him he would like to make the acquaintance of Mademoiselle de Beauvoir before they started working together as a group. He suggested a tearoom on the Rue de Médicis, across from the Luxembourg Gardens, five minutes from the Sorbonne. Maheu passed on the message but told Beauvoir he was afraid Sartre would take advantage of his absence to make off with her himself. "I don't want anyone to get in the way of my most precious feelings," Maheu said. He had talked about Sartre in glowing terms, but as far as women were concerned, he did not trust him an inch.

On the designated afternoon, Sartre waited in the tearoom, reading and smoking his pipe. He was taken aback when a fair-haired young woman walked up to him, introduced herself as Hélène de Beauvoir, and explained that her sister was unable to come. "How did you know I was Sartre?" he asked. Poupette, as everyone called her, looked sheepish. "Because . . . you are wearing glasses." Sartre pointed out that the man sitting in the other corner was also wearing glasses.

Sartre thought he knew why Simone de Beauvoir had not turned up, and he could guess how she had described him to her younger sister. He was right. Beauvoir had told Poupette that she would have no trouble recognizing Sartre. He was extremely short, he wore glasses, and he was "very ugly."[1]

Sartre was gallant, and took Poupette to see the new American film *A Girl in Every Port*. The conversation flagged. When she got home, Poupette told her sister that Jean-Paul Sartre was nothing like the lively dynamo Maheu had cracked him up to be.

This was not an auspicious beginning. Sartre could not stand being rejected by women. Throughout his life, he would never forgive his mother for betraying him, as he saw it, by marrying again, when he was eleven. Then there was that traumatic episode in La Rochelle, when he was twelve.

His father, Jean-Baptiste Sartre, had died when Jean-Paul was fifteen months old. Twenty-four-year-old Anne-Marie bundled up her little "Poulou" and went to live with her parents in Paris.² She belonged to the dynasty of Schweitzers, a Protestant family from Alsace (the famous Albert Schweitzer was her cousin), and like all the Schweitzers, Anne-Marie was tall and slim. Physically, Poulou would take after his diminutive father. And when he was two, he went almost blind in his right eye.

Poulou was the little prince in his grandparents' house, doted on and idolized by his mother, grandmother, and grandfather. In that patriarchal household—dominated by the lanky, bearded, and imperious Charles Schweitzer—Anne-Marie felt to Poulou like an older sister. She was financially dependent on her parents, and they condescended to her. There were three bedrooms in the house: the grandfather's, the grandmother's, and the one they called "the children's," which Anne-Marie shared with her son.

Anne-Marie gave Poulou her undivided attention. They told each other their troubles. She read to him. She played the piano for him. On rainy Sundays they would earnestly debate whether to go to the circus, a museum, or a movie. Charles Schweitzer would appear at the door of his book-lined study. "Where are you children off to?" he would ask. It was usually the movies.

"All I wanted to see was Anne-Marie, the young girl of my mornings," Sartre would write in his autobiography, *Words*. "All I wanted to hear was her voice."

She used to call me her attendant knight and her little man; I told her everything. More than everything. . . . I described what

I saw . . . I gave myself feelings for the pleasure of sharing them with her. . . . We had our myths, our habits of speech, and our ritual jokes. . . . I used to trot along looking tough, my hand in my mother's, confident that I could protect her.

When he grew up, Sartre intended to marry Anne-Marie. Then, in 1916, when he was eleven, she married again. For Sartre, this was a catastrophe. It broke his heart. The stranger who stole his mother was Joseph Mancy, a naval engineer. Until the day he died, Sartre would always hate his "Uncle Jo."

The following year, when Sartre was twelve, the awkward trio moved to La Rochelle, a small port town on the Atlantic coast. Sartre detested the place. His new classmates were the sons and daughters of local fishermen and oyster farmers. They did not like him—a prissy Parisian with a walleye and a funny way of speaking—and they did not hesitate to beat him up. It did not take Sartre long to become a tough little hoodlum himself.

In a bid for popularity, he stole money from his mother's handbag to treat the other kids to cakes from the local pastry shop. The provincial boys all seemed to have girlfriends, and Sartre told tall stories about his girl, back in Paris, with whom he had gone to a hotel and made love. They did not believe him. At school in La Rochelle, he picked out a pretty blond girl, the daughter of a ship chandler, and boasted about her to his classmates. They warned her of Sartre's interest.

Sartre never forgot that afternoon. He found the girl, Lisette, standing with a group of her friends. He was on his bicycle. Not sure what to say, he rode in circles around the group. Finally, she said: "Have you finished, you cross-eyed old fool, with your glasses and big hat?"[3] Her friends jeered.

The realization that he was ugly hit Sartre like a stone from a catapult. His adolescence was tormented by it. At the end of his teens, he made a decision. He told a girlfriend, Simone Jollivet, "Until last year I was very melancholy because I was ugly and that made me suffer. I have absolutely rid myself of that, because it's a weakness. Whoever knows his own strength must be joyful." He added, "I call that state moral health, because it is exactly like when one is in excellent physical health, one feels strong enough to bend lampposts with a single hand."[4]

Sartre, the future existentialist, had made a fundamental existential choice. If he could not seduce women by means of his physical assets, he would seduce them with words—*les mots.*

At sixteen, Sartre was sent back to Paris to his old school, the prestigious Lycée Henri IV, this time as a boarder. Among his classmates was Paul Nizan, equally talented and ambitious, and equally set on becoming a writer. For the next few years, Sartre and Nizan became inseparable friends.

As schoolboys, the young Sartre and Nizan took themselves for supermen. Convinced they were far superior to the common herd, they would strut around Paris for hours at a time, imitating their literary heroes, acting out roles, inventing a private language. Sartre gorged himself on adventure stories; Nizan introduced him to contemporary literature. They read each other's writing, and discussed narrative technique.

From Henri IV, Sartre and Nizan went to the equally prestigious Lycée Louis-le-Grand, for two years of hard cramming in preparation for the competitive entrance examination to the most elite all-male institution in the nation. Two years later, they moved together to the Ecole Normale Supérieure in the Rue d'Ulm, near the Pantheon, where they shared a study.

They were so often together that people mixed them up, though their only common physical attribute was a squint. Nizan's eyes rotated inward; Sartre's roamed outward. Whereas Sartre's wandering eyes were intensely disconcerting, Nizan's cross-eyed look was quite appealing. Sartre was stocky, and at 158 centimeters (five foot one), he was cruelly short. His skin was pale and dull, with pockmarks and blackheads, and he looked as if he needed a bath and a good sleep. Nizan, dark and handsome, dressed with a dandy's elegance and sometimes appeared at lectures in plus fours, dangling a monocle or twirling a malacca cane. Sartre greatly admired his friend's costumes, but did not try to compete.

By their early twenties, their temperaments were pulling the two friends apart. Sartre was in his element during the four years he spent at the Ecole Normale. He reveled in his newfound independence and enjoyed the security of an easygoing, elitist male community, in which he shone. He threw water bombs on friends in evening attire; he wrote a highly obscene sketch for the school's annual review, in which he acted the part of the school principal. The other *normaliens* would hear him singing in his fine tenor voice as he dashed between lectures, and playing the piano evenings in the common room. He once stepped into the middle of a fight because he saw an acquaintance, Maurice Merleau-Ponty, being picked on. And yet he was one of the leaders when it came to hazing, the semi-sadistic initiation rituals to which new recruits were subjected.[5]

Nizan, on the other hand, was profoundly unhappy in that environment. In his autobiographical narrative *Aden Arabie* (published in 1931, when he was twenty-six), Nizan, by then a Marxist, was scathing about the Ecole Normale, that "laughable and odious" institution with the esprit de corps of seminaries and regiments, where adolescents, tired after years of cramming for competitions, were taught vapid sophisms by stuffy professors who lived in the affluent western districts of Paris.[6]

Nizan had always been prone to melancholy, and at the Ecole Normale his moods grew darker. In one of the most tender and penetrating portraits Sartre would ever write, his foreword to the 1960 reprinting of *Aden Arabie* (Nizan was killed in battle in 1940), he was harshly critical of his own inability to understand the depths of Nizan's anguish. As a student, he preferred to see Nizan's rage and despair as emotional extravagance—an affectation, such as his wearing a monocle.

> My anger was only a bar of soap, his was real. . . . His words of hate were pure gold, mine were counterfeit. . . . We had superficial melancholies in common. . . . For the rest, I tried to impose my optimism upon him. I repeated to him that we were free. He didn't answer, but the slight smile at the corner of his mouth said a great deal about this idea.

In their shared study, whole days would pass when Nizan did not speak to his companion. Sartre was hurt. And when Nizan took a year's leave from the overheated atmosphere of the Normale and caught a boat to Aden, in Yemen, Sartre felt as if he'd been jilted.

Almost a year later, Sartre was alone in his study one evening, moping over a girlfriend, when Nizan burst in without knocking. Sartre was overjoyed. The two went out drinking. It was like old times. Over brimming beers, they again put the world on trial. Sartre thought they had taken up their friendship where they left off. But Nizan did not return to board at the Ecole Normale. Instead, he moved in with his fiancée's family, in Montparnasse. A few months later, he got married. Sartre was appalled. "I had made of bachelorhood a moral precept, a rule of life—thus it couldn't be otherwise for Nizan."[7]

Sartre was known for his brilliance, and was expected to come first in the *agrégation*. In June 1928, to everyone's astonishment, he failed the written exams. That was why he was sitting them again a year later, in the summer of 1929, at the same time as Paul Nizan, who had lost a year by going to Aden, and as Simone de Beauvoir, who had gained a year by taking her teacher's diploma at the same time, giving herself a double load.

Beauvoir had heard considerable gossip about Sartre and Nizan, those godless young men who mocked bourgeois hypocrisies and Catholic sanctities and only bothered to drop in on certain lectures. Around Sartre, in particular, there swirled rumors of drunken binges and visits to brothels. The third member of their trio, René Maheu, did not share their legendary reputation. Although he, too, held himself aloof from most of his fellow students, Maheu was slightly less intimidating.

In January 1929, Maheu had given a talk in class that provoked an animated discussion. Beauvoir was charmed by Maheu's slightly mocking voice, his "broad, liquid smile," and the "ironical twist he gave to his mouth."[8] Despite his well-cut suits, his ruddy complexion and blond hair lent him the air of a country boy. She wished she could get to know him.

One morning in spring, Beauvoir looked up from her books at the Bibliothèque Nationale and saw Maheu walk in. She watched him take off his blue overcoat and scarf and sit down to work. At lunchtime she saw him get up, leaving his books behind. Normally, she ate a sandwich in the gardens of the Palais Royal. That day, she went to the library café. Maheu flashed her a smile and cleared a place for her at his table as if they had arranged to meet. They talked about Hume and Kant.

After that, whenever he came to the library, Maheu would greet her warmly. Before the Easter break, he came and sat next to her in one of Leon Brunschvicg's lectures. (Sartre and Nizan boycotted these.) After Easter, when lectures resumed, he sat next to her again. He told her he was "an individualist." So was she, she said. He stared at her. "What? You!" He had been convinced that she was a good Catholic, devoted to good works. Not at all, she assured him.[9]

"Meeting with René Maheu, or with myself?" Beauvoir wrote in her journal that evening. "Who else has ever made such a strong impression on me? Why am I overwhelmed by this meeting, as if something had *really* happened to me at last?"[10]

She started to save the seat next to hers in the library. Maheu turned up most days. For weeks, he called her "Mademoiselle," in that slightly ironic voice of his. One day, he reached across, took her notebook, and wrote on the cover in large capital letters: BEAUVOIR = BEAVER. Her name resembled the English word, and she also worked like a beaver. From that day on, he called her Beaver, *le Castor*.

He told her about the "little comrades," as they called themselves. He had met them at the Lycée Louis-le-Grand, when he first came to Paris from the provinces, at the age of eighteen. They were now twenty-four. Maheu was "the Lama," Nizan "the Grand Duke," Sartre "the Little Man."[11] Maheu admired his two friends with a passion, especially Sartre, whom he thought a genius. But Sartre was very different from him, he explained. Sartre belonged to the Parisian bourgeoisie; Maheu felt like an upstart in that milieu. Maheu liked to enjoy life; Sartre never for a second stopped analyzing. Maheu liked the countryside and fresh air; Sartre didn't give a damn about such things.

There was something princely about Maheu. He reminded Beauvoir of Jacques, the cousin she had been in love with throughout her adolescence. They were both graceful, boyish characters, who often smiled in place of speaking. Both valued beauty—in art, nature, and people. To her, they were artists, poets.

Beauvoir's friendships had always been exceptionally formal. Even with her bosom friend, Zaza, whom she had known since the age of ten, she used the formal *vous* rather than the informal *tu*. (Zaza used *tu* with all her other friends.) And when they met or said good-bye, they shook hands. There was only one person who ever hugged or kissed Simone, and that was her exuberant Polish friend Stépha, who was extroverted and unrestrained to a point that left Simone a little dizzy.

Maheu made Beauvoir conscious of her body in a way she had never been before. He would put his hand on her arm and wag his finger in her face mockingly. He commented on her appearance, her clothes, her husky voice. He found it very appealing, he assured her. Beauvoir had never thought about her voice before.

She was equally conscious of Maheu as a physical presence. "I would watch him come striding through the gardens with his rather awkward grace; I would look at his ears, transparent in the sun as pink sugar-candy, and I knew that I had beside me not an angel, but a real man," she would write in her memoirs. His laugh was irresistible. "When he gave vent to his laughter, it was as if he had just unexpectedly dropped in on a strange planet and was making a rapturous discovery of its prodigious comicality."[12]

In the three weeks running up to the written examinations, they saw each other almost every day. On the rare occasions when Maheu did not work in the library, he would turn up at the end of the afternoon and invite her for tea or coffee.

Beauvoir was enchanted by their conversations. Maheu knew a lot about history and myth—more, she thought privately, than about philosophy—and had a wonderfully entertaining way of bringing the past to life. "My greatest happiness is Maheu," she wrote in her journal.[13]

He was also her greatest source of anguish. When they said good-bye at the end of the day, she felt sad. He was going home to his wife. He rarely talked about his personal life, but he had told her that Inès was five years older than he, and represented all the mysteries and paradoxes of femininity. He loved her. She was beautiful. She came from the Catholic nobility.

There were times when Beauvoir found Maheu disappointingly

conventional, particularly when it came to women. He admitted that bright women brought out a certain resistance in him. When Beauvoir told him about her tormented relationship with her cousin Jacques, Maheu said he thought she should marry Jacques. Society did not respect unmarried women. Beauvoir lent Maheu a recent English novel she had enjoyed, *The Green Hat,* by Michael Arlen. She admired its independent heroine, Iris Storm. Maheu did not. "I have no liking for women of easy virtue," he told her. "Much as I like a woman to please me, I find it impossible to respect any woman I've had." Beauvoir was indignant. "One does not *have* an Iris Storm!"[14]

The written exams were held in the middle of June. Beauvoir and Maheu walked into the library of the Sorbonne together. "Good luck, Beaver," he said to her gently. They found their seats. Beauvoir placed a thermos of coffee and a box of biscuits by the side of her desk. The topic was announced: "Liberty and Contingency." She gazed a while at the ceiling, and soon her pen was flying across the page. When they came out, she looked for Maheu, but he had disappeared.

The exams continued for several days. After the last one, Maheu called around at the Beauvoir family apartment, on the Rue de Rennes, and invited Simone for lunch. He was about to join his wife in Normandy, he told her, but when he got back, the little comrades were going to prepare for the orals together. Would she like to join them?

When he failed his *agrégation* the previous year, Sartre had been obliged to move out of his room at the Ecole Normale. He was now living in one of the student residences at the Cité Universitaire, on the southern edge of the city. On Monday July 8, 1929, Maheu turned up in the morning, as arranged, with Mademoiselle de Beauvoir. Sartre opened the door and greeted her politely, his pipe in his mouth. Paul Nizan looked at her dubiously through his tortoiseshell glasses.

Beauvoir was taken aback by the filth of Sartre's tiny student room. There were cigarette butts on the floor, and the air was thick with stale body odor and tobacco fumes. Books and papers were piled everywhere, and satirical sketches were stuck on the walls. They brought in a second chair for Beauvoir. The others took turns on Sartre's chair, desk, and narrow bed. Beauvoir, who had prepared for this all weekend, gave a close reading of Leibniz's *Discourse on Metaphysics,* feeling as nervous as if she were taking the actual oral exam.

At the end of the day, the men decided that Beauvoir needed a nickname. They teased her with various possibilities. Sartre wanted to call her Valkyrie. To him, she was like a Viking virgin warrior goddess. No, said Maheu. She was Beaver, *le Castor.* They clenched their fists about her head. It was official.

They devoted two days to Leibniz, and decided that was enough; then Sartre set about explaining Rousseau's *Social Contract.* Beauvoir proved by far the best at finding the flaws in Sartre's arguments. Nizan frowned and chewed his nails. Maheu looked at Beauvoir with frank admiration. Sartre accused her of making him trot out everything he knew. But Sartre clearly loved imparting his knowledge, and did so with passion. He knew how to untangle complicated ideas and make them comprehensible and exciting. And while he did so, he had the other three in fits of delighted laughter. "More and more, his mind seems to me quite extraordinarily powerful," Beauvoir wrote in her journal. "I admire him and also feel huge gratitude for the way he gives himself so generously."

The men did not hold themselves back in Beauvoir's presence, and Beauvoir was often shocked by the things they said. But she had been rebelling for years against the stiflingly conventional world in which she had been brought up. Their defiance was a tonic.

Their language was aggressive, their thought categorical, their judgments merciless. They made fun of bourgeois law and order; they had refused to sit the examination in religious knowledge.... On every possible occasion—in their speech, their attitudes, their gestures, their jokes—they set out to prove that men were not rarefied spirits but bodies of flesh and bone, racked by physical needs and crudely engaged in a brutal adventure that was life.... I soon understood that if the world these new friends opened up to me seemed crude, it was because they didn't try to disguise its realities; in the end, all they asked of me was that I should dare to do what I had always longed to do: look reality in the face.[15]

Beauvoir had never imagined that fierce intelligence could go along with such a sense of fun. When they stopped work, the men started singing, joking, and acting out different characters. Sartre put a jazz record on his gramophone, then they strolled over to the fun fair at the Porte d'Orléans and tried out the shooting gallery. Whenever Sartre scored a prize—an ugly bit of crockery or a dime novel—he gallantly handed it to Beauvoir.

On Wednesday afternoon the group gave themselves what they called "a very big recreation," at the Café Dupont, in the sleazy Pigalle district of Montmartre. The men drank beer; Beauvoir drank lemonade. She got into a fierce discussion with Sartre, and realized she was arguing with him for the sheer fun of it.

Sartre and Nizan started to plan the group's evening. Maheu cut the discussion short. He was taking the Beaver to the cinema, he said. "Fine, fine," said Nizan. "So be it," said Sartre.

On the bus ride back home that evening, Maheu told Beauvoir: "I'm happy you get on with the little comrades, but . . ."

"But you're the Lama, I know."

"You won't ever be one of the little comrades."

"Of course. I'm your Beaver."[16]

On Thursday morning, Nizan turned up with his wife, Henriette. To Beauvoir's dismay, this meant they did not work. Instead, they squeezed themselves into Nizan's car and went for a drive around Paris, stopping in a bar for a coffee and a game of Japanese billiards. The women did not warm to each other. Henriette Nizan thought that Beauvoir dressed atrociously, and seemed pathetically eager to copy the men—smoking, drinking, even adopting their private language.[17] For her part, Beauvoir had little interest in Henriette's worries about her new baby. She scrawled in her journal: "I spoke to her about her daughter with an air of sympathy, which apparently made her like me, and which amused Sartre and Maheu, who saw it as proof that I am feminine after all."

At lunch Beauvoir joined the men in a glass of beer. The Nizans dropped them back at Sartre's student residence and went home to Montparnasse. Beauvoir, Sartre, and Maheu settled down to work. It was hot. Sartre drew the curtains to keep out the sun. Maheu sprawled on the bed, handsome in his shirtsleeves. Sartre puffed at his pipe. For Beauvoir, in that semi-obscure retreat from the world, time seemed to melt away. She was at her brilliant best that afternoon, and she knew it. "I felt unleashed," she wrote in her journal.

At 8 P.M., she hurried off to the Bois de Boulogne where she was meeting other friends—a more conservative group of philosophers who were still practicing Catholics. Among those rowing on the lake that evening was Maurice Merleau-Ponty. It was Beauvoir who had introduced Maurice to Zaza, and that magical summer, while so much was going on in Beauvoir's own life, Maurice and Zaza were falling in love. But Zaza had been forbidden to join them that evening. Her family did not approve.

Zaza Lacoin, the third of ten children, came from a well-to-do, devoutly Catholic family. She and Simone had been best friends since the age of ten, when they rivaled each other as star pupils at the Cours Adeline Désir, a private Catholic girls' school in Saint-Germain-des-Prés, which placed far less emphasis on education than on prayer, the catechism, piety, and deportment. The girls were taught the piano, knitting, crochet, and etiquette at tea parties.

Monsieur de Beauvoir, an atheist, had wanted to move his two daughters to a secular school, which would have given them a better education without his having to pay fees, but Simone would not contemplate leaving her friend behind. She idolized Zaza. Whereas she herself was timid, childish, and in every way the model obedient pupil, the dark-haired Zaza was precocious and rebellious. Beauvoir would never forget the school musical recital at which Zaza, a talented pianist, played a piece her mother had insisted would be too difficult for her. When she finished a perfect performance, the triumphant Zaza, in front of all the teachers and parents, stuck her tongue out at her mother. Madame Lacoin merely smiled.

But when her daughters reached a marriageable age, Madame Lacoin turned into a tyrant. She had significant social aspirations for her daughters; nothing was more important than a good marriage. Before Zaza was allowed so much as to play a game of tennis with a group of young people, her mother needed to know that they came from good Catholic families.

The Beauvoir girls could not aspire to a bourgeois marriage, because they did not have a dowry. Their marriage prospects had plummeted in 1918, when the Bolsheviks overthrew the Czar in a dramatic revolution that rendered Georges de Beauvoir's Russian railway and mining stocks worthless. Most of his inheritance had been invested in these, and after the war he no longer had the capital to open his law practice again. For the rest of his life he drifted from one salesman position to another. The family struggled to keep up appearances, but Georges would tell his daughters bitterly, "You girls will never marry. You'll have to work for a living."

Looking back later in life, Beauvoir thought it the best thing that could have happened to her. When she left school, she decided to take the *agrégation,* which would mean a secure job as a secondary-school teacher in a state school. She wanted to study philosophy. The nuns at the Cours Désir were appalled. "To them a state school was nothing better than a licensed brothel," Beauvoir writes. "They told my mother that the study of philosophy mortally corrupts the soul."[18] She agreed to study classics and mathematics instead, at an all-female Catholic institution on the outskirts of Paris. Not for another year did her parents consent to let her study philosophy at the Sorbonne.

Zaza's parents would not let Zaza near the Sorbonne. They belonged to the traditional French Catholic bourgeoisie, who distrusted intellectuals, especially philosophers. They considered the classics, Greek and Latin, to be full of crudities. As for modern literature, they dreaded to think what effect it might have upon a young girl's imagination. While Beauvoir was studying Greek, Latin, philosophy, and pedagogy, Zaza's life became an endless round of church-going, tea parties, bridge games, picnics, and social visits. She had no illusions about the emptiness of her existence. She complained to Beauvoir that she could not sleep, and she suffered from frequent headaches.

Despite the differences between their families, the girls' friendship endured. A turning point came when Simone, at the age of nineteen, finally admitted to Zaza that she no longer believed in God. Zaza prayed for her soul, but remained loyal to her friend in the face of intense opposition from her mother. By the summer of 1929—Zaza and Simone were twenty-one—the situation had reached a crisis point. Madame Lacoin would no longer allow the godless Simone in their house. Nor would she allow Zaza to go boating in the Bois de Boulogne with Simone and her freethinking philosopher friends from the Sorbonne.

Sartre and Beauvoir were among seventy-six students across the nation who sat the highly competitive written *agrégation* examinations in philosophy in 1929. Passing the *agrégation* guaranteed lifelong tenure as a secondary-school teacher in France's state school system, and the number of successful candidates was determined by the posts available in the nation's high schools. Philosophy had a long and venerable tradition in France, and attracted the best and the brightest.

The results were displayed on the afternoon of July 17, an oppressively hot day in Paris. Twenty-six candidates had been successful, six of them women. This group was now eligible to proceed to the orals. Sartre, Beauvoir, and Nizan were among them. Maheu was not.

Maheu left Paris that same afternoon, telling Sartre to give Beauvoir his best wishes for her happiness. That evening Jean-Paul Sartre took Beauvoir out to celebrate their success. "From now on, I'm going to take you in hand," he said.

It was scarcely an atmosphere conducive to romance. The orals were famous for being extremely grueling. They involved four separate tests in front of a six-man jury. The hardest was *la grande leçon,* in which candidates pulled a topic out of a hat and were given five hours in the Sorbonne library to prepare a class lesson at the tertiary level. In addition, there were three close readings of texts, in Greek, Latin, and French, for which the students were given only an hour to prepare. The orals were public events. The best students, like Sartre and Beauvoir, had a large audience.

For those two weeks, while they prepared for their orals, Sartre

and Beauvoir barely left each other's company other than to sleep.
They went along to hear their friends perform. Between sessions,
they continued their own preparations—sometimes with Nizan, in
his study in the Rue Vavin, under his large poster of Lenin. But
mostly they preferred to be alone together.

They talked in bars and cafés that had always been out of bounds
for Beauvoir. She had only ever gone to the cinema to see serious art
films; Sartre now took her along to cowboy movies. They walked in
the Luxembourg Gardens, and strolled past the secondhand-book
stalls along the banks of the Seine, where Sartre bought her some of
the swashbuckling cloak-and-dagger historical novels he had loved as
an adolescent. "He was interested in everything and never took anything for granted," Beauvoir wrote later. "How cramped my little
world seemed beside this exuberantly abundant universe!"[19]

People tend to assume that it was Jean-Paul Sartre who transformed
Simone de Beauvoir from a dutiful daughter of the French bourgeoisie into the independent freethinker who did more than any
woman in twentieth-century France to shock that bourgeoisie. It was
not so. Sartre merely encouraged Beauvoir to continue down the path
on which she had already embarked. Even Zaza, who thoroughly disliked the "frightful, learned Sartre," had to admit that Simone had
chosen this route of her own accord. "The influence of Sartre might
have hurried things along a bit; that's all," she mused in her journal in
July 1929.[20]

Beauvoir also kept a journal, and those square-ruled notebooks,
written in her scarcely legible, forward-thrusting hand, reveal a young
woman who was prepared to go out on a limb long before she met
Sartre. Already at fifteen—the same age she set her heart on becoming a writer—she had realized she no longer believed in God. For a
long time she told no one. When she admitted her dark secret, at the
age of nineteen, it caused a major rupture between her and her
mother.

At nineteen, inspired by the French writers André Gide, Maurice
Barrès, Paul Valéry, and Paul Claudel—men who were now middle-
aged, but who, like her, came from the bourgeoisie and were also in

revolt against its hypocrisy—Simone de Beauvoir embraced "sincerity toward oneself" and the commitment to "calling a spade a spade."[21] She was already questioning marriage on ethical grounds. "For me a choice is never made, it is always being made. . . . The horror of the definitive choice, is that it engages not only the self of today, but that of tomorrow which is why basically marriage is immoral."[22]

By the age of twenty, Simone de Beauvoir had chosen a path that she increasingly realized would condemn her to loneliness. "I can't get rid of this idea that I am alone, in a world apart, being present at the other as at a spectacle," she wrote in her journal. "This morning . . . I passionately wished to be the girl who takes communion at morning mass and walks in a serene certainty. . . . The Catholicism of Mauriac, of Claudel, . . . how it's marked me, and what place there is in me for it! And yet . . . I do not wish to believe: an act of faith is the most despairing act there is and I want my despair to at least keep its lucidity. I do not want to lie to myself."

Beauvoir came from a world in which women were extraordinarily sheltered and constricted. As she would show in *Memoirs of a Dutiful Daughter,* men and women inhabited sharply divided worlds. Women could not vote. France's best educational institutions were for men only.[23] Women were expected to go to church; men could be atheists. Not only did women never go in bars, they did not even venture into cafés. (When Beauvoir set foot in a café for the first time in her life, at the age of twenty, she considered herself wildly rebellious.) Men drank and smoked in public; women did not. Women remained virgins until marriage; men did not. Unmarried women were pitied. And even if a young woman was beautiful and cultivated, the only way she could aspire to a socially desirable marriage was by means of a substantial dowry.

There were times when Beauvoir called her solitary rebellion "an intoxication." And yet she was aware that she was going to need extraordinary strength. "I would so like to have the right, me as well, of being simple and very weak, of being a woman," she confided to her journal. "In what a 'desert world' I walk, so arid, with the only oases my intermittent esteem for myself."

She sensed that for women love came at a cost, and that there was part of her that no man was ever likely to accept. "I speak mystically of love, I know the price," she wrote. "I am too intelligent, too demanding, and too resourceful for anyone to be able to take charge of me entirely. No one knows me or loves me completely. I have only myself."

The stakes were different for Sartre, as a male. He could indulge his romantic concept of love without risking his subjecthood. He dreamed of moonlit walks and tender talks on a park bench by the seaside. His fantasy was that he would take charge of a beautiful young woman, protect her, save her. He liked sentimentality, adoration, whispered sweet nothings. It reminded him of his doting childhood relationship with his mother. Even now, Anne-Marie still called him Poulou.

As a man, his sex life could be nearly separated off from his dreams of love. Sartre lost his virginity at eighteen, with a married woman who was thirty. She took the initiative. ("I did it with no great enthusiasm," Sartre said later, "because she wasn't very pretty.") After that there were prostitutes picked up in the Luxembourg Gardens. In his Ecole Normale years, Sartre and his friends regularly visited brothels. They felt contempt for these women. "We felt that a girl shouldn't give herself like that."[24]

When Sartre was twenty-one, he courted a young woman who lived in Lyon. Their romance was nourished by long narcissistic letters. "I love you to the point of madness," Germaine Marron wrote to him. "You find me simple, without affectations, which is true, but in fine Lyonnaise society I give the impression of a wild animal."[25] They became engaged. At twenty-three, Sartre, as a good bourgeois son, asked his mother and stepfather to formally request the girl's hand in marriage.

When Sartre failed his *agrégation* in the summer of 1928, the Marron family called off the engagement. "Instead of joining my friends at tennis I went by myself to a meadow with a bottle, and I drank," Sartre recalls. "I even cried. Cried because I had drunk, but it felt good.... I was relieved. I'm not sure of having acted quite correctly in this whole affair."[26]

Behind his fiancée's back, Sartre had enjoyed a tempestuous liaison with Simone Jollivet, a theatrical blonde who since the age of eighteen had worked as a courtesan in a fashionable brothel in Toulouse. Her clients would find her standing in front of the fireplace reading—entirely naked except for her Rapunzel-like hair. "Her cultured mind, her proud bearing, and the subtle technique she brought to her task knocked town clerks and lawyers flat," Beauvoir wryly reports in her memoirs.[27]

Jollivet was three years older than Sartre and had grand ambitions to be a writer. Sartre drew her up a reading list, encouraged her, lectured her. He saw his role as preventing her from botching her life. She risked being nothing other than a dreaming Madame Bovary; he would make her into an artist. She complained that his letters were "little lectures."[28] He wrote back: "Who has made you what you are? Who is trying to keep you from turning into a bourgeoise, an aesthete, a whore? Who has taken charge of your intelligence? I alone."[29]

Sartre took her along to the Ecole Normale ball one year. He appeared in spats, with Simone Jollivet on his arm in one of her sensational costumes. She created quite a stir. As a token of friendship, she gave Sartre and Nizan a lamp shade for their study, made out of a pair of skimpy lace purple panties—her own.

The *agrégation* results were displayed on July 30, 1929. Twenty-one students had competed for the orals (several of the eligible students had not turned up), and thirteen were successful. First place went to Jean-Paul Sartre. The runner-up, just two points behind him, was Simone de Beauvoir. There was a considerable gap between her and the third student. Paul Nizan came fifth.

Four of the thirteen successful candidates were women. It was a record. There were only eight women in France with an *agrégation* in philosophy. The head of the jury of examiners, Professor André Lalande, felt obliged to comment on the phenomenon. There had been no special indulgence shown to the women, he assured people. The written exams were anonymous, and it was impossible, he said, to determine the sex of educated people from their handwriting.[30]

The most staggering intellectual triumph that year was undoubtedly Simone de Beauvoir's. Having taken on a daunting double load, she was, at twenty-one, the youngest ever to pass the *agrégation*. She had been studying philosophy at a tertiary level for just three years. Sartre had been taking it for seven.[31] Unlike him, she had not had the rigorous intellectual training of two years of preparatory classes (*hypokhâgne* and *khâgne*) for the entrance exam to the Ecole Normale Supérieure, followed by the ENS itself. She was just a lowly Sorbonne student. Nor had she had a practice run at the exams.

It would emerge in later years that the 1929 jury had debated at length whether to give the prize to Sartre or to Beauvoir. The members had been inordinately impressed by the young woman's rigorous argumentation. Finally, they had decided on Sartre. He was, after all, the *Normalien,* and he was sitting the examination for the second time.

On August 5, 1929, Simone de Beauvoir left with her family for their annual vacation in Limousin. She loved that region of France. Her childhood summers spent with her father's family on the vast estate called Meyrignac, in the hilly countryside near Uzerche, were idyllic. That summer her grandfather was no longer there—it was his death she had been mourning that spring—and they stayed with her aunt and cousins in the second family house, La Grillère, four kilometers away from the village of Saint-Germain-les-Belles. Beauvoir knew it would probably be her last summer vacation with her family. The thought had once filled her with anguish. But this year, her future seemed wholly exciting.

She wandered in the fields and chestnut groves, breathing in the fragrance of freshly mown hay and honeysuckle, and feeling passionately happy. On the second day, a letter arrived from Sartre. Beauvoir wrote in her journal that she missed his presence. She had so many things she wanted to tell him. But she was not in love. "I need Sartre, and I love Maheu. I love Sartre for what he brings me, and Maheu for what he is."

When she did not hear from Sartre for several days, she was filled with anguish. "Why this silence, just after a letter where I let myself go?" Finally a thick envelope arrived, which gave details about his imminent visit.

She met his train from Paris on August 20. "Immense joy," she wrote, "and some timidity which made me artificial." The prospect of entertaining him in Limousin was daunting. Would he be bored away from Paris? On the first day, she suggested a walk. Sartre laughed at her. He was allergic to chlorophyll, he said, and the only way he could cope with it was to forget it. They would find a nice meadow and sit and talk. By the end of that day, Beauvoir could see that boredom would never be their problem. "I realized that even if we went on talking till Judgment Day, I would still find the time all too short."[32]

Sartre stayed at the Hôtel de la Boule d'Or in Saint-Germain-les-Belles, the village where Beauvoir's cousins went to mass each Sunday. Beauvoir would wake up at seven o'clock, remain awhile in bed, exhilarated by the thought of seeing him, then run over the meadows to meet him, thinking about all the things she wanted to tell him that day. If she was expected home for lunch, she took cider, cheese, and gingerbread for him to eat while waiting for her in the meadow. Sometimes, Poupette and their cousin Madeleine left him a picnic in an abandoned pigeon loft down the road from the house.

Sartre was an attentive listener, and Beauvoir found stories pouring out of her. They lay close together in the grass, and while the shadows lengthened around them, she talked about her life—her parents, Poupette, the Cours Désir, Zaza, Jacques. Sartre had a talent for seeing things from her perspective. When she told him about her cousin Jacques and the hopes she once had of marrying him, Sartre commented that it must be difficult for a woman with her background not to marry, but personally he thought it a trap. He admired her "Valkyrie spirit," and hoped she would never lose it.

Sartre was encouraging; he was also full of projects and plans for their future life together. They would have adventures and travels, he told her, and while they would work extremely hard, they would also lead dazzling lives of freedom and passion. He would give her everything he could. The only thing he could not give her was his person. He needed to be free.

It was clear that Sartre's help would not be the conventional sort. He scorned anything that smacked of conformity or conventionality. The idea of a regular job, with colleagues and a boss, was anathema to him. Nor did he want to be a professional literary man, scribbling away in a musty study lined with books. The thought of settling down in one place had no appeal. And though he had once been engaged, these days the idea of getting married, having children, and acquiring possessions horrified him. He had a mission: to be a great writer. Nothing else mattered. In order to write, he had to experience the world.

Sartre explained to Beauvoir his theory of liberty and contingency. It was the subject on which they had written in their exams, and he had been thinking about it for some time. As he saw it, individuals lived in a state of fundamental absurdity, or "contingency." There was no god; life had no preexisting meaning. Each individual had to assume his freedom, create his own life. There was no natural order; people held their destiny in their own hands. It was up to them to determine the substance of their lives, even the way they chose to love. It was frightening to be free. Most people fled from their freedom. But Sartre embraced his. He was not going to allow any preestablished code to determine *his* life. His life was going to be his own construction. Beauvoir thought this a beautiful philosophy.

In the first few days, they met in the mornings in the village square. Curious faces watched them behind curtains. Later they chose a more discreet place, a chestnut grove between La Grillère and the village. In Paris, Beauvoir had felt awkward when Sartre kissed her. But in those Limousin meadows, surrounded by birdsong, she enjoyed his soft kisses and caresses. "Now I accept without embarrassment the slightly disturbing sensation of being in his arms and feeling his power," she wrote in her journal. "My admiration and my faith in Jean-Paul are absolute, and my tenderness for my dear Leprechaun is without reservation."

Five days into Sartre's stay, the two of them were sprawled close together in a meadow when they saw Simone's parents walking toward them. They sprang up. Simone's father looked embarrassed. He told Sartre that people were gossiping, and he was afraid he had to ask him to leave the district. Simone flushed with anger and told her father that that was no way to talk to her friend. Her mother started to shout at her. Sartre quietly but firmly said he would leave as soon as he could, but he and their charming daughter were working on a philosophical inquiry, and they had to finish it first. The parents retreated to the house.

Sartre usually ate dinner at his hotel, and Simone went back to the house. After the meal, she would reappear with Poupette and their cousin Madeleine. Sartre organized endless high-spirited games. He had them improvising plays and acting out parts. Leading the way with his fine tenor voice, he got them to sing. "We laughed and laughed," Poupette would recall, "and the summer softly slipped away."[33]

Sartre left on September 1, and Beauvoir jotted down her thoughts and memories about those "perfect days." He had called her "my sweet love." He had told her he loved her, and assured her he would always love her. He said he was afraid of hurting her. "You do not know how tender your expression can be, dear little girl."

"This was the 'life' I was waiting for," she wrote. For the first time ever, she had met a man whom she considered her superior. She felt understood by him, loved and supported. Sartre would help her to be a strong, joyous Valkyrie. His love was full of promises, full of certitude. With him she felt a quite extraordinary harmony ("Oh! Much more than with the Lama or Jacques"). There was something incredibly vital about this man. He made her want to discover herself; he made her want to discover the world. With him, she knew she would never stagnate.

It was not "an overwhelming passion," she wrote in her journal. Not yet. It was not comparable to the "madness" and "obsession" she had once felt for Jacques. "But it's happiness." Most exciting was the feeling that through Sartre she had found herself. "Never have I loved so much to read and think. Never have I been so alive and happy, or envisaged such a rich future. Oh Jean-Paul, dear Jean-Paul, thank you."[34]

A week after Sartre left, late on a Friday evening, Beauvoir was on the platform of the railway station at Uzerche to meet Maheu. It was a mark of her new independence from her parents. Maheu was coming for the weekend, and he had invited her to stay with him—in two separate rooms in a hotel.

He stumbled out of a second-class compartment tired, unshaven, his coat slung over his shoulder, and his hat crooked. They caught a bus to a little hotel on the banks of the Vézère. Beauvoir heard him singing in the room next door as he washed and shaved, and she thought to herself how happy she was. After dinner—he was not hungry, and she ate most of his meal as well as her own—they climbed the hill to the church and looked at the stars. They talked for an hour in her room, then he kissed her hand tenderly, wished her good night, and went to his room.

The next day they walked by the river. He sang "So Blue" and told her stories about the Romans and the Gauls in that region. They had lunch at an inn. He climbed a tree. "I will never forget the young erudite René Maheu perched on a branch, his gray flannel trousers turned up, his hair in his face, his feet the color of the sunset," Beauvoir wrote in her journal. Her shoes were drenched, so she walked barefoot. Maheu threw pebbles into the water.

That evening at dinner, he ordered a bottle of Chablis Villages, 1923. When she got up from the table, her head was spinning. Maheu stretched out beside her on her bed. They lay close to each other, but Maheu did not make a move. He did not seem to want to leave, and she did not want to tell him to. He talked, and she gazed at him through a mist. After he left, she was sick. "Atrocious night."

The next morning was sweet. She loved his "Good morning, Beaver," his blue pajamas, his eau de cologne, and the soap he lent her. She was still not feeling well, and he was full of tender solicitude. He took her arm. He kissed her hair. He was, as usual, gay and witty, distant and close, ironical and tender, her "prince of lamas."

After he departed on the train, Beauvoir wrote in her journal: "It was like a dream lasting two days." She concluded: "I know exactly what he is, what Sartre is. But I'll talk about that later."

When she returned to Paris in mid-September, Simone de Beauvoir moved out of her parents' home and rented a fifth-floor room from her maternal grandmother at 91 Avenue Denfert-Rochereau, in Montparnasse. Her grandmother treated her exactly like her other lodgers; Simone could come and go as she pleased. Beauvoir bought some cheap furniture: a table, two chairs, bookshelves, an orange divan. Her sister, Poupette, helped her put up some bright orange wallpaper. Beauvoir pinned up a Michelangelo drawing Maheu had given her, and some satirical sketches by Sartre and Nizan. Stépha, her Polish friend, brought flowers, which Beauvoir put on the table, along with some books, her fountain pen, and her English cigarettes. She looked around rapturously. At last she was beginning her new life.

TWO

THE PACT

October 1929 – September 1932

On October 14, 1929, in that fifth-floor orange-papered room overlooking the plane trees on the Avenue Denfert-Rochereau, Beauvoir gave up her virginity.

Maheu's visit to Limousin had clarified things. She had been in love with him for months. He was a handsome man, and she frankly desired him. He was kind and affectionate. But he was married, and in any case, he vaguely disappointed her. More than once, he had said to her: "You mustn't judge me." She could never quite decide whether he was asking her a favor or giving her an order. But now she had met a man who was not afraid of judgment, a man who believed that his character was the sum total of his actions, a man who *asked* to be judged.

By the time Maheu left Limousin, Beauvoir had understood. She needed "Sartre and no one else." He might be the Little Man, but he lived life so intensely, he seemed bigger than any man she knew. He was burning with ambition, but not in the worldly sense. Material things did not interest him, nor did hobnobbing with famous people. Quite simply, he was convinced he was going to be a great man and that his task was to get on with it. Sartre needed his liberty, but he also wanted Beauvoir to embrace hers. This was not a man who was going to urge her to comply with social conventions.

She still loved her Prince of Lamas. Theirs was "the most tender of friendships." But he was bound by other people's opinions, and too eager to cut a figure in society. Intellectually, he did not satisfy her. "In everyday life, one could be bored with him. . . . One can't let oneself go, expansively, with this man."[1]

After Maheu left Limousin, she rationalized: "It is good that precisely with this sensual man there is nothing physical between us, . . . whereas with Sartre, who is not sensual, the harmony of our bodies has a meaning which makes our love more beautiful."

There were two weeks of "feverish caresses and lovemaking"[2] before Sartre left for Saint-Cyr, at the beginning of November, to begin his military service. Late every night, Sartre left Beauvoir's flat and went back to his grandparents, the Schweitzers, who had a large apartment in the Latin Quarter.

The young lovers talked a great deal about the future. Sartre did not suggest marriage. Instead, what he proposed was a "two-year lease." While he was doing his military service, they would see as much of each other as possible. Beauvoir, instead of entering the teaching profession straight away, which would mean being sent to the provinces, would remain in Paris, make a start on a novel, and do some part-time tutoring. Sartre had inherited a small legacy from his paternal grandmother, and would help Beauvoir out as much as he could.

At the end of those two years, when Sartre's military service was finished, he envisaged a period apart. He had applied for a position as a French teacher in a Japanese school in Kyoto, a job that would begin in October 1931. This would mean a separation for a couple of years. Then they would meet up in a new place—Athens or Istanbul, maybe—and live near each other again for a couple of years before striking out again by themselves. That way, their relationship would never degenerate into dull routine.

Beauvoir did not share Sartre's lone-hero dreams. She would have much preferred to undertake exotic adventures with him at her side. Her dream was the "Grand Amour," and she dreaded the idea of long separations. But for the time being, two years seemed a long way off, and she did her best to suppress her fears. She knew Sartre would regard them as a weakness.

Sartre had made clear from the beginning that monogamy did not interest him. He liked women (far more than men, he always said), and he did not intend to stop having affairs at the age of twenty-three. Nor should Beauvoir, he said. The love they had for each other was "essential," and primary. They were "two of a kind," each other's double, and their relationship would surely last for life. But they should not deprive themselves of what he called "contingent" affairs, meaning secondary and more arbitrary.

Sartre felt strongly that love was not about possession. To him, a more generous kind of love meant loving the other person as a free being. When Beauvoir raised the thorny question of jealousy, Sartre said that if they told each other everything, they would never feel excluded from each other's lives. They should have no secrets from each other. In their love affairs, doubts, insecurities, and obsessions, they should aim for complete openness. He called it "transparency."

Beauvoir found the idea as frightening as it was exhilarating. She valued truth and sincerity, but she also treasured her inner life. Throughout her adolescence she had learned to keep her thoughts to herself. She had long since stopped recounting her sins to her father confessor. And yet, here was Sartre wanting her to share her thoughts—*all* her thoughts—with him.

Did Beauvoir point out that they were not quite "two of a kind," that the stakes were not even, that society regarded women in a completely different light from men? Probably not at the time, though both of them knew it. Twenty years later, in *The Second Sex*, she would make the point that women were not the "other sex," but the "second sex." They were not seen as equal; they were viewed as inferior.

While Sartre did not want to lose a freedom he had already enjoyed for several years, Beauvoir could not even quite imagine what her freedom would look like. Her female friends all aspired to marriage, and Beauvoir was as contemptuous of spinsters—*vieilles filles*—as everyone else. She knew her parents would be ashamed if she did not marry. Many people would pity her. Even her close friends, like Zaza and Maheu, would be taken aback by the idea of her having an open relationship with Sartre. And she herself had to come to terms with the idea. "I had not emancipated myself from all sexual taboos," she admits. "Promiscuity in a woman still shocked me."[3]

Despite her professed disdain for marriage in her 1927 journal, Beauvoir had spent her teenage years hoping to marry her cousin Jacques. Up until her meeting with Sartre, she envisaged herself as a wife and mother, as well as a writer. And she had never aspired to sexual libertinage. On the contrary. Throughout their adolescence she and her sister, Poupette, had been mortified on those nights when their father did not come home. They knew that while their mother chafed and wept, he was escorting some mistress or other to the theater. At the age of twenty, Simone was aghast when she discovered that her cousin Jacques had been having an affair with one of those heavily painted young women who hung around bars. She was horrified to think that her Polish friend, Stépha, might actually be sleeping with her Spanish painter boyfriend, Fernando. When Stépha gently tried to enlighten her, Simone shut her eyes and put her hands over her ears. Even at the age of twenty-one, when she met Sartre, she was shocked to hear that the Nizans had an "open marriage." These people all maintained a public façade of married respectability; Sartre was proposing none at all.

Sartre, it seems, was surprised that Simone de Beauvoir accepted his terms. Ten years later, he analyzed his need for freedom with vaguely disconcerting self-mockery. Since his bookworm youth, he had taken for granted that he would one day be a great writer. Early on, he had understood that a male adventurer had to preserve his freedom. In everything he read—from Greek myths, classical tragedies, nineteenth-century novels, to the swaggering detective novels he devoured one after the other—the lone male hero steered his way through treacherous obstacles, the most dire of which were women. Sartre was determined, he writes, to avoid this trap himself.

It was all the more comical in that women certainly weren't running after me, indeed it was I who was running after them. Thus, in the few adventures that came my way at that time, after I'd gone to immense trouble to get round some young lady, I used to feel obliged to explain to her, like some dragon of virtue, that she must take care not to infringe my freedom. But within a short space of time, as I was good-natured, I'd make her a gift of that precious freedom. I'd say: 'It's the finest present I can give you.' . . . Happily for me, . . . circumstances independent of my will would intervene in time to restore me (after a bit of a drubbing) to that dear freedom, which I'd forthwith make haste to bestow upon some other young lady.

On one occasion I was hoist with my own petard. The Beaver accepted that freedom and kept it. It was in 1929. I was foolish enough to be upset by it: instead of understanding the extraordinary luck I'd had, I fell into a certain melancholy.[4]

It seems Beauvoir had no difficulty accepting the idea that they would not have children. Their relationship was on an entirely different basis. They were writers. They needed their freedom, and they needed a great deal of time, without distractions. Moreover, she saw that Sartre was disgusted by pregnant women's bellies, and by babies, which he said smelled of piss. Whether he influenced her on this is a moot point, but over the years, several of their friends would comment that Sartre and Beauvoir were visibly repelled by pregnant women. It is obvious in their writing.

Beauvoir felt desolate at the beginning of November, when she saw Sartre off on the train to Saint-Cyr. For the first two weeks, the conscripts were allowed no visitors. By the time Beauvoir was permitted to visit him, Sartre had been transformed into a soldier, in dark blue puttees and a beret. They were obliged to meet in a room packed with other soldiers and their families. Sartre was fuming at his loss of freedom and the waste of eighteen months. Beauvoir felt as if she were visiting a man behind bars.

In mid-November, Zaza Lacoin was seriously ill, with a high fever and delirium, in a small hospital in Saint-Cloud, southwest of Paris. The doctors called it meningitis or encephalitis; they were not sure. Beauvoir was convinced Zaza was suffering from a broken heart.

For the last five months, Madame Lacoin had put Zaza under an intolerable strain. Zaza and Merleau-Ponty were deeply in love. They had decided to get married in two years, after Merleau-Ponty had finished his *agrégation* and military service. But Madame Lacoin was not happy. Merleau-Ponty was an outstanding student and a practicing Catholic, but he was not wealthy, and though he aspired to a university position, his financial prospects were modest compared with those of Monsieur Lacoin, a businessman.

Madame Lacoin was also concerned about the social status of Merleau-Ponty's family. Zaza admitted she did not know much about them, except that Maurice's mother was a widow and that his father had been a naval officer, and Maurice was one of three children. She assured her parents there was no need to worry. "Knowing our family as he does, he would never have breathed a word about his feelings if for whatever reason it would not be admissible for him to enter it."[5]

Her mother was not satisfied. She arranged for Zaza to spend a year in Berlin, in the hope that she would forget this man. "It's so hard, Simone," Zaza wrote to her friend at the end of the summer of 1929. "One really has to believe in the virtue of suffering and to want to carry the cross with Christ to accept this without a murmur."[6]

Zaza was torn between her mother and the man she loved. Her extreme piety taught her obedience. In the face of all the difficulties, Merleau-Ponty, instead of battling with Zaza's mother, retreated slightly. Just when the tormented young woman most needed his reassurances, they were not forthcoming.

In October, Simone received a mysterious letter from Zaza: "Mama has told me something astonishing which I cannot explain to you now." In her next letter, Zaza asked: "Can children bear the sins of their parents?"[7]

At the beginning of November, Zaza fell ill. In the hospital she was allowed no visitors other than her family. When Beauvoir saw her again, at the end of that dreadful month, Zaza was laid out on a bier in the hospital morgue, her hands folded over a crucifix on her chest.

Beauvoir held it against Merleau-Ponty that he had not had the moral courage to support Zaza against her mother, and she made this quite clear in her memoirs. By 1958, when *Memoirs of a Dutiful Daughter* was published, Maurice Merleau-Ponty was a well-known left-wing philosopher (he no longer believed in God), with a teaching position at the prestigious Collège de France. In her memoirs, Beauvoir calls him "Jean Pradelle." In a further attempt to put readers off the scent, she calls him once by his real name: "My fellow pupils were Merleau-Ponty and Lévi-Strauss; I knew them both a little. The former I had always admired from a distance."[8] But she leaves the reader in no doubt that she did not admire the man she calls "Jean Pradelle."

Maurice Merleau-Ponty had remained close friends with Beauvoir over the years. When he read *Memoirs of a Dutiful Daughter,* in 1958, he wrote to her. He had reread the letters he and Zaza wrote each other during those painful months in 1929. (He called her by her real name, Elisabeth.) "Reading these, as well as your book, made me realize— intensely, to the point of despair—the extent to which I was passive, unconscious, and nonexistent in those years. Everything you say about me is true." At twenty-one, he had been too immature, he said, to deal with the pressures "Elisabeth" and her family were putting him under:

> I have never doubted that she was the woman I could have loved . . . but I was not ready to love somebody, not even her. . . . It would have taken some months for it to become love, for me to have been changed by her and by her presence. The attitude of her family, her own anxieties (which she hid from me more than she did from you), instead of touching me, they chilled me. . . . But there is something you don't know, which I myself did not know about at the time when Elisabeth fell ill, and which she had to bear all alone, without it being any fault of mine.[9]

Soon afterward, he and Beauvoir met over a drink, and—thirty years after those tragic events—Merleau-Ponty recounted the full story. In the autumn of 1929, the Lacoin parents did what many bourgeois families did before a marriage: they hired a private detective to investigate Merleau-Ponty's family.[10] The skeleton that emerged from the closet was deeply shocking to devout Catholics, who considered adultery a mortal sin. Madame Lacoin told Zaza, whereupon Zaza wrote Beauvoir those mysterious letters. Merleau-Ponty was told nothing until it was too late, and Zaza was dead.

Monsieur Merleau-Ponty was indeed a navy officer, and he and his wife lived in La Rochelle. They had one son. During her husband's long absences, Madame Merleau-Ponty fell in love with a university professor. He, too, was married, but it was a serious liaison, and conducted fairly openly. Madame Merleau-Ponty bore two children by him—first Maurice, then his sister Monique. The professor assumed financial responsibility for his children, but he could not give them his name.[11]

Back in November 1929, Beauvoir and Merleau-Ponty were both devastated by Zaza's death. At the time, Merleau-Ponty had no idea that Beauvoir held the loss partly against *him*. And Beauvoir had no idea what Merleau-Ponty was going through.

Beauvoir always felt that Zaza's fate could easily have been her own. Zaza was her shadow self, the self she might have been if Georges de Beauvoir had not lost his fortune. *Memoirs of a Dutiful Daughter* ends with the haunting words: "For a long time I believed that I had paid for my own freedom with her death."

It was Raymond Aron who suggested that Sartre and another friend of Sartre's, Pierre Guille, apply to do their military service in the meteorological division. Aron had completed a year of his military service as a meteorologist. It was not too bad, he told them.

For the first three months, Sartre and Guille were sent to train at the meteorological station at Fort Saint-Cyr. Aron was one of their instructors, and they annoyed him by throwing darts at him during lectures. Sartre chafed at being sequestered in his barracks, but he had to admit that wind velocity readings were easy, if tedious, and he had far more spare time than he had anticipated.

Saint-Cyr was so close to Paris that Sartre and Beauvoir managed to see each other most days. Three or four evenings a week, Beauvoir caught a train to Versailles, then a bus to Saint-Cyr, and she and Sartre had dinner together, sometimes with Guille and Aron, mostly at the Soleil d'Or, the large brasserie near the bus terminal. On Sundays, Sartre went to Paris.

After their training period, Guille was sent to Paris and Sartre to the meteorological station at Saint-Symphorien, near Tours. He shared a small house with two other conscripts, neither of whom he liked. But their supervisor, a civilian, gave them an entire week off every month, in addition to Sundays. Sartre spent all his spare time in Paris. And once a week, Beauvoir would catch the train to Tours.

When they were apart, they wrote to each other most days. Sartre

called her "my little wife" and "darling little Beaver." She called him
"my sweet little husband" and "most dear little being."

"My dearest, it is thundering, and I look constantly to the past, all
those beautiful days with you," Sartre wrote after one of his weeks in
Paris. He was feeling bored and restless, he told her, "like a swimmer
who realizes he is caught in seaweed."

"If one has to be ill, it's nice to do so just after you've left, my dearest love," Beauvoir wrote from her bed at Denfert-Rochereau, where
she was recovering from a sore throat and fever. She was thinking
about the "miraculous week" they had just spent together. "We'll be
seeing each other soon, won't we, my love? You promised, so I'm taking good care of myself. I love you. I love you."[12]

They wrote as though speaking to each other, and joked and
cavorted with prose. Sartre, about to turn up in Paris, sent a frivolous
note:

> *My little morganatic wife*
>
> *I'll be arriving at 12.15, Gare d'Austerlitz (up to you to check the time. . . . No,
> I take that back. The schedule's here in the drawer of the table where I'm writing;
> I can check it myself: it's 12:13). I'd be delighted if you could find time to meet me
> at the station. By the way, I hope to be in Paris for six days.*
>
> *If you have free time, we might go out together sometimes.*
>
> *With warm regards.*
>
> *PS: My dearest, I've read the description of your 1st chapter. If its style is as
> simple as the style in your letter—no more, no less—it will be excellent.*[13]

By the summer of 1930, Beauvoir was making troubled remarks in
her journal. "I cannot reconcile myself to living if there is no purpose
in my life. . . . Sartre talks to me as though to a very little girl. . . . I
have lost my pride—and that means I have lost everything."[14]

At first she had been overjoyed to fall in love with a man she
regarded as her superior. Now she was beginning to realize the dangers. The man who was considered the brightest of his year's crop of
bright young men at the Ecole Normale had a firm sense of his
genius. It was a word he used without embarrassment. "I looked upon
myself—though in all modesty, if I may say so—as a genius," he said
later. "I talked to my friends as a genius talks to his friends."[15] Sartre

had a strong personality, and his friends all too easily became what he called his "acolytes."

Sartre's sociability and generosity were legendary. Funny, playful, inventive, and a brilliant imitator, he would make people laugh till they cried. He loved to help and encourage people, and to give them things. But despite his warmth and gregariousness, he was disconcertingly self-sufficient. He didn't seem to need anyone. At least, not one particular person. He liked people around him, the hubbub of voices in the background. He needed to have a woman in love with him, and he also liked for her—even if he complained about it—to *need* him. But provided he was able to feel that he was loved, he was happiest when alone with his fountain pen, paper, and books.

His friends regularly accused him of indifference. His girlfriends at first basked in his attentions, then complained that he did not give them enough of his precious time. They would become possessive and jealous, and Sartre would grumble that they were too demanding. It was the pattern of his life.

Beauvoir did not like to complain. From the beginning of their relationship she made a supreme effort to see things from Sartre's perspective. It was partly because she felt she owed him everything. It was also because she was convinced that she loved him more than he loved her. She rationalized that she would not make a grievance out of an objective fact. After all, if she loved Sartre, it was partly because he taught her to look things squarely in the face.

It did not help that the first eighteen months of their relationship were a blur of arrivals and farewells on railway platforms. They had a short time to enjoy each other's company, then Sartre would have to return to his barracks. For Beauvoir, the only moments that counted were those she spent with Sartre. The rest felt as if she were killing time.

There was also a physical problem, one that filled Beauvoir with shame at the time, but which she would discuss with astounding openness thirty years later, in her memoirs. Sartre had awakened her physical appetites, and unless he was in Paris, they lacked opportunities to make love. On those days when she visited him in Tours, they were too shy to get themselves a hotel room in broad daylight. She suffered "tyrannical desires" and "burning obsessions," and was dismayed not to feel in control of her body. The fact that Sartre did not seem to suffer from the same problem made her more ashamed. "I was forced to admit a truth that I had been doing my best to conceal ever since adolescence: my physical appetites were greater than I wanted them to be."[16] Beauvoir, despite their pact, did not talk to Sartre about this.

Everything conspired to make her fall into a trap she would describe twenty years later in *The Second Sex*. There is a chapter on "the woman in love," a woman for whom love is a faith, who spends her life waiting, who abandons her life, even her *judgment,* to her man.

> The woman in love tries to see with his eyes; she reads the books he reads, prefers the pictures and the music he prefers; she is interested only in the landscapes she sees with him, in the ideas that come from him; she adopts his friendships, his enmities, his opinions; when she questions herself, it is his reply she tries to hear. . . . The supreme happiness of the woman in love is to be recognized by the loved man as a part of himself; when he says "we," she is associated and identified with him, she shares his prestige and reigns with him over the rest of the world; she never tires of repeating—even to excess—this delectable "we."[17]

In her memoirs—written at a time when she was seen by the whole world as a famously independent, intellectual woman—she describes her earlier self, in scathing terms, as an "ancillary being," and "intellectual parasite."[18]

The underlying existentialist philosophy of Beauvoir's memoirs—it was also the underlying philosophy of her relationship with Sartre—is that it is "bad faith" to look to another, whether a human being or a god, for a sense of salvation. As individuals we are free, and we act in "bad faith" when we try to avoid our freedom. It is not easy, freedom. It brings with it the anguish of choice. It comes with the burden of responsibility.

Looking back on the first eighteen months of their relationship, Beauvoir writes that Sartre had become her whole world. So fascinated was she by him that she forgot herself. She had ceased to exist on her own account.

• • •

The moment they met on the railway platform, in Tours or Paris, Sartre would grasp Beauvoir's hand and say: "I've got a new theory." Beauvoir would listen carefully, then point out the flaws she saw in his argument. This would be her lifelong role, and Sartre would come to rely on it heavily. Back then, he pointed out her lack of originality. "When you think in terms of *problems,* you aren't thinking at all," he told her.[19]

He had volunteered to "take her in hand," but now her dependence alarmed him. "You used to be full of ideas, Beaver," he said. He compared her to the heroines in George Meredith's novels, who, after struggling hard for their independence, finished up surrendering themselves to love. Beauvoir was mortified.

On the anniversary of Zaza's death, Beauvoir's journal was tear-stained. "If you were only here, Zaza. I can't bear it that you're dead." Simone's parents disliked Sartre, and fervently hoped she would wean herself from the strange-looking fellow and his bad influence. Her friends had dispersed. René Maheu had a teaching job in Coutances, Normandy. Stépha had married her Spanish boyfriend, Fernando Gerassi, and they had moved to Madrid. Her cousin Jacques had married. Poupette was something of a comfort. She was studying painting, and was working hard at it. Meanwhile, she and her girlfriend, Gégé, another artist, were sleeping around, trying to discover themselves.

Sartre's stepfather, Joseph Mancy, refused to have Simone de Beauvoir in the house. His stepson was not proposing to marry her; therefore she was quite simply a slut. Sartre did not take a stand, and continued to make weekly visits to his parents. His mother met him and Beauvoir from time to time, usually in the cafeteria of a Paris department store, but she was terrified that her husband might find out. After half an hour with them, she would scurry off.

The worst was that Beauvoir did not feel quite accepted by Sartre's friends. She could not be sure of this, but she always had the impression that Paul Nizan seemed to be slightly mocking her. And she had nothing in common with Nizan's wife, Henriette. Sartre's closest friend at the time was Pierre Guille, a fellow *Normalien,* with an *agréga-*

tion in French literature. He was handsome, like all Sartre's friends, male or female. (Sartre considered this a necessary condition for friendship.) Guille distrusted Sartre's philosophical theories, and laughed long and loud at some of the stilted passages in the novel Sartre was writing. Sartre took it well. The two men had a deep affection for each other.

Guille was twenty-four, the same age as Sartre, and in love with a forty-year-old married woman, Madame Morel. Sartre was attracted to her himself. Small and plump, with thick black hair and sparkling brown eyes, Madame Morel had grown up in Argentina—a lonely rich girl who used to ride her horse across the pampas. She was wealthy, hospitable, and full of life.

In her apartment on the Boulevard Raspail, she had put a room permanently aside for Guille. Sartre and Beauvoir often speculated as to whether she and Guille were actually lovers. They never knew. No one, not even Madame Morel's invalid husband and her two grown children, seemed to mind her closeness to Guille. Beauvoir and Sartre were frankly fascinated. What hurt Beauvoir was that she sensed Guille and Madame Morel's reservations toward her:

> Madame Morel did not bestow her friendship lightly, and I found favor more quickly with Guille. Even so, his regard was edged with a certain irony which often disconcerted me. Both of them intimidated me. . . . I did not have positive proof of this, but often in Madame Morel's presence I felt clumsy and adolescent, and was certain that she and Guille were passing judgment upon me.[20]

If Sartre's friends made Beauvoir feel naïve and awkward, it was Sartre's former lover, Simone Jollivet, the former courtesan, who shook her self-confidence most painfully. There seemed to be nothing Jollivet could not do. After seeing Charles Dullin give one of the best film performances of the decade as Louis XI in *The Miracle of the Wolves,* Jollivet harbored the wild dream of seducing him. Sartre dismissed this as a crazy fantasy. Dullin, a much older married man, was a famous actor and theater director. Still, a year later, by the end of 1928, Jollivet had become his mistress. Dullin doted on her. He bought her an apartment. Jollivet moved to Paris. She was now tak-ing acting lessons at Dullin's famous drama school, L'Atelier, in Montmartre, and writing a play.

The way Sartre talked about Jollivet threw Beauvoir into torments of jealousy. "He frequently set her up as an example to me when try-ing to goad me out of my inactivity."[21]

Sartre disliked jealousy. He believed it important for individuals to control their passions, not to let themselves be swept up by them. Otherwise, they were denying their liberty, he told Beauvoir, and reacting rather than acting.

Years later, Sartre told an interviewer that Simone Jollivet was his "first serious affair," and that with her he had experienced "the most unpleasant emotion that has ever laid hold of me and which, I believe, is most often described as jealousy."

He had asked her to stop sleeping with other men. "Do you own me?" Jollivet had retorted. "Am I supposed to sit here and wait for your occasional appearances? Are you prepared to abandon *L'Ecole Normale?*"

"I paced back and forth in her lush, heavily scented bedroom," Sartre recalled. "She was right, of course, and I knew it. I concluded that jealousy is possessiveness. Therefore, I decided never to be jeal-ous again."[22]

Sartre tended to see any violent emotion as an affectation. And he had no time for self-pity. Simone Jollivet once made the mistake of telling him she felt sad. The twenty-one-year-old Sartre had written back:

Do you expect me to soften before this interesting pose you decided to adopt, first for your own benefit and then for mine? There was a time when I was inclined toward that kind of play-acting.... Nowadays I hate and scorn those who, like you, indulge their brief hours of sadness. What disgusts me about it is the shameful little comedy rooted in a physical state of torpor that we play out for ourselves.... Sadness goes hand in hand with laziness.... You revel in it to the point of writing to me,

500 kilometers away, who will very likely not be in the same
mood: "I'm sad." You might as well tell it to the League of
Nations. . . . If, on your melancholy evening, you'd been made to
saw some wood, your sadness would have disappeared in 5 minutes. Saw away, mentally, of course. Stand erect, stop playacting,
get busy, *write*.[23]

Sartre was adamant that people should not use their emotions as
an excuse. Beauvoir would have a lifelong struggle with jealousy, but
she worked hard on herself. It made her all the more impatient with
jealousy in others.

After René Maheu's visit to Limousin that summer, his and
Beauvoir's platonic romance continued. In October 1929, Maheu
took up a teaching post in Normandy. He saw Beauvoir when he
came to Paris a few weeks later, but she did not disclose to him that
she and Sartre had become lovers. In December, Maheu read a letter
from Sartre on her desk that left the nature of their relationship in no
doubt. Maheu said he would never trust her again. Beauvoir wept. In
the New Year, when he heard that Sartre had just spent a week in
Paris, Maheu sent Beauvoir a note:

Forgive me for disturbing you amid all the tender and colorful
memories that are doubtless prolonging for you your own dear
love's passage. Nevertheless: can you be at home *on Wednesday
afternoon?* . . . I have some quite important things to tell you,
since it is possible I shall never see you again. For you must
understand that I have had my fill of the pretty situation that
now exists, as a result of that September of yours and the two
months of lying which followed it.[24]

Beauvoir copied the note for Sartre's perusal. She had little sympathy with Maheu, she told Sartre. This was "mere jealousy of a thoroughly disagreeable kind."

Sartre firmly believed that with willpower one could transcend all
emotions, discomforts, and obstacles. According to him, tears and

bad nerves were weaknesses. Seasickness was a weakness. We are free beings, Sartre said, and we can choose. He attributed almost no importance to physiological functions, and none at all to psychological conditioning.

With some reservations—she was prone to seasickness and tears— Beauvoir went along with Sartre's extreme voluntarism. As she writes in her memoirs, nothing compelled them to see things otherwise. They were young, in good health, with a lot of free time and enough money to do what they wanted. As philosophers, they were convinced that they appraised the world with a detached, objective gaze.

Beauvoir recalls a fierce argument in the Café Balzar between Sartre and his philosopher friend Georges Politzer. A Hungarian Jew who had emigrated to France as an eighteen-year-old, Politzer was far more politically conscious than Sartre. He pointed out that Sartre was in every way a product of the French bourgeoisie. Sartre said that this was nonsense. He despised the bourgeoisie. An intellectual could transcend class ideology, and he himself had done so. His sympathies were with the working class. He felt more comfortable among the common people. Politzer disagreed. "Politzer's shock of red hair glowed flamelike, and words poured out of him," Beauvoir writes, "but he failed to convince Sartre."[25]

For the next ten years, Sartre and Beauvoir maintained their belief in an almost absolute individual freedom. It took the cataclysm of the Second World War (in which Politzer, a courageous Resistance fighter, was tortured and killed by the Gestapo) to make them discover history. They finally understood that it was precisely because they belonged to the privileged bourgeoisie that they had been able to entertain their grand illusion for so long.

Whenever Sartre was in Paris, he and Beauvoir spent time with Madame Morel and Pierre Guille. Madame Morel had a car, and occasionally she, Guille, and Beauvoir drove to Tours to see Sartre. Beauvoir liked the handsome Guille a great deal, mostly because Sartre liked him so much.

Guille was discharged from his military service a few weeks before Sartre. He decided to celebrate by making a ten-day trip across France, visiting relatives and friends on the way. Madame Morel was happy to lend him her car, but she had to stay behind and look after her invalid husband. Guille asked Beauvoir if she would like to join him.

"A *real* car journey, the first trip of the sort I had ever made!"[26] Beauvoir was equally exhilarated by the thought of ten days alone with Guille. And then a complication arose. Two days before they were due to leave, René Maheu turned up. He was staying in Paris for a fortnight, without his wife, and planned to spend time with Beauvoir. They had patched up their quarrel months before. But now she had to break the news that she was about to go away with another man. Maheu issued an ultimatum. If she went, he would never see her again. She protested that she could not let Guille down. Her choice, Maheu said. The two of them went to the cinema and she wept throughout the film.

Once she and Guille set off, she cheered up. They drove through the hills of Morvan, stopping to see some sights. In Lyon, Guille spent the night with friends, and Beauvoir stayed with cousins, who teased her mercilessly. "Because I was traveling with a man they assumed that I must be familiar with every kind of vice, and the coarseness of their jokes took me aback. Over the dessert they offered me what they called a 'Grenoble nut': this turned out to be an empty nutshell with a condom inside."[27]

It was her first time in the South of France. She loved the bareness of Provence, the colors, the sight of cypresses bent by that fierce wind, the mistral. In her memoirs, she paints a picture of a particularly cozy evening in Les Baux. It was nighttime when she and Guille arrived. The wind was blowing hard. Lights twinkled down in the valley.

> A fire was crackling in the grate at the Reine Jeanne, where we were the only guests. We had dinner at a little table close to the fireplace, and drank a wine the name of which, "Le Mas de la Dame," I recall to this day.

In her old age, Beauvoir admitted to her biographer that she slept with Guille on that trip. Did she tell Sartre? "I didn't have to. He knew."[28]

The return to Paris was a shock. After "ten days of the closest intimacy," she and Guille were back with Madame Morel and Sartre, and a gulf opened up between them. Sartre had just heard that he had not got the teaching job in Kyoto, and was bitterly disappointed. And there was a nasty little farewell note from René Maheu.

Now that Sartre's Japan adventure had fallen through, his immediate future was in the hands of the French Ministry of Education. In March 1931, a teaching post opened up in Le Havre. Sartre decided to accept. Le Havre was at least not far from Paris. Then Beauvoir heard she had been assigned to a school in Marseille. She panicked. Marseille was eight hundred kilometers away. Marseille was exile.

She fell into such a state of anxiety that Sartre finally suggested they get married. That way they would be given postings in the same town. It was pointless to martyr themselves for a principle, he said. Marriage was merely a legal formality. In the long run, it would not seriously affect their relationship.

Beauvoir knew what marriage represented for Sartre. She had no desire to become the little wife he resented. She could also see that he was undergoing a crisis of his own. His dream of a posting in some exotic place had been dashed, leaving him with the prospect of years ahead as a schoolteacher in the provinces. "To have joined the ranks of the married men would have meant an even greater renunciation," Beauvoir writes. "Mere elementary caution prevented my choosing a future that might be poisoned by remorse."[29] She chose a less conventional future. They revised their two-year pact. This time it was for life.

That summer—Sartre was twenty-six and Beauvoir twenty-three—they crossed the French border for the first time in their lives.[30] Fernando Gerassi had invited them to stay with him in Madrid. (Stépha was temporarily back in Paris with their baby son.) Sartre paid their fares out of his grandmother's legacy.

"We're in Spain!" they kept saying incredulously, as they strolled around the town of Figueres on their first evening. They wandered around the poorest parts of Barcelona, convinced that the slums held the key to the soul of Spain. Beauvoir consulted her guidebook with manic thoroughness; she wanted to see *everything*. Sartre, after a morning of sightseeing, preferred to sit in a café and smoke his pipe, "soaking up the atmosphere," as he put it.

Beauvoir treasured the precious days alone with Sartre. When they got to Madrid, Fernando was waiting for them at the station, and after they deposited their bags in his apartment, he took them on a tour of the city. At the end of the afternoon, Beauvoir was in tears. "I was feeling nostalgic," she admits, "not so much for Barcelona as for my long private tête-à-tête with Sartre."[31]

They went to cheap restaurants and sampled grilled shrimps, black olives, and peach ice cream. They sat in cafés, where workers talked animatedly about a forthcoming revolution, and sipped Manzanilla, a pale-colored dry sherry. At the Prado, they admired the El Grecos, argued about the Goyas, and disliked the Titians. On Sundays they went to bullfights.

At the end of September, they took the train together as far as Bayonne, just over the French border. Then Sartre headed to Le Havre, and Beauvoir caught the express from Bordeaux to Marseille.

She stopped at the top of the flight of steps at the St. Charles station, and looked down at the scene below. "I was in Marseille—alone, empty-handed, cut off from my past and everything I loved. I stood staring at this vast unknown city, where I now had to make my own way, unaided, from one day to the next."[32]

Beauvoir embraced her solitude with the fervor of a young monk. She got herself a room within easy walking distance of her school, the Lycée Montgrand, near the Old Port. In the mornings she would stride through the ornate front gates, march into the staff room without greeting anyone, and sit in a corner with a book.

In her spare time, she went on long walking trips. In her memoirs, she describes this as obsessive behavior. "If I had given up even one trip through indifference or to satisfy a mere whim, if I had once asked myself what the point of it all was, I would have destroyed the whole carefully contrived edifice."[33] The exhausting rambles preserved her from "boredom, regret, and several sorts of depression."

Every Thursday and Sunday, whenever she did not have to teach, she left home at dawn in an old dress and canvas espadrilles, with a *Guide Bleu* and a Michelin map in her backpack, and walked as much as forty kilometers a day. She did not consider joining one of the town's walking groups. She never bought herself decent walking shoes. By herself, she climbed steep hills, strode along copper-colored cliffs, and clambered down gullies. Older female colleagues warned her that she could be raped. She pooh-poohed this "spinsterish obsession," and continued to hitch rides in passing cars.

One hot afternoon, she was trudging down a dirt road, and two young men pulled up. They said they would give her a lift as far as the next town. They drove a little way, then pulled off the main road, mumbling something about a shortcut. She realized they were heading for the only deserted spot in the area. When they slowed down at a crossing, she opened the door and threatened to jump out. They stopped and let her go. It was not the only occasion on which she extricated herself from a difficult situation just in time.

When her sister visited in November (Sartre paid her fare), Beauvoir marched her over the mountains. Poupette developed bad blisters, but did not dare complain. On one famous walk, she became feverish. Beauvoir finished the trek alone, leaving her sister shivering for several hours in a gloomy waiting room until a bus took her back to Marseille. It turned out to be the onset of influenza.

One brave colleague tried to pierce Beauvoir's solitary carapace. In *The Prime of Life,* published in 1960, Beauvoir called her "Madame Tourmelin," but otherwise she made no attempt to disguise her. The woman's real name was Suzanne Tuffreau.[34] She was one of the English teachers at the school, and with her brown hair, fresh pink complexion, thin lips, and tortoiseshell glasses, she looked, to Beauvoir, like an Englishwoman. She was thirty-five, twelve years older than Beauvoir, and crazy about Katherine Mansfield—both her work and her life. Beauvoir noticed that Tuffreau did not seem nearly as passionate about her husband, who was recovering from tuberculosis in a distant clinic.

Suzanne Tuffreau introduced Beauvoir to her friends. They often ate together, went to concerts and films, and, one weekend, made an excursion to Arles. Thanks to her new friend, Beauvoir moved into the room above Tuffreau's apartment—charming digs on the elegant Avenue du Prado, with a balcony overlooking the rooftops and plane trees. Tuffreau kept badgering Beauvoir to let her come hiking. Finally Beauvoir consented.

> She appeared complete with rucksack, studded shoes, and all the proper equipment, and tried to make me keep to the Alpinist's pace, which is very slow and steady. But we were not in the Alps, and I preferred to go at my own speed. She panted along behind me, and I derived a certain malicious satisfaction from her plight.... Spurred on by hatred, I walked steadily faster and faster; from time to time I stopped for a breather in the shade, but set off once more as soon as she caught up with me.[35]

Beauvoir's plucky colleague was not deterred. One evening, she invited Beauvoir to dinner at a famous fish restaurant. They ate grilled perch, drank copious quantities of local wine, talked in English; Tuffreau affectionately mocked Beauvoir's bad accent. Afterward, they weaved their way back to the Prado. No sooner had they stepped inside the older woman's apartment than she pulled Beauvoir to her in a tight embrace.

> "Come on, let's drop this pretense," she gasped, and kissed me passionately. Then she burst out about how she had fallen in love with me at first sight, and it was high time to have done with all this hypocrisy, and would I—she begged me—spend the night with her? Dazed by this impetuous confession, I could only mumble, "Think of tomorrow morning—what shall we feel like then?"
> "Must I kneel at your feet?" she cried, in a strangled voice.
> "No, no, no!" I screamed, and fled.[36]

Beauvoir *did* share Tuffreau's passion for Katherine Mansfield. That year, she read and reread Mansfield's journals, correspondence, and short stories, and found great romantic appeal in Mansfield's cult of the "solitary woman."

> When I lunched on the Canebière, upstairs at the Brasserie O'Central, or had dinner at the back of Charley's Tavern—a cool, dark place, its walls covered with photographs of boxers— I told myself that I, too, personified this "solitary woman." I felt the same while I was drinking coffee under the plane trees on the Place de la Préfecture, or sitting by a window of the Café Cintra down at the Old Port.[37]

Shortly before she died, Beauvoir, in conversation with her biographer Deirdre Bair, described her time in Marseille as "the unhappiest year of my life." She admitted she felt very unsure about Sartre:

> I did not want to leave Sartre, because I loved him then passionately, as well as intellectually, and I wanted to be with him. He was very sweet and very innocent and he often felt so sorry for the girls with whom he had other relationships. I think I was afraid that his natural sentimentality might make him a fool for some stupid girl's sobbing.[38]

It seems that while Simone de Beauvoir was dashing around mountain paths, Sartre was practicing the art of seduction. Beauvoir did not do much reading that year in Marseille, and in the end she discarded the novel she was writing, but by the time she left there, she felt better about herself. "Separation and loneliness had not destroyed my peace of mind," she writes in her memoirs. "I knew that I could now rely on myself."[39]

THREE

OLGA KOSAKIEWICZ

October 1932–April 1937

Sartre had been living in Le Havre for eighteen months, and he made it very clear, to himself and others, that he was passing through, not settling in. He did not dislike the place. It was a handsome old town in those days (before large sections were destroyed in the war), and he liked to go for long walks around the docks, observing the sailors' cafés, bars, and whorehouses. But if he chose to live in the seedy Hotel Printania it was because of its proximity to the railway station. And when Simone de Beauvoir took up a teaching job in Rouen, in October 1932, she, too, found herself a hotel (equally squalid) within earshot of the "reassuring whistle of trains."[1]

The railway station was once again the focal point of their lives. On Thursdays there was no school, and as soon as classes were over at midday on Wednesdays, one of them would make the hour-long trip either to Rouen or Le Havre. At midday on Saturdays, when school was out, they headed to Paris (either staying at Madame Morel's or sharing a hotel room for the night.) On Sunday evenings they were back at the Gare Saint-Lazare. Feeling slightly dejected, they'd settle into their separate blue upholstered compartments on their separate trains and bury their noses in detective novels. By the time they inserted their keys in their respective hotel room doors, their provincial towns were asleep.

•　　•　　•

His students at the Lycée François I in Le Havre had never met anyone like Sartre. They were fascinated by this small, round man who turned up to school in an old tweed jacket—no tie—sat on the front desk, his legs swinging in the air, and threw ideas around, without ever looking at any notes, as if he were talking to friends. He was not like other adults. He took ideas very seriously, but did not take his position of authority seriously at all. He never failed the students and almost never gave them below-average grades. He even let them smoke in class.

There was nothing of the snob about him, and there did not seem to be a subject that did not interest him. He took the view that everything told you something about contemporary civilization. "Go to the movies often," he told them.[2] His voice was metallic but clear, with wonderful projection, and somehow quite mesmerizing. He was a brilliant imitator, and so funny and inventive that he managed to bring laughter even into a philosophy class.

Sartre did not seem to care about the things other adults cared about. Those students who got to see his hotel room were shocked by its Spartan austerity. He told them he had few possessions and no interest in material acquisitions. He had very regular work habits, but prided himself on being able to work anywhere—on a train, under a tree, in noisy cafés.

He did not seem to like working in his room. At lunchtime, he could nearly always be found at Le Havre's famous old café, the Guillaume Tell, with its plush red banquettes and stained-glass windows. In the evenings, he was generally at the Café de la Grande Poste. He would eat a simple dinner—usually a sausage, sauerkraut, and fried egg with a beer—then get out his pipe and start writing. His students knew he was working on a novel that contained his ideas about contingency and freedom. Some evenings, he would meet two or three of them in his café. He'd ask questions, and they'd find themselves chatting about all sorts of things. He was encouraging, and made them realize they had choices. Sometimes they played poker, or Sartre taught them bawdy songs.

One of his teaching colleagues had gotten Sartre keen on boxing, and Sartre encouraged his students to become his sparring partners. As he liked to tell people: "The fact that I was their teacher didn't stop them punching me in the face as hard as they could."[3]

•   •   •

Colette Audry was a colleague of Beauvoir's at the Lycée Jeanne d'Arc in Rouen. Nizan knew her from communist circles, and had talked about her warmly to Beauvoir. At first Audry did not warm to the brisk Parisian who came up to her in the staff room and introduced herself. She thought Beauvoir very bourgeois, except for her rapid-fire voice, which wasn't bourgeois at all.[4] For weeks, Beauvoir felt intimidated by this assured young woman who went around in a felt hat, tailored trousers, and a leather jacket, and who seemed always to be on her way to a political meeting. Audry was a committed Trotskyite; Beauvoir knew nothing about politics. Audry had deco-rated her studio apartment with loving care; Beauvoir basically camped out in her room at the Hôtel La Rochefoucauld. But before long, the women were regularly having lunch together at the Brasserie Paul, and finishing it off with a game of Russian billiards at the far end, among the men, before they left to prepare their classes for the next day.

As Audry said later, she enjoyed Beauvoir's company, her laughter, and the ferocity with which she loved or despised people. It seemed to Audry that there were no limits to Beauvoir's courage and deter-mination. Beauvoir had discarded one novel and bravely embarked on another. Audry had no doubt that her friend would be a published writer one day.

When Sartre came to Rouen, they sometimes went out as a three-some. "Soon the three of us were exchanging ideas so fast it some-times made my head spin," Audry recalls. Beauvoir had explained that she and Sartre had a contract based "on truth, not on passion," but Audry could see the tenderness between them, as well as the intellec-tual sparks. "Theirs was a new kind of relationship, and I had never seen anything like it. I can't describe what it was like to be present when those two were together. It was so intense that sometimes it made others who saw it sad not to have it."[5]

In her memoirs, Beauvoir writes that Sartre was fascinated by Audry, and they often discussed her. She does not say that Sartre and Audry had a brief affair, and that for a while, she and Audry were quite jealous of each other.[6]

• • •

Sartre's philosopher friend Raymond Aron (who had encouraged him to go into meteorology) was on a brief visit back to Paris when he pointed to Sartre's apricot cocktail and said: "You see, my dear fellow, if you are a phenomenologist, you can talk about this cocktail and make philosophy out of it!" Aron had a fellowship at the French Institute in Berlin, where he was studying "phenomenology." This school of thought, associated with the German philosophers Husserl and Heidegger, maintained that one could talk in a concrete way about any subject whatsoever. Sartre, who wanted nothing more than to apply philosophy to everyday life, was pale with excitement.

Sartre wasted no time in applying for a fellowship to the French Institute, and he was successful. By the time he arrived in Berlin, in September 1933, Hitler was chancellor, swastikas were flying from government buildings, and Nazis were marching in the streets. In May, there had been a vast bonfire of Jewish and communist books in front of the opera house. Sartre was appalled by Nazism, but convinced it could not possibly last long. He had little interest in politics.

That year, he once again lived the collective life he had so enjoyed at the Ecole Normale. "I re-found the irresponsibility of my youth," he said later of his stay in Berlin.[7] But he also worked hard. His schedule rarely varied, seven days a week. In the mornings, from 9 A.M. to 1:30 P.M., he studied phenomenology. In the middle of the day he took a few hours off, walked by the River Spree or explored the city, and wrote letters. From five to nine in the evening, he worked on his novel. He was writing a second draft.

The French scholars were housed in a charming villa. In the evenings, Sartre and his friends threw themselves into Berlin nightlife. Brought up by Alsatian grandparents, Sartre had always loved heavy German cooking—pork, sausages, sauerkraut, and rich chocolate cakes. And he was extremely fond of German beer.

He had been keen to get himself a German girlfriend but found that he lacked the language skills. He had learned German at school and could read it, but he spoke it badly. "Stripped of my weapon, I was left feeling quite idiotic and did not dare attempt anything. I had to fall back on a French woman," he wrote later. "What sympathy I felt for the naïve remark a frustrated Hungarian once made to the Beaver: 'If you only knew how witty I am in Hungarian!' "[8]

The French woman, Marie Ville, was the wife of one of his colleagues at the institute. She was a dreamy, waiflike creature, so disconnected from the real world that Sartre called her "the moon woman." He liked her amorphousness. For him, "drowning women," as he called them, had an almost "magical attraction."[9]

Whatever Jean-André Ville, a mathematician, thought of his wife's affair with Sartre, it was not easy for Beauvoir.[10] In February 1934, she wangled herself a medical certificate and spent two weeks in a frozen Berlin. She had been there only a few days when Colette Audry sent word that the school authorities were asking about her. If they found out that she was not at home in bed after all, she'd risk being fired. Audry urged Beauvoir to return. So did Sartre. Beauvoir refused. "I shook with rage at the idea of being forced to make any concessions to prudence, and stayed where I was."[11]

Sartre introduced his two girlfriends to each other. He assured Beauvoir that though he and Marie Ville felt very close, they knew the relationship had no future. Beauvoir returned to Paris, and there were no repercussions at her school.

Rouen is the town where Flaubert has Madame Bovary go almost demented with ennui. Simone de Beauvoir, too, was suffering from provincial boredom. As she writes in her memoirs, she was twenty-six and had nothing to distract her—"no husband, no children, no home, no social polish."[12] Meanwhile, Sartre was happily ensconced in Berlin, involved with another woman.

On free days, Beauvoir sometimes spent eight hours cloistered in her room, reading and writing in a fug of smoke. With Sartre's guidance, she was reading Husserl and phenomenology. She was taking German lessons from a German refugee she had met through Colette Audry. And she was writing a novel (once again, it did not seem to be coming together) that explored the conflict between love and independence.

At weekends she sometimes went to Paris to see Pierre Guille, with whom she was once again intimate. "I used to tell him everything that had happened to me," Beauvoir writes in her memoirs, "and if I needed advice, it was to him that I turned. I placed great trust in his judgment, and he occupied a most important place in my life." He would come to the Gare Saint-Lazare to meet her. Beauvoir surmises that if rumors began to circulate in Rouen about her being the mistress of a wealthy senator, it was because she was often seen with Guille, who had a "very fine presence."[13]

That year, Beauvoir befriended one of her students, a boarder. "The little Russian," as the other teachers called her, sat at the back of Beauvoir's baccalaureate philosophy class—pale, ethereal, and sullen looking, her long blond hair hanging over her face. At first Beauvoir thought her listless and uninteresting. The girl rarely opened her mouth in class, and the work she passed in was so scant that Beauvoir had trouble assessing it. No one was more surprised than Beauvoir when Olga Kosakiewicz handed in an essay on Kant that was the best in the class.

Olga was enchanted by their new philosophy teacher, who was young and beautiful, and came to class—unlike the other teachers—wearing makeup and elegant suits. Sparkling with vitality, Mademoiselle de Beauvoir seemed to know everything; she seemed to have read everything. And she dropped intriguing hints about her life—her year in Marseille, long solitary walks by the sea, her habit of writing in cafés. To seventeen-year-old Olga, who was feeling atrociously trapped in her Rouen boarding school, Beauvoir represented a world beyond the stifling horizons of Rouen. She seemed exuberantly free.

One day, after a class test, Olga burst into tears. It was becoming clear to Beauvoir that the girl was very timid, with no confidence in her own abilities. Beauvoir suggested that they meet in the Brasserie Victor the following Sunday. They talked at length. Olga was intelligent and articulate, but seemed quite bewildered and lost in life. Beauvoir felt sure she could help her.

She did, and Olga ended up doing well in her baccalaureate, particularly in philosophy. Before they parted for the summer, the two women spent several evenings in each other's company, playing chess and table tennis, going for long walks, sitting in bars and listening to music. Olga had no idea what she wanted to do with her life. She loved reading, and used language with ease. Beauvoir lent her books (Stendhal, Proust, and Baudelaire) and encouraged her to write. Olga began some prose poems.

In the summer of 1934, Olga returned to her family home in Laigle, a small town in Normandy, while Beauvoir spent her vacation in Germany, then Crete, with Sartre.[14] In her first letter to her, Beauvoir asked Olga not to call her "Mademoiselle" anymore. "You are much too close to me for this formal word to be suitable any longer." She added: "I'm deeply attached to you, but did not know to what extent until you left. I miss you, almost painfully. Not only are you one of the most admirable people I know but you are one of those people who enrich the existence of those around them, and who leave a big emptiness behind them."[15] Beauvoir wrote to Olga several times that summer, encouraging her to enjoy her new independence. ("It can be marvelous, some evenings, to be in a provincial café, a woman alone, eating fried eggs and listening to bad music. One day, you will know these pleasures, I'm impatient for you to experience them."[16]) Olga started letters to Beauvoir, then tore them up.

"Why tear up letters?" Beauvoir asked, in August. "I want you to know that there is not one of your facial expressions, not one of your feelings, and not one incident in your life that I do not care about. You can be certain that when you sit down to eat, there is someone who would be extremely interested in knowing what kind of soup you are eating. Naturally this someone would love to get long and detailed letters."

She had talked about her to Sartre, Beauvoir told Olga. "I've made plans for the new school year. We will go to Le Havre together. We'll go for long walks, and we will see each other very often."

In October 1934, Olga took a room in Rouen and began her new life. Her parents had persuaded her to study medicine, and though she did not have the slightest interest in the subject, she was going to prepare for the entrance examinations. She was in many ways immature, but she had an unusual capacity for listening and understanding. With her came "a new perception of the world," Beauvoir told Sartre, "a world rethought in an absolutely unexpected way by an original little consciousness."[17]

After a year abroad—he called it his "Berlin holiday"—Sartre was back in Le Havre, considerably podgier. ("I was a real little Buddha."[18]) Beauvoir was happier than she had been for some time. Sartre was not.

Later, he would refer to this period of his life as "the gloomy years."[19] The excitement of Berlin was over, and he was back at his old school. (Raymond Aron had taken his place while Sartre was in Berlin.) Sartre was painfully conscious that time was marching on. In his arrogant youth he had written in his journal: "Whoever is not famous at twenty-eight must renounce glory forever."[20] Now he was twenty-nine, going on thirty, and no one had heard of him. Paul Nizan had published a second book, *Antoine Bloyé,* and it was receiving even higher praise than his first. Sartre had been writing diligently for years, and all he had to show for it was a novel that had done the rounds of publishers to no avail, and two drafts of a second novel that Beauvoir, Guille, and Madame Morel agreed was still not right.

Beauvoir thought it a good idea for Sartre to write a philosophical novel, but so far Sartre's writing was too symbolic, dry, and dull. Couldn't he convey his ideas by writing a story like the detective stories they so loved, which portrayed real life? Sartre finally understood what he was doing wrong. In his third draft, he would set the novel in Le Havre, and base the main character, Antoine Roquentin, on himself.

He tried to rekindle his affair with Marie Ville, who was back in Paris with her husband, but she was fed up with Sartre. She now felt he had made her life unnecessarily difficult in Berlin.[21] Sartre felt frustrated about his writing and frustrated about his life, including his relationship with Beauvoir. He liked to tell himself she felt the same:

> We were weary of that virtuous, dutiful life we were leading, weary of what we then called the "constructed." For we had "constructed" our relations, on the basis of total sincerity and complete mutual devotion; and we would sacrifice our impulses, and any confusion there might be in us, to that permanent *directed* love we had constructed. At bottom, what we were nostalgic for was a life of disorder.[22]

One afternoon in November 1934, they were sitting on the terrace of
Les Mouettes, their favorite seafront café in Le Havre. The sea was
dark green and choppy. Seagulls were circling and shrieking. Sartre
started to complain about the monotony of his life. What had happened to the gay irresponsibility of his student days? Where had his
dreams gone? This was not the great man's life he had anticipated. He
still hadn't written anything good. What was he? A provincial schoolteacher! He liked teaching and was fond of his students, but he
despised institutions, headmasters, senior masters, colleagues, and
parents. Like it or not, he told Beauvoir, they were prisoners of the
bourgeois world. They taught fourteen hours a week, took a trip
abroad every summer, and their pensions were guaranteed by the
state. They were almost thirty, and their paths were preordained.
They might as well be married. What adventures could possibly lie
ahead? Beauvoir was soon in floods of tears.[23]

Sartre had put his novel aside in order to finish a philosophical
essay on "The Imagination," commissioned by an academic publisher.
The subject made Sartre wonder about the role of hallucination and
dreams. He talked to Daniel Lagache, a friend from the Ecole
Normale who had specialized in psychiatry. Lagache suggested Sartre
take mescaline, a hallucinogenic drug, to see for himself what hallucination was like. It might conceivably be slightly unpleasant, Lagache
warned, but the effect would wear off in a few hours.

In February 1935, Sartre went to Sainte-Anne's Hospital in Paris
for a mescaline injection. For several hours he lay in a dimly lit room
under observation. He did not hallucinate in the rose-tinted way he
would have liked; instead, everyday objects took on grotesque shapes
and forms for him. The clock became an owl, his umbrella turned
into a vulture, and in the corner of his eye, crabs and polyps swarmed.
Beauvoir waited for him in Madame Morel's apartment on the
Boulevard Raspail. When Sartre turned up that afternoon, his friends
were shocked to see that he was not at all his usual self. He spoke in a
dull, flat voice and stared fixedly either at the telephone cord or at
Beauvoir's crocodile-skin shoes.

For weeks, Sartre did not seem interested in anything. One weekend, Colette Audry accompanied Beauvoir to Le Havre. "We walked
along the beach collecting starfish," Beauvoir recalls. "Sartre looked as

though he had no idea what Colette and I—or indeed he himself—
were doing there."[24] In Paris, they went to an exhibition of Fernando
Gerassi's paintings, and the whole day Sartre sat slumped in a corner,
his face blank. Finally, he admitted that he was fighting off serious
depression. He still had freakish visions. Houses had leering faces.
Lobsters trotted along behind him. Beauvoir, used to Sartre's insistence that the mind controlled the body, was impatient. "Your only
madness is believing that you're mad," she told him.[25]

A doctor advised Sartre to avoid being alone. He did seem far better in company. He knew Beauvoir too well to put himself out, but
with their friends, particularly younger people, he made a real effort
to be entertaining, and he temporarily forgot his neuroses.

In Le Havre, Sartre's friends were a handful of baccalaureate students. One of his favorites was Jacques-Laurent Bost, a charming
young man who was the youngest of ten children from a well-known
Protestant family. His father was the chaplain at their school. His
elder brother Pierre, a novelist and playwright, worked as a reader for
Gallimard. The handsome Jacques-Laurent, his mother's favorite,
was known by all and sundry as "Little Bost."

In Rouen, Sartre started to spend time with Olga Kosakiewicz.
They enjoyed being together, and everyone benefited. Sartre felt
reinvigorated in Olga's presence, Beauvoir was relieved to see Sartre
more cheerful, and Olga liked to feel needed.

Before she even set eyes on Sartre, Olga had encountered the legend. Beauvoir had talked about him and the couple they formed.
Sartre knew that. As he wrote later, his relationship with Beauvoir
appeared "fascinating" and "crushingly powerful" to the people
around them. "Nobody could love one of us without being gripped by
a fierce jealousy—which would end by changing into an irresistible
attraction—for the other one, even before meeting them, on the basis
of mere accounts."[26]

The man Olga encountered was at his seductive best. His lobsters
gave him a poetic aura. Olga liked the idea of eccentric artists and
bohemian madness. It went with the dark Russian soul she made so
much of. Sartre was also hilariously funny. Sometimes they acted little scenes together: a lone Englishwoman meeting a famous adventurer in the middle of the desert, and so on. He would listen to

her for hours, encourage her, and offer to help her. "Sartre had some-thing of a medieval knight about him," Olga said later. "He was very romantic."[27]

That summer, Sartre and Beauvoir went walking in the Tarn region, north of Montpellier. Lobsters followed Sartre along the mountain tracks. Worse, he discovered he was losing his hair. "When I noticed it—or rather when the Beaver noticed it with a shriek at the Trou des Bozouls—it was a symbolic disaster for me. . . . For ages I used to mas-sage my head in front of mirrors: balding became the tangible sign for me of growing old."[28]

Lobsters gave way to the Little Russian. For two years, from the spring of 1935 to the spring of 1937, Sartre was completely obsessed. As he put it, his "strange black mood . . . turned to madness."[29]

Who was this young woman, Olga Kosakiewicz, who managed to fascinate first Beauvoir then Sartre? Her father was a Russian aristo-crat, an officer of the Csar. Her mother, who was French, had gone to Kiev to be a governess in a family of aristocrats, and ended up marry-ing one of the sons. Olga was born in Kiev on November 6, 1915.[30] Her sister, Wanda, was born in 1917, the year of the Russian Revolution. Soon after, the Kosakiewicz family joined the exodus of Russian nobles and dissidents to France.

Victor Kosakiewicz bought a sawmill in Laigle, Normandy. The business did not do well. The girls grew up hearing romantic stories about the magical country they would still be living in, were it not for the evil communists. They felt exotic in France, and superior.

Ever since September 1934, when Olga took a room in town, she and Beauvoir had been spending all their spare time together. In her memoirs, Beauvoir explains the intensity of their relationship by the provincial backdrop against which they were both floundering. "Her feelings toward me quickly reached a burning intensity," she writes of Olga.[31] The fact is, her own were also strong. "There are at the pre-sent time only two people in the world who count in my life," she told Olga, "and you are one of them."[32]

She took the girl to the theater and movies. They drank vast quan-tities of cherry brandy in each other's rooms. "One night we drank so much of the stuff that Olga, after leaving me, rolled head over heels down the stairs and slept there at the bottom till one of the other tenants kicked her awake," Beauvoir writes in her memoirs.[33] They sometimes went to dance bars, and Olga, a superb dancer, tried to teach Beauvoir.

Beauvoir would describe those evenings in fictional form in her first published novel, *She Came to Stay*. Xavière, the exhibitionist young girl, loves nothing more than to dance. "She did not dislike having people take them for Lesbians when they entered a public place; it was the kind of shocking behavior that amused her," Françoise, the Beauvoir character, muses. Xavière soon has them on the dance floor:

> She certainly enjoyed attracting attention and was deliberately holding Françoise tighter than usual, and smiling at her with flagrant coquetry. Françoise returned her smile. Dancing made her head spin a little. She felt Xavière's beautiful warm breasts against her, she inhaled her sweet breath. Was this desire? But what did she desire? Her lips against hers? This body unresisting in her arms?

In July 1935, Olga failed her medical preliminaries, and her parents decided she would have to come home. It was then that Sartre made a suggestion to Beauvoir. Why didn't they take on Olga themselves? She was not interested in medicine, but it seemed she had talent for philosophy. With their two salaries, they could afford to support her. All they needed, since she was twenty and still a minor, was her parents' consent. Beauvoir, it seems, did not sense the danger ahead. "I would help you to work well," she promised Olga. "What an interesting year you could have."

Beauvoir went to Laigle to see Olga's parents. She told them that Olga was intelligent, and she thought she could help her. Olga did not value herself enough, Beauvoir said, and she lacked motivation.[34] But if she did something she liked, she would surely do well.

Marthe and Victor Kosakiewicz were frank about their worries. They did not know what to do with Olga. She never did any work. Nothing interested her. When they tried to talk to her about her future, they met with complete indifference. Olga had spent the sum-

mer daydreaming, they said. She would hum to herself, then get up
and dance for a few minutes. She read a little, but only in brief bursts.
She played tennis and went for long walks. At least—and they were
grateful for this—her violent outbursts were less frequent than in the
previous year. They thought perhaps Mademoiselle de Beauvoir was
right: she was the only person who could give Olga a sense of purpose.
If Beauvoir could afford to support Olga, they were deeply grateful.
"I do not understand how, at twenty, she can accept the beautiful gift
you want to give her," Marthe Kosakiewicz wrote to Beauvoir. "I
would have liked her to show more independence."[35]

Beauvoir had moved to the Hôtel du Petit Mouton, a charming
place with exposed wooden beams, leadglass windows, and rickety
but cheerful furnishings. In October 1935, she rented a room there
for Olga. She and Sartre bought Olga a shelf full of philosophy books.
Together they drew up her schedule.

It was the beginning of the "trio." Their relations were suddenly
placed on an entirely different footing. Beauvoir had originally been
Olga's teacher, then they had become friends, and around this time
they became occasional lovers. Sartre had been courting Olga as well,
and now he also became her teacher. Olga was financially dependent
on them both. Her feelings toward them were a mixture of gratitude,
reverence, defiance, and resentment. Authority figures always
brought out the rebel in her.

At first, Beauvoir writes, the trio had a magical sheen to it:

> Olga's enthusiasms swept away our provincial dust with a
> vengeance: Rouen began to take on a glimmering, iridescent
> appearance. She would open her door to us with great cere-
> mony, offer us jasmine tea and sandwiches made from her own
> recipe, and tell us stories about her childhood and the Greek
> countryside in summer. We in turn told her about our travels,
> and Sartre went through his entire repertoire of songs. We
> made up plays and in general behaved as though we were twenty
> again.[36]

In terms of Olga's studies, Sartre and Beauvoir had been quite
unrealistic. They expected her to study in isolation, without fellow

students and without the supportive structure of university life. But Olga lacked motivation at the best of times. Beauvoir knew Olga's limits, and would stop her lessons after an hour and a half. Sartre's lectures, however, went on and on, and after three hours, Olga would start to nod off. Sartre chided her. Reproaches merely had the effect of paralyzing Olga. She did less and less work. After some months, Sartre and Beauvoir were forced to abandon their plan.

They continued to support her financially. From now on, Olga whiled away her time sleeping, listening to music, dancing, worrying about her future, and trying to steer a path through the impossibly contradictory roles—friend, lover, muse, and protégée—that had been thrust upon her by two older and much stronger personalities.

Years later, on one of the rare occasions Olga Kosakiewicz consented to an interview, she commented that she, her sister Wanda, and Jacques-Laurent Bost were submerged by their two larger-than-life mentors. "We were all like snakes, mesmerized," she said. "We did what they wanted because no matter what, we were so thrilled by their attention, so privileged to have it."[37]

Colette Audry looked on from afar. "I saw enough to know that it was an awful experience for Olga," she recalls. "The poor girl was too young to know how to defend herself really."[38]

At that time, Sartre understood "authenticity" to be pure, unreflective spontaneity—the capacity to be entirely caught up in an immediate feeling. On that basis, he concluded that he was not authentic. "With everything that I feel, before actually feeling it I know that I'm feeling it," he wrote in his notebook. "And then, bound up as I am with defining and thinking it, I no longer more than half-feel it. . . . I fool people: I look like a sensitive person but I'm barren. . . . I know it—and often I'm weary of it."[39] He believed this was the source of his attraction to "drowning women"—tentative, tremulous women who felt intensely and could hardly articulate their feelings.

To Sartre, Olga represented radical authenticity. He philosophized about liberty; Olga *was* liberty. He was eternally analyzing his behavior; she was swept by pure, violent feelings. Whereas he projected himself toward the future, she lived in the present. She refused to make plans, and despised routines, responsibilities, and social duties. Sartre and Beauvoir's methodical work habits horrified her. Olga happily spent three hours washing her hair with egg yolks. Her willpower, such as it was, mostly took the form of refusals. She would refuse to sleep, drinking tea all night to keep herself awake, or refuse to eat, saying she did not want to put on weight. Her health, diet, and body were major preoccupations.

Olga's narcissism fascinated Sartre. There were times when he felt a violent desire to *be* her, "to feel those long slender arms from within."[40] He saw his own body through her eyes. When he first came back from Berlin, Guille had teased him about his paunch. At the time, Sartre had found it amusing. No longer. Olga was horrified by fat people. Sartre was also painfully conscious of his thinning hair.

"I placed her so high . . . that, for the first time in my life, I felt myself humble and disarmed before someone," Sartre wrote later. He abandoned his ultrarationalism and strode eagerly toward passion. "I entered a world that was blacker, but less insipid."[41]

As time went on, Beauvoir felt increasingly stifled by the trio. Sartre's Berlin passion had at least been out of her sight. With Olga, Sartre "experienced feelings of alarm, frenzy, and ecstasy," and he confided all his ups and downs to Beauvoir. She writes: "The agony which this produced in me went far beyond mere jealousy."[42]

Sartre was determined to supplant her in Olga's life, and Beauvoir took the view that she might as well let him. She could not bear dissension between herself and Sartre. She tried hard to see things through Sartre's eyes, but soon realized that she and Sartre simply did not see things the same way. Whereas she saw through Olga's childlike behavior, Sartre took Olga's every whim seriously. For two years, there were quarrels and reconciliations, with Beauvoir in the unenviable middle position. If she sided with Olga, Sartre became furious. If she sided with Sartre, Olga sulked for days.

There were moments when Sartre seemed a complete stranger to her. Beauvoir tried to take comfort in the thought that his relationship with Olga was a mirage, like the lobsters. But if that were so, what did it say about her own relationship with him? "At times, I asked myself whether the whole of my happiness did not rest upon a gigantic lie."[43]

In the next few years, Sartre and Beauvoir would both paint fictional portraits of Olga. In Sartre's novel *The Age of Reason*, Mathieu Delarue is a thirty-four-year-old philosophy teacher in Paris. He's balding, has a paunch, and keeps telling himself with disgust, "I'm getting old." He's been with his girlfriend, Marcelle, for seven years. She is "his comrade, his witness, his counselor, and his critic," and they have a pact to tell each other everything. But Mathieu is in love with Ivich, a pale blond, frail young woman, the daughter of a Russian aristocrat, whose hair smells of egg yolks.

Mathieu is always analyzing people. He can never forget himself. It has been a long time since he forgot himself while making love to Marcelle. She tells him there's something slightly sterile about the way he thinks. "Everything is so neat and tidy in your mind. It smells of clean linen; it's as though you had just come out of a drying-room."

Ivich is emotional and unpredictable. Mathieu yearns to know what the world is like from inside her head. "If I could be granted a wish," he tells her, "it would be that you should be compelled to think aloud."

He is terrified of her judgment. "You used to look at me above the forehead, just at the level of the hair," he tells her. "I've always been so nervous of getting bald.... I thought you had noticed a thinning patch and couldn't take your eyes off it." When she looks at another man, he is eaten up with jealousy. He tells himself he could not endure life without her.

Beauvoir freely admitted that her novel *She Came to Stay* was very close to reality. Despite the minor fictional elaborations, the novel, with its rich use of dialogue, gives a far more vivid picture of the lived experience of the trio than Beauvoir's memoirs.

Pierre and Françoise, intellectuals immersed in the world of Paris theater, have an open relationship, and tell each other everything. At the beginning of the novel, Pierre says he's tired of all his affairs that go nowhere. "With the exception of my relationship with you, everything about me is frivolous and wasteful," he tells Françoise.

"I no longer enjoy these affairs," said Pierre. "It's not as if I were a great sensualist, I don't even have that excuse!" He looked at Françoise a little sheepishly. "The truth is that I get a kick out of the early stages."

Françoise's young friend Xavière is about to return, unwillingly, to her family in Rouen. Pierre suggests to Françoise that they "take her in hand." They form a trio. Soon Pierre's personal neuroses come to the fore:

"It's too ridiculous," he said, "she really makes me uncomfortable, that little devil, with her philosophy that makes less of us than dust. It seems to me that if I could get her to love me, I'd be as sure of myself as I was before.... To make her love me would be to dominate her, to enter her world and conquer in accordance with her own values." He smiled. "You know the need for this kind of victory is a mania with me!"
    "I know," Françoise said.

The novel's only radical departure from reality is the ending. Françoise goes up to the gas range in Xavière's room—Xavière is about to go to sleep—and quietly turns on the gas. It's so psychologically unconvincing, this murder, that it completely lets down the novel. But it shows Beauvoir's need to get her rival out of her system. Astonishingly, she dedicated the book to Olga Kosakiewicz.

Among their various inventive games, Sartre and Beauvoir used to conjure up a character they called Petit Crâne—Little Noddle—a handsome, upright man, a man of action rather than words, who thought little and spoke little, and in the place of ambition had small, obstinate desires. When Little Bost joined their circle, they joked that Little Noddle had materialized in real life. "Light as that young man's presence is, you feel something like a vacuum when he goes," Sartre observed to Beauvoir.[44]

Little Bost was tall, with jet-black hair that fell in his face, green eyes framed with dark lashes, and a dazzling smile. He never pushed himself forward, and did not like to talk about himself. Sartre and Beauvoir attributed his reticence and integrity to his Protestant Huguenot upbringing. He did not have an original mind, and he was always afraid of saying something stupid. But he thought he would like to be a writer, like Sartre, whom he idolized.

In October 1935, Marc Zuorro landed a teaching post in Rouen and joined their circle. He was a friend of Pierre Guille and Madame Morel's, and over the years Sartre and Beauvoir had sometimes met him in Paris. Zuorro, too, was a handsome fellow. He had a beautiful singing voice, and firmly believed he would one day be a famous opera singer. From his future lofty heights, he looked down on the world, mocking everyone, including Sartre and Beauvoir, who appeared to acquiesce in its mediocrity. "Despite this he affected to treat his friends with the greatest consideration," Beauvoir writes. "We were amused by his love of intrigue, his indiscretions, and his scandal-mongering."[45]

She warned Olga: "The handsome Zuorro...will surely try to catch you in the nets of his dirty little intrigues."[46] Indeed, Zuorro quickly added to the atmosphere of tension and jealousy that was growing, like thick brambles, around the trio. He moved into the Hôtel du Petit Mouton and struck up a friendship with Olga. Zuorro could see that Sartre was interested in her, far more so than he publicly let on. The competition spurred Zuorro on. He played Olga his classical records. In the street, he sang her arias from operas. The stories he told her were even more extravagant than Sartre's.

Sartre would watch the two of them going off somewhere, arm in arm, and became wildly jealous. Beauvoir did her best to mollify him.

Sartre and Beauvoir had continued, every year, to apply for teaching posts in Paris. Beauvoir, who knew that her chances were not helped by her living in hotels and consorting with a former student in seedy

Rouen dance bars, was astonished when, in the early summer of 1936, she was offered a post at the Lycée Molière, a girls' school in the affluent sixteenth arrondissement of Paris. Sartre was also promoted, but to a school in Lyon. He decided to turn this down in favor of a less prestigious job in Laon, an hour from Paris by fast train. He calculated that taking the more modest job would give him a better chance of being considered for a Paris post the following year.

Beauvoir moved into the Royal Bretagne Hotel in the Rue de la Gaîté, near the Montparnasse station. Zuorro, who had also landed a post in Paris, installed himself in a more expensive hotel in the nearby Rue Delambre. Little Bost was going to study philosophy at the Sorbonne, and he lived ten minutes away, in his brother Pierre's apartment in the Place Saint-Germain-des-Prés.

Sartre insisted that Beauvoir bring "the daughter of the Cossacks" to Paris.[47] Beauvoir half hoped that Olga's parents would make her go back to Laigle. But Olga was almost twenty-one, and eager to move to the big city. Beauvoir rented a small room for her in the Royal Bretagne, and Olga found herself a part-time job as a waitress. Sartre spent every spare moment in Paris. He and Olga would often spend whole nights together, wandering the streets of Paris till dawn.

They called themselves "the Family." Like most families, theirs was rife with tensions and rivalries.

Sartre's obsession with Olga was devastating for his ego. She told him repeatedly that she was not in love with him. She rarely let him touch her. For more than two years he had waited patiently, making tentative efforts to seduce her. Occasionally, when her defenses were down, he managed to kiss her. But Olga never slept with him.

In Rouen, Zuorro had made a great show of his courtship of Olga. In Paris, Zuorro finally realized he was homosexual. He had always been keen on Bost. Now he declared that Bost was his undying passion.

Bost was embarrassed—this was not a passion he reciprocated—and he began to hide from Zuorro. Olga was hiding these days from Sartre. Bost and Olga had always been a little wary of each other. One of the things that distanced them was Bost's wholesale admiration for Sartre. But things now took a different turn.

One evening, Zuorro peeped through the keyhole of Olga's room in the Royal Bretagne and saw exactly what he had feared: Bost and Olga locked in an embrace. At Christmas, Zuorro accompanied Sartre and Beauvoir to the ski slopes of Chamonix. The three of them shared a hotel room ("a bare, bleak barn of a place, with three beds in it"), and Zuorro loudly cried himself to sleep.[48] On that vacation, Sartre even shed a few tears himself.[49]

For the next few months, Zuorro went around raging and sobbing, then took to prowling around Montparnasse with a revolver in his pocket.[50] Sartre suffered the most ferocious jealousy he had ever known. He had never made public his real feelings for Olga. Now he acted as if he did not mind. He even encouraged Bost. To Beauvoir, he fumed and despaired.

What made things worse, far worse, was that Gallimard rejected Sartre's novel *Melancholia* (the future *Nausea*). He had been working on it for four years, and had staked everything on it. With Beauvoir's encouragement and advice, he had completely reworked it three times. She was convinced that it was now a first-rate novel. Sartre was heartbroken.

By February 1937, Beauvoir was at her wits' end. She was working very hard—at school most mornings by eight-thirty, and in her spare time trying to finish a collection of novellas—and she felt strangely exhausted. One evening, she was having a drink with Bost at the Café Sélect, in Montparnasse, when a shiver ran through her. She spent the next few days in bed, sweating and in severe pain. Every day she felt weaker than she had the day before. Her doctor finally became alarmed. She was taken by ambulance to a hospital in Saint-Cloud, on the edge of Paris.

It turned out to be an extremely serious case of pneumonia. One of her lungs had collapsed, and the other was damaged. If the good lung failed, she could die. For weeks, Beauvoir floated between consciousness and unconsciousness, relieved to lie between fresh sheets, with nurses to look after her, removed from the daily crises of the trio.

Her mother visited every morning. Olga and Madame Morel came in the afternoons. When Sartre was in Paris, he saw her every day. His

tenderness and solicitude reassured her. But he remained preoccupied. "It was the last stage of my passion for O," he wrote later. "I was
nervy and restless, each day I used to wait for the moment of seeing
her again—and beyond that moment for some kind of impossible
reconciliation. The future of all those moments spent waiting for the
train in the station at St-Cloud was that impossible love."[51]

Her doctor wanted to send Beauvoir to a sanatorium. She wanted
to convalesce in Paris. The doctor reluctantly agreed. Sartre moved
her to a more comfortable hotel, the one in which Zuorro lived, on
the Rue Delambre. During the Easter vacation, when Sartre was in
Paris, he carried Beauvoir's lunch over from the Coupole, taking great
care not to spill it on the way.[52]

That Easter, in 1937, Olga's sister, Wanda, came for a visit to Paris.
She had grown more beautiful since the time Sartre met her in a
dance bar in Rouen. Whereas Olga was delicate and graceful, Wanda
was plump and comely. But her face was exquisite. Unlike her sister,
Wanda was only semiarticulate. "It was pathological," she told an
interviewer, years later. "I could not talk, and not at all with Sartre."[53]
She was an adolescent from the provinces, she explained to her interviewer, and this was Paris, the intimidating capital, and there was
Sartre, equally intimidating, who never stopped talking. She felt completely out of her depth.

One day, Olga was looking after Beauvoir, and Sartre suggested to
Wanda that he show her Montmartre. She was a good walker and
could happily trudge for kilometers, but that day Sartre exhausted
her.[54] He took her to his favorite place, Le Café Rouge. At one point,
he suggested they act out roles. She would be his mother; he would
be her daughter. "I was horribly shocked," Wanda recalls.

The memory of that afternoon still made Wanda shudder when
she was fifty-six. On the way home, in the back of a taxi, Sartre put
his arm around her shoulders, pulled her over to him, and planted a
kiss on her lips. Wanda, a twenty-year-old virgin, was appalled.[55]

For the rest of her vacation, Wanda dreaded bumping into Sartre
on the street. She hid in her sister's hotel room, refusing to go out.

Olga, who was quite bitter these days about Sartre's manipulative behavior, was furious on her sister's behalf. After Wanda returned to Laigle, Olga tackled Sartre about it.

He penned Wanda an icy letter from the Dôme. "Calm down," he told her. He would not be seeing her again, nor her older sister. If destiny should cause them to meet on the street, he would cross the road. So he had spoiled her Paris holiday? She had spoiled it herself! Or at least, her sister had, by telling her all those nasty things about him. He had never had any intention of playing the seducer. That role did not suit him, he already knew that. If anything, he had been rather bored by the idea of taking her out. And he had never for one second imagined that she loved him![56]

With her collapsed lung, Beauvoir missed an entire term of teaching. For weeks, she was bedridden. Sartre wrote her tender letters. "Do you feel well, are there roses in your cheeks?" he asked. "Don't forget to take a little walk around your armchair. And when you've had a good trip around it, sit down in it."

It was Zuorro and Bost who took her out for the first time. "They walked me as far as the Luxembourg Gardens, each supporting me by one arm," Beauvoir writes. "The fresh air and sunlight were quite overwhelming, and I could hardly keep my balance."[57]

She was still weak and gaunt in mid-April, when she took the train south to convalesce, on doctor's orders, in a warmer climate. In the little Provençal town of Bornes-les-Mimosas, she gorged herself with good food and lay in the sun reading Faulkner's short stories. A few days later, defying her doctor's strict orders, she slung her knapsack on her back and set off on a walk. Sartre urged her not to tire herself out. "Eat well, my Beaver, turn your back to the sea, walk three little kilometers, then sit down."

From Laon, Sartre was determinedly courting Wanda, despite his protestations to the contrary. Every day, he worked on his short stories, then spent from one to three hours writing to "the littlest Kosakiewicz." Near the end of April he told Beauvoir there had been two letters in his mailbox that afternoon:

Yours was very short, my darling Beaver, but so blissful it was a joy to read. Wanda's was long (about like the previous one) and very appealing. That girl seems to have a lazy but considerable intelligence, because each of her letters shows progress over the previous ones. I'll send it to you as soon as I've answered it.

Years later, Sartre told his biographer John Gerassi (the son of Fernando and Stépha) that when Olga went off with Bost, he was excruciatingly jealous for six months. In order not to succumb to despair, he felt obliged to form a romantic relationship with Olga's sister, Wanda.

"Why did you feel obliged?" Gerassi asked.

"Because the woman I loved had refused me," Sartre said. "They look very alike, you see, and so it had to be her. It could not be anyone other than this sister."[58]

FOUR

THE PROSPECT OF WAR

May 1937–September 1939

In May 1937, Sartre's gloomy years came to an abrupt end. "Everything began to smile on me."[1] He announced to Beauvoir, still convalescing in the south, that Gallimard had decided to publish his novel *Nausea* after all.[2] "Today, I walk the streets like an author." One of his short stories was going to appear in the summer issue of Gallimard's prestigious journal, the *Nouvelle Revue Française*. And he had landed a new teaching post. After eight years of exile in different towns—eight years of hanging about on railway platforms—he and Beauvoir would finally both be in Paris.

In the summer, they spent six weeks in Greece, three of those weeks with Bost. They slept in the open. Sartre and Bost raced each other down the marble steps of the Acropolis. They traveled to the Cyclades islands on decrepit old boats. (In the choppy seas, Beauvoir invariably heaved her guts up, and Sartre would accuse her of self-indulgence.) Beauvoir planned exhausting excursions, to which Sartre mostly good-naturedly concurred. (When he did not, she admits she was capable of shedding "tears of pure rage."[3]) On the island of Santorini, they set off on their longest walk, one they would never forget. The sun was blazing mercilessly, and by the time they reached the ancient ruins of Thera they were parched and exhausted. Then they had to walk halfway across the island to catch a bus back. The last straw was when they strayed from the path and lost their way, whereupon Sartre threw one of his short, sharp temper tantrums. "This is a fine sort of lark," he said. "I came out here to make the Grand Tour, and now you've got me playing at Boy Scouts."[4] By the time they got to the village of Emborio, and stumbled around the baking, shuttered streets looking for a place to eat, they felt half dead.

Sometimes Bost and Beauvoir went off by themselves, exploring or swimming, while Sartre stayed in a café and worked. That summer, he wrote to Wanda every day—hundreds of pages in all—colorful, humorous letters full of tenderness.[5]

While Beauvoir traveled around Alsace for ten days with Olga, Sartre went back to Paris to look for a room. Beauvoir's hotel, the Royal Bretagne, was full, as were most of the long-term rental hotels in Montparnasse, and Sartre was pleased to discover the Hôtel Mistral, on the Rue Cels, a tiny street between the Avenue du Maine and the Montparnasse Cemetery. "It doesn't look very promising, has a shabby stairway and motheaten halls," he told Beauvoir, "but the rooms are large, clean, and much better furnished than those at the Royal Bretagne, with a sofa, rug, bookshelves on the walls."

When Beauvoir came back to Paris, they moved in, taking rooms on different floors. "Thus we had all the advantages of a shared life," Beauvoir writes in her memoirs, "without any of its inconveniences."[6]

Their favorite cafés—the Dôme, Coupole, and Sélect—were close by, on the Boulevard du Montparnasse. Just around the corner from the Mistral, on the Avenue du Maine, was a large, noisy brasserie, the Café des Trois Mousquetaires. For the next few years, these cafés were as familiar to them as their hotel rooms. "What never wearies me," Sartre would write, "is to sit on chairs which belong to nobody (or, if you like, to everybody), in front of tables which belong to nobody: that's why I go and work in cafés—I achieve a kind of solitude and abstraction."[7]

Now that they lived in the same city, they had to be careful not to encroach on each other's private space. Their days were strictly scheduled. On the whole, they did not see each other before they left for school. Sartre tended to be irascible when he first got up, and preferred his own company at breakfast. "I can hardly endure even the Beaver," he confessed in his journal. "I have been known, when she'd be waiting for me at the Rallye, to pop in to the Café des Trois

Mousquetaires and quickly gulp down a coffee and croissants, in order to remain for a moment still wrapped up in myself and last night's dreams."[8] Their afternoon writing hours were equally sacred. Lunch times and evenings, after eight P.M., were their sociable hours.

They had long ago decided that the most satisfying form of communication was tête-à-tête. If Sartre was eating with Wanda at the Coupole, or if Beauvoir was seeing Olga at the Dôme, there was no question of the other's spontaneously joining them. And time limits were sacrosanct. Their friends constantly complained that when their time was up, they were expected to melt away, making way for the next person.

Sartre was teaching at the Lycée Pasteur in Neuilly, an affluent western district of Paris, close to where his parents lived, in Passy. His mother, Anne-Marie, wanted him to have lunch every day at her house, after he'd finished his day's teaching, but he could not abide his nagging stepfather. "I convinced my mother that it would be quite enough if I came for lunch on Tuesdays and dinner on Sunday evenings," he told Beauvoir. "She asks only a brief bit of afternoon for herself, which is reasonable, because these days she's being extremely kind."[9]

Beauvoir saw her parents less often, and did not enjoy her visits. Georges de Beauvoir had become bitter and disillusioned with his life, and often made jibes about Simone's writing, which never found a publisher, and her ignominious free union with Sartre. "You'll never amount to more than a Worm's whore," he flung at her.[10]

Nausea was published in April 1938. The dedication read: "To the Beaver." Les Nouvelles Littéraires called it "one of the distinctive works of our time." Paul Nizan (whose third novel, La Conspiration, was also a contender for the prizes) hailed Sartre as a "French Kafka." Sartre and Nizan were both considered to have a good chance of winning the prestigious Prix Goncourt. Neither did.

When Sartre's story "The Wall" appeared in the Nouvelle Revue Française, André Gide told the editors he thought it a masterpiece. "Who is this new Jean-Paul?" he asked. "It seems to me we can expect a lot from him."[11]

• • •

Simone de Beauvoir dazzled her students at the Lycée Molière. She came to class in elegant, tight-fitting suits and exuded a "brilliant, piercing, bold intelligence." She never looked at her notes, and spoke so fast that the students sometimes begged her to slow down. Bianca Bienenfeld, the best student in Beauvoir's 1938 baccalaureate philosophy class, thought her like "a ship's prow speeding through the waves."[12]

That spring, Bienenfeld wrote Mademoiselle de Beauvoir a letter. She was tremendously inspired by philosophy classes, she said, and would like to continue her studies at university. Might it be possible for them to meet and talk after school? The reply came by express delivery. Beauvoir suggested a brasserie in Montparnasse.

Bienenfeld was sixteen, small and pretty, with a mass of curly auburn hair. Her parents, hoping to escape the anti-Semitism they had experienced in Poland, had come to France when Bianca was a baby, and her father, previously a medical doctor, had done well in the pearl business. They were a cultured, well-read family. Bienenfeld was also a talented pianist. Beauvoir responded to the girl's passion and intelligence. "I respect her wholeheartedly," Beauvoir told Bost, "and there are a whole lot of occasions when I do not have the impression of talking to a young girl."[13]

The two women were soon spending every Sunday together. "Waking up Sunday morning was a joy for me," Bienenfeld would write in her memoirs. "I would run to catch the Metro at Passy station, near my family's house. . . . I was so terribly impatient for the end of my ride; I don't think I have ever felt so strongly about any other ride in my entire life."[14] She got out at Edgar-Quinet and ran all the way to the "seedy-looking Mistral."

Beauvoir told her about Sartre, explaining that they loved each other but did not want to live together, they did not believe in marriage, and did not want children, and they had affairs with other people, and were never jealous. Bienenfeld was fascinated by the stories about their past trio with Olga, and astonished when she learned that Sartre was now courting Olga's younger sister. She thought the Kosakiewicz sisters sounded lazy and capricious, and she could not understand Sartre and Beauvoir's generosity toward them. In every way, Beauvoir struck her as courageous and admirable:

> From the very first months I identified myself ardently with Simone de Beauvoir. I did everything to get closer to her, to such an extent that my classmates later made fun of the speech habits I had picked up from her. . . . Around June, even before graduating from high school, I knew I wanted to get a degree in philosophy and teach, just like her.[15]

At the end of June, after Bienenfeld graduated from school, the two women went on a backpacking trip in the Morvan region, in Burgundy. They hiked about twenty kilometers a day, in mountainous terrain. Bienenfeld found it hard going. Beauvoir urged her on with a hint of impatience. It rained for the whole five days. They stayed in little pensions sharing a bed. "It was during this trip that we began, shyly at first, our physical involvement," Bienenfeld writes. She was soon telling Beauvoir that she would never love anyone else as much as she loved her.

In July 1938, Sartre remained in Paris to finish a volume of short stories and to see Wanda Kosakiewicz, who was coming to stay at the Mistral for a week. Beauvoir was going hiking in the mountains of Haute-Savoie with Bost, who had proved to be one of their few friends, male or female, who could keep up with her. Sartre saw her off on the night train.

The following evening, Sartre ate at the Coupole while reading a detective novel. After dinner, he took out his pipe and wrote to Beauvoir:

> I didn't much like saying goodbye yesterday, you absurd little globe-trotter; you'd still be with me right now, full of good little smiles, if you didn't have that strange mania for gobbling up kilometers. Where the devil are you, anyway? This morning I was mourning for you because it was gray out and I imagined you at the summit of your little mountain looking up, with a

stubborn expression, at a sea of gray clouds, like a fisherman gazing at his cork bobbing on the water.... I love you very much, absurd little thing.

Afterward, Sartre went for a long walk, then caught the metro back to the hotel. There was no message from Wanda, he told Beauvoir the next day ("I was a bit annoyed"), and Olga's room was dark. He wondered if Wanda had changed her mind about coming:

> I began to downplay the fun I'd have the next day with Wanda, through a compensatory phenomenon I know very well by now: ever since the Olga affair I immediately blot out anything with the slightest resemblance to passion, be it no more than jangled nerves, in a sort of abiding fear. It's not just with Olga but with the whole world that I have "counter-crystallized." So I went to bed regretting, as part of the act, that I wouldn't be able to work the following days if Wanda should come.

It transpired that Olga had gone to meet Wanda, who turned up on the evening train. Sartre woke to find a note from Wanda suggesting they meet at the Dôme at two in the afternoon, and one from Olga asking for money. He found the two sisters sitting on the terrace of the Dôme. He and Wanda walked to the Rue Mouffetard "affectionately entwined."

Sartre's next letters, addressed to Beauvoir *and* Bost, announced an unexpected turn of events. He had allowed himself to be distracted by a young actress, Colette Gilbert (his interest was piqued by the fact that Maurice Merleau-Ponty was also pursuing her), and Wanda had gone home to Laigle early, in a huff.

Meanwhile, Sartre told Gilbert he loved her, but that there was no room for her in his life with Beauvoir and Wanda. As Sartre told his two readers, Gilbert nevertheless spent three nights with him, in his room at the Mistral:

> It's the first time I've slept with a brunette, actually *black-haired*, Provençale as the devil, full of odors and curiously hairy, with a little black fur patch at the small of her back and a very white

body, much whiter than mine. . . . Very lovely legs, a muscular and absolutely flat stomach, not the shadow of a breast, and, all in all, a supple, charming body. A tongue like a kazoo, which unreels endlessly and reaches in to caress your tonsils.[16]

Sartre was fairly sure that on their last night together, before she left for vacation, he had taken Gilbert's virginity. ("How can I tell you in terms delicate enough not to shock Bost?")

Around midnight she suddenly became very nervous, pushed me away then drew me back and finally said, "It bothers me that I'm not yours. I would like you to enter me." "You want me to try?" "You're going to hurt me, no, no!" But I tried gently. She moaned. . . . After a moment she said louder, "No more, no more, let me be, please." I stopped and said to her, "But you're no longer a virgin."[17]

At seven the next morning, he accompanied Gilbert to the station. When they said good-bye, her eyes filled with tears. Back at the hotel, he found blood on his sheets.

Sartre was infatuated by the theater of seduction, and he knew it. He described it as a "literary labor," which, much like writing, involved fine words, adroit silences, and skilled use of viewpoint. The difference, he reflected in his journal, was that seducing women did not make him feel noble. "I'd come back from a rendezvous, mouth dry, facial muscles tired from too much smiling, voice still dripping with honey and heart full of . . . disgust."[18] Writing, on the other hand, made him feel worthwhile. When he first heard that *Nausea* was going to be published, he told Beauvoir: "I feel more likeable with this than the sort of happiness that comes to me through the bounty of a good woman. I . . . can think of myself with pleasure."[19]

His desire to seduce was only partly due to his sense of ugliness. As a child he had learned to please the adults around him with his little antics. He writes in *Words* that early on, he became "a buffoon, a clown, a sham." Even before his walleye was noticeable, he had gone to considerable lengths to win little girls' hearts through his talents as an actor and storyteller. In his adolescence, his hated stepfather once made the casual remark that Sartre was like him: "He'll never be able to talk to women."

> In a child's life there are always words of this kind, thrown out absent-mindedly, which are like the absent-minded smoker's match in some forest . . . and which set the whole lot ablaze. I'm not so sure that this pronouncement wasn't one of the main causes, in later life, of all those conversations I stupidly wasted in spouting sweet nothings—just to prove to myself that in fact I did know how to talk to women.[20]

Sartre's dream was to be "a scholarly Don Juan, slaying women through the power of his golden tongue." Since he himself felt so hideously ugly, it was essential that the women were beautiful. ("An ugly man and an ugly woman—the result is really . . . rather too conspicuous."[21]) The only problem, he admitted, was that once he had conquered a woman, he scarcely knew what to do with her. "To be honest, for a long time—and perhaps to this very day—nothing struck me as more moving than the moment at which the avowal of love is finally wrenched forth."[22]

Sartre's lifelong practice of harsh self-analysis was disconcerting—slippery, almost. His friends ended up admiring if not his behavior then at least the merciless lucidity with which he scrutinized himself. But what did it add up to? Critics have regularly discussed Sartre's self-excoriation. Was it exhibitionism? Was he taking responsibility for his actions? Or was it a form of exoneration?

Sartre had been courting Wanda for over a year, and their relationship was still unconsummated. Like her sister, she was horrified by his unhealthy diet, which she blamed for his bad skin. She made it clear that physically, he disgusted her. This made Sartre all the more determined in his pursuit.

Feeling contrite about making her jealous with Gilbert, he took the train to Rouen. Wanda consented to meeting him there for the weekend. They shared a room at Le Petit Mouton (where Beauvoir and Olga had once lived). They even shared a bed. Wanda let him contemplate her naked body, but she resisted any incursions. "To tell the truth, I gain territory each time," Sartre reported to Beauvoir.[23]

After Wanda caught the train back to Laigle, Sartre had a few hours to kill before returning to Paris. It was a dreary, gray Sunday. He sat in the Brasserie de l'Opéra and wrote a tender letter to Wanda. He called her his "dear little marvel." He had been wandering the streets of Rouen, missing her, he said. He could still see the charming little smile she had flashed him when she left. He imagined her in the train, downhearted to be returning to Laigle. "I love you, my dear little Wanda." He believed, or *wanted* to believe, that she was at least a bit fond of him. *Was* she?[24]

Wanda was persuaded to return to Paris for a few more days. However, Sartre wrote to Beauvoir (still in the mountains with Bost), progress had been stalled:

Little Kosakiewicz displays the mental faculties of a dragonfly, and I'm finding it heavy going. I so wish you were here, I want to feel your arm in mine and tell you little anecdotes and hear your comments. Last night was painful.... I was deliberately very affectionate with her, first on La Butte, and then at the College Inn, but all in vain. There at the end, my tenderness made her shudder with displeasure.

They had spent the evening drinking. Wanda looked very pretty, "in an angelic little jacket." Afterward, in her room at the Mistral, Sartre tipped her back on the bed and kissed her. She dashed to the bathroom, and Sartre heard her vomit. He supposed the rum and sherry had upset her stomach. The next afternoon, he met her at the Dôme. "I froze her out all day, abruptly dropping my game and declaring that we were through unless she became more loving with me. She promised anything I wanted."

Sartre and Beauvoir had arranged to meet at the railway station in Marseille on the morning of July 30. They were going to take a boat across the Mediterranean to Morocco. "I'm feeling a sort of departure anguish right now, the whole year's behind me," Sartre wrote to her.

"O charm of my heart and my eyes, mainstay of my life, my consciousness and my reason, I love you most passionately, and I need you."

Beauvoir had been having an enjoyable time in the Savoy with Bost. He was waiting for her at the station at Annecy, "tanned and looking very nice in his yellow pullover."[25] For the first few days they had risen at six in the morning and hiked grueling distances. They wound their way through gorges, climbed narrow mountain paths, scrambled across screeds of rock, and traversed stretches of snow. In a hailstorm, they hurried down a steep mountain, sliding down slippery ferns, and Beauvoir gashed her left hand on a rock. Bost washed the wound with spirits, bandaged her hand with a handkerchief, and insisted they find a doctor in a nearby hamlet. One afternoon, Bost threw up from sheer exhaustion, and Beauvoir had a violent nosebleed. In the evenings, after a hearty dinner washed down with local wine, Bost smoked his pipe and filled in their travel log, while Beauvoir wrote letters. In fine weather, they slept in a small tent. When it was wet, they took a room in an inn. On the fifth night, it was pouring, and they slept in a barn. Beauvoir would write to Sartre from Albertville:

Something extremely nice has happened to me, which I didn't at all expect when I left: three days ago, I slept with little Bost. It was I who suggested it, of course. Both of us had been wanting it: we'd have serious conversations during the day, and the evenings would be unbearably oppressive. One rainy evening at Tignes, in a barn, lying on our bellies ten centimeters from each other, we gazed at each other for an hour, putting off the moment of going to sleep with various pretexts; he was chattering madly and I was vainly searching for the casual propitious phrase that I couldn't bring myself to articulate—I will tell this to you better when I see you. Finally I looked at him and laughed stupidly, and he said: "Why are you laughing?" and I said: "I was trying to picture your face if I suggested that you sleep with me," and he said: "I thought you were thinking that I wanted to kiss you and didn't dare." After that we floundered around for another quarter of an hour before he decided to kiss me. He was simply astonished when I told him I'd always felt incredible tenderness towards him, and he ended up telling me last night that he had loved me for a long time. I'm very fond of him. We spend idyllic days, and nights of passion. But have no fear of finding me sullen, disoriented or ill at ease on Saturday; it's something precious to me, something intense, but also light and easy and properly in its place in my life, simply a happy blossoming of relations that I'd always found very nice.[26]

The following weekend, Beauvoir and Sartre, on their way to Tangiers, stood in the bow of the boat, underneath the shooting stars, watching the moon disappear into the sea. Sartre showed no signs of jealousy, but told Beauvoir, without any real reproach in his voice, that by sleeping with Bost she was being "ignoble" to Olga. Had Beauvoir considered how complicated her life was going to be in the coming year?

It was true, what Sartre said. Beauvoir and Olga had remained close friends, despite their ups and downs over the years. (They had long since ceased being lovers.) And it mattered a great deal to Olga that Bost was faithful to her. But Beauvoir kept thinking of the previous summer, when Bost had been with them in Greece. They had crossed from Marseille to Piraeus in a rickety boat called *Cairo City*, and she had gazed at the sleeping Bost with longing. Throughout those three weeks with Bost, she had been painfully conscious that Bost was a delightful young man of twenty-one, and she was about to turn the ripe old age of thirty.

This summer she *was* thirty, and she would never forget the way Bost had murmured "I love you" at the station at Chambéry. She felt as if her youth had been returned to her. She was not going to spoil it with remorse.

Tangiers, Casablanca, Marrakech, Fez, Ksar el Souk, Meknès: they marveled at the shuttered palaces, the mosques, the labyrinthine streets and noisy marketplaces, the veiled women, the donkeys struggling under their loads. In the stifling heat of August, there were few

European tourists in Morocco. Sartre and Beauvoir tried to spend the hottest part of the day in cafés, reading, writing, and drinking mint tea. In Meknès, Sartre stayed and worked in their hotel while Beauvoir went off for the day by herself, steeling herself against the inevitable harassment by Arab men. She had completed her book of novellas that year, while teaching, and she was giving herself a break from writing. Sartre had finished his volume of short stories, and was now writing a daring article for the *Nouvelle Revue Française* in which he attacked the establishment Catholic writer François Mauriac. In years to come, the article would be considered among his most brilliant pieces of literary criticism.

They moved between two worlds, European and Arab. In the native shantytowns, they came across the worst poverty they had ever seen. They told themselves that the French were responsible. They made a twelve-hour trip south, crossing the burning desert in a bus that felt like a furnace, and the driver, the only other European on board, insisted that they sit next to him. They were horrified by the tyrannical way he treated the Arabs to whom he delivered goods along the route.

When Beauvoir heard a love song on a crackling little radio in an Arab bar, she fought back tears. She thought constantly about Bost. "In three weeks I have forgotten none of your smiles, your kisses," she wrote to him. "I am about to go to bed, I have a terrible desire to see you. You remember Emborio, how hot and thirsty we were, how we were tortured by our need for shade and water. Well! That is nothing beside the kind of anguish I feel tonight. My love, my love, how I wish you were here, your body pressed against mine."[27]

Bost wrote that he was reading and rereading her letters with the most perfect joy. He was having "a devil of a time" with her handwriting. He felt like a bad Hellenic scholar, who needed a dictionary to read Greek texts.

> But I'm not very irritated. . . . On the whole when I read your letters, I'm in a state of mad joy, in a way I never thought I would feel about anyone. I love you *tremendously,* I want you to know that and to feel it strongly and to take pleasure in that. I really enjoy writing to you. When I write, I can visualize your

face. I suspect there's an idiotic smile on mine. I don't care. Write to me often. I will too. . . . I don't try to imagine the places you write to me about, nor to imagine you in Casablanca and Marrakech, but I can hear you speaking to me. I haven't lost the reality of your voice, nor your face, and I easily picture you on the road going down from Tignes to Bourg-St-Maurice, when you were telling me things about yourself. I would like to hug you and to kiss you until it hurts. . . . I love you and I kiss you.[28]

He had a hard time getting to sleep the previous night, he wrote. "I tossed and turned until three in the morning in the tent and got up at one point to drink. I had an incredible desire to have you beside me in the tent, and two months seems interminable."[29]

In Fez, Beauvoir learned that Bianca Bienenfeld's mother had come across a love letter Beauvoir had written to Bienenfeld, and had raged about this "spinster with peculiar habits."[30] The publishing house Grasset had rejected her novellas (already turned down by Gallimard), saying they lacked originality.[31] A tender letter from Bost helped her face these bits of bad news stoically.

But an unusually warm letter from Olga left her uneasy. Bost was now with Olga in Marseille, in a dilapidated hotel overlooking the Old Port. Beauvoir was anxious. How did he feel, she asked Bost, strung between two women? There were moments, Bost replied, when he felt very bad about it.

In October 1938, back in Paris, Beauvoir and Bost stole as much time together as they could. They spent several nights at the Hôtel du Poirier, in a charming square in Montmartre, well away from Olga's daily stamping ground. They roamed the canals and wandered beside the Seine. Beauvoir felt insecure at times, realizing that she had complicated Bost's life, and convinced that she loved him more deeply than he loved her. Bost tried to reassure her. He had wanted this relationship every bit as much as she did. "I'm happy with my life now."[32]

At the beginning of November, Bost had to leave for military service in Amiens. And this time—unlike when Sartre did his—the

prospect of war hung over them. Bost was a soldier at the bottom of
the hierarchy. Normally, for a man with his education, it would have
been natural to climb the ranks to officer status. But Bost, fiercely
democratic in spirit and stubborn as a mule when it came to making
what he considered "compromises," firmly refused to do so. He did not
want to give orders, he said. He wanted to belong to the common herd.
He and Beauvoir both knew what this decision meant. In wartime, he
would be among the first men to be offered up as cannon fodder.

Bost came to Paris most Sundays. Some weekends Beauvoir went
to Amiens to see him. Olga was always scrounging up money to go to
see Bost herself, and frequently it was Sartre or Beauvoir who paid
her fare. From now on, Bost had to juggle his free time among Olga,
Beauvoir, and his parents. ("The pastor" and "the pastoresse," as he
called them, lived at Taverny, twenty kilometers northwest of Paris.)
This meant habitually lying to Olga.

Sartre and Beauvoir regularly discussed Olga's situation. What was
the exact nature of false happiness such as Olga's? What freedom did
she have within it? Should Beauvoir feel remorse about her affair
with Bost? Sartre usually came up with rationalizations that appeased
Beauvoir's conscience. Olga had been furious when Sartre had first
starting courting Wanda, and she was still angry with him. Sartre
took the view that there were some people one simply had to lie to.

Sartre was urging Beauvoir to write about her own life. One day that
summer, the two of them had been sitting in the Dôme discussing
their writing. Sartre leaned forward, Beauvoir recalls:

> "Look," he said, with sudden vehemence, "why don't you put
> *yourself* into your writing? You're more interesting than all these
> Renées and Lisas." The blood flushed up in my cheeks; it was a
> hot day, and as usual the place was full of smoke and noise. I felt
> as though someone had banged me hard on the head. "I'd never
> dare to do that," I said. To put my raw, undigested self into a
> book, to lose perspective, compromise myself—no, I couldn't do
> it, I found the whole idea terrifying. "Screw up your courage,"
> Sartre told me, and kept pressing the point.[33]

It was a bold idea, some thirty years before intimate self-revelation became commonplace. At first Beauvoir worried that it was self-indulgent. And there were other people's feelings to consider. But in the autumn of 1938 she suddenly felt a strong desire to write about the complicated relations between the four people she knew best in the world—Sartre, herself, Bost, and Olga. She wanted to write a novel about freedom, love, friendship, and jealousy. She wanted to explore the question of the "Other" that she and Sartre were always discussing. Sartre thought it an excellent idea.

People think of *She Came to Stay* as a novel about the trio that Françoise and Pierre form with the whimsical young Xavière. But a fourth character in the novel is just as important, and he's by far the most tenderly portrayed. Gerbert, with his green eyes and shock of soft black hair falling over his eyes, resembles Jacques-Laurent Bost to the letter.

In the novel, Xavière puts an end to the tortures of the trio by falling in love with Gerbert. "I'm always fond of what belongs to me," she tells Françoise pointedly. "It's restful to have someone entirely to yourself."[34] Olga had said exactly the same thing to Beauvoir.

Soon after that, Françoise goes on a hiking trip with Gerbert. One wet night, the two hikers throw their sleeping bags close together on some hay in a barn. The candle flutters. They suddenly feel awkward with one another. Gerbert asks Françoise why she is smiling. She plucks up her courage:

"I was smiling—wondering how you would look—you who loathe complications—if I suggested your sleeping with me."

"I thought you were thinking that I wanted to kiss you and didn't dare," Gerbert said.[35]

Back in Paris, Gerbert tells Françoise: "I've never loved any woman the way I love you, nowhere near the way I love you." This was truly the novelist's revenge.

One sunny afternoon, Françoise is reading on the terrace of the Dôme. When she opens her handbag to pay, she discovers that the key to her writing desk is missing. Her heart misses a beat. She runs back to the hotel, rushes up the stairs, opens the door of her room, and finds her desk ransacked. Letters from Gerbert are scattered all over the carpet.

"Xavière knows." The walls of the room began to whirl. Searing, bitter darkness had descended on the world. Françoise dropped into a chair, crushed by a deadly weight. Her love for Gerbert was there before her, black as treason.

In the novel, Françoise is so upset by Xavière's knowing the truth that she murders Xavière in order not to have to face her accusing eyes. And yet here was Beauvoir, the writer, effectively *telling* Olga that she was having an affair with Bost.

No one knew better than Olga how much the novel was true to reality, with some bits of dialogue taken straight from life. Nevertheless, to Olga, Beauvoir and Bost would always insist that the romance between Françoise and Gerbert was pure invention. Olga must have often wondered: Where did the truth lie in this bewildering hall of mirrors? First came the flattering dedication: "To Olga Kosakiewicz." And then the epigraph from Hegel: "Each conscience seeks the death of the other."

While she was in love with Bost, Beauvoir was also having a passionate affair with Bianca Bienenfeld. (Bost knew about Bienenfeld, but Bienenfeld did not know about him.) Bienenfeld was eighteen now, and studying philosophy at the Sorbonne. She saw Beauvoir three times a week, and their lovemaking was ardent.

For their Christmas 1938 vacation, Sartre and Beauvoir went to Mégève. (Beauvoir asked Bost to write to her, "Mme Sartre," at the hotel Les Primevères.) Bienenfeld was staying in a youth hostel at Mont d'Arbois, on the other side of the mountain. Some mornings, the three took skiing lessons together. Bienenfeld looked charming on the slopes, with her curly red hair wrapped in a little headscarf. One afternoon she came back to their hotel, and Sartre explained phenomenology to her while Beauvoir thumbed through magazines. After dinner, Bienenfeld lay on their bed and free-associated, and Beauvoir and Sartre psychoanalyzed her. On New Year's Eve, they invited Bienenfeld to a celebratory dinner with them in their hotel. It was too late to go back up the mountain, so Bienenfeld wrapped herself in an eiderdown and slept on the floor.

When they got back to Paris, in January 1939, Sartre started to court Bienenfeld seriously. Bienenfeld was flattered. This was Jean-Paul Sartre, Simone de Beauvoir's idol. At the Sorbonne, Bienenfeld's three closest men friends were Sartre's former pupils, all of whom thought the world of him. In January, Sartre's book of short stories, *The Wall*, came out (dedicated to Olga Kosakiewicz). His name was in all the newspapers. Reviewers talked about his brilliant, innovative writing.[36]

Sartre was "a master of the language of love," Bienenfeld would write years later, in her memoirs. "Just as a waiter plays the role of a waiter, Sartre played to perfection the role of a man in love."[37] She no longer noticed his wandering eye or the blackheads on his face and neck. He told her she had beautiful eyes. He said he found her slightly hunched posture touching. He called her all sorts of funny nicknames.

They walked across the cobblestones of Montmartre to the Café Rouge, and in that cozy interior, next to the large warm stove, he declared his love for her. He asked whether she thought she could fall in love with him. Bienenfeld said she might be able to, but she did not want to hurt Beauvoir—not ever. Sartre assured her that the Beaver would not mind at all.

He talked about consummating their relationship. Bienenfeld, who was still a virgin where men were concerned, writes in her memoirs that she felt an anticipatory thrill. They chose the day. As they walked down the Rue Cels towards the Hôtel Mistral, Sartre remarked that the hotel chambermaid would be in for a surprise, for he had taken another girl's virginity the day before. "I shuddered inside," Bienenfeld says, "but I said and did nothing."

Bianca Bienenfeld Lamblin wrote her memoirs, *A Disgraceful Affair*, in the early 1990s, after having read the newly published correspondence between Sartre and Beauvoir. She had been horrified to learn what they had said to each other about her behind her back, while professing their tender love to her. Her account of that afternoon was no doubt colored by these insights:

> When we got to his room, Sartre undressed almost completely and stood by the sink to wash his feet, raising first one leg, then

the other. I was intimidated. When I asked him to draw the curtains a bit to shut out some of the light, he refused flatly, saying that what we were going to do should be done in broad daylight. I hid behind the curtain of a closet to undress. . . . I did not take off my pearl necklace, which unfortunately displeased my partner—he made fun of me because this last adornment seemed ridiculously childish to him, or maybe he was annoyed because they were natural pearls, and he was scornful of my father's business, I don't know. I was distressed and did not understand why he was not his usual, gentle self; it was as if he wanted to brutalize something in me (but also in himself) and was driven by a destructive impulse.[38]

Sartre got nowhere with her that day. He earnestly explained the difference between a vagina and a clitoris. Bienenfeld thought him like a teacher, or "a doctor preparing for an operation." A few days later he achieved his goal. Bianca Lamblin writes that she was never able to enjoy sex with Sartre. When she looked back on this period of her life, after far happier sexual experiences with her husband, it seemed to her that Sartre's practice of coitus interruptus was part of his inability to let go of himself, and even an aspect of what she came to regard as his sadism. She points out that he could have simply worn a condom.[39]

Behind Wanda's back, Sartre created a new trio. "My love," he wrote to Bienenfeld, "*Our* future is *your* future."[40] The old patterns began again. Sartre would knock on Beauvoir's door at nine in the morning to tell her about his evening with Bienenfeld. The girl confessed to Beauvoir that she was in love with Sartre but did not feel passion toward him, and she was afraid Sartre could not accept that, and she was scared of losing him, and could Beauvoir please explain things to him so he would understand?

Until Sartre came between them, Beauvoir had nothing negative to say about Bienenfeld. Now she frequently complained about her to Bost. The three of them had endured a tense evening at the Café Rouge, she wrote to him in his barracks at Amiens. The conversation was forced, and Bienenfeld was irritating. "She does not realize that effusions of tenderness work with two but not with three. . . . She took our hands, squeezed them, let them go, took them again, being careful to share herself evenly."[41]

To Beauvoir, it was beginning to seem as if the Kosakiewicz sisters would be her lifelong bête noire. In her letters to Bost, the "Kos" factor was an anguished refrain. Every time Bost had a brief leave, it was agony for Beauvoir. "My love, . . . do try to spend as much time as you can with me; can't you tell K that you'll be arriving later than you'll actually be coming? . . . I would love to meet you at the station and spend the first moments with you."[42]

Bost did not always tell her his plans. On his first leave, he saw Olga before seeing Beauvoir. He did not dare to tell Beauvoir until the last minute. She was upset, and told him she felt like his mother, "the pastoresse," someone to whom he only ever told things afterwards, when they were *faits accomplis.*[43]

And then there was "the littlest Kosakiewicz," as Sartre called her. She had become his new obsession. If Wanda was still not sure what she felt about Sartre, she *was* sure what she felt about Beauvoir. She did not like her. In fact, she loathed her, she told Sartre, who did not hesitate to pass this information on.

In the spring of 1939, Wanda came to live in Paris. Sartre supported her financially. "You would make a good little painter," he told her. He arranged for her to take lessons, and for Poupette, Beauvoir's sister, to share her art studio with her. When Wanda asked him what exactly was the nature of his relationship with Beauvoir, he assured her that they were no more than friends. Then he told Beauvoir what he had said.

The whole situation was "grimy," Beauvoir fumed to Bost. She felt betrayed. She blamed Sartre's women, who, as she saw it, obliged Sartre to tell lies. And she resented the way the Kosakiewicz sisters talked about her. "It's very unpleasant for me to feel dismembered by these two consciences." Bost, for once, had no sympathy:

I was rather indignant that you protest about the judgments and the conversations that Wanda and Kos might have about you and Sartre, and also about me. I think that you must come over to them as shifty and dubious to the highest degree, and that it's with justification, since they have been so deceived in every sense.[44]

Beauvoir was mortified. A week later, she and Bost had an even more upsetting exchange. She had written to him describing the pleasant Sunday she had spent with Bianca Bienenfeld. The young woman had come to the Mistral as usual, at midday, looking very beautiful, Beauvoir said, in a blue dress and mauve coat. They went to the Coupole and ate a sumptuous lunch, with a bottle of champagne. Then they went to the Flore for a coffee. They must have been flirting with each other rather obviously, because a group of men started to mock them, with coarse gestures. Back at the Mistral, they called by to say hello to Sartre, who was working in his room, still in his nightshirt.

Then we went down to my room where we engaged in some illicit embracing. I think ultimately that I'm not a homosexual since sensually I feel almost nothing, but it was charming and I love being in bed in the afternoon when there is lots of sunshine outside.[45]

Bost wrote that the word *charming* had stopped him in his tracks. It seemed to him "dreadfully obscene" for Beauvoir to talk about Bienenfeld in that way. He went on to say that he was glad the Beaver had mentioned feeling some remorse about Olga. He had been grappling with his guilt to the point of feeling quite sick about it. The last time he saw Olga, she had been unusually straightforward and sincere with him. He had felt ashamed.

His letter provoked an attack of anxiety that Beauvoir described as "pathological." She read it in the evening, just before going out with Olga. For hours she felt numb. When she climbed into a taxi at the end of the evening, she struggled to retain her tears until she reached her room, and then she dissolved in a paroxysm of weeping. She woke up in "a despair that was absolutely morbid." She had lunch with her mother and just managed to control herself until she left. As she went down the stairs, she felt tears coming on like a wave of nausea. The only thing she was able to do, she told Bost, was to go home and cry.

The reason I commented on my physical relationship with Bianca . . . was precisely because I didn't want you to misunderstand me. I have only *one* sensual life, and that is with you, and for me it is something infinitely precious, and serious, and weighty, and passionate. I wouldn't be able to be unfaithful to you, because that would make you into one episode of this life whereas you *are* this life. I don't want another, I am totally engaged in it, deeply, and with great happiness.

. . .

And before finishing with this subject, even though it embarrasses me a little, I must be clear about one other thing. With Sartre, too, I have a physical relationship, but very little, and it is mostly tenderness, and—I'm not quite sure how to put this—I don't feel involved in it because he is not involved in it himself. That is something I have explained to him often enough. That's why I can say that the only sensual life I have, and have ever had, is with you, and I need you to take it seriously and to know that I take it seriously, with all my soul.[46]

She admitted that she was frightened of Bost's remorse toward Olga. She was afraid it would go along with a vague hostility toward her. She would prefer not to see him than to feel she deserved his reproaches, but the idea of not seeing him was absolutely odious to her. "It is not a pleasant situation."

"This morning, for the first time, I slept with her," Sartre announced. It was late July 1939, and he was with Wanda in the south of France. "The result was that I left her on her bed, all pure and tragic, declaring herself tired and having hated me for a good 45 minutes." He had sneaked out to a café to write to Beauvoir.

Marseille was full of the Beaver, he told her, and he felt very emotional sitting in places where they had dined together. With Wanda it was "perfect love, gazing into one another's eyes, holding hands."

For now I'm relentlessly devoting myself to my personal life . . . Wanda is almost always charming and affectionate, and it is very nice sleeping with her, which happens to me morning and evening for the moment. She seems to get pleasure out of it, but it kills her, she lies on her bed dead to the world for more than 15 minutes after her revels. The thing is, it takes the violence of arguments or the touching quality of reconciliations for me to feel alive. Last night we had a terrific argument, but it was worth the effort.[47]

He and Wanda generally did not get to sleep till three in the morning. They woke up at seven and made love, he got dressed around ten and went to the post office, then to a café to write. Wanda showed up around noon, and they spent afternoons reading and sightseeing. She rested an hour before dinner, while Sartre wrote clandestine letters. They went to dinner, usually at Charley's Tavern, then sat drinking in the Old Port, looking at the lights. Sartre regretted that he had to tear up all incoming letters, even those Beauvoir asked him to keep. "It's impossible to hold on to them: we share the room and Wanda wanders around every morning while I'm still asleep."

Sartre had been courting Wanda for two years. It was his longest seduction ever. This time, unlike with Olga, he had attained his goal.

At the beginning of August 1939, Wanda went back to Paris, and Beauvoir joined Sartre in Marseille. Bost came down for a few days, on leave. He considered war inevitable, and he and Sartre joked about whether it would be worse to return from the war without legs, without arms, or with one's face blown apart. Beauvoir was horrified.

Bost said that things were going unusually well between him and Olga. He thought Olga was developing new confidence as an actress. At Beauvoir's suggestion, Olga was taking acting workshops at Dullin's school, known as L'Atelier, and Charles Dullin considered her promising. Olga seemed at last to be committed to Bost, and this meant he felt more committed to her. He asked Beauvoir to burn all his letters to her, and said he was going to burn hers. "It would be too ignoble if ever anything should come out; it would be abject. . . . I don't regret anything, but I would feel profoundly guilty if Kos ever suffered because of me. It embarrasses me to say this to you, but I can tell you anything. I know what you are like."[48]

After Bost left, Sartre and Beauvoir were sitting one evening in the Old Port when who should walk past but Paul Nizan, with a large rubber swan under his arm! He was with his wife and two young children, on their way to Corsica. They had a drink together. Nizan, usually so gloomy, was convinced that Germany would be on its knees in no time. Sartre and Beauvoir were astonished, and heartened, by his optimism. They watched him walk off, the swan under his arm. It would be the last time they saw him.

They went to stay with Madame Morel in her villa at Juan-les-Pins, near Antibes. The large garden ran down to the Mediterranean. Sartre tried to teach Beauvoir to swim. He himself could swim quite a distance, but he would suddenly become terrified of the slimy creatures he imagined lurking in the depths, and would swim back in a panic.

In Juan-les-Pins, Beauvoir kept bursting into tears. The prospect of war was terrifying. It seemed to her she was losing her men, if not to the Kosakiewicz sisters then to the Germans. Sartre was obsessed with Wanda to the point that Beauvoir wondered what exactly she herself meant to him now. And Bost seemed to be hinting that his and Beauvoir's relationship was just an affair, and that only his relationship with Olga was serious. For Beauvoir, that summer was miserable.

War had been on the horizon for years. Everyone knew it was coming—everyone, that is, except Sartre, who kept assuring his friends it would not happen. "It's impossible that Hitler is thinking of starting a war, given the mental state of the German population. It's bluff," he assured Bienenfeld on August 31, 1939. He and Beauvoir were back in Paris. Bienenfeld, distraught with worry, was with her parents in Annecy.

That same day, Bost was called up. The next day, Friday, September 1, German troops marched into Poland. Posters went up around Paris giving the order for general mobilization of all fit men between the ages of eighteen and forty. In the afternoon, Sartre went back to the Mistral to pack. He and Beauvoir went down to the cellar and fetched two knapsacks and Sartre's ski boots. There were soon clothes, cans of food, tobacco pouches, notebooks, and books all over the floor.

After packing, Sartre went to a café and wrote to Bienenfeld. "I will come back to you. I'm the faithful type, and you'll find me again when the time comes, exactly like the person you left at the station square in Annecy. Nothing can change us, my love, neither you, nor the Beaver, nor I.... I'd like you to know that I love you passionately, *forever*."

His farewell with Wanda was emotional. "I'm terribly afraid you'll forget about me," he told her.[49] He promised to write to her every day, and asked her to try to do the same. He privately worried that she might have to go back to her family in Laigle. He had promised that he would support her in the coming year, so she could continue her painting in Paris, but he feared that if he were out of teaching for long, he would not be able to afford to do so.

Sartre spent his precious last hours with Beauvoir. They had dinner together, then went to bed at ten P.M. in Beauvoir's room, set the alarm, and tried to sleep. At three A.M. they dressed quickly. Sartre kept chewing on his nails. They slung his knapsacks over their shoulders and went for a morning coffee at the Dôme. It was a final glimpse of prewar Paris. From now on, cafés were to close at eleven P.M.

Paris was dark and silent. The moon had disappeared behind clouds, and the streetlights had been dimmed. The café windows were covered with heavy blue curtains. In a subdued Montparnasse, the Dôme was an island of noise and smoke. Men in uniform had sprung up as if from nowhere, and were sitting at tables talking. A couple of prostitutes were plying their trade. Sartre and Beauvoir sat down on the terrace and ordered coffees. She felt as if they were in a Dos Passos novel, Beauvoir said.

At four-thirty A.M. they took a taxi to the mobilization depot at the Place Hébert. A policeman told them to go to the Gare de l'Est. They walked. Dawn was breaking. The sky was pink. They expected to find a crowd at the station, but the hall was almost empty. There was not a uniformed man to be seen. Sartre explained that three-quarters of the men had already been called up. The whole thing felt

Kafkaesque, he said. No one had come to fetch him away. It was almost as if he were leaving of his own free will.

There was a train at 6:24 A.M., but since no one else seemed to be taking it, Sartre decided to take the 7:50 A.M. train. They went and had another coffee. Sartre assured Beauvoir once again that he wouldn't be in any danger in Nancy. This was simply another of their separations. They would write to each other regularly. She would send him parcels of books.

By the time they returned to the platform, there were more people around, including men with knapsacks. Near the entrance gate, a few couples held each other tightly. Beauvoir felt tears pricking her eyes. Sartre pressed her to him, then she watched him walk down the platform with a rapid, determined step. He looked small and vulnerable, and she could tell from his back that he was tense.

She turned around and walked toward the exit. She thought to herself that even if she cried for hours, she would not have finished crying. She would walk and not stop, or her heart would burst.

FIVE

WAR

September 1939 – March 1941

"La Guerre!" It was Sunday afternoon, September 3, 1939. That morning, Britain had declared war on Germany. Now France had too. Beauvoir took one look at the headlines and burst into tears. Her immediate thought was that Bost would be killed. "My love, if anything bad happens to you," she wrote him from the Flore, "there will never be any more happiness for me in this life." As a reservist, Sartre was in less danger, but for how long? If *he* were killed, Beauvoir told herself she would commit suicide. The thought was strangely consoling.

The young men had left, and in the next few days thousands of civilians fled the city, in cars stacked with suitcases. Paris had become a city of women, old people, and the infirm. Gas masks were distributed. In the cafés, clients had to pay as soon as they were served, in case the air raid siren sounded. Streetlamps were reduced to a dim yellow glow, the size of a candle. A midnight curfew was enforced.

Beauvoir had never envisaged the war lasting longer than a few months, and now people were talking about several years. She heard some women discussing the telegram they would receive if their husbands were killed on the battlefield. For weeks she was ravaged by dread, unable to settle down to any work. She lived for letters from Sartre and Bost. "History burst over me," she writes, "and I dissolved into fragments."[1]

For eight months it was the "Phony War"—neither war nor peace. There was a constant whiff of nightmare, and yet the enemy remained invisible. Sartre came up with the theory that just as modern music was without harmony, modern war was without death.

"The war *interests* me," he wrote from Alsace. "I feel I'm in a foreign country, which I'm going to explore bit by bit."[2] As usual, he had adapted well to communal life. There were four others in his meteorological unit, and they were billeted with an old priest. "An odd bunch. Who knows how many years I'll live with them? They aren't unlikable."[3] He called them his "acolytes." Apart from a meteorological reading every three hours—releasing a red balloon into the air, observing it through binoculars, and telephoning the wind direction to the artillery unit—they had little to do. On their first Sunday they walked in the countryside, and the acolytes picked plums while Sartre smoked a cigar. "My sole worry is I'll get fat."[4]

He settled into a work routine of ten to eleven hours a day, and made good progress on his novel *The Age of Reason*. He told Beauvoir he would send her chapters as soon as the postal service became more secure. The war gave him a new perspective, and for the first time he was keeping a journal. He was enjoying the freedom of writing spontaneously, following his thoughts where they led him. In addition, he was writing at least three letters a day.

He had finished the Kafka books he had brought with him, and was enjoying the journal of André Gide that Beauvoir had sent him. Yes, he would forward it to Bost when he had finished it, as instructed. (All three of them were keeping journals, and wanted to read others, for models.) He wrote a list of other titles he would like to read. There was no hurry; the Beaver should not send them all at once. Were there any new detective novels? And would she mail him the latest *Nouvelle Revue Française,* four notepads, and fifty envelopes?

"Believe it or not, when you wrote you would not survive me if there were some disaster, I felt a profound peace," Sartre admitted to Beauvoir. "I wouldn't like to leave you behind, not because you'd be a free little consciousness sauntering around the world and I'd be jealous, but because you've persuaded me you would be in an absurd world. . . . But don't worry, I was thinking about all that in the abstract, since I'm in a charming Alsatian village, very secure and comfortable. Besides, I also think, in the long run, that I'd definitely want you to go on with your own little life without me: a life cut short does seem, after all, a loss of something good. The fact is, in any case, I've never felt so intently that you are me."[5]

For years he had used the notion of "oneness" to assuage Beauvoir's occasional doubts about their relationship. "If there had been a need to feel how much we two are one, this phantom war would at least have had the virtue of letting us see that," he wrote in another letter. "It answers the question that was tormenting you: my love, you are not 'one thing in my life'—not even the most important—because my life no longer belongs to me, because . . . you are always *me*."[6]

Their tenth anniversary (dated from the first time they made love) was October 14, 1939. Looking back, Sartre realized more than ever what he owed to Beauvoir. He did not hear from her for three days, and afterward he wrote in his journal: "My irritation about the lateness of Wanda's letters is dreamed up. This, this is serious. Felt the world without the Beaver (not that I thought her dead but simply, there was no letter and I live her world and mine through her letters); it was a desert."

Two days later he wrote: "I felt today that all my courage and even my appetite for experiencing the war come from the certitude of being understood, supported, and approved by the Beaver. If this approbation were not there, everything would fall apart and I'd be adrift."[7]

Sartre was greatly relieved to hear that as a civil servant he would continue to receive his full teaching salary while in the military. "I'll know that all of my little family has enough money and security, and I won't have the feeling—which was really beginning to gnaw at me— that it is you who are supporting the burden of the whole community," he told Beauvoir.[8] The Kosakiewicz sisters would be able to stay in Paris. Olga could resume classes at the Atelier and try to establish herself as an actress. Wanda could continue her painting lessons. Neither would have to find a job.

In November, Sartre traversed a dark period. His eyes were hurting him. He was already almost blind in his right eye, and the fear hung over him that one day he might lose his sight altogether. But it did not occur to him to stop working for a few days, to rest his eyes. Instead, he took to writing with his eyes closed.

His main source of torment, however, was not his eyes, but Wanda. He was dependent on her letters, with their large, childlike handwriting. When he read, "I love you passionately" or "You must treat me like an adult," he felt warm inside. He did not care about her atrocious spelling and grammar.[9] He did not mind her preening about her "Russian soul." He needed her to tell him she loved him. By the beginning of November she was no longer writing every day. He was very far away, she wrote. He might as well be on another planet. She also made it clear that Roger Blin, one of the most talented young actors at her sister's Atelier, was courting her. Sartre confided to his journal:

> Yesterday, . . . at about two o'clock I received a letter from her which ends like this: "I must stop, because I can see the top of B[lin]'s head surfacing; people clutch at him as he passes, but his gaze is fixed upon me and he is walking softly in my direction with a crab-like determination. Till tomorrow." That serial-story ending—"continued tomorrow"—threw me into a bout of jealous prophecy: I was sure something was going to occur between them. At once I wrote an irreparable letter, which I finished by tearing up. Today I reverted to a more balanced view.[10]

Sartre would wonder, afterward, about the "paroxysm of passion" he suffered that November.[11] His reaction to his jealousy was a pattern he knew well. He told himself he did not care and would not miss Wanda, and he hurled her little person into the void. As usual, he was unable to fool himself. The buoyant confidence he needed to write had completely deserted him. He lost all desire to start a new chapter of his novel. When he tried to imagine his postwar life without Wanda, it felt as if his world had shrunk. A vital dimension was missing.

He did his best to rationalize. An affair with Blin would probably not mean all that much to Wanda. "It's obvious . . . that her life is me—

less perhaps through the tenderness I inspire in her than through the intellectual and material need she has for me," he told Beauvoir.[12] "She may deceive me, but for the moment I've become legendary to her, she 'bows low' to me, as you know, and that provides her with her solemn, romantic little myth. Don't destroy that for me, please."[13]

In his journal—he called them his "war notebooks"—Sartre was making notes for the philosophical treatise that would become *Being and Nothingness*. A central argument was that relations with other people always involve conflict. The love between two people is necessarily a conflict:

> Each one wants the other to love him but does not take into account the fact that to love is to want to be loved and that thus by wanting the other to love him, he only wants the other to want to be loved in turn. . . . Hence the lover's perpetual dissatisfaction.[14]

Sartre saw love as a battle in which two free subjects each try to get hold of the other's freedom while at the same time trying to free themselves from the hold of the other. The scenario recurs throughout his work, just as it would recur throughout his life.

When Sartre left Paris, Beauvoir, feeling terribly alone, had written to Olga in Laigle, enclosing money for the latter's fare to Paris. Two days later, Beauvoir returned to the Mistral at midnight to find a note from Olga under her door: "I'm here, in room 20, at the end of the corridor." The two fell into each other's arms and talked till three in the morning.

Olga had always disliked the Mistral, so Beauvoir moved with the Kosakiewicz sisters to the Hôtel du Danemark, on the Rue Vavin. The rooms were larger and more comfortable, and the hotel was closer to their favorite café, the Dôme, but Beauvoir felt sad to leave the home she had shared with Sartre. "I felt as though I were separating from you," she wrote to him. "We'll both go back to the Hôtel Mistral, my love, won't we? We'll live together again? Promiscuously?

Little being, dear little creature, I love you so much—I can't stop cry-ing today."[15]

With the men away, the women saw more of one another. Beauvoir was having breakfast in Olga's room one morning when Wanda came in. The three spent an enjoyable hour together. One evening, Wanda accompanied them to the Jockey, a dance bar in Montparnasse. Beauvoir found her strangely appealing with her skimpy black pull-over, fresh complexion, short blond hair, and childlike expressions. For the entire evening, Beauvoir could not stop looking at her. She thought she could understand the attraction Sartre felt.

But she struggled with resentment. She herself was earning her income and working hard. The Kosakiewicz sisters, however, sup-ported by her and Sartre, seemed to lack the slightest drive. Wanda shared Poupette's rundown artist studio near the Jardin des Plantes. (Beauvoir paid the rent.) Poupette had done a splendid portrait of Wanda working at her easel, but this was a rare sight. "She works for only one hour every three days," Beauvoir reported to Sartre.[16] Olga had resumed her classes at the Atelier, and Dullin was encouraging, but Olga suffered from terrible anxieties. She was always telling Beauvoir about the latest catastrophe at a rehearsal. Either she had lost her voice or she had a dizzy spell or she had forgotten her words. She needed constant reassurance.[17]

Beauvoir took great pleasure in writing to Sartre and Bost, and bundling up parcels for them—books, notebooks, tobacco, and any-thing else they might ask for. Occasionally these letters or parcels were "official," but mostly they were clandestine. The "Kosaks" (as Sartre and Beauvoir called the sisters) had no idea that Beauvoir cor-responded almost daily with Sartre and Bost. Meanwhile, Olga airily declared that long-distance relationships were abstract and unreal, and she would write letters to Bost only when she was in the mood.

After a morning's teaching, Beauvoir would pick up her clandes-tine mail from the local Poste Restante. Whenever she could, she went straight to a café to reply. One afternoon, she posted her letters to Sartre and Bost, then went to meet Olga, who also had had a letter from Bost, and hers was longer. As Olga folded it away, Beauvoir glimpsed the words "My dear love." She felt as if she had been physically struck. To her, Bost wrote "Dear Beaver." She tried to reason with herself that Bost loved her as much as he did Olga, and that she should be satisfied with that. After all, she didn't give him all her love, either. But try as she might to be reasonable, she found that Bost's love for Olga remained an open wound.

Women were not allowed to visit their husbands at the front. They needed a safe-conduct pass to enter the war area, or they risked jail, and soldiers were punished if their women tried to see them. Women were also not supposed to know where their husbands were located; war censors opened letters randomly to ensure this. Nevertheless, in response to her pressing entreaties, Sartre sent Beauvoir instructions in code. "Emma" would like to see her in November, he wrote. He hoped she would have more luck than Emma's friends Bernard and René Ulmann, and Maurice, Adrien, and Thérèse Héricourt. He was spelling out the town of Brumath.

On October 31, Beauvoir got up at six-thirty A.M., and dressed quickly. The Boulevard du Montparnasse was still in darkness as she walked toward the taxi stand; the Dôme and the Rotonde were just opening. She left from the Gare de l'Est, on the same train Sartre had taken two months earlier. She had faked illness in order to get a medical certificate and time off school, and had wangled a false certificate of residence in order to obtain a safe-conduct pass. It had not been easy.

The train was packed with military men. Beauvoir read Dickens's *Barnaby Rudge*, looking up periodically to admire the autumn colors of the countryside. At one moment she suddenly realized that she was going to see Sartre and felt pure happiness.

It was almost midnight when she stepped onto a deserted platform in Brumath, cutting an unusual figure with her high heels, blue turban, and dangling earrings. Only then did she remember that the troops had curfew after nine P.M. She walked past the Lion d'Or hotel—Sartre had mentioned the place in letters—and knocked on the door. No one answered. Two soldiers passing on patrol flashed a light at her and asked to see her papers. She told them she was from Paris. So were they, they said. They escorted her to several hotels before she found a room. Nervous and exhausted, she slipped between the icy sheets.

Sartre had told her that he ate breakfast at seven A.M. at the Taverne du Cerf. Beauvoir set her alarm and made her way there at the crack of dawn. Her heart beat furiously when she saw the familiar small body come up the street, walking fast, as usual, with a pipe in his mouth. He had grown a scrubby beard, which looked dreadful. He was not expecting her so soon. Her telegram had not arrived.

Sartre was in uniform, which meant that they could not go into a café together. They went to Beauvoir's freezing hotel room. She felt very anxious. Would she be able to extend her twenty-four-hour permit? Sartre said the police in the area were strict. After an hour, he had to go back to his barracks. When he came back to Beauvoir's hotel at eleven A.M. he had shaven off his beard.

In the end, Beauvoir managed to stay four days. They talked their heads off. Sartre explained his latest philosophical ideas. When he had to be back at the barracks, Beauvoir read his novel, noting down criticisms and suggestions. They read each other's journals. Beauvoir's was more about daily events; Sartre's was more reflective. He encouraged her to probe deeper. This was a good time for them to look back on their lives, he said. How, for example, did she think hers was shaped by her being a woman?

They discussed their complicated love life. Beauvoir confessed to the anguish she felt about Bost's love for Olga. She was already afraid she would hardly get to see Bost on his leave, because of Olga, and she dreaded the emotional derangement she knew she would feel. Sartre did not think she need be ashamed of her feelings, but she should not forget that she had *chosen* her relationship with Bost. In fact, Olga was necessary for the relationship's equilibrium. Bost could not give all of himself to Beauvoir because she had not given all of herself to Bost. She had him, Sartre.

Beauvoir also admitted that she was very upset about Sartre's forthcoming leave. "And you," she asked Sartre, "how will it be possible to see you almost all the time, with just a little time for Wanda as you said?"[18] She felt sad that they were going to have to hide away in Paris, out of Wanda's sight. She found it demeaning that the Kosakiewicz sisters must not know that Sartre was spending most of his leave with her. Sometimes she felt a huge desire to be alone in the world with Sartre, just the two of them.

Sartre handed her a pile of letters to read, from Wanda and Bienenfeld. He felt tender toward Wanda, he said, but she was twenty-two, immature and unstable. By the end of the war, she was likely to be "dead, crazy, or gone off with some other guy."[19] As for Bienenfeld, he wrote to her regularly—sometimes copying out whole passages from his letters to Wanda—but she left him cold these days.

Sartre was able to procure them a room together for only two out of the four nights. Those two nights at the Boeuf Noir, in that charged atmosphere of war, were unusually passionate. They made love. "I'm happy, my love," Beauvoir wrote, as soon as she got back. "Never have I cared so strongly or so joyfully for you. . . . Never, never have I felt so fully merged with you."[20]

Sartre liked to think of her in their room—"all alone and totally naked, the little expressions that cross your face, the tender smiles, your little arms around my neck." His next few letters were equally affectionate. "My little flower, never have I loved you so much as in the past few days. . . . Your little husband loves you."[21]

"The truth is," Beauvoir admitted to Sartre, "I've developed a certain taste for such relations."[22] She was not talking about their own; she knew Sartre hated her to be clinging. She was referring to what Sartre called her "harem of women."[23]

Beauvoir had no doubts about her heterosexuality, but she often wondered whether she was also a "wolf trap"—Madame Morel's term for homosexuals, which Beauvoir and Sartre had adopted. As a teacher, Beauvoir aroused an extraordinary number of schoolgirl crushes. Women told her she was beautiful. Men rarely did—to the point that she was currently conducting a poll, getting her women friends to ask men how they responded to her physically. Sartre had never made her feel particularly desirable. Even Bost could make disconcerting comments at times. She had recently started to wear a turban (it was shaped like a turban, but was actually a headband), and had sent a photo to show Bost. He wrote that he had taken one look at it and laughed till he cried. "You look like a lesbian, a cocaine addict and a fakir, too."[24]

Beauvoir enjoyed sex with beautiful young women—there was no doubt about that—but she always told herself that women were a poor substitute for the real thing. When she wrote to Sartre about her love affairs with women, her tone—ambivalent and condescending—was just like his. Part of her pleasure was that she felt almost as if she *were* Sartre. Shortly before Christmas 1939 she reported to him on the night she had just spent with Bienenfeld:

We went to dinner at the Knam, we talked, and I made a real effort. Moreover, I was in a good mood and tired at the same time, so that I was entirely myself, unadorned. She always finds me funny at such times—and is quite enchanted. We returned to her place, went to bed and talked a bit, then moved on to embraces. I found it really charming to sleep in her room like that, though I slept quite badly since she moves around and snores. . . . We woke up at about 8.30, and like a sated man I discreetly avoided her caresses. I wanted to have breakfast and work (I feel I can get right into your skin at such moments).[25]

These days, Beauvoir was more enthusiastic about Nathalie Sorokine, yet another young woman in her baccalaureate class who had developed an infatuation with her. Sorokine had Russian parents and Slavic good looks. She was tall, with blond hair, a strong, muscled body, awkward gestures, and a tomboy attitude toward fighting. Her blond fringe hid a scar. She had a temper that made Olga look mild.

Sorokine had done well in her baccalaureate, and was eager to continue with her studies. Her mother, who was divorced and struggling to make an income, wanted her to get a job. Beauvoir said she would pay the girl's tuition fees. Just after the war broke out, Sorokine enrolled at the Sorbonne.

Beauvoir was soon reporting that Sorokine wanted more than hand-holding and kissing on the lips. "There's nothing to be done," she told Sartre. "She wants to sleep with me."[26]

I've honestly been slow to yield—I'm not getting vainly carried away—but I can't find any fault with her, merely limits. If I were free, I'd surrender myself enthusiastically to this affair. Yesterday I was smitten and she could sense it—it made her really happy. . . . I told her a heap of things about what prostitutes and brothels are—

all of which she listened to with rapt interest. She's rereading *Intimacy*. . . . She's sensitive to the style, and was delightedly quoting me expressions of yours that she finds charming. She asks me to explain the obscenities—but only in my room, with her face turned to the wall. I call her a frightened doe, which drives her wild with rage.[27]

By January 1940, the two women were having a full-fledged affair. "I've a very keen taste for her body," Beauvoir admitted.[28] With Sartre, she played up the sexual aspect of her lesbian affairs. With Bost, she played it down. She told Bost it was strange to be loved and admired by all these young women, but deep inside herself, she knew it was not her they loved. What they desired was the reflection they saw in her of their own future. They were in love with her freedom.

By February 1940, French soldiers had been away from their families for five or six months, and were getting bored and edgy. The Germans had still done nothing. What were they waiting for? There were rumors of a spring offensive.

Until the last minute, the men did not know whether they would have a home leave, and if so, how long it would be. Married men were to be given priority. At first it looked as if Sartre and Bost might be in Paris at the same time. Then it seemed that they might not come at all. Finally, Sartre was able to tell Beauvoir he would arrive in Paris on Sunday, February 4, for ten days.

Beauvoir was tense. "I have the feeling that he only exists in dream," she wrote in her journal, "or at least that this business of his leave only exists in dream."[29] She and Sartre had arranged to stay at the Mistral, their old haunt. The Kosakiewicz sisters never went near there. Beauvoir would tell Olga that she was going to Limousin. Sartre wrote several letters to Wanda before he left, and asked his acolytes to mail them, one a day, from the war zone.

On Sunday morning, Beauvoir collected a suitcase with Sartre's civilian clothes from his mother and took it over to the Mistral. In the afternoon, at five P.M., she was at the Gare de l'Est, waiting in the dingy basement café, too nervous even to write in her notebook. Finally, there was Sartre, at the top of the stairs, in a filthy military greatcoat and shoes that were several sizes too big.

For the next four days they were together every minute, except when Beauvoir was teaching, during which time Sartre visited his mother. Each morning they went to the Café des Trois Mousquetaires on the Avenue du Maine, and read each other's novels, pencils in hand. In Beauvoir's novel *She Came to Stay*, Pierre Labrousse, Sartre's thinly fictionalized counterpart, was no idealized portrait. Quite the contrary. Beauvoir showed Sartre's insecurities and manipulative behavior close up. Sartre did not seem to mind. He thought she needed to rewrite the opening section, but for the most part he thought the novel very good.

On Friday evening, Sartre left to spend three days with Wanda. He had told her that he had only six days' leave, and he was spending the first three with her and the last three with Beauvoir.

"It doesn't upset me," Beauvoir wrote in her journal. "I don't have the feeling that these days have been taken from me." However, the following day, when she and Sartre met briefly at the Dôme (officially Sartre was seeing his mother), she lost her tranquility. Sartre did not conceal his strong feelings for Wanda, and Beauvoir left the café feeling extremely dejected. Was the trio scenario she had depicted in *She Came to Stay* never to end? The next two days dragged by. She slept atrociously and had a headache that never went away. In her journal, she wrote of "the naked distress caused by absence."

On Tuesday morning she woke up "terribly tired and anxious." She spent the morning teaching, then took a taxi to the Dôme to meet Sartre. His mood had not changed. He was feeling bad about all the lies he had told Wanda, especially as she seemed sincerely to love him. He was beginning to wonder whether it might not be better to spend one's life faithful to one person.

He and Beauvoir spent their last evening together talking in a café. Chased out just before midnight, curfew hour, they went back to the Mistral. For a long time they sat up and talked. Sartre did not want to go to bed in case sleep took them over. He wanted them to treasure every minute together. Finally they went to bed and slept.

On Thursday, after an early breakfast at the Café des Trois

Mousquetaires, Sartre put on the uniform his mother had cleaned for him and he and Beauvoir went to the Gare de l'Est. The station was packed with couples saying good-bye. "It's moving, and primitive, this elemental separation of the sexes, with the men being taken away and the women returning to town," Beauvoir wrote in her journal. "One senses the ardent night behind them, and the lack of sleep, and the nervous fatigue of the morning."

She and Sartre had not had ardent nights. "You were able to see that I'd changed," he wrote her one week later. "Perhaps the power of our physical relationship is fading slightly, but I find that it's becoming tidier."[30]

He was anxious to show that this did not affect his love for her. "Your little face, eyes brimming with tears, which I saw across the shoulders of the soldiers in my compartment, completely overwhelmed me with love," he told her. "How beautiful it was, my darling Beaver, I know of nothing more beautiful in the world than that face, and it made me feel so strong and filled me with such humility to think that it was *for me* that it was so beautiful."[31]

The day after Sartre left, there was a violent snowstorm. Beauvoir had not heard from Bost. For weeks she had been anticipating his visit with a mixture of anguish, anticipation, and burning desire. They had not seen each other for six months. After she had visited Sartre in Brumath, she had pressed Bost to let her come see him. He had said no. She pressed harder. He still said no. Since then, for the last two months, he had been at the front. He and his comrades had permanently frozen feet, their nerves were jangled, and in their boredom they were drinking too much. She had written to him daily, and he had written almost as often, sometimes in excruciating conditions. "I love you and you cannot know how happy I am that you love me and how much that changes my life," he assured her.[32] Beauvoir wondered, what was it going to be like for them to meet?

On Friday afternoon she was taking her last class for the day when one of the cleaners knocked and came in. She walked up to the teacher's desk and whispered that a "Monsieur Bost" was waiting in the visitors' parlor. "My hands started to tremble and my heart to thump, and I had the greatest difficulty in continuing on the subject of sociology—that last quarter of an hour passing in the strangest agony of impatience," Beauvoir wrote to Sartre afterward. "I rushed down—and there, all solitary amid the green settees and mirrors of a vast visitors' room, I found Little Bost waiting for me."

They went for a long walk in the snow—by the Seine, along the Canal St. Martin, and to the Gare de l'Est, where they had a coffee in the dreary basement café that had come to mean so much to Beauvoir. Bost did not seem to notice his surroundings. He talked manically—about life at the front, his comrades, the officers, everything but himself.

By dinner, he had become slightly calmer. He wanted to know all about Sartre, the Kosakiewicz sisters, and everyone else. He and Beauvoir spent a "tender and passionate night" in the Hôtel Oriental on the Place Denfert-Rochereau. "It's pretty sumptuous—elevator and fine, warm rooms with velvet drapes and a pink counterpane," Beauvoir reported to Sartre, "but I slept very badly because of the stifling heat—and also, I think, because my nerves were overwrought."[33]

The next day, she showed her companion Sartre's notebooks, and Bost read passages with "wild exhilaration." She told him the latest stories about Bienenfeld and Wanda. "From the standpoint of principle he finds us infamous," she wrote to Sartre, "but his heart's with us."

We went to the Nox, sat down at a table and talked—gently, so gently. He was truly moving: seeking in you, and me, hopes for later on; talking about his comrades—and about himself and his moods out there, his regrets and his joys—by fits and starts, without the volubility of the previous day, but drawing things from his innermost depths. I was moved to tears (actually shedding a couple) and was feverish—I'd drunk a lot of toddies and other alcohol—but I didn't lapse into pathos.

She and Bost spent three days and nights together, staying in different hotels each night. Bost left her on Monday evening, in front of his brother Pierre's apartment in the Place Saint-Germain. He was going to spend the next six days with Olga, who was under the impression that he had just arrived in Paris.

For the next few days, Beauvoir dreamed about Bost. She missed his kisses, longed for his body, and envied Olga. But she knew it was fair this way, and Bost's tenderness had left her feeling strong. "There's one thing of which I'm now sure," she told Sartre. "Bost forms part of my future in an absolutely certain—even essential—way."[34]

She was forgetting the rules. Their "contingent" affairs were not meant to become "essential."

Just as Beauvoir was feeling calmer at last, Sartre plunged into another crisis. He had left Paris smitten with Wanda. No sooner was he back in the war zone than his nightmare came true. He was faced with days in a row of silence from her. No letters. And then came a bombshell—a four-page screed foaming with rage.

It seemed that Sartre's past had caught up with him. Colette Gilbert, the actress with whom he had had an affair the previous summer, had told the whole story to Marcel Mouloudji, an eighteen-year-old drama student at L'Atelier, who was a close friend of Wanda's. Gilbert claimed that Sartre had virtually raped her. She even showed Mouloudji the love letters Sartre had written her.

Mouloudji felt more than friendship for Wanda Kosakiewicz. In his memoirs, *Le Petit Invité,* he writes that he was besotted with her.[35] He loved her Russian-doll manner, her laughter, and the short blond hair that made him think of a thatched roof. He was daunted by her intellectual language; it seemed she could talk analytically about the slightest thing. On Friday nights they often went together to the famous Bal Nègre, on the Rue Blomet, and he would watch her shimmying around the dance floor with her African and West Indian partners. To him, she was inaccessible, a sort of goddess. She had introduced him to the Sartre clique, that intimidating group who went around saying "vous" to one another. Wanda talked about Sartre with wonderment. But Mouloudji had no idea that she and Sartre were lovers.

Mouloudji passed on Gilbert's story, and Wanda seemed to react calmly enough at the time. Only decades later, when Sartre's letters to Beauvoir were published in 1983, did Mouloudji discover that Wanda was not as indifferent as she had made out, and the reason why.

"I am doing my best not to let this obscenity fill me with childish loathing," Wanda wrote to Sartre, "but I just can't help feeling a terrible physical anguish."[36]

Feeling alarmed and ashamed, Sartre tried to retain his dignity with a show of anger. He told Wanda that he, too, had a right to be angry. Why had she listened to Mouloudji's version of things rather than his? Wanda should reread his letters. How could she doubt his love?

He wrote Colette Gilbert a blisteringly nasty letter. "I never loved you," he fumed. "I found you physically pleasant though vulgar, but I have a certain sadism which was attracted to your vulgarity nonetheless. I never—from the very first day—intended to have anything but a very brief affair with you.... My letters, which were exercises in passionate literature and gave the Beaver and me many a good laugh, did not entirely deceive you."[37] He sent the letter to Wanda, asking her to find out Gilbert's address and send it on. And he sent a copy to Beauvoir.

He had been "a grubby bastard" with Wanda, he lamented to Beauvoir. He was thoroughly ashamed of his behavior with Gilbert, and with women generally:

> What need did I have for that girl? Wasn't it simply to play the neighborhood Don Juan? And if you excuse me because of sensuality, let's just say, first of all, that I have none, and that minor skin-deep desire is not an acceptable excuse.... It seems to me that up to now I've behaved like a spoiled brat in my physical relationships with people. There are few women I haven't upset on that score.... As for you, my little Beaver, for whom I've never had anything but respect, I've often embarrassed you, particularly in the beginning, when you found me rather obscene. Not a satyr, certainly. That I'm quite sure I'm not. But simply obscene.

In a flurry of letters, Sartre begged Wanda to understand how fragile she made him. He loved her. He could not bear to think he disgusted her. "You well know that I'd walk all over everyone (even the Beaver) . . . to have a good relationship with you."

He quoted this comment in his next letter to Beauvoir. "The end justifies the means, but I was not proud to have written that," he con-

fessed.[38] When he did not hear from Beauvoir for five days, he started
to worry about *her*.

> I'm in an odd state, I've never been this uneasy with myself
> since I went crazy.... My sweet, how I need you.... I love you.
> I'm afraid I must seem slightly underhanded to you with all the
> lies I'm entangled in.... I'm afraid you might suddenly ask
> yourself... isn't he perhaps lying to me, isn't he telling me half-
> truths? My little one, my darling Beaver, I swear to you that
> with you I'm totally pure. If I were not, there would be nothing
> in the world before which I would not be a liar, I would lose my
> very self. My love, you are not only my life but also the only hon-
> esty of my life.[39]

He was greatly relieved when a firm but forgiving letter from
Beauvoir came the next day. "You mustn't be too afraid that your letters have a pretty good whiff of reprimand," he replied, "you've got to
rub my nose in what I've done. Or else, aren't you my little moral
conscience any more?... I feel that this whole period will be set to
rights, stamped, buried, only when we two have been able to talk
about it together. It's as though you have a little seal and have to
stamp everything I see."

He assured her he would not be having any new affairs for a good
while. The whole episode had made him realize once again how much
their relationship meant to him. As for "conjugal" relationships,
Wanda was more than enough.[40]

Intent on tidying up his emotional life, Sartre wrote to Bianca
Bienenfeld, announcing that they were finished.

Beauvoir saw Bienenfeld shortly afterward. "She restrained herself
with astounding guts—but she was transfigured by anger. And honestly, I don't know what got into your head," she chided Sartre. "That
letter, with its moral exhortations and protestations of esteem, was
quite unacceptable.... She was humiliated that you didn't even take
the trouble to explain things to her properly. Humiliated and disgusted by the passionate letters you were writing her only a fortnight

earlier. I found it desperately unpleasant. . . . She knows there's a lie somewhere and is wondering what the truth is—she's not without her suspicions even with respect to me."[41]

A few days later, Beauvoir admitted she was not innocent either. "I never blamed you for making the break, since after all that's what I'd advised you to do. But I blamed us—myself as much as you, actually— in the past, in the future, in the absolute: the way we treat people. I felt it was unacceptable that we'd managed to make her suffer so much."[42] Beauvoir would become even more convinced of this in the future, when Bienenfeld suffered a major nervous breakdown.

At the end of March 1940, six weeks after his first leave, Sartre was back in Paris on another home leave. On April 9, in the train taking him back to Alsace, he and his comrades heard that the Germans had invaded Denmark and Norway. The "Phony War" was over. Bost never had a second home leave.[43]

For one more month their lives continued more or less as before, except for a drama on the home front. Olga was having an affair. She and Wanda tried to hide it from Sartre and Beauvoir, but Beauvoir eventually found out. The man was Niko Papatakis, a heart-stoppingly handsome fellow, half-Greek, half-Ethiopian, who hung around with the theater and film people at the Flore and danced at the Bal Nègre with such grace and lack of self-consciousness that he put all the other men in the shade.[44]

What did Sartre think? Beauvoir wanted to know. Should she tell Bost? She and Bost had vowed to be open with each other, and she felt very uncomfortable knowing something he didn't. She did not want to be complicit in Olga's guilt. And if Bost ever found out, he would be angry that Beauvoir had kept it from him.

Sartre was shocked. Wasn't Olga a bit disgusted with herself for cheating on Bost at the very moment when Bost was in grave danger of being blown up? Sartre was also angry that Wanda had hidden the affair from him.[45] But his advice was not to tell Bost. He did not think Beauvoir had the right to say anything unless she was prepared to replace Olga in Bost's life, if Bost decided to leave her. But Beauvoir could not do that, because she had him, Sartre, and one could not have two "absolute" relationships at the same time. He thought it better that Olga tell Bost herself, on his next leave. That way Bost would at least have the opportunity to talk it over with her. A man at the front did not need to be emotionally weakened.[46]

A few days later, still mulling over the question, Sartre, out of the blue, pointed to two other culprits in the whole story. Where Olga was concerned, he told Beauvoir, their guilt was absolute. However much Olga might at times irritate them, they had partly made her the person she had become. They had created the situation in which she lived, and they maintained her in a bubble of lies. In his opinion, they could never feel enough remorse toward the little vixen.[47]

In his memoirs, *Tous les désespoirs sont permis,* Niko Papatakis writes that he had an affair during the "Phony War" "with a young actress, of Russian origin, . . . a member of the Sartre clan." Because he was not French, he had not been called up, and he was one of the few young men to be found in Paris. The women were throwing themselves at him.[48]

In his eighties, Papatakis is still a handsome man, occasionally to be seen at the Café de Flore. "Olga was sexy," he recalls. "Not beautiful, but sexy. She had a Slavic charm. You know, mysterious, without really being so. Her figure was androgynous, almost boyish. She had no breasts to speak of. She had a very attractive, deep voice. I think she liked to seduce."

Papatakis believes their affair lasted a couple of months. Since Olga tried to hide it from Beauvoir, they did not go out much together, especially not in Montparnasse. But Papatakis remembers going with Wanda and Mouloudji to the Bal Nègre, where they were not likely to bump into Beauvoir.

He found Wanda far less appealing than her sister. "Olga seemed a bit lost in life, and Wanda even more so. She gesticulated a lot, I remember, and tried to keep up with her sister."[49]

"My little one, I was completely worn down yesterday," Sartre wrote to Beauvoir. German planes had dropped a bomb on a town fifteen kilometers away, but that was not what was worrying him. It was Wanda. She had a lesion. They would not know how serious it was until she was X-rayed. She had written to him. "Dear God, how I wish you would come, come at any price."

> It's odd, she is becoming more and more "my child," as O. was at one time for you. This time, I've had enough of brushing her off with sweet talk each time she needs me. I've just written to her that if she wants it, and if the delays aren't too great, I was ready to marry her to get three days of leave. I don't imagine that will be very nice for you; though it's purely symbolic, it does make me look committed up to my ears. I for one don't like it at all.... But I've told you and my mind's made up: I want to do everything I can for W. from now on.[50]

Sartre was informed that there would be no marriage leaves while the battle was raging. He begged Wanda not to feel abandoned, either materially or psychologically. "You are my whole life, my love," he wrote to her.[51] He asked Beauvoir to give her money.

On May 10, 1940, the Germans invaded Holland, Belgium, and Luxembourg. That same day, Bost and his friends were transported by convoy to the woods near Sedan, close to the Belgian border. Nervously, they assured one another that the Maginot Line was the most impenetrable line of defense in history.

But the Maginot Line was incomplete. It did not run along the Belgian border. On May 12, the Germans swept around it, through the Ardennes forest in Belgium, and into France. The French divisions found themselves surrounded and isolated. On land they were shelled; from the air they were bombarded.

Sartre wrote Beauvoir a second letter in the evening of May 12: "My darling Beaver, you sent me a really pathetic little letter, so distressed, my dearest.... Where exactly is Bost at the moment?"

On May 21, 1940, Bost was wounded, hit in the abdomen by flying shrapnel. He was pulled from the front lines, bleeding badly, and carried by relays of stretcher bearers to a Red Cross station. From there, he was taken by ambulance to a military hospital, where he was operated on. The surgeon told him he was lucky to have survived.

"It gave me a hell of a shock to get your letter," Sartre told Beauvoir a few days later.[52] Like her, he wondered whether Bost was understating the severity of his wounds, but he thought it a good sign that Bost had been able to scrawl her a brief note. Provided he survived, this was the best thing that could have happened to him. At least, he would be away from enemy lines for the next few weeks.

During the following days, Bost's regiment was almost entirely wiped out. Two days after Bost was wounded, Paul Nizan, also on the Belgian front, was killed by a German bullet.

Late in the evening of June 9, 1940, Beauvoir got back to the Hôtel du Danemark to find a note in her mailbox. Bianca Bienenfeld had been looking for her all day. Would Beauvoir come straight away, whatever the time, to the Flore?

There were no taxis on the deserted streets, so Beauvoir took the metro to Saint-Germain-des-Prés. She burst into the Flore and found Bienenfeld with friends, looking very distressed. Her father had inside knowledge that the Germans were about to enter Paris. The schools in Paris were going to close. Bienenfeld and her father were leaving Paris the next day in his car. It was less urgent for Beauvoir—she was not Jewish—but they hoped she would pack her bags and join them.

That was the moment when the bitter truth finally hit home for Beauvoir. France was defeated, humiliated, on its knees, about to surrender to the Germans. And Sartre would inevitably become a prisoner of war. She wept hysterically. For a while, she was totally out of control.

The next day, she joined the Bienenfelds in their car. It was the famous exodus. Almost three million people took to the roads, heading south or west. The Bienenfelds headed west. They were going to Quimper, in Brittany. Beauvoir asked them to drop her in Laval, the nearest point to her friend Madame Morel's country house, La Pouèze, fourteen miles from Angers.

On June 14, Paris fell to the Nazis. Within days, France surrendered. On June 22, the eighty-four-year-old French military man

Marshal Henri-Philippe Pétain signed an armistice with the Germans. The Nazis were to control the northern section of France, including Paris, and a large section in the south would be governed by the French, with Pétain at the head. The capital of the so-called "Free Zone" was Vichy. Whether Pétain realized it at the time or not, he had signed up for almost complete collaboration with the Nazis. Beauvoir sat around in La Pouèze listening to the news bulletins, reading detective novels, and weeping.

By the end of the month, Beauvoir was impatient to return to Paris. She was sure there would be messages from Sartre and Bost waiting for her at the hotel. She even imagined that one or both of them might have made his way back to Paris.

She accepted a lift for part of the way from a German military truck. The back section, under the tarpaulin, was packed with French refugees. They could not move, the air was stuffy, and the smell of gasoline turned her stomach. Beauvoir threw up.[53]

All that awaited her at the Hôtel du Danemark was a cheery letter from Sartre dated June 9. She fled to her room and sobbed her heart out. The Nazi flag, with its large swastika, was flapping over the Senate in the Luxembourg Gardens. The streets were deserted. Never had Paris felt more grim. Never had Beauvoir felt more utterly alone.

During those first difficult days, Beauvoir would sit on the terrace of the Dôme, gazing across the street at the Rodin statue of Balzac, and fantasize that Sartre would materialize behind the statue, dressed in his blue uniform and beret, his knapsack slung across his shoulder, and walk toward her smiling.

She was given another teaching job, and was relieved to spend her mornings at the Lycée Duruy. She telephoned the Bost household, in Taverny. One of Bost's sisters said that Bost had been moved to a military hospital in Carpentras, near Avignon. Beauvoir rang Olga in Laigle. The town had been bombarded and their windows had been shattered, but the Kosakiewicz family was safe.

Nathalie Sorokine returned to Paris, and Beauvoir had never been more pleased to see her. Sorokine was an inveterate thief, and she proceeded to steal two bicycles, one of which she gave to Beauvoir.

Beauvoir learned how to ride it, and soon the two women were swooping around the empty streets of Paris on their new wheels.

On July 11, Beauvoir received a penciled note from Sartre. The envelope had been opened, and at first she did not recognize the handwriting. He had been taken prisoner on June 21, his thirty-fifth birthday, the day before the Armistice. He seemed in good spirits. "If I'm writing in pencil, it's not that a shell shattered my pen, but that I lost it yesterday. . . . I have high hopes of seeing you again soon, and everything is fine with me. . . . I love you with all my might."[54] Only later did he tell her that the prisoners were sleeping on the bare floor, with almost nothing to eat, and that they were in a "strange emotional state."[55]

People were beginning to come back to the city. On July 18, Olga arrived from Laigle. There had been standing room only on the train. Beauvoir wrote in her journal:

> I go to school by bicycle and return in the pouring rain. At the hotel, there's a note from Kos, telling me she's here. She quickly comes down from her room, we go to the Dôme, she has a beautiful new raincoat, a red scarf around her hair, she looks very nice and I am happy to see her.

They spent the rest of the day in cafés, anxiously talking. In the evening, they returned to Beauvoir's hotel room. Olga brewed some tea. They shared Beauvoir's bed, and slept badly. Beauvoir's war journal ended there.

Over the next few weeks, Beauvoir and Olga were involved in something Vichy France regarded as a crime of the highest order. Olga was pregnant. The man in question was Niko Papatakis. The affair was over.[56] Even if the father had been Bost, Olga did not want a child. She was going to have to have one of those illegal, dangerous back-alley abortions that every woman in France dreaded. Under the Vichy government, it was even more difficult than usual to find a willing abortionist.

Beauvoir managed to obtain an address. The abortionist was a skinny old woman, and Beauvoir and Olga were terrified that she might not be sufficiently conscious of hygiene. They moved temporarily into Beauvoir's grandmother's vacant apartment at Denfert-Rochereau, where they spent "two sinister weeks."[57] In her next novel, *The Blood of Others,* Beauvoir would include an abortion scene, and Sartre would work a gnarly old woman abortionist into the novel he was writing, *The Age of Reason.*

"Getting your letters gave me back my joy," Sartre wrote to Beauvoir. "You are my life, my little sweet, my whole life."[58] Communication was sporadic. Prisoners were authorized to write only two postcards a week. Sartre sent longer letters from the local civilian post office, but this required "cunning and the right opportunity."[59]

In mid-August, he was transferred to Stalag XIID, a prisoner-of-war camp near Trier, in Germany. The prisoners' conditions were much improved. Sartre was cheerful, he assured Beauvoir, and neither bored nor hungry. In fact, he had never felt so free. He liked his fellow prisoners, he had found a good chess partner, and had become a good bridge player. He boxed or wrestled for three-quarters an hour every day. He was reading Heidegger (the Nazi officers had been only too pleased to give him a fine hardback edition of *Being and Time*) and was writing his own philosophical treatise, *Being and Nothingness.* He was having fun mounting a Christmas mystery play. His closest friends were two priests—a Jesuit and a Dominican. On Tuesday evenings he gave philosophy lectures to an audience made up almost entirely of priests.

"I'm not at all miserable, I even have loads of pleasant moments, but I'm hard as a pebble. To melt into water, it's you, tender little Beaver, you alone I'd need to find again. If I find you again, I find my happiness again and I find *myself.*"[60]

In Paris, Beauvoir got on with her life as well as she could. Most of her friends had left. René Maheu was teaching philosophy at a high school in Fez, Morocco. Stépha and Fernando, known to be communists, had fled to New York. Colette Audry was in Grenoble with her husband. Poupette was trapped in Portugal. (She had gone to visit her boyfriend, Lionel de Roulet, and the borders had closed a week later.)

Beauvoir taught in the mornings. Some afternoons, she went to the Bibliothèque Nationale and grappled with Hegel, so she could keep up with Sartre's latest thinking. Otherwise she sat in one of the booths at the back of the Dôme, revising *She Came to Stay*.

She spent two evenings a week with Olga, who had a small role in Charles Dullin's production of *Plutus*, at the Atelier. Wanda was painting Beauvoir's portrait. "We have very polite relations at present," Beauvoir told Sartre, "though she has given me a face shaped like a gourd."[61]

Two other evenings were spent with Nathalie Sorokine. The girl was wildly jealous. She could not stand being just one more person slotted into Beauvoir's inflexible schedule. "I've been working it out," she told Beauvoir. "You give up slightly less than a hundred and fortieth part of your life to me!"[62] Beauvoir explained in vain that she was writing a novel and had courses to prepare. Sorokine riposted: "You're nothing but a clock in a refrigerator!"[63] She was often waiting outside Beauvoir's hotel room when Beauvoir left in the morning, at eight A.M., and would loiter outside the gates when Beauvoir came out of school. There were frequent arguments, and the residents of the Hôtel du Danemark would hear the sounds of scuffles and fighting coming from Beauvoir's room. No one had any doubts as to the nature of hers and Sorokine's relationship. The women were causing something of a scandal at the hotel.[64]

Bost returned to Paris in September 1940. "After so many months exclusively in female company, it was wonderful to pick up a friendship with a man again," Beauvoir writes. Bost and Olga took a room together at the Hôtel Chaplain, on the Rue Jules-Chaplain. Wanda moved there, too. They were five minutes from Beauvoir at the Hôtel du Danemark.

Bost was given a temporary teaching job. He and Beauvoir had lunch together every day except Thursdays, when she went to her parents. On Saturday nights they had a secret tryst at the Poirier, an old hotel in the Emile Goudeau Square in Montmartre. They loved this square, with its chestnut trees, cast-iron fountain, and rundown artist studios where Picasso, Braque, and Modigliani had painted at the beginning of the century.[65] For Beauvoir, this was the high point of her week.

Soldiers in gray-green uniforms strutted around the city. There were large green street signs in German. Shopping for food involved ration cards and long queues. The hotels were freezing, and Beauvoir slept in her woolen ski pants. Petrol was almost nonexistent, and the only cars on the street were taxis and emergency vehicles. In the cafés everyone was talking about the prisoners, the conditions of the prison camps, and whether any of them was likely to be released before the end of the war. There were rumors that they were starving to death.

Signs went up in shop windows: OUT OF BOUNDS TO JEWS. Jewish workers were fired from factories, and Jews were debarred from public office and the liberal professions. Public servants, which included teachers, were asked to sign an affidavit swearing that they were neither Jews nor Freemasons.

Beauvoir had finished another draft of her novel *She Came to Stay* and was polishing the finer details. "But what a need I have of your judgment!" she told Sartre. "Alone in front of my text, I get to feel pretty sick of it in the long run."[66] She was helping Bost write film scripts. He was hoping to break into journalism and screenwriting.

She was not unhappy, she wrote, but she was not leading her true life, which was so full and rich and gay. Her true life was Sartre. She was waiting for him all the time. "I have constant nightmares about you. You come back . . . but you don't love me anymore and I'm filled with despair. At times, not knowing when I'll see you again has me literally fighting for breath. . . . I scan every street corner for you. I live only for the moment when I set eyes on you again."[67]

Beauvoir had not seen Sartre for eleven months. One evening, at the end of March 1941, she returned to the Hôtel du Danemark and found a note in her mailbox in his handwriting. "I'm at the Café des Trois Mousquetaires." Her heart stopped. She ran all the way to the café ("a reddish glow behind its thick blue curtains") and almost fell through the door.[68] Sartre was not there. A waiter handed her a note.

Sartre had waited two hours, then gone out. He would be back shortly.

There were civilians as well as military men in the Nazi prison camps, and the Nazis were releasing civilians if they proved themselves unfit for military action. Sartre and a priest friend of his had organized forged papers and passed themselves off as civilians. At the medical examination, Sartre made the most of his near-blind right eye, pulling at his eyelid, exposing the expanse of white, and complaining of dizzy spells. The doctor had signed his release papers.

Sartre had come back to Paris a changed man. It frightened Beauvoir. Never had the two of them seemed so far apart. He was impatient, intransigent, full of moral strictures. He was shocked that she had signed an affidavit declaring she was not a Jew, and disgusted to hear that she occasionally bought food on the black market. He had not come back to Paris to enjoy his freedom, he told her, but to *act*. He wanted to organize a resistance group. They had to expel the Germans from France. Beauvoir thought him deluded. Had he *still* no idea how powerless they were as individuals?

"That evening, and the next day, and for several days thereafter, Sartre completely baffled me," she would write in her memoirs. "We both felt that the other one was speaking in a completely different language."[69]

SIX

OCCUPIED PARIS

March 1941–September 1944

Sartre wasted no time in making contact with other intellectuals interested in forming a resistance group. Maurice Merleau-Ponty was back in Paris—freed from his prison camp when he contracted pneumonia—and he knew some young philosophers who had already formed a group called "Under the Boot." Bost also had friends who were eager to take action against the Germans. In the end, a dozen or so people turned up to the first meeting in Beauvoir's room at the Hôtel Mistral, where she and Sartre were living again. Most of them, like Bost, were in their mid-twenties, ten years younger than Sartre and Beauvoir.

A couple of the members, including the hotheaded Corsican philosopher Jean-Toussaint Desanti, wanted to manufacture bombs and hurl grenades, but the group quickly decided that this was beyond their capacity. Their weapons would be words. They would collect information and distribute news bulletins, inciting Parisians to resist German power.

They called their group Socialism and Liberty. Sartre had been deeply marked by collective life in the prison camp, which he considered a kind of socialism, and for the first time he thought of himself as a socialist. He did not mind that some members of the group were Marxists. Their aim was not to form a political party, he pointed out, but to expel the Germans from France. Discussion at the weekly meetings was sometimes fierce, but Sartre never tried to impose his own views.

It was usually Dominique Desanti, Jean-Toussaint's wife, who typed the leaflets; Bost and his friend Jean Pouillon printed them on a duplicating machine, and members of the group distributed them across Paris, preferably at the doors of factories, at dawn. They soon had fifty members. For better secrecy, they modeled themselves on the communist network, splitting up into groups of five.

They made overtures to the communist resistance movement, but word came back that the communists did not trust Sartre, who by his own admission had sat around in his prison camp reading Heidegger (a Nazi supporter), and who probably bought his release by agreeing to spy on French resistants. Sartre was horrified by this rumor.

He arranged meetings with other resistance leaders, and Beauvoir sometimes went with him. "All these groups had two things in common," she writes, "a very limited effective strength, and extraordinary lack of common caution. We held our meetings in hotel rooms or someone's study at the Ecole Normale, where walls might well have ears. Bost walked through the streets carrying a duplicating machine, and Pouillon went around with his briefcase stuffed full of pamphlets."[1]

That summer, Sartre and Beauvoir crossed into the so-called Free Zone, run by the collaborationist government of Marshal Pétain. Sartre hoped to establish contact with some resistance members in the south, in order to make Socialism and Liberty part of a larger organization. The border was formally closed, but they sent ahead bicycles (illicitly supplied by Sorokine) and camping equipment (lent by Bost), and were led across the border at night by a guide to whom they paid a small fee. For the next few weeks they cycled long distances up hills and along bumpy roads, eating even less well than in Paris. Among the people on Sartre's list of contacts were the prominent left-wing writers André Gide and André Malraux. Neither showed much interest in Sartre's plans. Malraux (who was not yet a member of the Resistance) told Sartre that Russian tanks and American planes were needed to combat Hitler, not well-meaning groups of intellectuals.

Resistance was dangerous work, and it became clear that the risks they were taking were far greater than any influence they might have. "We had the feeling we were shouting in the desert," Dominique

Desanti recalls.² As a group, they felt isolated. In May 1942, nineteen-year-old Yvonne Picard, a former student of Beauvoir's, resigned from the group to join the much larger and more effective communist resistance. One week later, she was arrested by the Germans. Her friends never saw her again.

Soon after that, reluctantly, the group decided to disband.³ The Marxist members, including the Desantis and their friend François Cuzin, went to work for the communist Resistance. Cuzin, a brilliant young philosopher, joined a major resistance group in the south. In July 1944, the Germans laid an ambush. Cuzin and his comrades were first tortured, then executed.

Although Sartre would not sign the declaration that he was neither a Jew nor a Freemason, he did not lose his job, and was sent back to the Lycée Pasteur. It turned out that the inspector general of education was a resistant. In October he transferred Sartre to the more prestigious Lycée Condorcet, where Sartre prepared students for the Ecole Normale.

After a morning's teaching, Sartre and Beauvoir installed themselves in a café to write. Their favorite was the Flore, on the Boulevard Saint-Germain, with its red chairs and mirrors. The café was not well known in those days, and German soldiers almost never set foot in it. But the best thing was its warmth. The four winters of the Occupation would prove unusually severe, with snow and ice on the streets of Paris. Coal was rationed, and power cuts were common. In the middle of the Flore sat a large potbellied stove, which the owner kept well stoked with his supply of black-market coal.

Sartre and Beauvoir worked mostly upstairs, on the second floor, where it was quieter. They sat at opposite ends of the room so they would not be tempted to talk, and—in the fug of tobacco fumes, amid the jangle of coffee cups, the hubbub of conversation, and the distraction of people making their way to the toilet or phone—they wrote. Both used fountain pens. Sartre's handwriting was small, neat, and professional. Beauvoir's jagged calligraphy was almost impossible to decipher. Even Sartre complained about it.

On the table beside their sheaf of papers were a small porcelain teapot, a cup and saucer, and an ashtray. Like everyone else, they smoked. Tobacco was scarce during the war, and Sartre would scour the café floor for cigarette butts to stuff in his pipe. Beauvoir liked the feel of a cigarette in her hand, but she did not inhale, and did not mind if she had to go without cigarettes altogether.

Dominique Desanti, a former member of Socialism and Liberty, was thoroughly inspired by Sartre and Beauvoir. One day she plucked up the courage to ask Sartre if he would read the first fifty pages of a novel she was writing. Sartre took her manuscript, and made an appointment to meet with her the following week:

> The table he used to sit at—it was virtually reserved for him— was opposite the clock. . . . He'd been there a while, absorbed by his writing, and I sat some way off. At another table Simone de Beauvoir was also writing; she made a little sign to me. He had not lifted his head. . . . At 11.30 on the dot, exactly the time he'd told me to meet him, he screwed the cap on his fountain pen and gave me a welcoming smile, showing that he had registered my presence. I went over to his table, he ordered me a tea, and took my manuscript out of his briefcase.

Sartre said encouraging things, then asked Desanti if she planned to make writing her vocation. Yes? In that case, he would make some more substantial criticisms. He was gentle and encouraging, she recalls, and he soon had her laughing at some of the weak passages in her writing. His criticism was kind, and utterly to the point. He tapped his pipe on the table, filled it (his nails were filthy, she noticed), and made several attempts at lighting it. "Writing is an occupation without respite," he told her as he handed the manuscript back. "I like to teach. But at some level I am always thinking about what I am writing. . . . At every moment you must be ready to dive back into it. Look at the Beaver."[4]

It was an affectionate joke in their circle, writes Desanti, that the Beaver was always beavering away. It was clear that Sartre admired her for it.

●　　　●　　　●

"My relationship with Wanda is perfect," Sartre declared. Although he and Beauvoir had moved back to the Mistral, he spent most nights in Wanda's room at the Hôtel Chaplain. "She is absolutely charming with me, in a proprietary way; I feel like a beloved cat or Pekinese," he told Beauvoir. "I've decided to have her give up painting, which she hates, and have her do theater work."[5] Sartre's collection of short stories, *The Wall* (1939), had been dedicated to Olga; the trilogy he was writing, *Roads to Freedom,* was dedicated to Wanda.

Beauvoir would maintain a lifetime of silence about Wanda. Her memoirs scarcely mention the young woman who played such a major role in Sartre's wartime life. But she vented her spleen in the novel she was writing. The title itself, *L'Invitée* (published in English as *She Came to Stay,* but whose literal translation is "the woman guest"), hints that this particular "guest" overstayed her welcome. When Beauvoir first began her novel, in 1938, Xavière was modeled entirely on Olga. Over time, Xavière had acquired some of Wanda's traits. Later in life, Beauvoir would tell her biographer, Deirdre Bair, "Too many people . . . entirely overlooked the fact that the most unpleasant aspects of Xavière came from my prickly relationship with Wanda."[6]

Sartre and Beauvoir's own sexual relationship was over. Beauvoir tried to rationalize: "It is pretty much accepted that in men habit kills desire."[7] Her father had turned away from her mother in the same way. She remembered her young mother glowing with happiness—a happiness five-year-old Simone vaguely associated with the bedroom from which her mother had just emerged. By the time Beauvoir was an adolescent, the idyll was over. Georges de Beauvoir had lost interest in his wife and started to frequent prostitutes. "Her senses had grown demanding," Beauvoir would write sympathetically of her mother. "At thirty-five, in the prime of her life, she was no longer allowed to satisfy them."[8]

When Sartre came back from the war, Simone de Beauvoir was thirty-three, and had to accept, once and for all, that the man she most loved no longer desired her.[9] For years, their sex life, such as it was, had limped along without sparkle. Neither of them had any doubt that this was because of Sartre, not Beauvoir. They discussed what they called his "sexual indifference" or "sexual coldness," and attributed it to Sartre's complete inability to lose his self-consciousness about his body. He was incapable of "letting go." On vacation, he would never relax on the grass or the sand, and he almost never sat in an armchair to read. For him, he admitted, sex involved "a slight touch of sadism," since his partner yielded her body to him, and he never yielded his.[10]

"It was rather deep friendship than love," Beauvoir would explain to Nelson Algren, a more passionate lover, a few years later. "Love was not very successful. Chiefly because [Sartre] does not care much for sexual life. He is a warm, lively man everywhere, but not in bed. I soon felt it, though I had no experience; and little by little, it seemed useless, and even indecent, to go on being lovers."[11]

At the age of sixty-nine, in a taped conversation with Beauvoir intended for publication, Sartre was quite candid about his lack of priapic drive:

> I was more a masturbator of women than a copulator.... For me, the essential and affective relation involved my embracing, caressing, and kissing a body all over.... As I was reasonably well equipped sexually my erection was quick and easy, and I often made love, but without very great pleasure. Just a little pleasure at the end, but pretty feeble.... I should have been quite happy naked in bed with a naked woman, caressing and kissing her, but without going as far as the sexual act.[12]

Certainly, Beauvoir's life could not have been more different from her mother's. She was no dependent wife, languishing at home. If Sartre had his twenty-four-year-old Wanda, Beauvoir had her twenty-five-year old Bost. Nevertheless, try as she might to make it so, their situation was not parallel. Sartre spent almost every night with Wanda; Beauvoir spent only one night a week with Bost. Sartre's relationship with Wanda was public: Beauvoir's relationship with Bost was clandestine. Even her relationship with Sartre was largely hidden. Sartre did not want Wanda to know the extent of their intimacy.

These days, Sartre's woman was Wanda. Bost's woman had always been Olga. Beauvoir was behind the scenes, undeclared. Almost like a mistress. But paradoxically it was Olga and Wanda who were the kept women. Not only was Beauvoir financially independent, but she was also constantly shelling out money in their direction.

•   •   •

With their pooled civil servant salaries, Beauvoir and Sartre were completely supporting Olga and Wanda, and helping Bost and Nathalie Sorokine as well. In July 1941, Beauvoir's father died, leaving no money. Françoise de Beauvoir, at the age of fifty-four, became entirely dependent on her eldest daughter.

Beauvoir decided that she and Sartre could not afford to keep eating out. To make ends meet, she moved, in the Mistral, to a room with a small kitchen. She borrowed saucepans, crockery, and utensils from Poupette's studio (Poupette was still in Portugal), and for the first and only time in her life took it upon herself to shop and cook. She enjoyed the challenge of foraging for food, shopping with ration cards, and making edible meals out of their meager provisions. "What a windfall it was if I stumbled on a beet or a cabbage!" she writes.[13] Bost and Sorokine often helped.

Beauvoir writes that she constantly felt hungry during the war. Sartre seemed better able to go without food. Madame Morel regularly sent food parcels from La Pouèze. Sometimes the package, held up in the mail, would arrive stinking, with a putrefying rabbit or purplish sausages inside. Too hungry to be proud, Bost and Beauvoir, would wash the meat with vinegar and try to disguise the taste in a spicy stew. Sartre once walked in and caught sight of this operation. "It's a rotting carcass!" he exclaimed, and insisted that they fling it out.

After dinner, the entire clan could mostly be found at the Flore. They never sat together as a group. They met in pairs, out of earshot from one another. Sartre might be at a table with Wanda, Beauvoir at another with Sorokine, Olga at another with Bost. They greeted one another when they came and went, but otherwise left one another alone. "We had always possessed—and were always to keep—the taste for conversation à deux," Beauvoir writes. "We would enjoy ourselves over the most idiotic topics—always provided that the two of us remained uninterrupted by any third party. . . . When you have to discuss things with several people at once, conversation, except in very special circumstances, tends to become mundane."[14]

There was another reason to talk in pairs: the group was beset with tensions and jealousies. The Kosakiewicz sisters got on less well since

Wanda had become Sartre's girlfriend. "Wanda always suffered from being the younger sister," Olga told a friend.[15] As Wanda herself said, her position in the Sartre clique was tenuous at best. "I arrived in a world where everything was already set up, where everyone had his or her relationship with everyone else. I was just the 'littlest Kosakiewicz.' I felt very awkward and very isolated. My only bond with all these people was through Sartre."[16]

Nathalie Sorokine was a divisive figure. She had not been pleased when Sartre came back from the war. Before she met him, having heard so many stories about him from the family, she was disdainful. "Fancies himself as a phony genius," she said scornfully.[17] When she finally met him, in 1941, she played all sorts of games to seduce him. It did not take long. She had already seduced Bost.[18]

As well as her relationship with Beauvoir, Sorokine had a boyfriend these days, a wealthy young man whom her mother hoped she would marry. But already they were arguing. Sorokine continued to seduce everyone in sight (including Wanda's admirer, the young Mouloudji).[19] At the same time, she remained obsessively jealous of Beauvoir.

Beauvoir would dedicate her second novel, *The Blood of Others,* to Nathalie Sorokine. Hélène, the young protagonist, is willful, egocentric, and an incurable bicycle thief. She first sees Jean Blomart (who resembles Sartre) sitting in a café with a book in front of him. She asks him if he would mind fetching her pale blue bicycle from a nearby courtyard. She is late for dinner with her parents, she says. He believes her. Soon she has him in her bed.

It is not until Beauvoir moved into the realm of invention that Hélène becomes a positive character—heroic, even. Blomart is active in the Resistance. It's at first to impress him that Hélène becomes politically active. In the course of the struggle, she learns the meaning of solidarity and fraternity. One night, she insists on going out on a mission, despite the unusual risk, and is mortally wounded by the Germans. Sitting beside her bed while she is dying, Blomart agonizes about the part he played in this tragedy. "It was my fault," he tells her. "I could have stopped you going." But Hélène is a transformed woman. "You did not have the right to decide for me," she tells him, smiling. "I would make the same choice again."

• • •

In March 1942, Nathalie Sorokine's mother lodged an official complaint to the Vichy Ministry of Education, accusing Beauvoir of corrupting her daughter, a minor. She claimed that Beauvoir had seduced her daughter and then acted as a procurer, passing Sorokine to her men friends—Sartre and Bost. Moreover, she claimed, her daughter was not the first young women to be subjected to this treatment.[20]

It had taken Madame Sorokine two years to discover the exact nature of the goings-on in the Sartre-Beauvoir circle, but one thing she had always known: "Since the day my daughter first set eyes on Mlle de Beauvoir, she became a stranger to her family."[21]

It turned out that Sorokine's boyfriend, whom Sorokine had just ditched, had divulged the details to her mother. Over the time they had been together, Nathalie had told him plenty of wild stories. Yes, he assured Madame Sorokine, Beauvoir and Nathalie had been lovers. Before Nathalie, there had been Olga Kosakiewicz and Bianca Bienenfeld.[22] In each case, Beauvoir had seduced the girl, then introduced her to Sartre, who also slept with her—or tried to. Sorokine had gone to bed with both Sartre and Bost. Now Sartre was sleeping with Olga's younger sister, Wanda.

Madame Sorokine's complaint took the form of a lengthy and detailed report. The Ministry of Education took it seriously, and brought in the police, who interrogated all the members of the "family"—Beauvoir, Sartre, Sorokine, Bost, Olga, and Wanda—as well as the Kosakiewicz parents and the principals of Beauvoir's schools. They even went around to the various hotels Beauvoir had inhabited over the years and questioned some residents.

Sartre and Beauvoir discussed their best strategy. The members of their clique were carefully primed. Each in turn duly denied everything, telling the police well-honed lies.

Beauvoir said that Sorokine was an excellent student, and they had become friends. Like some other of her pupils, Nathalie had developed an "exalted admiration" toward her, but Beauvoir had never responded to the girl's appeals. On the contrary, she had directed her toward "normal sexual relations." Yes, Beauvoir knew Sartre and

Bost. Sartre had been her lover for six years, and was now a good friend. Bost had never been her lover. Yes, Nathalie also knew these men, but they were just friends.

Nathalie Sorokine endorsed this story. She was deeply indebted to her former teacher, she said. If Mademoiselle de Beauvoir often came to her hotel room in the winter of 1940, it was because Beauvoir's own room was freezing. Sorokine said yes, she had told her former boyfriend that she and Beauvoir had been lovers. That was because he wanted to marry her, and she wanted to get rid of him. Mademoiselle de Beauvoir had advised her to invent that story so he would be disgusted and leave her alone.

Sartre said he could state for a fact that Mademoiselle de Beauvoir had never had unusual tendencies toward women. Bost said he had known Beauvoir since 1935, and they had an excellent friendship. He was a former student of Sartre's and saw a lot of him. No, he had never received money from Mademoiselle de Beauvoir. He had never been her lover. And he could not imagine that Beauvoir and Sorokine had ever had sexual relations.

Olga assured the police that Beauvoir had never made advances to her of an unusual type and had never introduced her to any man with the aim of procuring. Wanda said she had been Sartre's girlfriend for the last three years, and she could not believe that Simone de Beauvoir had "peculiar habits." It seemed to her that Mademoiselle de Beauvoir was the victim of calumny.

Monsieur Kosakiewicz was outraged that Madame Sorokine should implicate his daughters in this business. He and his wife felt nothing but gratitude and deep respect toward Mademoiselle de Beauvoir.

Nothing could be proved, and the case was dismissed. Moreover, Beauvoir's teaching credentials were impeccable. Nevertheless, the rector of the University of Paris, a supporter of Marshal Pétain, decreed that it was inadmissible to keep Beauvoir in the teaching corps. She was unmarried and had lived for years in a relationship of concubinage with Sartre. She did not have a permanent home, she lived in hotels, corrected her students' work in cafés, and at a time when France was urgently trying to restore moral values, she taught the homosexual writers Proust and Gide.

In June 1943, after twelve years of service, Simone de Beauvoir was dismissed from the Vichy government teaching corps.[23] In progressive circles, this gave her a certain cachet. Her position would be restored in 1945, after the war, but Beauvoir never went back to teaching.

Nathalie Sorokine soon had a new boyfriend. It was Sartre who introduced her to Jean-Pierre Bourla, a Spanish Jew who had been his student at the Lycée Pasteur. They made a striking pair. Sorokine was tall, blond, and Slavic; Bourla was short, dark, and Latin. The "kids," as Sartre and Beauvoir called them, quarreled often—it was impossible not to quarrel with Sorokine—but Bourla's gentleness and generosity were having a visible softening effect on her. The family had never seen her so happy.

Bourla had an almost manic energy. He wanted to study philosophy. To Sartre's and Beauvoir's amusement, he devoured Hegel and Kant as if they were detective novels, and still managed to understand them. He wrote poetry, encouraged by his friend, the Jewish poet Max Jacob. Bourla was "tumultuous, irritating, passionate, childish, clumsy, frantic," writes Beauvoir. "He liked to be alive."[24]

In June 1942, a new Vichy law decreed that all Jews in Occupied France had to wear the Star of David. They no longer had the right to own a residence or maintain a bank account, and were forbidden to enter public places—including restaurants and cafés. For Jews, there was a curfew at eight in the evening. The following month, in Paris's worst dawn raid during the Occupation, the Gestapo and French police rounded up some twenty thousand Jews and transported them to Nazi death camps.

Bourla looked more Spanish than Jewish, and he continued much as before. He did not wear a yellow star, he ignored the Jewish curfew, and he spent hours each day at the Flore. His father, a wealthy businessman, was convinced that they were protected by influential friends in the Spanish embassy. One day Jean-Pierre Bourla was outlining his plans for the future. "What if the Nazis win the war?" Sartre asked him. Bourla replied: "A Nazi victory does not enter into my plans."

• • •

It was illegal to cross the border between the Occupied Zone and the Free Zone without special permission, but in the summer of 1942, Beauvoir and Sartre sneaked through again, this time with Bost. They went cycling in the Pyrenees, sleeping in barns. Just as before, food was in short supply, and it was difficult for them to scrounge up enough to eat. Sartre was plunged in *Being and Nothingness,* and he often stayed behind to work in a café while Beauvoir and Bost went off by themselves.

One day Sartre wrote in a meadow while the other two, battling a strong wind, climbed to the summit of the Midi de Bigorre. They came back to find him still writing. "He had knocked off heaven knows how many pages, wind or no wind," writes Beauvoir, "and felt very pleased with himself."[25]

She and Sartre returned to Paris, leaving Bost to see friends in Lyon. A few days later, he was caught trying to slip across the border and spent two weeks fretting, half-starving, in a local prison.

Back in Paris, Beauvoir was dismayed to learn that the manager of the Hôtel Mistral had rented her room to someone else. She spent days scouring Montparnasse for a similar arrangement. There was nothing. In the end she found a room with a tiny kitchen that doubled as a bathroom in a squalid hotel, the Aubusson, on the Rue Dauphine. The walls were peeling, there was a dim yellow bulb in the ceiling, and at night she heard mice scampering around.[26]

The "kids"—Sorokine and Bourla—loyally moved with her, taking a room on the floor below. Sorokine insisted that Beauvoir come downstairs, tuck her in, and kiss her goodnight. Bourla would say: "And me? Don't I get a kiss?" And Beauvoir would kiss him, too.

In an essay called "Paris Under the Occupation," which he would write at the end of the war for British readers, Sartre tried to describe what it felt like to live in a city occupied by the Nazis. He was aware that many English people, who after all suffered atrocious bombardments, thought that the French had not had too hard a time of it. "I would like to explain to them that they are wrong, that the Occupation was a terrible ordeal, that it is not certain that France can get over it and that there is not one Frenchman who has not often envied the fate of his English allies."[27]

He was not asking the English to pity the French. Of course not. But he wanted to explain what it meant to live in humiliation, to have to look on passively while the fate of one's country was in the hands of others. In prison camp, he had seen the shame at firsthand. The French military prisoners felt they had let down France. The Polish and Czech prisoners openly called them cowards. And yet, Sartre pointed out: "The three biggest powers in the world took four years to defeat Germany; wasn't it natural that we gave way at the first onslaught, we who faced it on our own?"

The Vichy collaborators tried to rub French noses in their inferiority, he wrote. Worse, under the Occupation it was almost impossible for the French to avoid a degree of complicity with their occupiers. Even the peasants who worked the fields to feed the French were inevitably providing food for the enemy at the same time. It meant that the French lost their pride. "Those who congratulate us ironically for having escaped the war cannot imagine with what ardor the French would have liked to take up combat again."

Sartre had enjoyed writing and producing a play when he was in his prison camp. The French prisoners understood and appreciated his covert resistance message. Now he was keen to get a similar message past the German censors and onto the Paris stage. He wanted the French people to throw off their paralyzing guilt. They should stop seeing themselves through the eyes of the occupiers and realize that they were free to shake off their shackles.

In the spring of 1942, Olga Kosakiewicz played a small role in a play directed by the talented young director Jean-Louis Barrault. He was encouraging, and one day she asked him how she might go about obtaining more significant roles. "The best way," Barrault said, "would be to get someone to write a play for you." When Olga told this to Sartre, he immediately said: "Why not me?" He and Olga no longer spent time together alone, but she was part of the family, and he liked the idea of giving her a lucky break.

Sartre knew the German censors would never allow a play about the Occupation, so he decided to convey his message through Greek mythology. He would write about Orestes's return from exile to his native Argos, a plague-ridden city ruled by the tyrannical Aegisthus and his consort, Clytemnestra. Orestes, in dialogue with Jupiter, comes to realize that the gods are not just. Throwing off the gods and assuming his freedom, he slays Aegisthus and Clytemnestra, his own mother. His act of violence frees the citizens of Argos and releases them from their plague.

Barrault agreed to direct *The Flies* but said he did not think the twenty-seven-year-old Olga up to the part of Orestes's sister, Electra. It was a demanding role, and Barrault worked with professional actors only. Sartre stood firm: Olga came with the play.

Rehearsals began. Barrault kept losing his temper with Olga. Behind Sartre's back, he muttered comments about Sartre promoting his mistress. Barrault was soon putting his energy into a production that was a far safer bet with the Vichy government, *The Satin Slipper,* an epic drama by the reactionary Catholic playwright Paul Claudel.

Finally Sartre decided to end their contract. "All this is my fault," he wrote Barrault. "I do not generally like to talk about my private life and my silence reinforced this misunderstanding. I want to tell you . . . that Olga has never been and will never be my mistress; it's <u>her talent alone</u> that I wanted to serve."[28]

Charles Dullin agreed to take the play on. He himself played Jupiter. Dullin worked patiently with Olga, and she threw herself into the part. Nonetheless, Dullin's temper was famous, and occasionally he erupted. Olga would burst into tears and threaten to give up. Their outbursts, writes Beauvoir, were "halfway between a family quarrel and a lovers' tiff."[29] The other students in the Atelier would look on jealously, hoping Olga would prove inadequate to the task.

Dullin was taking a big risk. Sartre was an unknown author, and Olga an unknown actress. The production was costly (involving a large crowd of extras), and the play was decidedly controversial. The opening night was June 3, 1943, at the Théâtre de la Cité. (The Vichy administrators had insisted that this theater change its name from the Théâtre Sarah Bernhardt, after the Jewish actress.) "How tense I was when the curtain went up!" Beauvoir recalls. Olga, under the stage name of Olga Dominique, performed beautifully. It was a triumphant beginning to her career.

To the audience that night, a fresh breeze seemed to be blowing across the stage. "It was impossible to mistake the play's implications," writes Beauvoir. "The word Liberty, dropped from Orestes' mouth, burst on us like a bomb."[30]

Dominique Desanti agrees. "Yes, Sartre had to make compromises because of the German censors. But what could he do? Some writers chose to maintain silence throughout the Occupation, in order not to compromise at all. That was a noble stance. But we young people were so excited that Sartre was speaking out. And to us, his message was clear."[31]

If Beauvoir did not care all that much about losing her teaching job in the summer of 1943 it was because she and Sartre had entered a far more exciting sphere than the world of classrooms, blackboards, and chalk. In June, a couple of weeks after *The Flies* opened at the Théâtre de la Cité, Sartre's weighty philosophical tome *Being and Nothingness* was published, dedicated to "The Beaver."

The book would not make a real impact until after the war, but some readers already recognized that it represented a landmark. Sartre had applied philosophy to everyday life, taking examples from the world around him. His portrait of a waiter in a café would become famous. Slightly affected, bearing his tray aloft, bending forward with eager solicitude to take a new order: was he free? Was he merely acting a role?

In August 1943, *She Came to Stay* appeared in the bookshop windows. After thirteen years of writing and rewriting, with dozens of drafts relegated to the back of her shelves, Beauvoir was a published author at last. For a brief time, she admits, she melted eagerly into her public image:

> One literary columnist, discussing new books from Gallimard, referred to me as "the firm's new woman novelist." The words

tinkled gaily around in my head. How I would have envied this serious-faced young woman, now embarking on her literary career, if she had possessed any name other than my own—but she *was* me![32]

She Came to Stay seeded the Sartre-Beauvoir legend. There were not many reviews—the censored wartime press did not exactly embrace this decadent novel—but the word flew around that it was a roman à clef, drawn from Beauvoir's open relationship with Sartre and the trio they had once formed with Olga Kosakiewicz, to whom the book was dedicated, the same woman, people said, who was acting the part of Electra in Sartre's play *The Flies,* at the Théâtre de la Cité. Rumor had it that Sartre, whose play hinted at a frisson of incest between Electra and her brother, Orestes, was now sleeping with Olga's younger sister, Wanda. The people in the Flore "looked somewhat askance at me," Beauvoir writes.[33]

There were polarized reactions to the novel. Some thought it immoral and exhibitionist; others thought it a courageous act of resistance to the Vichy ideology of "work, family, country." One thing was certain: Beauvoir, with her very first novel, had surrendered the last shreds of bourgeois respectability.

The book caused a frenzy of gossip. "It's Sartre portrayed in his entirety," the anthropologist Claude Lévi-Strauss told a friend, "and he comes over as a vile bastard."[34] Raymond Queneau noted in his journal: "Extraordinary veracity of the description, total lack of imagination. Even when S de B attributes a different childhood to one of her characters, it belongs to someone else—for example, the childhood of Gerbert (J-L Bost) is Mouloudji's."[35] As a portrait of an iconoclastic group of people, the novel was thought by Michel Leiris to be the French equivalent of *The Sun Also Rises.* But he observed that it lacked clarity on a central question: "Pierre and Françoise have been together for ten years. Are they people who still have a sexual relationship, or who don't anymore? . . . Without this basic information, it is difficult to understand how the equilibrium of the trio works."[36]

Françoise de Beauvoir had already had to face the ignominy of having her daughter expelled from the teaching profession. Now she had to endure another round of comments from family and friends. "Until *She Came to Stay* came out she knew almost nothing at all about my life," Simone de Beauvoir writes. "She tried to persuade herself that at least as far as morals were concerned I was 'a good girl.' Public rumor destroyed her illusions."[37]

Beauvoir heard that *She Came to Stay* was a serious contender for the Prix Goncourt. This was the Vichy period. Jewish writers could not be published; their names could not even be mentioned in any piece of writing published under the Vichy regime. Although Beauvoir was disgusted by this, she writes, "If I had been awarded the Prix Goncourt that year I should have accepted it with wholehearted jubilation."[38]

In the autumn of 1943, Sartre briefly put aside his trilogy and, in two weeks flat, wrote *No Exit,* a dazzling one-act play. An instant success, it would become a French classic, repeatedly revived on Paris stages.[39]

The three characters—one man and two women—are in Hell. They arrive one after another to find themselves locked in a room furnished with ugly antiques. At first they are relieved. They expected torture instruments and burning coals. Then they understand. There are no mirrors, no books, no toothbrushes, no distractions. All they have—for the rest of yawning eternity—is one another.

Garcin is a coward who desperately wants to be seen as a hero. Estelle is a narcissist who lives for the desire of men. Inès, a lesbian, likes to see others suffer. She is the first to understand their plight. "Each of us is a hangman for the two others," she says. Near the end of the play, Garcin utters the famous Sartrean quip: "Hell is other people."

Sartre wrote the role of Estelle for Wanda to play. For a year now, she had been going along to Dullin's classes at the Atelier and acting in minor roles. She did not show her sister's talent, but Sartre thought it only a matter of time. He wanted to give her a start.

A young actress friend, Olga Barbezat, played Inès. Sartre asked Albert Camus to play Garcin and to direct the play. The first rehearsals took place in December 1943, in Wanda's room at the Hôtel Chaplain.

•   •   •

"One would hardly dare to invent two figures in a drama of such con-
trasting physical appearance as Sartre and Camus," Arthur Koestler
writes. "Sartre looked like a malevolent goblin or gargoyle, Camus
like a young Apollo."[40]

Camus had walked up and introduced himself to Sartre at the
dress rehearsal of *The Flies.* He was thirty and recently arrived from
Algeria. His latest novel, *The Outsider,* was causing a splash. Sartre had
written an appreciative review of it. Camus had also played a courageous role in the Resistance, editing the underground newspaper
Combat.

Sartre liked Camus immediately. So did everyone in the Sartre
clan. Camus was a warm and passionate Mediterranean man. His
roots were Spanish, French, and Algerian, and his accent sounded
southern French. He was sensitive, funny, tragic, and full of stories,
which he told in spicy language. His charm was extraordinary. "You'd
be at a party, and you'd look around," his publisher, Robert Gallimard,
recalls, "and suddenly you'd see that nearly all the women in the room
were clustered around Camus."[41]

Wanda had not heard of Camus before they started rehearsing.
Over Christmas, she read *The Outsider* and thought it marvelous. She
was fascinated by Camus—his exotic North African origins, his lifelong struggle with tuberculosis, the vulnerability beneath his swaggering surface.

Camus had no idea that Wanda and Sartre were lovers. One
evening at the Flore, he confided to Sartre that he was captivated by
Wanda's "Russian soul." He even used the word *genius* to describe her.[42]

Sartre's and Beauvoir's social horizons began to open up. Through
Camus, Sartre joined the writers' resistance group, the CNE—the
National Committee of Writers. He became friendly with the former
surrealist writers Michel Leiris and Raymond Queneau, who were
five or six years older than he was.

Sartre and Beauvoir were invited to dinners at Michel and Zette
Leiris's apartment, on the Quai des Grands-Augustins, overlooking

the Seine. Leiris introduced them to Picasso, whose studio was just around the corner. On several occasions they had lunch with Picasso and his mistress, Dora Marr, in a Catalan restaurant up the street. "Picasso always welcomed us with sparkling vivacity," writes Beauvoir, "but though his conversation was gay and brilliant, one didn't exactly talk *with* him. It was more a case of his holding forth solo."[43]

For the first time in her life, Beauvoir entertained in her own home. She and the "kids" had moved to a much nicer hotel, La Louisiane, on the Rue de Seine, in the heart of Saint-Germain-des-Prés. Several of the Flore regulars lived there, including Mouloudji and his new girl-friend. Beauvoir had a large corner room on the third floor, with a kitchen and a view of rooftops. The day she moved in, Sartre spilled a bottle of ink and the manager had the carpet removed, leaving bare parquet flooring. Beauvoir did not mind. "None of my previous retreats had come so close to being the apartment of my dreams," she writes, "and I felt like staying there for the rest of my life."[44]

The room contained a divan, bookshelves, and a massive table, covered with books and papers, with Beauvoir's bicycle propped against it. One evening, Beauvoir cleared the table, took her bike down to Sorokine's room, and had their new friends around for a meal. Leiris and Queneau came with their wives; Albert Camus was there, and so were Sorokine and Bourla, Bost, Olga, and Wanda. Bost stood in front of a huge bowl of beans, dishing out with a ladle. Camus burst out laughing. "It's like the army barracks," he said.[45]

That spring, they had a series of orgiastic all-night parties, which they called "fiestas." Everyone saved up his or her coupons, so they could amass what seemed like prodigious quantities of food and drink. The surrealist writer Georges Bataille hosted the first party. Olga, Wanda, and Camus were the dazzling dancers in the group. Sartre sang lewd songs and danced a parody of the tango; Dora Marr mimed a bullfighting act; Queneau and Georges Bataille fought a duel with bottles. Leiris was so drunk he fell down the stairs. Once midnight struck, the revelers were imprisoned until dawn by the cur-few. In the early hours of the morning, some of the company crept upstairs to sleep.

Two weeks after Bataille's party, Bost's mother lent them the family house at Taverny. "For a septuagenarian and clergyman's widow she was remarkably broadminded," Beauvoir writes. "She locked up her antique furniture and precious knick-knacks, put away some chessmen that normally stood on a table, and went off somewhere else for the night."[46] In June, Simone Jollivet and Charles Dullin threw a party in their grand apartment. Jollivet, who was already showing signs of the alcoholism that would destroy her, was drunk before the guests arrived.

At the first fiesta, Camus disappeared upstairs with Wanda. At the second, just before dawn, Olga went looking for Bost and found him on a sofa in a dark corner feeling up a young Algerian actress. Olga started to shout and scream, Mouloudji recalls, and people came hurrying out of the bedrooms, rubbing their eyes with sleep and wonder.[47]

"What a carry-on. The little Sartre group is in an uproar," Raymond Queneau reported in his journal the next day. "Bost has broken up with Olga K. etc. Discussions. Tragic atmosphere at the Flore this evening."[48]

At the fiestas, the revelers tried hard to forget that in those sinister curfew hours, Paris belonged to the men in gray. As Sartre pointed out in "Paris Under the Occupation," the Gestapo carried out their raids with almost unfailing politeness:

Towards midnight one heard the sound in the street of late passers-by hurrying to get home before the curfew, and then there was silence. And we knew that the only footsteps clacking past outside were *their* steps. It is difficult to convey the impression that this deserted town could give, this *no man's land* plastered against our windows and which they alone inhabited. The houses were never exactly a protection. The Gestapo often performed their arrests between midnight and five in the morning. It felt at each moment as if the door could open, letting in a cold blast, a bit of night, and three affable Germans with revolvers. Even when we did not talk about them, even when we did not think about them, their presence was among us.

In February 1944, the rehearsals for No Exit came to a standstill. Olga Barbezat, the actress who was to play Inès, went to a party one evening at the home of a fellow actor. She did not know that he was active in the Resistance until the Gestapo swept in and arrested everyone present. Their host was never seen again. Olga Barbezat was taken to Fresnes, the prison just outside Paris that was known for torturing and executing members of the Resistance. She was there for three months before being released. Out of solidarity, Camus refused to continue with the play. Sartre handed it over to professionals at the Théâtre du Vieux Colombier.

One hideous night at the end of March, Bourla was arrested. He had gone to see his father in the fashionable Paris district of Neuilly, and because of the curfew, he stayed over. Just before dawn, the Germans came crashing through the door. Bourla, his father, and his sister were arrested and taken to Drancy, the internment camp on the northern outskirts of Paris where, just ten days earlier, Bourla's poet friend Max Jacob had died of pneumonia.

Beauvoir and Sartre were at La Pouèze spending Easter with Madame Morel when they heard about Bourla's arrest. Beauvoir writes of her "agony and despair." Sartre tried to persuade her that, fundamentally, death at nineteen was no more absurd than death at eighty. Beauvoir was not convinced. She tortured herself with questions about Bourla and his fate. "Why had he stayed with his father on that night of all nights? Why had his father been convinced he ran no danger? Why had we believed him?"[49]

Sartre and Beauvoir were in La Pouèze. On the nights of April 20 and 21, the northern districts of Paris were bombed by the allies. The noise was deafening, Bost wrote to Beauvoir. He was terrified. He could imagine nothing worse than being buried under a pile of rubble. The Kosakiewicz sisters were implacable. Bost admired them. He'd seen Nathalie Sorokine at the Flore, looking haggard. Someone had told her that Bourla had been transferred from Drancy to the prison at Villeneuve-Saint-Georges. She was hoping against hope that it was true. (In fact the Bourlas had already been transported to Auschwitz.)[50]

Olga was still giving Bost a hard time about the Algerian actress, he wrote. It was tiring. As for Wanda, there had almost been a scandal that morning at the Hôtel Chaplain:

Tell Sartre that this morning Camus was in bed with Wanda, who was saying to him in her half-sleep, "We sleep like two little angels," when they were woken by a battering on her door and the voice of the manager saying: "Monsieur Sartre, I've been calling you for an hour! Monsieur Sartre, you're wanted on the phone!" It seems that Camus leapt out of bed and took at least an hour to recover.[51]

For money, Bost was churning out love stories under a pseudonym. Work on his war novel was advancing slowly. He looked forward to showing Beauvoir what he had written.

Wanda's affair with Camus did not last long. (Camus fell in love with the beautiful twenty-one-year-old Spanish-French actress Maria Casarès, whom he brought to the next fiesta.) Nevertheless, Sartre was hurt. It was a turning point in his relationship with Wanda. "She made the break inevitable by becoming Camus's mistress," Sartre said later, adding that he had also grown tired of her "pathological rages." He knew that he sometimes provoked this behavior. Still, he found it tedious.[52]

Sartre and Wanda soon went their separate ways, but Sartre would support Wanda for the rest of her life, spend time alone with her twice a week, and take her on vacation for two or three weeks every year. All in all, he would write six plays for her, giving her the only roles she would ever have. In 1965, he would buy her an apartment.

Wanda had plenty of other lovers, but she never ceased to be jealous of Sartre's other women. The one she hated most, with a passion, was Simone de Beauvoir.

Food, coal, and gas had become even more scarce. Restaurants and cafés were obliged to close three days a week because of electricity shortages. The Allied air forces were pounding French factories, industrial targets, ports, and railway stations—anything useful to the Germans. The Nazi flag was still flying over the Senate. The

Germans had not yet withdrawn. But liberation was in the air. The Anglo-Americans were advancing on Paris.

On the evening of Friday, August 25, 1944, Sartre, as a member of the resistant writers' group, the National Theater Committee, was at the Comédie Française. He and others had put up a barricade to protect the theater from German sabotage. Bost and the women—Olga, Wanda, Beauvoir, and Sorokine—were in the room Bost shared with Olga at the Hôtel Chaplain. Bost had rigged up a kind of stove. For fuel, they used old newspapers. It was a challenge to cook on the contraption. Dinner consisted of potatoes. While they were eating, the radio announced that General de Gaulle had arrived in Paris that afternoon and had given a speech at the town hall.

The group heard cheers and shouts in the street, and went down. A throng of people had gathered at the Vavin intersection, in front of the Dôme. Church bells pealed. Some people lit a bonfire in the middle of the street and danced around it, singing and laughing. Then a voice called out, "Tanks coming!" The fire was stamped out, and people ran for safety. The lights in neighboring houses were turned off. Armored cars filled with SS men clattered past. There was sniper fire. Red Cross ambulances whizzed by with wounded people.

The next day, the French tricolor flew from the summit of the Eiffel Tower. De Gaulle marched down the Champs-Elysées accompanied by French and American troops. Sartre watched from the balcony of the Hôtel du Louvre. Beauvoir went with Olga to the Arc de Triomphe, where, arm in arm, they joined the cheering crowd. Shots rang out. Beauvoir and Olga ran. People crumpled onto the street. Sartre and his colleagues retreated inside the building and lay flat on their bellies.

These were euphoric yet frightening days. Before the Germans withdrew, there was violent fighting in the streets. Sartre and Beauvoir took notes and combined their impressions for a series of articles they wrote for *Combat,* under Sartre's byline.[53] On the Boulevard Saint-Germain, an old man who could not run fast enough was shot down by German soldiers. Meanwhile, the French were taking revenge on those deemed to be collaborators. At the bottom of the Boulevard Saint-Michel, a middle-aged woman whose hair had been shaved off was shaking her head from side to side saying, "No, no, no!" Sartre was disgusted by this "medieval sadism." Did people think this was patriotism, these low acts of vengeance towards women who had supposedly slept with a German?

Paris was liberated, but the war continued. In September, the Allied air forces obliterated large sections of Le Havre, killing thousands. The Germans fired the world's first long-range ballistic missiles on London. It was "a ravaged world," Beauvoir writes.[54] "No blade of grass in any meadow, however I looked at it, would ever again be what it had been."[55]

SEVEN

FAME

November 1944–January 1947

"Go and see Camus. He wants to send you to America for *Combat!*"
Hardly able to contain his excitement, Bost was calling down from
his first floor room to Sartre, who had just walked into the courtyard
of the Hotel Chaplain.[1] The United States State Department was
going to pay for eight French Resistance journalists to spend two
months in the United States to report on the American war effort.
"Shit! I'll *run* over there!" Sartre said. Beauvoir had never seen him so
elated.

Sartre had been fantasizing about America since his boyhood.
Back then, his voracious reading of adventure stories made him realize that if he was to be a bona fide hero, he needed to go to that conti-
nent. "In Paris you don't often see a Redskin leap out with feathers
on his head and a bow in his hand," he told Beauvoir in his old age.
"So I began to dream that I would go to America, where I'd fight
with roughnecks and come out of it safely, having knocked around a
fair number of them. I often dreamed of that."[2]

As young writers, he and Beauvoir had been hugely influenced by
American literature—particularly Hemingway, Dos Passos, Steinbeck,
and Faulkner. Their reading left them fascinated by the country itself.
"America . . . was the future on the march," Beauvoir writes. "It was
abundance, and infinite horizons; it was a crazy magic lantern of legendary images."[3] America was jazz, the blues, skyscrapers, movies, and

magical names like Memphis, New Orleans, and Chicago. They could not wait to go there.

The military DC-8 landed at La Guardia Airport in the late evening of Saturday, January 13, 1945. It was Sartre's first flight. The trip had taken two days and involved three stops. The plane was nonpressurized, and the air pockets had been alarming.

The eight French journalists—six men and two women—stumbled off the plane, tired, shabby, and disheveled. Their hosts from the Office of War Information (OWI) whisked them in limousines through the neon shimmer. Sartre, nose pressed to the window, was astonished to see barber shops open at that hour. "You could have your hair cut or washed or you could be shaved at eleven o'clock at night," he told Beauvoir.[4] They alighted at the Plaza Hotel, on Fifth Avenue, opposite Central Park. Bellhops ushered them through the revolving door. In the foyer, milling about, were women in low-cut evening dresses and men in dinner jackets. The ragged Europeans had entered another universe.

The following day, after a luxurious American breakfast, Sartre ventured out with a couple of his colleagues. It was Sunday, freezing cold, and there were few people about. "I was looking for New York," he wrote, "and I could not find it." The long straight streets all looked the same. "New York is for farsighted people," Sartre decided, "people who can focus to infinity."[5] The snow under their feet was a dirty gray color. Litter blew about in the wind.

On Monday their American hosts wasted no time in marching the shabby-looking French group down Fifth Avenue to do some shopping. Sartre had arrived in a wretched sheepskin jacket. From now on, he got around New York in a smart pinstriped suit.

The French were only now realizing the full extent of the austerity they were suffering back home. "With large glasses of whisky, they seemed intent on blotting out four years of privations," Henriette Nizan recalled. "For them, America was like a country fair. Night clubs, pretty girls."[6] Henriette had fled to the United States with the Nizans' two children in 1940, after Paul Nizan was killed. She saw a lot of the visiting French journalists, who had accompanied Sartre, and was soon having an affair with one of them.

Sartre was representing the right-wing newspaper *Le Figaro,* as well as the left-wing *Combat.* He felt a little nervous among these trained journalists. He was grateful to the Americans for funding his trip, but determined that this should not get in the way of his objectivity. And he was scared of naïve generalizations. "How can one talk about 135 million Americans? You need to have spent ten years here and we're here for six weeks."[7] All in all, he would write thirty-two articles while he was in the United States.[8]

At first he stuck to simple observations about the country. Cigarettes were rationed, and petrol was apparently in short supply, he reported, but there was plenty of food. Fruit and vegetables were abundant, and New Yorkers ate vast quantities of meat. The streetlights were dazzling. The buildings were overheated. At night, he boiled under his thin blankets. Didn't the Americans know about eiderdowns and fresh air?

Sartre knew the best way of getting to know America. But he did not speak English. How could he possibly get himself an American girlfriend? He and his colleagues had been in New York only a few days when they were invited to the OWI offices for a radio interview, in French. A vivacious young woman, Dolores Vanetti, welcomed them to the French broadcasting section. She was tiny, even shorter than Sartre, with a golden-brown complexion and a radiant smile. The eight French journalists filed into the recording studio, she recalls, and at the end of the line was a little man, by far the smallest of the bunch. "At some point he knocked against something and dropped his pipe, then he picked it up and that's when we started talking. I don't remember what we said to each other, but whatever it was, once it was said he asked me whether we could see each other again."[9]

Sartre had landed on his feet. Vanetti had been brought up in France and had worked before the war as an actress in a theater in Montparnasse. Sartre thought of her as a "mulatto." Her parents were Italian and Ethiopian, though Vanetti had learned, in race-conscious America, to keep quiet about the Ethiopian part. She was married to a wealthy American doctor, Edward Ehrenreich, but her marriage was floundering. She had spent the war years in New York, and had lots of friends among the French expatriate community, including Claude Lévi-Strauss, Fernand Léger, Marcel Duchamp, André Breton, and his wife, Jacqueline Lamba. Breton had published some of Vanetti's poems in his surrealist magazine *VVV*. They liked to explore Manhattan's antique shops together.

Sartre set out to charm her. "He was in a state of constant effervescence," Vanetti told Sartre's biographer, Annie Cohen-Solal, years later. "He kept telling all sorts of stories to amuse you and draw you into his life. He was always looking for the things that could please you, going out of his way for you, and always giving his very most."[10]

After a week in New York, the French journalists were taken on a six-week trip across the country in a chartered military plane. They traveled north and south, east and west; gazing at bridges and dams; inspecting army training camps, armament factories and infantry schools; attending concerts, university debates, a meeting of Midwestern farmers, and numerous cocktail parties. A highlight for them was visiting film studios in Hollywood; another was a hair-raising descent into the Grand Canyon in a little plane in stormy weather, with the pilot asking the passengers: "Are we touching on the left? Are we touching on the right?"[11] They were even invited for an evening at the White House with President Roosevelt. "What strikes one first of all is the deeply human charm of this long face, at once hard and delicate, the eyes shining with intelligence," Sartre wrote. "He loves France: in his youth he biked all over its roads."[12] Less than a month later, Roosevelt would be dead.

Sartre was astonished by the immensity of the country, the extremes of wealth and poverty, the social conformity, and the level of discrimination against blacks. "In this land of freedom and equality there live thirteen million untouchables," he wrote. "They wait on your table, they polish your shoes, they operate your elevator, they carry your suitcases into your compartment, but they have nothing to do with you, nor you with them."[13]

In early March, when the other journalists left for home, Sartre returned to New York to see Vanetti. He was in love, and with her as his guide, he soon fell in love with New York as well. Vanetti acted as his interpreter, helped him read the newspapers, and took him to her favorite haunts. They drank vodka at the Russian Tea Room, listened to jazz at Jimmy Ryan's and Nick's Bar while sipping scotch, watched people jitterbugging in Times Square, and visited Harlem. Sartre would always say: "Dolores gave me America."[14]

The war was still raging, and mail, sent by boat across the Atlantic, was extremely slow. Beauvoir hardly heard from Sartre while he was away. To find out what he was doing, she read the reports he wired in to *Combat* and *Le Figaro*. She also heard bits of news from Camus, with whom Sartre had brief conversations when he filed his stories over the phone.

At the end of February, Beauvoir went to Portugal for five weeks. Her sister, Poupette, had married her boyfriend, Lionel de Roulet. Roulet was working at the French Institute in Lisbon and had invited Beauvoir to give some lectures there. She wrote several articles on Spain and Portugal, which appeared in *Combat*.

The sisters had not seen each other for almost five years. Poupette was shocked by Simone's threadbare clothing and wooden clogs, and took her shopping for new clothes. Portugal was wealthy compared with France, with an abundance of food, leather, silks, and other quality goods. "Never in my life had I surrendered to such a debauch," Beauvoir would write in her memoirs. "My lecture tour was very well paid, and in one afternoon I assembled a complete wardrobe."[15] She returned to Paris with shawls and knitted sweaters for her women friends, and shirts for the men. It was the beginning of April, and to Beauvoir's dismay, Sartre was still not home.

Sartre wrote to say he was staying on for two more months, till the end of May. Bost was away, freezing at the front with the American military, covering the war for *Combat*. Beauvoir sought consolation in the arms of Michel Vitold, a Russian-born actor the same age as Bost, who was playing the part of Garcin in *No Exit*. Vitold, too, had love problems. They put their bicycles on the train and cycled around the Auvergne region. Among other things, they talked about the play Beauvoir had written, *Useless Mouths*.[16] Vitold was going to direct it later that year.

That spring, René Maheu returned to Paris. He had spent most of the war years in Morocco, teaching philosophy at a high school in Fez. He had fallen in love with one of his students, and though he had no intention of divorcing his wife, the girl was about to join him in Paris.[17] Maheu and Beauvoir were delighted to see each other again. They roamed in the woods outside Paris, and for the first time, they went to bed together. A few months later, when her novel *The Blood of Others* was published, Beauvoir would inscribe Maheu's copy: "To my very dear Lama, in memory of spring 1945, very confidentially, S de Beauvoir."[18]

On May 7, Germany capitulated. Bost was in Dachau a few hours after the Americans, and sent back horrified reports for *Combat.* None of their deported friends was among the emaciated survivors transported from the camps to the Paris reception center at the Hôtel Lutétia. "I was ashamed to be alive," writes Beauvoir, and "just as frightened of death as before."[19]

She had begun a third novel, *All Men Are Mortal,* about a man who drinks the elixir of immortality. At first he is elated and then, unable to die, he feels more and more disconnected from everyone around him. He no longer shares their hopes and illusions, and finds himself envying *real* men, whose lives have the weight of mortality hanging over them. As a philosopher, Beauvoir knew that death gave life meaning. She needed to convince herself of this at an emotional level.

At the end of May 1945, Sartre returned to Paris brimming with stories about America, and with a second suitcase stuffed full of food and clothes, including a tailor-made suit for Beauvoir. He had heard from his mother while he was abroad, but only now did she tell him that his stepfather, Joseph Mancy, had died in mid-January, shortly after Sartre left. Anne-Marie knew what the trip to America meant to her son, and had not wanted him to feel obliged to come home early. He was moved by her thoughtfulness.

Sartre hated turning forty, that June. He resigned from his teaching job, determined to earn his living by writing from then on. But he was in the doldrums. His affair with Vanetti had collapsed because of

Beauvoir. Vanetti had said she could not accept another woman in Sartre's life. Before they parted, she had asked him not to write to her.

Years later, Vanetti observed that Sartre returned to France in a "troubled, unsettled, undecided" state, and that all three of them— she, Sartre, and Beauvoir—were "all of these and much worse."[20] As if Beauvoir's position were not already insecure enough, Bost went to New York in June, sent by *Combat,* and had a brief fling with Vanetti himself. He started to tell Beauvoir that he, too, had fallen a bit in love with her, then realized his mistake. Beauvoir looked devastated.[21]

In July, Sartre cracked, and wrote to Vanetti. She replied with a loving letter. In early August, the Americans dropped atom bombs on Hiroshima and Nagasaki. Japan surrendered. The war was over at last, and to Beauvoir, the world had never felt more terrifying.

"The war really divided my life in two," Sartre said in his old age. "It started when I was thirty-four-years old and ended when I was forty, and that really was the transition from youth to maturity."[22] Before the war, Sartre was unknown. After the war, he was famous. It happened almost overnight. "We were astonished by the furore we caused," Beauvoir writes. "My own baggage weighed very little, but Sartre was now hurled brutally into the arena of celebrity, and my name was associated with his."[23]

Their names were everywhere. *Existentialism* had become a buzzword. Sartre's play *No Exit* had been the talk of the theater season. In September and October 1945, Beauvoir's novel *The Blood of Others,* and the first two novels of Sartre's trilogy, *The Age of Reason* and *The Reprieve,* all appeared at the same time in the bookstore windows. At the end of October, Beauvoir's play *Useless Mouths* opened at the Théâtre du Vieux Colombier, with Olga in the lead female role.[24] And the news kiosks sported a new journal, *Les Temps modernes* (named after the Charlie Chaplin film *Modern Times*), with Jean-Paul Sartre as editor-in-chief, and Simone de Beauvoir among the names on the editorial committee.[25] Sartre had always maintained that everything, however banal, shed light on society. The aim of the journal was to comment and take a position on "modern times."

On October 29, Sartre was billed to give a talk at the Club Maintenant. The title of his talk, "Is Existentialism a Humanism?" was staid, and Sartre expected his audience to be small. It was a warm autumn evening. Sartre took the metro there. When he turned the corner, he was taken aback to see a vast crowd milling outside. It took him fifteen minutes, battling his way through the mob, to reach the podium.

Sartre talked animatedly and unpretentiously, as if he were in front of his students. He pointed out that though the word *existentialism* was highly fashionable, almost no one knew what it meant. Surprisingly, it usually had connotations of decadence. He had heard about a lady who, feeling frazzled, had uttered a swear word, and by way of apology, declared, "I must be becoming an existentialist."[26]

In truth, existentialism was neither a pessimistic nor a negative philosophy, Sartre told the audience. Its doctrine was that since God does not exist, man makes himself. There is no a priori human nature or essence. We are not born cowardly or lazy; we choose to be these things. "Man is responsible for what he is.... We are alone, without excuses. This is what I mean when I say that man is condemned to be free."

If many people disliked this philosophy, Sartre went on, it was because they preferred to make excuses for themselves, to tell themselves that circumstances were against them. "I have not had a great love, or a great friendship, but it's because I did not meet the right man or woman," they would say. "If I have not written very good books, it's because I haven't had the leisure time to do it." According to Sartre, they were lying to themselves about their freedom. This was "bad faith."

Existentialism was not about possibilities or intentions, Sartre said, but about concrete projects. No one was a genius unless it was expressed in his or her works. The same applied to love. "There is no love except that which is constructed, there is no possibility of love except that which is manifested in a loving relationship." Hence the existentialist slogan: "Existence precedes essence."

The room was crowded and hot. In the jostle and excitement, chairs were broken and people fainted. It was, one journalist quipped, "a *No Exit* situation." A hip young jazz trumpeter, Boris Vian, would immortalize that evening in his first novel, *L'Ecume des Jours* (*The Froth of Passing Days*). In the novel, Paris is crackling with excitement: its new intellectual star, Jean-Sol Partre, is to give a talk. He has written a book called *Vomit*. The event is sold out, and there's a vigorous black market in forged invitations. People arrive via the sewers; some parachute in on a special plane. The Duchess of Bovouard and her circle, sitting in the gallery, attract excited looks from the crowd. Blasts from an elephant trunk announce Partre's arrival. He makes his way to the stage.[27]

After that memorable evening, not a week went by without some gossip about the existentialist couple in the tabloid newspapers. Sartre and Beauvoir could no longer walk in the street without photographers darting in front of them or people asking for autographs. When they went into a café or restaurant, people stared, nudged one another, and whispered. The newspapers reported that the two writers were now frequenting the Pont-Royal, instead of the Flore.

No sooner had the curfew been lifted than new cellar jazz clubs and dancing places sprang up in Saint-Germain. According to the tabloids, these were full of young drifters called "existentialists," who spent their days in existentialist cafés and their nights listening to existentialist jazz. A wild and gloomy bunch, they sometimes resorted to existential suicides.

It was no coincidence that existentialism struck a chord in the postwar world. Sartre's readers had experienced the Holocaust and the atom bomb. Having discovered history, with its most savage face, they had lost their faith in eternal progress. What was so refreshing was that existentialism acknowledged the horror and absurdity of the human condition, while at the same time insisting on individual freedom and choice.

Ignored in 1943, *Being and Nothingness* now became a fashionable book, especially among the young, where Sartre had a cult following. The communists said Sartre was a nihilist, who "wallowed in nothingness." Conservatives saw him as godless and depraved.

Beauvoir was known mostly because of Sartre, but she also greatly enhanced the public's interest in him. This strikingly handsome woman—who had come second in the *agrégation* the year Sartre had come first, who wrote books in cafés alongside Sartre, who shared his ideas about liberty and contingency, and whose first novel had portrayed their scandalous relationship—was an essential ingredient in Sartre's iconic stature. *Samedi Soir,* the new sensationalist postwar tabloid, disparagingly called her "la grande Sartreuse" or "Notre-Dame de Sartre."

Sartre and Beauvoir had become a famous couple, yet their relationship had never been more precarious. Three decades later, looking back on the many women in Sartre's life, Beauvoir told him that Dolores Vanetti was the hardest of all for her to accept: "You were immensely attached to her. Furthermore, she was the only woman who frightened me. She frightened me because she was hostile."[28]

Sartre's introduction to the first issue of *Les Temps modernes,* a manifesto of "committed literature," was dedicated to Vanetti. Readers wondered who she was, this Dolores, whose name was emblazoned at the top of the first page of the new magazine. Beauvoir had hoped Sartre would come skiing with her at Christmas, in Mégève. Instead, on December 12, he took the train to Marseille, then boarded a military cargo boat to New York. He was going to spend two months with Vanetti.

In her letters to Sartre, Beauvoir admitted that it was hard for her to contemplate the idea of more time apart: "It's especially in the mornings on waking that it causes me a little anguish." But she did her best to appear calm and breezy. She was busy with *Les Temps modernes,* finishing her novel *All Men Are Mortal,* and editing Sartre's lecture "Is Existentialism a Humanism?" for publication. "I'm very happy with our life and with you," she declared bravely. "I want you to have a good stay over there."

She was seeing friends, she told him, and had spent a "marvelous evening" with Camus:

> It bowled me over that he should be so affectionate, and that we should be so intimate and talk so easily. We had dinner Chez Lipp, drank at the Pont-Royal, then took a bottle of champagne to the Louisiane and drank it till 3 in the morning. He talked a lot about himself—private life and literary life—in a way that

touched me. And it made me want to write good things—it gave me a great thirst for life—that one can be such good friends with somebody for whom the same things count as for you. If everything works out well, we'll go and spend a fortnight winter-sporting in February—he seemed really to like the idea too.[29]

Underneath the feisty bravado, a loneliness seeps through Beauvoir's letters. Her room at the Louisiane was icy cold; the hotel was not heated. She had felt very bad after an evening with Bianca Bienenfeld, who was back in Paris with her husband, having spent the war in hiding. Bienenfeld was a changed woman, Beauvoir told Sartre. Soon after the trio collapsed, Bienenfeld had had a nervous breakdown. Five years later, she was still not better:

> She's suffering from an intense and dreadful attack of neuras-thenia, and it's our fault, I think. It's the very indirect, but pro-found, after-shock of the business between her and us. She's the only person to whom we've really done harm, but we have harmed her. . . . She weeps all the time—she wept three times during the dinner, and she weeps at home when she has to read a book or go to the kitchen to eat. . . . At times, she really looked quite mad—bottling things up, anxious, but with moments of repressed tenderness and mute appeals that tore at my heart-strings. It's important to see a lot of her, and I'm going to try because I'm filled with remorse. I'm describing this to you very badly, but I know you'd have been very upset and full of sympa-thy for her.

In the late 1940s, Bienenfeld's psychoanalyst, Jacques Lacan, would come to the same conclusion. It was his view that Sartre and Beauvoir had had a quasi-parental relationship with Bienenfeld, and Bienenfeld's traumatized reaction was partly because they had bro-ken the incest taboos by sleeping with her.

Nathalie Sorokine, who also had a room at the Louisiane, was pregnant and about to leave for California to join her boyfriend, a handsome American GI who hoped to become a screenwriter. In the last year, Sorokine had made a sport of seducing GIs. She could not wait to get to the land of plenty.

Beauvoir and Bost were still occasional lovers, but he was away a great deal, and they were no longer as intimate. Over dinner one night, he confessed that if he had appeared somewhat indifferent recently it was because he did not feel he had any place in a life in which Sartre loomed so large.[30]

At Christmas, Beauvoir went to Mégève with Bost, Olga, and Wanda. The Kosakiewicz sisters rarely put on skis; they mostly lay on the terrace, sunbathing. Beauvoir and Bost would go off together, taking local trains and cable cars, sweeping through fields of fresh snow to lunch in little chalets, and returning to the hotel at sunset.

Beauvoir told Sartre she was "bursting with tenderness" for him. She kept thinking of him skiing beside her on those same slopes in the past, wearing a blue ski suit she could still see as if it were yesterday. These memories had a "rather harrowing" effect on her. "I'd so like to think that we'll come back here together some day, just the two of us on our own and perfectly happy." She wished they could go away for several months, somewhere where they could write. She had dreamed so long of traveling with him, and now their travels were more often than not apart. She missed working beside him at the Flore.

"Like you, I feel we must make changes in our lives," Sartre wrote back. "Only my mother and Wanda keep me from leaving with you to work anywhere at all for six months a year. But between that and the daily Café de Flore, there are intermediary positions."

After three weeks in Mégève, Beauvoir returned to Paris. She was tanned and healthy, she wrote to Sartre, and "stunningly handsome." She saw to business matters, mostly his, and then, at the end of January, took the train to Marseille, from where she flew—*her* first flight—to Tunisia. She had been invited by the Alliance Française to give lectures in Tunis and Algiers. But she was worried. She had not heard a word from Sartre, and was banking on a letter waiting for her in Tunis:

Try to keep a long time reserved *for me* at the beginning of March—I'd so like to be alone with you, either at La Pouèze or anywhere else. I'm always anxious, even before trips I enjoy—I wouldn't like life to separate us. My dear love, my sweet little one, do whatever you think best—bearing in mind how much I love you. I kiss you most passionately—I'll write from Tunis.

Two weeks later, she was on the edge of the Sahara desert and about to travel around the south of Algeria. She had seen many interesting things, and attendance at her talks had been overwhelming: "the wild success of existentialism—people fought with their bare hands to get into my lectures!" she told Sartre. But she *still* had not heard from him. Nothing for two months, no letter since he set foot in America. Fifteen years' experience had taught her that he was an "unblemished marvel," and she knew there must have been some hitch. "Only I'm a bit distraught every night to feel that I'm cut off from you. A swift word, my dear little one, my love. Don't forget me. Don't forget how passionately I love you. I kiss you with all my might—and for a long, long time."[31]

When Beauvoir returned to Paris, Sartre was still not back. Bost was traveling with a group of journalists in Italy. Olga was with her parents in Laigle, feeling feverish and tired. Sorokine had left for America. Camus was about to go to New York. Beauvoir worked and "moped a bit."[32] She tried to write at the Pont-Royal, but the barrels that served as tables were hardly conducive to serious work. It was there, at the bar, that Raymond Queneau introduced her to Boris Vian, whose novel *L'Ecume des Jours* (featuring Jean-Sol Partre and the Duchess de Bovouard) Queneau thought quite brilliant. Beauvoir told Vian that they would like to publish an excerpt of it in *Les Temps modernes*. Soon afterward, she was invited to a party at the Vians':

> By the time I arrived, everyone had already had quite a bit to drink; his wife, Michelle, her long, silky blonde hair spread over her shoulders, was smiling beatifically ... I too drank manfully while we listened to American records.[33]

It was dawn when Beauvoir left the party. She and Jean-Bertrand Pontalis (a former pupil of Sartre's and a future psychoanalyst) went to a café in Saint-Germain to sober up. Beauvoir told him about Vanetti and wept floods of tears.[34]

Everyone around him knew how infatuated Sartre was this time. Henriette Nizan, who had left New York and was back with the two children in Paris, encountered Sartre's mother, Madame Mancy, in Saint-Germain-des-Prés. Madame Mancy asked her point-blank, "Rirette, I would like to ask you: would Dolores Vanetti make a good wife for Poulou?"[35]

Sartre's voyage to New York on the *Liberty* had taken eighteen days. The weather was stormy and the sea was rough. He was not seasick. "It's surely a matter of will," he joked to Beauvoir. But he was unable to write. "You get the impression that the wind and the rocking empty your head." He couldn't even read. "I don't just mean Malraux, but not even the detective novels I'd brought along." He walked around the deck staring at the sea, chatting to his fellow passengers, and trying to keep his balance. One evening he gave a lecture on existentialism. "I must be *truly* famous, poor little Beaver, because though I'm only identified by mangy tags on my suitcases, the whole ship knew who I was."

In the evenings, he got drunk with his shipboard companions and tried to seduce the wife of the Brazilian consul. ("She's thirty-five and beautiful, with the pampered look of an Egyptian dancing girl. Stupid, actually, and terribly flirtatious.") She ended up preferring his better-looking rival, the ship's captain. Sartre was mortified. "I couldn't stop seeing myself with horror as an insect. The sea air must really turn a person slightly batty."[36]

To pay for his trip, Sartre had arranged with French Cultural Relations in New York to give some lectures on French literature. He had become famous since his last American sojourn, and the Americans were eager to hear about this new European intellectual fashion, existentialism. Sartre's books had not yet been published in English, but some of his writing had appeared in American journals, and *No Exit* was about to be staged in New York. Wherever he went—Harvard, Princeton, Yale, and various venues in New York—the lecture theaters were packed.

The press trail built up a picture of an intriguing personality. A flattering photo in *Time*—Vanetti's favorite photo of Sartre—bore the caption "Philosopher Sartre. Women swooned." If the "Bible" of existentialism was Sartre's 724-page treatise, *Being and Nothingness,* the article declared, its "foremost disciple" was "authoress Simone de Beauvoir, who lives in the same hotel on the same floor as the master."[37]

After Sartre's talk at Carnegie Hall, *The New Yorker*'s "Talk of the Town" columnist reported:

Mr. Sartre, a rumpled little man who wears tortoise-shell glasses with very large lenses, wound a shepherd's-check scarf around his neck as soon as he stepped down from the lecture platform. He told us at once that he approves of New York without qualification. "Here there are no restaurants of an exclusively intellectual clientele," he said, "so it is easy to keep out of fights. Also, the hotels have the very good custom of throwing out the guests after a sojourn of three or five days. I prefer three. If one takes the precaution of leaving no forwarding address, it is impossible for anybody interested in literature to find one. So one never risks being bored. One is free to promenade oneself in the streets but relieved of the necessity of conversation. That is, if one has taken the precaution not to learn spoken English. I have guarded myself well from it, although I read. Two phrases only are necessary for a whole evening of English conversation, I have found: 'Scotch-and-soda?' and 'Why not?' By alternating them, it is impossible to make a mistake."[38]

Harper's Bazaar paid Beauvoir a generous fee to write a portrait of Sartre. Her short essay, translated by Malcolm Cowley, was given the alluring title "Jean-Paul Sartre: Strictly Confidential." Had Beauvoir set out to create a legend, she could not have done it better. Sartre, she declared, was "a new sort of figure in life and letters."

He hates the country. He loathes—it isn't too strong a word—the swarming life of insects and the pullulation of plants. At most he tolerates the level sea, the unbroken desert sand, or the mineral coldness of Alpine peaks; but he feels at home only in cities.

Sartre, she went on, affirmed himself as "consciousness and pure liberty":

From the very beginning, Sartre was fiercely determined to be a free man; he kept clear of everything that might burden him down or chain him to one place. He has never married; he has never acquired any possessions; he doesn't own so much as a bed or a table, a picture, a keepsake, or a book. Nevertheless, he has always spent his money as fast as he earned it, and sometimes a little faster. . . . One characteristic that impresses all his friends is Sartre's immense generosity. He gives without reckoning, gives his money, his time, and himself; he is always ready to be interested in others, but he doesn't wish for anything in return; he doesn't need anybody.

Vanetti was jealous of Beauvoir, and Sartre rarely mentioned her. It was on this, his second trip, Vanetti says, that she fell in love. She was seeking a divorce, and hoped to marry Sartre. Meanwhile, she was terrified of roving photographers employed to provide evidence of adultery.

Sartre was staying in a midtown hotel. At weekends the two either remained holed up in Vanetti's uptown apartment out of sight of the doormen ("she calls me the prisoner," Sartre told Beauvoir) or they went to Connecticut to stay with her friend Jacqueline Lamba, a talented painter, who had separated from André Breton and was now living with the American sculptor David Hare.

I get up around 9 o'clock and never manage, despite all my efforts, to be ready before 11 (bath, shave, breakfast), I go to some appointment, and I lunch with Dolores or various people wanting to see me. After lunch I take a walk all alone till 6 o'clock around NY, which I know as well as Paris; I meet Dolores again here or there and we stay together at her place or in some quiet bar till 2 in the morning. I'm drinking heavily, but without any problems so far.

His letters were full of mixed messages. "Dolores's love for me scares me. In other respects she is absolutely charming and we never get mad at each other. But the future of the whole thing is very grim. . . . Au revoir, my dearest, my darling little Beaver, au revoir. I'm at my best with you and I love you very much. Au revoir, little one, I'll be so happy to be with you again."

At the end of February, Sartre wrote that he was busy giving lectures and writing articles. He would tell her more when he got back:

> I'll also tell you about Dolores, who is a poor and charming creature, really the best I know after you. At present we are involved in the agonies of departure, and I'm not having fun every day. . . . Her passion literally scares me, particularly since that's not my strong suit, and she uses it solely to her disadvantage, but she can display the candor and innocence of a child when she is happy. . . . I yearn to go home, I'm half dead from passion and lecturing.

Sartre postponed his return by two weeks—ostensibly to give lucrative lectures in Toronto, Ottawa, and Montreal. He did not tell Beauvoir that Columbia University had offered him a job for two years, and that he had considered the proposition seriously. Nor did he tell her that he had asked Vanetti to marry him.

Since Vanetti was not yet divorced, they agreed that Sartre would return to Paris and they would spend three or four months together later in the year. After that, they would see. On March 15, 1946, Sartre went home, this time by plane.

"I seem to be working at half speed," Beauvoir wrote in her journal. "It's so annoying to have obstacles in one's head."[39] She had constant headaches and was plagued by bad dreams. Sartre's conversation was full of Vanetti. Such was their harmony, he told Beauvoir, that when they walked around New York together they always wanted to stop and go on again at exactly the same moment. Beauvoir was frightened. At parties, with the slightest amount of alcohol, she would weep into her glass.

One day—she and Sartre were about to go for lunch with

friends—she blurted out, "Honestly, who means the most to you, Dolores or me?" Sartre told her: "Dolores means an enormous amount to me, but it's you I'm with." Beauvoir thought he meant that he was respecting their pact, and she should not ask more than that. She could barely pull herself together during lunch, and used the fish bones as her excuse for being unable to swallow. She saw Sartre watching her uneasily. That afternoon, when they were alone again, he told her he thought it was obvious that they were together; it did not need explaining.[40]

So many aspects of their past seemed to Beauvoir to be unraveling. They were too famous to be able to work quietly in cafés. When Sartre got back from America, it was in the din and smoke of the Méphisto, a new jazz cellar on the Boulevard Saint-Germain, that he read the last chapters of her novel *All Men Are Mortal*. But this was about to change. Some months earlier, Sartre had agreed to share an apartment with his mother. Anne-Marie Mancy had found a fourth-floor apartment at 42 Rue de Bonaparte, on the corner of Place Saint-Germain-des-Prés. In May 1946, they moved in.

After fifteen years of living in Spartan conditions in hotels, Sartre was suddenly living the bourgeois life. From his large study at the far end of the apartment, he looked across the cobblestone square to the old church, the terrace of the Deux Magots, and right up the Rue de Rennes. The living room was fitted out with his mother's fake Louis XVI furnishings, which he hated. The large oak desk and black leather armchair in his study had belonged to his stepfather, whom he hated. But the apartment was very comfortable. He enjoyed having access to a piano again. For the first time in his life, he began to build up a library. Until then he had always given his books away.

Anne-Marie Mancy was ecstatic. "This is my third marriage," she told friends proudly.[41] From now on, it was she who bought Sartre his ties and shirts. Her old Alsatian maid, Eugénie, who had a small bedroom at the other end of the apartment, took care of Sartre's washing and ironing. His mother glowed with pleasure when Sartre occasionally had lunch or dinner with her. "She was completely devoted to her son," Beauvoir writes, "just as she had been to her husband, and she liked to believe that she was necessary to him."[42] Beauvoir and Madame Mancy had never warmed to each other.

Sartre had only just moved into his new abode when he heard devastating news. Olga was about to begin rehearsals for a new production of *The Flies,* but she had been feeling weak for some time. Now chest X rays showed tuberculosis. Both lungs were infected. Olga was just twenty-nine, and facing possible death.

She was sent to the Beaujon hospital in Clichy, on the northern outskirts of Paris, and given a pneumothorax, an operation that involved cutting a hole through the chest wall and using a tube to collapse the affected lung by pumping air into the pleural cavity. Bost had no time to enjoy the success of his novel, *Le Dernier des Métiers* (*The Last Profession*), based largely on the letters he'd written to Beauvoir during the war. He went to visit Olga every day and Beauvoir often went with him. In those dark days, the two were a great comfort to each other.

After Sartre got back from America, he received a letter from Jean Cau, a twenty-one-year-old student who was preparing for the competitive entry exam to the Ecole Normale. He wanted to know if Sartre could use a secretary. The two met. Sartre liked the eager young man with his ironic smile, sense of humor, peasant good sense, and working-class southern accent. He agreed to employ him for three hours each morning.

"Sartre's secretary! Never has a title been worn so comically. Never under the sun will such a 'boss' appear again." After Sartre's death, Jean Cau would paint an affectionate picture of his generous, trusting boss.[43]

The arrangement was to last eleven years. Cau would turn up at 42 Rue Bonaparte at ten A.M. on the dot, climb the four flights of stairs, and ring the bell. Madame Mancy, "the very beautiful, tall, elegant, adorable 'little mama,' with her superb bearing, fine ankles, blue eyes, and her clear and musical voice," would come to the door. On occasion, it was Eugénie who let him in, in which case Cau invariably found Sartre and his mother playing a duet—usually Schubert or Chopin—on the upright piano in the living room. Cau's arrival would interrupt the idyllic scene. Sartre would lower the lid and cry, "To work!"

More often Cau would go straight to the foldup bridge table in the drawing room, which was separated from Sartre's study by an opaque glass door, and would already be going through the mail when Sartre emerged from his room, unshaven and in pajamas and a badly tied dressing gown. He'd been working, and now he was heading to the bathroom for his morning ablutions. His fast walk, head bent forward, always reminded Cau of a boxer: "He does not walk, he charges."

When Sartre had slept at home, Cau would open the study door and reel, slightly nauseated, from the stench of sleep and tobacco. If Sartre had slept at a girlfriend's, he would turn up around the same time as Cau. On those mornings, Cau writes, Sartre was in such a huge hurry to get to work that he often went straight to his desk without even bothering to take off his jacket and tie.

Cau was dumbfounded by Sartre's capacity for work. He worked, Cau says, "like a mule." All morning he would smoke like a train, either a pipe or cigarettes, and drink tea from a thermos on his desk. He wrote by hand, rarely crossing things out. If he didn't like what he was writing, he preferred to start again, on a fresh page. He disliked messy drafts.

It was Jean Cau's job to ward off the outside world. Sartre would tell him: "I simply don't have time, Cau, to write that letter" or "to see that fool" or "to argue with that moron" or "to bore myself stupid with those jerks." Cau had to convey the message more delicately.

Cau's other task was to manage Sartre's finances. If Sartre was careful with his time, he was profligate with his money. Cau had never seen anything like it. "Generosity? I don't know. Sartre didn't *give* money. He strewed it." Like all Sartre's friends, Cau was astonished to see that Sartre went around with wads of banknotes in his pockets—as much as a couple of thousand dollars. Sartre never let others pay for meals, and he left huge tips for the waiters.

Instead of an advance for each book, Gallimard gave Sartre a monthly allowance. At the beginning of the month, there was a flurry of check signing. Ever since she had stopped teaching, Beauvoir had been financially dependent on Sartre. Then there was Cau's salary to pay, and a monthly allowance for Wanda. Bost and Olga sometimes asked for a "loan," which they rarely paid back. Other friends were always asking for help with this and that—medical bills, travel, or some emergency. Sartre never hesitated. He signed a check or handed over the cash. By the end of the month, he regularly ran out of money. Cau recounts that Sartre would come barging out of his study:

"Cau, I haven't a dime. Is there any money around, by any chance?"

"Zero."

"Shit! Are you sure? You've done the rounds?"

"Yes. Nothing to be scraped from anywhere."

"Oh well, too bad. I'll borrow from Eugénie."

And he plunged down the corridor that led to the other end of the little apartment in the Rue Bonaparte.

At one P.M., Sartre would go off for lunch, either with Beauvoir or another woman friend, and Cau would leave for the day. Sartre would be back at four-thirty in the afternoon, when Beauvoir would turn up and work at the little bridge table, transported to Sartre's study. Beauvoir started work immediately. Sartre sometimes sat at the piano for an hour and practiced a Bach prelude or a Beethoven sonata, then set to work. They worked till 8 P.M. Just across the square from the Flore and the Deux Magots, they recreated the café atmosphere at home.

In the summer of 1946, Sartre and Beauvoir went to Switzerland and Italy. Beauvoir was finishing her historical novel, *All Men Are Mortal.* Sartre was writing two plays. *The Victors*—dedicated to Vanetti, with a leading role for Wanda—was about the courage of the resistants during the war and the torture many of them had endured. *The Respectful Prostitute,* inspired by the famous Scottsboro case in Alabama, in which nine black youths were falsely accused of raping two white prostitutes, portrayed racism in the American South. The title caused a scandal (the play was obliged to run under the title *The Respectful P.*), and the play itself aroused cries of "anti-Americanism." Sartre was taken aback by the accusations. "I am not anti-American," he said. "I don't even know what the word means.... I have just devoted two whole issues of my review, *Les Temps modernes,* to the United States. The writer's duty . . . is to denounce injustice everywhere, and all the more so when he loves the country which lets this injustice happen."[44]

In the evenings in Rome, Sartre and Beauvoir dined with Italian friends, including the writers Elio Vittorini, Carlo Levi, and Ignazio Silone. Marked by the bitter memory of Italian fascism during the war, Italian intellectuals were nearly all communist sympathizers. In France, the Communist Party, which was fiercely Stalinist, attacked independent left-wingers like Sartre. In Italy, the atmosphere was quite different. The Italian Communist Party, far more all-inclusive, regarded fellow travelers as friends. It made life much more pleasant for the intellectuals. Throughout their lives, Sartre and Beauvoir would always feel comfortable in Italy.

Sartre spent three weeks with Wanda, and Beauvoir went hiking by herself in the Dolomites, staying in inns and mountain huts. Once more she experienced "the noise of pebbles rolling down the screes . . . the gasping effort of the long climb, the ecstasy of relief when the haversack slips from the shoulders . . . the early departures under the pale sky."[45] As usual, the long exhausting walks helped her to find an inner serenity. For her, it was a form of meditation.

She and Sartre had arranged to meet in Paris on the morning of Sunday, August 24, and planned to spend the day together. Unfortunately, Wanda (worried about Olga, who was to have a second pneumothorax) understood things differently, Sartre explained to Beauvoir:

Around 10 o'clock (perhaps just slightly later) I'll be at the Deux Magots. I'll stay with you till noon. The catastrophe is that W. doesn't understand "till the 24th" as we do. To her it means *"including the 24th."* Which means that, to end things on a good note, I think we'd better give her that much. We'll gain her good mood for a time—because she *is* in a good mood these days (the play, a new hotel). I'll meet you on the morning of the 25th and we'll stay together till Monday evening without seeing a soul. . . . Don't be cross with me and don't be upset that I gave in: she'd just heard about her sister's pneumothorax, which came as a blow, we were on the verge of a frightful scene and I simply gave in.[46]

In the autumn, Beauvoir accompanied Sartre back to Rome. "I had never seen Rome in the gentle October light," she writes.[47] They stayed at the old Minerva Hotel, in the center of town, and spent peaceful days writing.

Les Temps modernes might have looked sober with its plain white cover and black-and-red print, but like its editor-in-chief, it was never stuffy. Sartre set out to break down the divide between so-called "serious literature" and journalism. Alongside articles on politics, literature, sociology, and psychoanalysis was a humorous column by Boris Vian, autobiographical pieces by people from all possible walks of life (a prostitute, a thief, and so on), and articles on the latest jazz, literature, and films from America. In no time, *Les Temps modernes* acquired a reputation throughout Europe for being fresh and stimulating.

To Beauvoir, this collective editorial project was "the highest form of friendship."[48] It was a privileged way for her and Sartre to communicate with their contemporaries, to take part in current debates. "I would read an article that made me angry and say to myself immediately: 'I must answer that!' " Beauvoir writes in her memoirs. "That's how all the essays I wrote for *Les Temps modernes* came into being."[49]

Every two weeks, on Sunday afternoons at five-thirty, the editorial committee would crowd into Sartre's study on the Rue Bonaparte. They argued heatedly, laughed, and drank a great deal. It seemed to the others that Sartre breathed ideas. Meetings would often last until one in the morning, when Sartre and Beauvoir would still be full of steam. The others were exhausted.

Sartre had little interest in the practical management of the magazine. Maurice Merleau-Ponty took over the day-to-day direction.[50] The other highly energetic member of the team was Simone de Beauvoir. She came up with ideas for articles, read through the pile of submissions, and wielded her editor's pen with skill. It was a great deal of work in addition to her own writing, but she relished it.

•   •   •

By the summer of 1946, Beauvoir was wondering what to write next. She wanted to write about herself, and Sartre encouraged her. Once again, he asked her: What did it mean to be a woman?

She answered, a little impatiently, that for her it did not mean much. She led the same sort of life as her male friends, she was just as privileged, and she had never felt inferior because of her femininity. "All the same," Sartre insisted, "you weren't brought up in the same way as a boy would have been; you should look into it further."

Beauvoir was sure she could dispense with the question quickly. She went to the Bibliothèque Nationale and looked up everything she could find on the condition of women and the myths of femininity. She was there for weeks and was astonished by her findings. "It was a revelation. This world was a masculine world, my childhood had been nourished by myths forged by men, and I hadn't reacted to them in at all the same way I should have done if I had been a boy."[51]

Such was her interest in the subject that she put her memoir project to one side and embarked on what she thought would be a long essay. It was to become a thick book, a twentieth-century landmark called *The Second Sex.*

Beauvoir had greatly envied Sartre and Bost when they flew off to the United States, and was thrilled when Philippe Soupault, a French surrealist writer and journalist who had lived in the United States during the war, managed to arrange a series of lectures for her at American universities. She was to leave in January 1947.

She was also extremely nervous. Four months was a long time to be away. She felt as if she were leaving her life behind. It did not help that while she was away, Vanetti was coming to Paris to live with Sartre.

She wondered, would she be able to immerse herself in American life as Sartre and Bost had done? Unlike Sartre, she had a good command of English, even if her accent was thick. But whereas Sartre had been looked after there—first by the Office of War Information, then by Vanetti—Beauvoir was on her own.

The final weeks passed in a whirl. It was a tumultuous time. The cold war divided French intellectuals and split up friendships. There were endless discussions about Soviet communism versus American imperialism, the Soviet gulag versus the American atom bomb.

Relations between Sartre and Camus were already strained because of politics. Then, in October 1946, Beauvoir writes: "a tumultuous newcomer burst into our group."[52] Arthur Koestler and his wife were visiting Paris for a few weeks. Koestler's novel *Darkness at Noon,* a chilling look at Stalinist Russia, was a best seller in France. Koestler and Camus were close, and shared a virulent anticommunism. Sartre and Beauvoir often went out with them. Koestler and Camus would harangue Sartre about his sympathy with the Soviet Union, telling him he was an apologist for Stalinism. They drank vast quantities, and their arguments were fierce.

Beauvoir gave in to Koestler's aggressive seduction ploys and spent a night with him. She would write about the episode, with a thin fictional disguise, in *The Mandarins.* In the novel, Anne Dubreuilh is about to leave for America, and feels nervous, insecure, and lonely. Her one-night stand with the condescending and sadistic "Scriassine" is a vivid evocation of alienated sex.[53]

One night, at a party, Camus picked a fight with Merleau-Ponty, accusing him of justifying the Moscow show trials. Sartre stood up for Merleau-Ponty. Camus left in a rage, slamming the door behind him. Sartre and Bost ran after him, but Camus refused to come back. It was their first major falling out, and would not be the last.

Before she left for America, Beauvoir went to say good-bye to Olga, who was undergoing "heliotherapy"—exposure to fresh air and sunshine—in the Leysin sanatorium high up in the Swiss alps. Her bed had been wheeled out onto the balcony, where she spent hours each day breathing in the icy air. A few months earlier, she and Bost had married.[54] It was a romantic gesture in the face of possible death, and a practical one as well. For Bost, it was easier to visit Olga in conservative Swiss sanatoria if they were married.

After twenty-four hours in that sinister white building filled with death and despair, Beauvoir felt crushed. She was relieved to take the train back to Paris.

•   •   •

It was a severe winter. Violent storms obliged some flights to turn around halfway across the Atlantic. On the evening of January 24, 1947, Beauvoir and Sartre went out to the airport at Orly. She was tense. Sartre kissed her and left. Then came the announcement that due to bad weather the flight would be postponed until the following evening. Beauvoir returned to Paris and spent the evening with Sartre and Bost, feeling as if she were floating between two worlds.

Twenty-four hours later, she was finally sitting in a forty-seat cargo plane. She opened her notebook. "Something is about to happen," she wrote. "You can count the minutes in your life when something happens."[55]

The flight was long and tiring, with stops in the Azores and Newfoundland. Beauvoir was apprehensive, and takeoffs and landings were an ordeal. Her ears hurt, and her temples throbbed. She wrote to Sartre from the airport at Newfoundland. "Do you remember that hall where I'm writing to you, with its pale blue walls? . . . I find your tracks everywhere and that's another way of feeling how tightly joined we are. . . . I really feel I shan't be separated from you for an instant—nothing can separate us."[56]

On the descent into New York, Beauvoir felt frightened and queasy. The plane pitched. Peering out of the little round window, she could make out houses and streets. She told herself she would soon be walking down those streets. The woman next to her murmured that the engine was making an odd noise. The plane turned, leaning on one wing. Beauvoir thought: "I don't want to die. Not now. I don't want the lights to go out." Then she felt the thud of the wheels touching the runway.

EIGHT

WABANSIA AVENUE, JAZZ, AND THE GOLDEN ZAZOU

January 1947—Summer 1950

A woman from the French Cultural Services met Beauvoir at the air-port, and the two of them had a lobster dinner, then Beauvoir deposited her suitcase in her midtown hotel room, and plunged alone into the Manhattan night. She walked down Broadway to Times Square. The streets were full of people. But she felt like a phantom. Nothing seemed quite real, and she was invisible in this crowd. On her previous travels—in Rome, Madrid, even in Francophone Africa—she still thought of Paris as the heart of the universe. No longer. This was another world.

Over the next few days, everything astonished her: the silence of the traffic ("no horns"), the uniformed doormen who stood at the entrance to apartment buildings as if they were palaces, the elevator employees ("it's difficult to receive clandestine visits"), the women's very high heels ("I'm ashamed of my Swiss shoes with the crepe soles I was so proud of"), the friendliness of total strangers, the speed of restaurant service ("You can eat anything, anywhere, very quickly—I like that"). She tried to pierce the façade of this strange culture, while mocking her little ruses. "I don't like the taste of whiskey; I only like these glass sticks you stir it with. Yet until three o'clock in the morning, I drink scotch docilely because scotch is one of the keys to America. I want to break through the glass wall."[1]

She knew the best key: an American lover. Sartre had found himself one with enviable ease. Why did it seem to her so difficult?

> If I want to decode New York, I must meet New Yorkers. There are names in my address book but no faces to match. I'll have to talk on the telephone, in English, to people whom I don't know and who don't know me. Going down into the hotel lobby, I'm more intimidated than if I were going to take an oral exam.[2]

As she roamed Manhattan and Brooklyn by herself, she took pleasure in seeing the things Sartre had seen. "It's you I meet everywhere about New York," she told him, "and it's you again whom I love when loving the skyscrapers."[3]

Vanetti was about to fly off to join Sartre in Paris, and Beauvoir was determined to meet her. Vanetti reluctantly agreed to come to the Sherry-Netherland, on Fifth Avenue, where the two women talked until three in the morning. They were nervous, and drank one whiskey after another. "I like her a lot," Beauvoir told Sartre, "and was very happy because I understood your feelings—I could appreciate them, and honored you for having them." A day or two later, she was invited to a cocktail party in Vanetti's home. "I was very moved to be entering that apartment where you'd lived for so long. . . . Dolores was as cute as a little Annamite idol and really charming to me—I'd like to know what she was actually thinking." Vanetti was certainly kind. She even arranged for Beauvoir to write some articles for American newspapers, for supplementary income.

The last time they met, Vanetti was surrounded by suitcases, about to leave for the airport, and dreading the long flight ahead. "I really do find her extremely pleasant and likeable," Beauvoir wrote. "Just a bit too much of a 'little dame,' as Bost puts it, for my own taste. But if you're male, and what's more driven by an imperialistic passion of generosity, you couldn't find anyone more appropriate."[4]

Beauvoir particularly liked Richard Wright, the black American writer, and his wife, Ellen. Their apartment on Charles Street, in

Greenwich Village, became her home away from home. Julia, their five-year-old daughter, was "a real little marvel." ("Even I who don't like children am friends with her.")⁵ The Wrights introduced Beauvoir to their circle of friends—left-wing intellectuals, nearly all Jewish, and all vehemently anticommunist—and Beauvoir found herself invited to their apartments. To her surprise, she saw that all these people had a typewriter, a record player, and a good collection of jazz.

She was immediately drawn to Bernard Wolfe's haunted face and generous spirit. Wolfe had been Trotsky's secretary down in Mexico, and had co-written a book on black hip culture, *Really the Blues*, with his friend Mezz Mezzrow, a white jazz clarinetist brought up in Chicago's black culture.⁶ Beauvoir asked Wolfe where she could hear good jazz, and he took her to a Louis Armstrong concert at Carnegie Hall. This was a rare occurrence, and tickets were hard to come by. Beauvoir was touched by what she saw as yet another example of staggering American kindness to strangers.

Her visit was featured in *The New Yorker*. Intimidated by the thought of meeting "Sartre's female intellectual counterpart," her interviewer admitted thinking he was "set for a grim half-hour." "Well, surprise! Mlle de B. is the prettiest Existentialist you ever saw; also eager, gentle, modest, and as pleased as a Midwesterner with the two weeks she spent in New York."⁷

In mid-February, Beauvoir left New York on a lecture tour. "My heart is as torn as if I were leaving someone special," she wrote. "I didn't think I could love another city as much as Paris."⁸

She was in Chicago for thirty-six hours. It was the end of February, so the streets were covered in snow and the wind cut like a razor. She did not feel like seeing the city by herself. Friends in New York had given her the address of a writer, Nelson Algren. Algren was thirty-eight, a year younger than Beauvoir. She had been warned that he was a moody, difficult fellow.

Beauvoir plucked up her courage and dialed. A man answered. She blustered into the phone with her thick French accent. The man hung up. She dialed again and spoke louder. "Wrong number," he said. After three tries, she was crimson with embarrassment, and asked the hotel operator to help. "There's a party here that would like to speak to you," the operator told Algren. He was used to misplaced calls in thick accents from Polish immigrants who had never used a phone before, and was busy cooking something on his stove. This time, he listened more carefully to what he later described as that "hoarse screech."[9] To Beauvoir's relief, he sounded more friendly.

That evening in the hotel bar, she saw a tall blond man with wire-frame glasses and a leather waistcoat come through the door and look her up and down with surprise. Beauvoir told him she was tired of luxury hotels and elegant restaurants. Would he show her the real Chicago?

Algren took her to Chicago's Bowery—to a strip club, a Negro bar, and a "gangster tavern," where music blared out from the jukebox and a variety of tramps, crooks, drug addicts, and whores propped themselves up at the counter. He felt at home in places like this, Algren said. These people were his friends.

Between his mumbling Midwestern drawl and her strong French accent, they had trouble understanding each other. At first she plied him with questions, and he answered laconically. But by the end of the evening, he was telling her about his life. He was born in Detroit, he said, and brought up in a poor immigrant district on the South Side of Chicago. His mother was Jewish and his father Swedish, but he did not feel either. During the Depression, after graduating in journalism from the University of Illinois, he had traveled in the South, hopping freight trains, and had served a four-month term in a Texas prison for stealing a typewriter. Back in Chicago, he was involved in a communist writers' group. It was the best time of his life. During the war, he had served in the army in France. He did not speak French, but he liked the French. On his way to and from Europe, he had stopped in New York. Otherwise, he had scarcely left Chicago.

They arranged to see each other the following afternoon. Beauvoir had to attend lunch with people from the Alliance Française. As soon as she could, she asked the French consul to drop her off at Algren's. The consul drove her to the Polish district, past warehouses, vacant lots, and rows of squalid wooden houses with scruffy backyards. At 1523 West Wabansia Avenue she stepped out into the snow, waved good-bye to the consul, and knocked on the door. The place was a hovel.

A fire was crackling in the black potbellied stove in the kitchen. The linoleum floor was covered with newspapers. "I was trying to clean up a bit," Algren said. He ushered her into the other room. There was a bright yellow chair, books, papers, a typewriter, a record player. On the bed was a colorful Mexican blanket. Beauvoir wished they could get under it and spend the afternoon there.

Instead, Algren showed her his neighborhood. She slipped on a patch of ice, and he took her arm. When their ears felt as if they would fall off with the cold, they went inside a bar and warmed up with stiff drinks. Beauvoir had not been able to get out of a dinner appointment with the French consul, and she resented it. Algren saw her to a taxi, and kissed her good-bye. He wanted her to come back in a few weeks. "If you do not I will come to Paris one day after you."[10]

The following morning, Beauvoir was on the train crossing the country to Los Angeles, remembering Algren's boyish smile. Before leaving the hotel, she had not seen the parcel Algren had left for her at the front desk. She had told him she was scared of seeing him again: wouldn't the parting be too painful? The parcel contained inscribed copies of his books, along with a tender note, which he was to forward to Los Angeles. He hoped very much to see her again, he said, even if the parting were painful.

After two days and nights on the train, Beauvoir arrived in Los Angeles at eight in the morning. Nathalie Sorokine, who was pregnant when Beauvoir saw her off from Paris two years earlier, was now living with her husband, Ivan Moffat, in Westwood, Los Angeles. She was at the station ("her hair and face magnificent, but more enormous than ever") and drove Beauvoir to their apartment, where Moffat was waiting with breakfast on the table. Their little girl was being looked after by a nanny.

Moffat, who was proving to be a successful screenwriter, had liked Beauvoir's novel *All Men Are Mortal,* and proposed to his producer friend George Stevens that they make a film of it together. (In the next few years, the two men would produce such classics as *A Place in the Sun, East of Eden,* and *Giant.*) There was talk of Claude Rains and Greta Garbo in the lead roles. "It would mean at least $30,000 for me," Beauvoir told Sartre. "Doesn't that make your head spin? We'd live for a whole year in America, you and I."[11]

A few days later, Moffat lent the women his big red Packard, and they set off. With Beauvoir navigating, they drove to San Francisco, then to Lone Pine, on the edge of the Nevada desert, where one afternoon, Moffat and George Stevens loomed up in Stevens's big car, a little later than the appointed meeting time, having stopped for several whiskeys on the way. They were wearing cowboy hats, red-and-black-checked shirts, and neckerchiefs. Beauvoir would write about that wondrous desert meeting in *America Day by Day.*

They went back to Los Angeles for a time, and then Moffat drove the women across a deserted Los Angeles bathed in the early light of dawn, and dropped them at the Greyhound bus station. Beauvoir and Sorokine set off on a three-week tour: a bus to Santa Fe, Houston, Natchez, and New Orleans; a plane to Florida, then a bus up to New York, with Beauvoir giving lectures along the way. The two women got on surprisingly well.

After she left Los Angeles, Beauvoir wrote and told Moffat how close she had felt to him, and how sad she felt to leave him. "While you were here I consciously became fonder and fonder of you and attracted by you," he replied. He wished they could have spent "a whole night in each other's embrace."[12]

Ivan Moffat, ten years younger than Beauvoir, could not help but respond to "the ardor and the vitality of her face, and those marvelous blue eyes and lovely smile and laughter."[13]

Her lecturing schedule was strenuous, but Beauvoir, untiring, was grateful for the opportunity to talk to American intellectuals. The *Daily Princetonian* reported:

> The elegant and attractive Simone de Beauvoir, the female ambassador for Existentialism in the United States, made the conquest of Princeton's linguists yesterday afternoon, while bombarding them in fast French about the responsibility of the

writer. "In France today," Mme de Beauvoir told her audience, "it is no longer permissible for the writer to stand apart and isolate himself in his ivory tower."[14]

Beauvoir pointed out that after the war, French tribunals had shown no mercy to French intellectuals who had collaborated, whereas other kinds of collaborators—war profiteers, for example— were treated comparatively leniently. In France, they had understood that an intellectual has a serious responsibility. As existentialists, she and Sartre believed that writers must be "committed." Words were actions. Writers had to take sides.

While Beauvoir was traveling around, imparting her message to university audiences across the country, she was meeting many people and asking many questions. Over cocktail parties and dinners, she chatted with faculty members and graduate students. Whenever she found herself alone, she sat in restaurants and bars or lay on her bed in hotel rooms, reading American literature and making notes. The book she would write about her trip, *America Day by Day*, gives a vivid sense of the kinds of conversations she was having, as well as her private reflections. When it was translated into English in 1953, most American critics (including the Francophile Mary McCarthy) resented what they saw as Beauvoir's facile generalizations and her sense of French superiority. In recent years, several American critics have hailed the book as "a forgotten gem."[15]

Beauvoir was also making notes for the essay she was writing on women. The experience of a different culture was proving invaluable. She was observing things with fresh, foreign eyes, and seeing the relationship between the sexes from an entirely new perspective. To her astonishment, she had come to the conclusion that women were less free in the United States:

I'd imagined that women here would surprise me with their independence. "American woman," "free woman"—the words seemed synonymous. At first, . . . their dress astonished me with its flagrantly feminine, almost sexual character. In the women's magazines here, more than in the French variety, I've read long articles on the art of husband hunting and catching a man. I've seen that college girls have little concern for anything but men and that the unmarried woman is much less respected here than in Europe.... Relations between the sexes are a struggle. One thing that was immediately obvious to me when I came to America is that men and women don't like each other.... This is partly because American men tend to be laconic, and in spite of everything, a minimum of conversation is necessary for friendship. But it's also because there is a mutual distrust, a lack of generosity, and a rancor that's often sexual in origin.[16]

In mid-April, Beauvoir was back in New York, staying at the Brevoort, an old hotel near Washington Square. She rarely spent an evening by herself. As well as the Wrights, she was seeing a lot of Bernard Wolfe and enjoying nights of jazz and ardent discussion. Wolfe took her to a marijuana party. She smoked several cigarettes, inhaled conscientiously, and felt nothing at all. Nevertheless, at four in the morning, she found herself passionately kissing Wolfe in front of her hotel.

Beauvoir was apprehensive about returning to Paris. Sartre's letters said ominously little about his feelings for Vanetti. Beauvoir, due to leave on May 10, begged him to "fix up a nice return" for her. She wanted to go away with him for two weeks—anywhere. "All I ask is to have you for a fortnight to myself."[17]

On Monday, April 28, she received an unusually loving letter. "My little sweet, dear heart," Sartre wrote. "I just want you to know that I'm filled with joy at the thought of seeing you again." He had booked her back into her pink room at the Louisiane, and would be waiting for her at the airport bus terminal. "We'll get back together as though we'd parted the night before. I am so happy when I'm with you, my little one."[18]

"How happy I've been feeling since Monday," Beauvoir wrote on Wednesday. "In ten days you'll be there, I'll touch you, I'll speak to you—I'm in raptures. You see, more than the Liberation, more than my journey to New York, it's you every time who are the most astonishing experience in my life, and the strongest and the deepest and the truest."

On Saturday, May 3, she went out for breakfast and returned to the Brevoort to find a cable waiting for her from Sartre. The situation with Vanetti was difficult, he said. Could Beauvoir postpone her return for a week?

Beauvoir did not write back until Thursday, May 8, "I was really shattered when I found your cable." She told Sartre she had suffered a "dreadful breakdown" and cried all day, "an anguish I just couldn't manage to cast off."

I found the idea of returning earlier than you wanted so unbearable, that on Saturday it made me quite ill when I couldn't exchange my seat. But on Monday I groveled to everybody so successfully that by Tuesday it had all been fixed. So I'll be at the Gare des Invalides at about 10.30 on *Sunday 18th*. . . . I really do want to feel completely calm and free of problems in Paris, at least during the first days. I beg of you, my love, fix everything nicely so that we can be on our own for a long time, and nothing spoils the happiness of being back with you.

She told Sartre she was going to Chicago for a few days. "The guy I liked there has been entreating me for two months to go back." What she did not tell Sartre was that when she got Sartre's cable, she was overcome with longing to be wrapped in loving arms. She first thought of Bernard Wolfe. She gathered all her courage and called him, hinting that they could perhaps take a brief trip away somewhere. He blustered excuses, clearly nervous that his wife would find out. When she put down the phone, she was damp with sweat.

She had paced the room nervously, then picked up the phone again. "I can come and spend three or four days in Chicago this week," she told Nelson Algren. "What do you think?"[19] He sounded very happy. He would meet her at the airport, he said.

She arrived in Chicago at mid-morning on May 10, and Algren was nowhere to be seen in the airport. She waited. Eventually it became clear that she was going to have to make another of those awful phone calls. She began to fumble in her handbag for her address book, thinking that it had been a dreadful mistake to come back to Chicago, when a tall figure appeared in front of her and said hello.

Algren was mortified to find her there waiting for him. He had rung the airport, he said, and they told him there was no flight from New York for an hour. He had even turned up forty minutes early. He sat down beside her. As Beauvoir herself has pointed out, Anne Dubreuilh's reunion with Lewis Brogan in *The Mandarins* is closely based on real life:

> I smiled at him. "We aren't going to stay here all morning, are we?"
>
> "No," he said. He thought for a moment. "Would you like to go to the zoo?"
>
> "To the zoo?"
>
> "It's near here."
>
> "And what will we do there?"
>
> "We'll look at the animals and they'll look at us."
>
> "I didn't come here to exhibit myself to your animals." I got up. "Why don't we go to some quiet place, where I can have some coffee and a sandwich, and we'll look at each other?"
>
> He, too, got up. "That's an idea!"

Beauvoir desperately wished Algren would suggest going back to his house. He didn't. In the taxi, he was silent. Beauvoir worried about spending four days with this stranger.

"We should stop off at the hotel first and leave my suitcase there," she said. On the phone from New York, not wishing to appear as if she were throwing herself at him, she had asked Algren to reserve a hotel room for her. Of course she hoped he would ignore the request.

Algren gave her an embarrassed smile and said it was hard to find a room in Chicago. He took her to an ugly cafeteria. After that they went to a baseball game. Then they went to a bowling alley. The day wore on. In the late afternoon, tired, cold, and frustrated, Beauvoir insisted that Algren ring for a hotel room. He helped her check in to the Hotel Alexandria, on Rush Street, in North Chicago. Surely, she thought, he would find an excuse to go up to the room with her? ("I could have given him twenty.") But he left her in the foyer. Beauvoir lay on the bed, listening for the sound of his steps in the corridor. They never came.

• • •

They had dinner that evening in a little Polish restaurant, then went to a bar. Algren had just fronted up to the gaming table when a group of his down-and-out friends, men and women, turned up. They talked excitedly to Algren, and Beauvoir could not understand a word they said. She was on the point of abandoning all hope when later, in a cab on their way to yet another jazz bar, Algren pulled her toward him and kissed her.

Anne Dubreuilh's body feels as if it were rising from the dead. In the jazz bar, she sips her whiskey, unable to focus on the music, encumbered by a "brand-new body," which is "too large, too burning." At last she is under the Mexican blanket with Brogan:

> Suddenly, he was no longer either awkward or modest. His desire transformed me. I who for a long time had been without taste, without form, again possessed breasts, a belly, a sex, flesh; I was as nourishing as bread, as fragrant as earth. It was so miraculous that I didn't think of measuring my time or my pleasure; I knew only that before we fell asleep I could hear the gentle chirpings of dawn.

Beauvoir and Algren would always call May 10 their "anniversary." The next day, Algren slipped a cheap Mexican ring on Beauvoir's finger. She told him she would wear it till the day she died. He called her "Simone, honey." She called him her "local youth." Algren laughed and imitated her accent. "Local use."

Apart from the *New Yorker* article, Algren knew almost nothing about Beauvoir, Sartre, or that worldwide craze, existentialism. For Beauvoir, it was intensely refreshing to be with a man who desired her first and foremost as a woman. Anne Dubreuilh muses: "I, who always question myself suspiciously about the feelings I inspire in others, never wondered who it was Lewis loved in me. I was certain it was myself. He knew neither my country, my language, my friends, nor my worries, only my voice, my eyes, my skin."

Beauvoir had to return to New York, but she did not want to leave Algren, so he came, too. He had never flown before, and was afraid of

heights, but once on the plane, he enjoyed himself. They spent passionate days and nights at the Brevoort. Beauvoir showed him her
favorite New York haunts. It was fascinating for her to see the city
through the eyes of a man from Chicago.

"It's funny that we get along so well," Algren told her. "I've never
been able to get along with anybody."[20] There were brief moments
when he became sullen and morose, and Beauvoir would feel panic
rising in her and wonder what she had done wrong. But she could see
that his moodiness was defensive. She liked to think she was the only
one who understood him.

On the plane back to France, she opened Algren's Chicago under-
world novel, *Never Come Morning*, and read the loving inscription he
had made to her. She leaned her forehead against the window, with
the blue sea below her, and wept. "Crying was sweet because it was
love," she wrote to her "beloved local youth" from the pale blue airport lounge in Newfoundland. It felt like a dream, she said, but it was
not a dream, so they would never have to wake up.[21]

Her return was painful. It was springtime, the sun was shining, and
lilies of the valley and bunches of asparagus were being sold on the
streets of Paris, but the cars were old, the window displays looked
anemic, the Louisiane was dingy, and Sartre was cold.

Vanetti was still in Paris, and appeared to have no intention of
leaving. Sartre listened to Beauvoir's stories about America, but he
volunteered little information himself, and evaded her questions. It
seemed that Vanetti was pressuring him to marry her, and he was not
at all sure what he wanted. He was in love, but not prepared to give
up his life for her, and Vanetti was not willing to accept anything less.
"Poverty. Anxiety. No doubt about it: I was home," Anne Dubreuilh
thinks to herself in *The Mandarins*.

After three days of weeping and heartache, Beauvoir decided she
needed air—country air. She packed her bags again, including a pile of
books and notebooks, and took a train to Saint-Lambert, a quiet village in the valley of Chevreuse, southwest of Paris. She installed herself in a blue-and-yellow inn, down the hill from the old stone
church. In the nearby woods were the ruins of an ancient Benedictine

convent, the Abbey of Port-Royal-des-Champs. The playwright Jean Racine, an orphan, had received a fine education from those nuns, and wrote about his solitary walks through the forest there. The area breathed the spirit of religious retreat. In her Catholic youth, Beauvoir had gone into retreat every year—to pray, tell her beads, meditate, and write down the outpourings of her soul. Thirty years later, she knew what she needed to try to restore her serenity.

For the two weeks he had promised Beauvoir, Sartre divided his time between Saint-Lambert and Paris. Whenever he was in the country, Vanetti would phone from Paris, weeping and making threats. After those two weeks, Sartre returned to Vanetti. Beauvoir remained in the village, on and off, for the next two months—with regular trips to Paris for *Temps modernes* meetings and to see friends.

In the country, surrounded by birdsong, cows, and the scent of roses, she worked on *America Day by Day*. Bost and Olga spent time with her. (Olga was home from the sanatorium, feeling much better.) Sartre came once a week, and they walked through the forest, along the paths Racine had taken, and Beauvoir tried to understand what was going on in Sartre's head.

She cursed the "dreadful Atlantic Ocean" between her and the man she desired. "I cry because I do not cry in your arms," she wrote to Algren. "This is not sensible at all, because if I were in your arms I should not cry."[22]

She admitted to Algren that she was doing a lot of weeping, but she rarely mentioned Sartre, and never mentioned Vanetti. There was a great deal that she did not tell Algren. When she talked about her life it was in the same whimsical, self-mocking tone that Algren himself used. One afternoon, friends came to visit her in the country, she told Algren in her idiosyncratic English, and there was a dramatic, beautiful storm:

The storm had gone on my nerves, and I drank much. . . . When the other friends left I became a storm myself, and poor Sartre was very bored with me who spoke about life and death and everything in a rather mad way. . . . You see, it has never been very easy for me to live, though I am always very happy—maybe because I want so much to be happy. I like so much to live and I

hate the idea of dying one day. And then I am awfully greedy; I
want everything from life, I want to be a woman and to be a
man, to have many friends and to have loneliness, to work much
and write good books, and to travel and enjoy myself, to be self-
ish and to be unselfish. . . . You see, it is difficult to get all which
I want. And then when I do not succeed I get mad with anger.[23]

Her emotional storms were rather more protracted than she let on
to Algren. That summer, there were moments when Beauvoir's anxiety "bordered on mental aberration." For the first time in her life, she
took drugs to fight off depression. For some time Sartre had been
taking Benzedrine, a stimulant that pilots took to keep awake when
flying. He gave her some. The pills seemed to help her work, though
she wondered if they were making her anxiety even worse.

In July, Sartre finally saw Vanetti off on a boat from Le Havre. She
warned him that either she would *never* come back or she would come
back for good. For months, Sartre brooded. Beauvoir was reminded
of the dark days when he had been followed by lobsters. "I wondered
in terror if we had become strangers to one another."[24]

In September 1947, Beauvoir returned to Chicago for two weeks.
Algren took her on a thorough guided tour of that city—including
the country prison, the electric chair, a police lineup, and a psychiatric
hospital—and she took notes for her book *America Day by Day*. She
called Algren's humble abode the "Wabansia goat nest." There was no
bathroom. They washed themselves at the kitchen sink. Algren showered twice a week at the local men's boxing gym, and arranged for
Beauvoir to take an occasional bath at a friend's place.[25]

He wanted her to stay in Chicago and marry him. She tried to
explain that her life was Paris, that in Chicago she would be lost and
uprooted, that she could never cope with what she saw as "the harsh
loneliness of America."[26] Algren found this hard to accept. Beauvoir
worried that if she could not give him her life she did not deserve his
love.

•   •   •

By the time Beauvoir was back in Paris, at the end of September, a new woman had appeared in Sartre's life. As screenwriter of *The Chips Are Down,* Sartre had gone to the launch at the Cannes film festival. He was photographed reading on that fashionable promenade, La Croisette. One day, a feisty twenty-four-year-old American journalist had come up to him, explaining that part of her job was to assemble details for future obituaries. "Here's an opportunity," she told him with a grin. "You can influence what people say about you *before* you die!" Sartre gave her his phone number at the Rue Bonaparte.

Beauvoir must have been extremely relieved. Sartre's two-and-a-half-year obsession with Vanetti seemed finally to be over. He was no longer faithful to her. Beauvoir was once again Sartre's loyal confidante—the one to whom he complained about the demands of his women.

Journalist Sally Swing, who was currently based in Paris, found herself slotted into Sartre's schedule on Wednesday evenings (till Thursday mornings) and from Saturday afternoon till Sunday afternoon. "He treated women like a chest of drawers," Swing recalls. "You're in the top drawer. She's in the bottom drawer. I hated it. It made me mad."

But she was crazy about him, she says. When he imitated people, he had her rolling on the floor with laughter. He wanted to psychoanalyze her. ("No way!") They played duets—he at the piano, she on the violin. ("Stop playing like a bloody German!" she said to him.) They acted out roles. She thought him "a wonderful lover."[27] (Decades later, Swing would read in Sartre's published correspondence to Beauvoir that he found her too sexually demanding.) When they spent the night together, they slept at her apartment on the Rue Grenelle, never at his mother's.

Beauvoir dedicated *America Day by Day* to Ellen and Richard Wright, and handed it in to her publishers in January 1948. Then she plunged into her essay on women, which she now saw as a book. She was inspired to work even harder than usual because she and Algren planned to travel together for four months, from May to September. She wrote to him that since they both liked to do the planning, she had come up with a scheme: "We'll cut the days in two parts, you'll plan the nights (I heard you were not bad at it), and I'll obey your plans in a very submissive way, and I'll plan the days, and you'll follow me the same way. What do you think of it?"[28]

Sartre's new play, *Dirty Hands,* opened on April 2 at the Théâtre Antoine. Sartre had insisted that Wanda play the lead female role, even though the director did not think she was capable. The weeks leading up to the play had been filled with anxiety. And then, to everyone's surprise, Wanda had acted like a star. Tickets sold out, and critics proclaimed *Dirty Hands* one of the most important plays to have come out of France in a long time. For Wanda, it was a personal triumph. "That is good," Beauvoir wrote Algren, "since the whole thing was done for her."[29]

While Sartre was writing the third volume of his trilogy and making notes for future books, he was heavily involved in politics. He had become one of the leaders of a new movement called the *Rassemblement Démocratique Révolutionnaire* (RDR). The idea of the RDR was that Europeans must not allow themselves to be pawns in the cold war being waged between the two great enemy powers, the United States and the Soviet Union. The Europeans wanted peace, and they must make their voices heard.

That summer, when the Soviet blockade of Berlin had the world poised yet again on the edge of war, the RDR gained considerable popular momentum. "We think that it is man who makes history," Sartre said, "and that *this war* . . . is absurd and unjustifiable."[30]

Sartre and Beauvoir had been making elaborate plans. From May to September 1948, Vanetti was coming to stay with Sartre in Paris. (He had warned Sally Swing that he would not be able to see her then.) During this time, Beauvoir was going to travel with Algren—down the Mississippi to New Orleans, then to the Yucatán, Guatemala, and Mexico.

And then, just a few days before the two women were due to swap continents once again, the plans went awry. Vanetti wrote to say that she had decided not to see Sartre under these conditions. Sartre, who saw this as a rejection, threw himself into the arms of his other American woman, Sally Swing. Beauvoir, faced with a new choice—being with Sartre instead of Algren—started to have doubts. Four months, after all, was a long time to be away from Sartre. After talking it over with him, she decided to cut her trip back by two months. She did not dare tell Algren. She would break the news to him later.

There was another delicate subject she had to broach with Algren, one that made her shy. "I am just a little afraid you'll laugh at me," she told him. On her previous visit, they had made love without taking any precautions. She had told him not to worry. ("If I had caught a baby, I should have gone to some surgeon and it would have been quickly fixed up.") But this time they were going to be traveling, and "it would be terrible if anything happened."[31] What did he think they should do? Did Americans have any sophisticated new method of contraception? She did not want to lessen his pleasure in any way. Algren wrote back and said he would use one of the traditional methods—withdrawal or condoms.

But Beauvoir wanted him to be "as free as free can be," and made other plans. On her way to Chicago she flew to New York, where Stépha Gerassi had made an appointment with a gynecologist, and Beauvoir had herself fitted with a diaphragm.

The voyage down the Mississippi was blissful. Lulled by the watery landscape, she and Algren made love often, and drank whiskey on deck. Algren took photographs with his new camera (none of which turned out), and Beauvoir translated one of his short stories for *Les Temps modernes*.

In Mexico City, Beauvoir was relieved to get a cheerful letter from Sartre. He did not seem to be pining for Vanetti. He was indignant about events in Palestine (the Arab armies appeared to be winning the war in the Middle East, and Sartre feared the Jews' dream of a homeland might yet be crushed) and indignant that the French newspapers seemed far more interested in Princess Elizabeth's sojourn in Paris. Sally Swing was part of the fleet of journalists covering the British royal visit. He was seeing a lot of her—he called her "the little one"—but her sexual demands were killing him, he told Beauvoir. He punctiliously did as he was told, but it was boring.

Here's my schedule: She lands at my place (Rue B.) around 5 in the evening, exhausted by her life as a journalist, her clothes in tatters, her calves scratched, her feet all blistered, her face spattered; she covered eight kilometers through the brambles of the Trianon to surprise Elizabeth at lunch, and she reached it dog tired, to find 50 journalists who had come in by the front door; or else she battled it out with the police. . . . She collapses on my bed and drops off with the sleep of Sorokine, by which I mean that I come and go, cough, light my pipe over and over, and she only wakes up at eight o'clock when I shake her. Sometimes, at 7.30, she draws grating notes out of a violin while I play the piano. . . . Then she takes a bath. . . . At 8.30, departure, search for taxi, dinner. . . . She adores eating. Then, at almost eleven, another taxi, where she loses some trinket (day before yesterday her bag with 30,000 francs, yesterday her hat). Then we search and take action, and we find or do not find the object (the hat found; the bag not). Then invariably, whether I go back to my mother's or sleep at the little one's place, I mount and submit. The mornings are pleasant: sun, the Arc de Triomphe in the distance, the greenery, the rooftops, her balcony, and then an American orange juice, American coffee, and departure: I get a taxi, go back to my mother's, drink some of Dolores's American coffee and work.[32]

Time was passing, and Beauvoir had still not said anything to Algren about her return date. Finally, on a long, dusty bus journey between Mexico City and Morelia, she clumsily announced that she had to leave him two months earlier than planned. Algren made some flippant comment, and Beauvoir did not at first realize how betrayed he felt. When she found herself exploring Morelia's old streets and squares without him, she still did not understand what was happening.

By the time she did, it was too late. For the rest of the trip she saw plenty of the famous Algren sullenness. He told her he could not love her on her terms, and she kept weeping. She wanted to talk things over openly and honestly; he had no patience with her obsession with talk. Near the end of the trip, during a particularly disagreeable Sunday lunch at the Tavern on the Green in New York, she told him she would leave the next day if he wanted her to. He burst out that she had not understood anything. "I'm ready to marry you this very moment."[33]

The return flight was nightmarish. Beauvoir stuffed herself with sleeping pills and still did not sleep. She was not sure she would see Algren again. Had she, in her foolishness, destroyed the greatest passion she had ever had?

On July 19, from her "toothpaste pink" room at the Louisiane, Beauvoir wrote to Algren that she and Sartre were leaving in a week (on July 23) for a two-month working trip in North Africa. She hoped he would write to her. Once again, she tried to explain to Algren why she could not give him her whole life:

> I could not love you, want you, and miss you more than I do. Maybe you know that. But what you have to know too, though it may seem conceited to say it, is in which way Sartre needs me. In fact, he is very lonely, very tormented inside himself, very restless, and I am his only true friend, the only one who really understands him, helps him, works with him, gives him some peace and poise. For nearly twenty years he did everything for me; he helped me to live, to find myself, he sacrificed lots of things for my sake. . . . I could not desert him. I could leave him for more or less important periods, but not pledge my whole life to anyone else. I hate to speak about it again. I know that I am in danger losing you; I know what losing you would mean for me.

The next day, July 20, Beauvoir sent Algren a wire. Plans had changed. Would it be possible for her to come back to Chicago for a month?

His wire had the effect of a bombshell: "No, too much work."[34]

Why had Beauvoir changed her plans yet again? On July 20, Vanetti had phoned Sartre from New York. She was sobbing into the phone. She could not bear to be away from him any longer, she said. Would he agree to spend a month with her in the south of France? Sartre said yes.[35]

Beauvoir had cut back her trip with Algren to be with Sartre, and now Sartre was leaving her high and dry. Sartre felt bad about it and offered to pay her fare back to Chicago. But whereas Dolores won this round with Sartre, Beauvoir lost with Algren.

On Friday the twenty-third, the day she and Sartre had originally planned to fly to Algiers, Beauvoir wrote to Algren with an invented story:

> I hope you were not angry at my wire, honey, I'll tell you what happened. If I had to come back to Paris in the middle of July, it was because Sartre needed me for working at a movie script from his last play. I told you I always wanted to help him when he asked, and then that is one of the ways of earning my life; my books would not be enough for me to live on. . . . But then suddenly, Tuesday, the producers changed their mind; there were arguments and quarrels, and the script is not to be done just now. Sartre has to stay here and discuss business before beginning the job, if he ever begins it, so he was terribly remorseful of having asked to me to come back . . . and he proposed to me to fly back to Chicago if I wanted, helping me with the money of the trip.

She did not mention Vanetti. In letters to Algren, she never mentioned her. What *is* surprising is that fifteen years later, in *Force of Circumstance,* she told the truth. When Algren, along with all her other readers, read about the woman Beauvoir called "M," and learned the extent to which Beauvoir had lied to him, he would never speak to her again.

After Sartre spent a month with Vanetti in the south of France, he and Beauvoir went to Algeria for six weeks. Bost joined them for a time. They swam in the ocean, toured the country, and worked, in front of a fan or in the shade of the trees.

Back in Paris, Beauvoir wrote most mornings at the Deux Magots, then had lunch and a break, and at four P.M. she went to work at

Sartre's. At eight P.M., she emerged for an evening's sociability. "What is really fine in Paris is this evening life, in the cafés," she told Algren. "When you have worked all day long, you just go on the Boulevard Saint-Germain, and without any appointment, you are sure to meet some friends with whom you can spend some time before sleeping."[36]

Beauvoir had Paris's café life; Algren had lonely Chicago. Beauvoir had Sartre; Algren had no one. He wrote that he felt the need to have a woman of his own. He did not think he would ever love another woman as much as he loved Simone, but "no arms are warm when they're on the other side of the ocean."[37] He hoped he would remarry one day.

His letter did not make her happy, Beauvoir wrote back, but she understood, and everything he said was fair. "You will be a nice fate for any woman, and I should have chosen that fate for myself heartily if other things had not made it impossible for me."[38]

Algren's letters grew warmer again. He sent loving parcels to Beauvoir (and even to her mother), with tobacco, books, chocolate, and fine whisky concealed in a bag of flour. They agreed he would come to Paris the following May.

Beauvoir had lived in hotels for eighteen years, and she decided she'd had enough. The places were badly heated. The Louisiane was damp and musty, and her pink room needed a good coat of paint. In October 1948, she moved into a small fifth-floor apartment on Rue de la Bûcherie, one of the ancient, narrow streets near the Seine, in the Latin Quarter. It was a poor Arab district in those days. As dusk fell, Beauvoir would hear the strains of Arab music coming from the second-floor café across the street, the Café des Amis. There were frequent street fights. Her building was shabby, and her ceiling leaked when it rained. But she loved having her own place. From one of her windows she looked across to the Seine, the quays, and the turrets of Notre-Dame.

She put red curtains up at the windows and bought two white armchairs. The room looked cozy with the green-bronze lamps designed by Giacometti, the cubist watercolor Fernand Léger had given her, some colorful Van Gogh and Picasso prints, and her books.

From the ceiling beams she hung the colorful objects she had brought back from her travels in Mexico and Guatemala. From now on, she worked at home in the mornings. In the evenings, she sometimes ate at home. "I cook nice meals: chiefly, already cooked vegetables and cold ham," she told Algren. "But I don't know very well how to manage the can-opener, I broke already two of them."[39]

When the studio below became vacant, the Bosts moved in. The three often had dinner together in the café in the cobbled square, which looked out across the trees to Notre-Dame. Things seemed perfect until Olga had another X ray and discovered she still had a hole in her lung. Half crazed with fear and frustration, she went back to Laigle to convalesce in the country air.

Soon after Algren came into her life, Beauvoir stopped sleeping with Bost. At first Bost (who never had any shortage of girlfriends) was hurt—jealous, even. He had never seen Beauvoir so much in love. But their own relationship had been more tender than passionate for some time now. They would always remain the closest of friends.

Beauvoir would dedicate The Second Sex to Bost. She told him he was the least macho of all the men she knew.[40]

"One is not born, but rather becomes, a woman." It was to be the most famous sentence in The Second Sex. As an existentialist, Beauvoir did not believe in "human nature." Her argument was that "femininity" is a social construct. Biology had no answer for the question: Why is woman the Other?

Her central thesis was that in all cultures, even those said to be matriarchal, man is regarded as the Subject, and woman as the Other.[41] She explored the data of physiology, psychoanalysis, history, and Marxist theory and found no satisfactory reason for this. Her conclusion was that otherness is a fundamental category of human thought. No group can set itself up as the One, without setting up another group as the Other.

She was working long hours on this book, determined to finish it before Algren's visit to Paris, in May 1949. Her research was vast, and yet she wrote The Second Sex in just two years. For her, this book was far easier to write than a novel. Fiction involved careful point-of-view

writing and considerable emotional energy. *The Second Sex* required
research, a lucid mind, and organizational powers. For that, she was
well trained.

Since her framework was existentialist, her yardstick was freedom.
Her premise was that the ultimate goal of any responsible human
subject should be "sovereignty." But this was complicated. If a woman
was not free, it could be for two reasons. Her lack of freedom could
be inflicted, in which case it constituted oppression. Or it could be
chosen, in which case it represented a moral fault. In both cases, it
was an absolute evil.

Like Sartre, she argued that freedom requires moral courage. It is
easier to forgo one's liberty and become a *thing*. As Beauvoir made
clear, for women there were advantages to be gained from playing up
to men, living through men, being kept by men. "It is an easy road; on
it one avoids the strain involved in undertaking an authentic existence."

Several chapters in *The Second Sex* ("The Narcissist," "The Woman
in Love," "The Mystic") demonstrate the various ways women choose
to avoid their freedom. But if *The Second Sex* is shot through with
ambivalence, it is because Beauvoir shows that freedom itself is full of
insurmountable obstacles for women. Society was not yet ready for
the free woman.

One of the best chapters in the book, surely, is "The Independent
Woman," in which Beauvoir talks covertly about herself. She sums up
the central problem thus:

> The advantage man enjoys . . . is that his vocation as a human
> being in no way runs counter to his destiny as a male. . . . His
> social and spiritual successes endow him with a virile prestige.
> He is not divided. Whereas it is required of women that in
> order to realize her femininity she must make herself object and
> prey, which is to say that she must renounce her claims as a sov-
> ereign subject.

In other words, whether she is a sovereign subject or an unfree
object, woman cannot win. As Beauvoir portrays her, the independent woman suffers from an inferiority complex when it comes to

"femininity." She can see that her intelligence and independence intimidate men. She knows that if she conducts her sex life too freely, she will be seen, humiliatingly, as "easy." And she is only too aware of the double standard in society when it comes to aging.

Beauvoir knew plenty of women who lived through men, who foisted the burden of their existence onto a man. She herself knew the temptation. She also knew the price of independence. Indeed, as *The Second Sex* shows poignantly, the independent woman was doomed to feel divided.

Sartre had always thought of Michelle Vian as the wife of their friend Boris. The Vians made a beautiful, bohemian, hip young couple. But by the beginning of 1949, there were rumors that the marriage was crumbling.

In May, the Vians threw one of their famous parties. Sartre watched as Michelle danced the swing and the jitterbug in a little red dress and the very high heels she always wore. She was petite, with shapely legs, blue eyes, a warm smile, and long blond hair. Later that evening, Sartre said to her: "You're always in motion. Stop dancing a moment, and come and talk to me." Michelle smiled and sat on the edge of the sofa, beside him. She wore theatrical makeup, like an actress. "But I'm boring," she said. "I have nothing to say."

Behind her extroverted façade, Michelle was painfully insecure. Her voice was sweet and clear, but she rarely spoke unless spoken to. Since the war, Boris Vian had become famous as a novelist and jazz trumpeter. He was also known for his humorous column in *Les Temps modernes*. By contrast, Michelle felt stupid. She was not a writer. She did not even have her baccalaureate.

She and Boris were twenty when they met at Capbreton in the summer of 1940, the summer when Paris fell to the Germans and Michelle's ten-year-old brother drowned in the currents. Her mother blamed Michelle, who was supposed to have been watching him. It was a trauma Michelle would never get over.

When America joined the war, and jazz was outlawed in occupied France, Boris and Michelle became part of the "Zazou" movement—young people whose resistance to the Germans took the form of dressing provocatively, listening clandestinely to American jazz, and dancing the swing at underground parties. Michelle loved English and everything to do with the Anglo-Saxon world—British detective novels, American films, American jazz. She helped Boris translate his favorite jazz songs. As Zazous, Boris wore high collars and tiny English-knotted ties and Michelle bleached her hair peroxide-blond and took to wearing the highest heels she could find.

They married in July 1941. Both were virgins. Boris wore a condom, but it burst, and Michelle became pregnant that very night. Boris was not ready to become a father. By the time their son, Patrick, arrived, in April 1942, Boris was making his mark as a jazz trumpeter. After the Liberation, when the new basement dance cellars sprang up in Saint-Germain-des-Prés, he and Juliette Greco became the stars at the famous club, the Tabou. A bevy of pretty girls hung around the stage door, and threw themselves at Boris Vian.

When Michelle complained about Boris's affairs, he snapped that she should take a lover herself, and learn something about sex. She said she had no interest in sleeping around; she loved *him*. At one of their parties, he pushed her toward a sixteen-year-old jazz clarinetist, André Reweliotty. During the summer of 1946, Boris was writing his second novel, and was busy. He invited Reweliotty on vacation with him and Michelle. Reweliotty and Michelle made love in the sand dunes.[42]

In April 1948, a second child, Carole, arrived.[43] The marriage deteriorated further. Michelle turned more and more to Reweliotty. He was too young to give her the validation she needed, but he was a loving man, and he was faithful.

Then, in May 1949, after the party where they had talked on the sofa, Jean-Paul Sartre, the most famous intellectual in France, phoned Michelle and asked her out. On their first evening together, they talked for three hours in the bar of the Pont-Royal. For a whole month, until Sartre left on a trip with Vanetti, he and Michelle Vian saw each other almost every day. Sartre did not touch her. They talked. Michelle was deeply moved. Sartre seemed so gentle, so sensitive to her feelings.

•   •   •

In May 1949, Algren came to Paris. The family had never seen Beauvoir look so soft and happy. "She was always asking Algren: 'Are you alright? What would you like?' " Michelle Vian recalls. "They gazed into each other's eyes and held each other's hands like young lovers."

Algren was nervous about meeting Sartre, but when the Little Man put his arm on Algren's back and guided him jovially into their first bar, Algren immediately felt at ease. He was especially fond of Olga and Michelle, who liked to speak English with him. Olga listened to his stories wide eyed. Michelle conscientiously acted as his interpreter in the group. Algren called her "the Golden Zazou."

The first volume of *The Second Sex* came out in June 1949. Beauvoir's scandalous reputation was sealed. Even the title of the book shocked people. By talking frankly about the female body and female sexuality, Beauvoir had broken major taboos. She was considered even more outrageous than her cross-dressing female writer predecessors George Sand and Colette.

Beauvoir was roundly attacked. "Unsatisfied, frigid, priapic, nymphomaniac, lesbian, a hundred times aborted, I was everything," she writes, "even an unmarried mother." She received hundreds of letters. People told her that her problem was that she did not believe in God. Some offered to cure her frigidity. Others offered, in the coarsest possible terms, to assuage her labial appetites. The Vatican blacklisted the book. The conservative Catholic writer François Mauriac told a member of the *Temps modernes* editorial board, "Your employer's vagina has no secrets from me."[44] Even Camus thought the book preposterous. ("Camus ... a Mediterranean man, cultivating Spanish pride ... accused me of making the French male look ridiculous."[45]) The fact that Beauvoir had discussed abortion was particularly shocking. Since she and Sartre had both written about abortion in their fiction, people had already come to the office of *Les Temps modernes* asking for addresses. The secretary had put up a sign: WE DO IT ON THE PREMISES, OURSELVES.

Algren arrived at the height of it all. Beauvoir and Sartre had almost stopped going into cafés; people pestered them. But with Algren there, Beauvoir went out a great deal. When the two of them went into a public place, people would point to her and snicker. She was glad Algren could not understand what they were saying, and relieved when they left on a two-month trip to Italy, Algeria, Morocco, and Tunisia. On their return from North Africa, they stayed a few days with Bost and Olga, in their cottage at Cabris, in the hills of Provence. Bost and Olga were amused by Algren's wild stories, most of which demonstrated his heroism. Bost called him "Tough Algren."

In mid-September, Beauvoir accompanied Algren to Orly Airport, feeling as if her heart would burst. Algren told her: "I've never been so happy; I've never loved so much."[46] During a stopover on his way home, he heard that his novel *The Man with the Golden Arm* had won the National Book Award.

While Beauvoir was with Algren, Sartre was traveling for three months in Central America with Vanetti. Before he left, he told Michelle Vian: "I'm going to put some order in my life."[47] When he came back, in October, he started to court Michelle seriously.

"I did not speak. I had no confidence. I was silent, always smiling, lost," Michelle Vian recalls. "Sartre taught me to speak. He told me my ideas were good. It was his view that people must think, and talk. I found him very exciting. I didn't care about handsome. I liked his lips. They were the same type as Brigitte Bardot's. The upper lip the same size as the lower lip. Like his mother's. . . . When I saw him coming, my heart began to beat. I'd think to myself, here's joy, here's fun."[48]

One evening in late December, in a taxi coming home after a nightclub, Sartre kissed her. By now, Michelle was well and truly in love. Shortly afterward, Sartre took her home to his place. It was the afternoon. His mother was away. They made love.

Sartre left the next day to spend New Year's Eve at La Pouèze. Bost and Beauvoir were working across the table from each other, translating Algren's novel *Never Come Morning*. Madame Morel, who was famous for her hospitality, was happy to let them work all day long. Sartre was absorbed in an essay he was writing about Jean Genet, a man he saw as an existential hero, since from his unfavorable beginnings (illegitimacy, public assistance, delinquency, prison, pederasty), Genet had, by choosing to write, made something positive out of what others had made of him. It was a Sartrean obsession: the idea of self-invention in the face of humiliation and stigmatization.

Sartre was writing frequent letters to Michelle, his "little charm." He could not stop thinking about that marvelous afternoon—her dress, her hair and mouth, her mysterious smile. He wanted to make her happy. He wanted her never to feel alone. It was new for him, he said, this need he felt for someone else. It was physical, as if he had contracted an illness. He missed her, in his body.[49]

By February, Michelle realized she was pregnant. With Sartre, as with Boris, she became pregnant the very first time she slept with him. Sartre could not believe it at first. He had practiced his usual method of contraception, coitus interruptus, and thought it foolproof. "Of course, it wasn't safe at all," says Michelle Vian. "Sartre would withdraw, and ten minutes later, he would make love again. We didn't know it back then, but it takes only a drop of semen. . . . You can see what the sexual act represented for me. Danger."[50]

Sartre asked whether she wanted to keep the baby. Michelle knew he disliked children. She had seen her marriage destroyed by her pregnancies. And she already had two children. It was enough, she told Sartre. That meant an abortion. Sartre said he would ask Beauvoir for addresses. Michelle was shocked. "Don't tell the Beaver," she said. "Not yet." Michelle said she would ask her medical-student brother for help.

Sartre was about to go away again. He and Beauvoir were leaving in early March to spend two months in sub-Saharan Africa. Michelle begged him to postpone his departure a few days. Couldn't he stay until after the abortion? She frightened, she said. But Sartre was firm. He could not let Beauvoir down. He had disappointed her the previous summer. (He did not go into details.) "I can't do it to her."

"I was angry," says Michelle Vian. Sartre left, and her brother performed the abortion. Michelle became infected and was feverish for days. From Algeria, Sartre sent orchids. From the depths of black Africa, he wrote tender letters. "I didn't reply," says Michelle. "Maybe once or twice, no more. I have photos of me at that time, looking incredibly sad. It was the end of the fantasy."

Not long before, she had broken off her affair with André Reweliotty, explaining that she was in love with Sartre. Reweliotty had been very upset. Now Michelle went back to him. She did not tell him she was sleeping with Sartre. And she did not tell Sartre she was sleeping with Reweliotty. "It was a total secret," she says. "I had a double life. Two different worlds."[51]

It was Beauvoir who wanted to see the Sahara, and it was she who had rushed around and made the bookings. She and Sartre spent four days crossing the desert in a truck, leaving each morning at around five, just as a bright red sun was rising in the mountains. In Tamanrasset, one moonlit night, they were taken to see the Touareg chief in his tent in the desert. The Touareg men were tall and proud faced, with only their dark eyes visible above their indigo veils. In Gao, Mali, Sartre came down with high fever. While he was in bed for two days, scarcely conscious, Beauvoir worked. They took a plane to Bobo-Dioulasso. A violent midday storm soaked their beds and brought out the cockroaches. That evening Beauvoir and Sartre were dropping with fatigue when they returned to their room. "Sartre barely closed his eyes all night," Beauvoir writes. "His bed was still wet, the jazz across the road deafened him, and above all he was frightened of the cockroaches that were trotting about on the ceiling. He spent the night reading."[52]

They no sooner arrived in a place than they dived into the local Poste Restante. Sartre was tormented because Michelle was not writing. Beauvoir was tormented by the silence from Algren. "Surely . . . your witty prose is lost in some place of the Sahara," she wrote to him, "or maybe some Negros enjoy laughing at it while eating each other."[53]

In early May, Sartre flew back to Paris from Casablanca. Beauvoir made a sentimental journey to Fez, where she and Algren had been so happy together. "If I had got letters, it could have been a sweet pilgrimage," she wrote to him afterward. "The way it was, it just broke my heart. I walked in all the little streets we liked so much, where we were happy together, and I wanted you so much that I enjoyed nothing and just felt like crying to death."[54]

In Paris, to her relief, there were two thick letters from Algren.

Vanetti's divorce had come through (Sartre had paid for it) and she was living in Cannes, on the Côte d'Azur, wanting Sartre to marry her. But Sartre was in love with Michelle. To Beauvoir, he complained that Vanetti was too demanding, always wanting more from him—more money, more time. But he felt guilty toward her, and agreed to spend a few weeks with her in June and July. Michelle was upset. "I thought you broke with her last year!"

"You have to do these things gradually," Sartre said.[55]

Sartre broke up with Vanetti during the summer of 1950. Beauvoir was away, but Bost was on hand to witness it. There were no dramatic scenes, he reported to Beauvoir, and it seemed to him that Sartre was almost a bit disappointed by that. Vanetti had wept once, on Bost's shoulder. She seemed surprised that Sartre no longer loved her, but she did not express bitterness. She kept saying that Sartre had changed. He had become even more fanatical about his work. Nothing else seemed to interest him anymore.

Bost had a contract to write a guide book, *Spain Day by Day*, in the same series as Beauvoir's book on America.[56] He needed a car, and Vanetti had a car, and she felt in need of a companionable vacation. The two were going to spend two months traveling around Spain together. Bost hoped she would not bash his ears about Sartre. "I kiss you tenderly," he signed off to Beauvoir. "My best regards to Tough Algren!"[57]

Across the world, Beauvoir was having a terrible time. Back in January, she had made a bad mistake. She had written to Algren with a request. She was scared of his answer, she told him, which would make her either very happy or very sad. She had reminded him that

when they were in Tunisia he had said that she must come back to
Wabansia Avenue, but not too soon. She had a favor to ask him:

> I have to ask you to let me come as soon as June. It is not whim,
> you know. Sure, I am impatient of melting in your arms again—
> I long for you—but if I wished to come soon just from my long-
> ing, I should not demand, I should just suggest. I don't like to
> be demanding, and you know I try not to be much, honey. Now
> I demand. The point is Sartre *has to* go away this summer for
> three months, no later than June, and he asks me, very demand-
> ingly, to go away when he does—not to wait until he is back. . . .
> And sure he has no right at all to ask anything from you, but you
> see how it is for me: since I decided not to break, even for love
> sake, the long friendship I have with him (and which he needs
> very much, as you could feel), it would be stupid and unkind not
> to act in a real friendly way. . . . *Trust me,* Nelson. If I say it is
> *important* for him, so it comes to be for me.

Algren had agreed, which made Beauvoir very happy. But over the
next few months, Algren's letters were less frequent. Just before she
was due to leave, the Korean War broke out. The whole world
seemed yet again headed for war. She thought of canceling her trip.
Sartre persuaded her to go.

She arrived in Chicago, and Algren was strangely distant. He made
love to her, but without tenderness. On the second night, Beauvoir
asked what the matter was. No, it was not that he loved anyone else,
he said, but something was dead. He was tired of her turning up only
to leave again. He had waited for her with indifference, and he did
not feel much when he saw her again. His ex-wife wanted him back,
and though he was weary of women, he was thinking they might
marry again.

On the third night, they tried to make love, and Algren could not.
Beauvoir panicked. "It was so pitiful that it horrified me," she wrote
to Sartre. "I brooded over my horror for a good part of the night,
then as soon as Algren woke up tried to talk to him; but he hates
explanations—he just runs away."[58] They did not try again.

The heat in Wabansia Avenue was stifling, and Algren's morose presence was suffocating. Beauvoir fled the house, but the streets of Chicago were so hot she thought she would melt into the tar. The newspapers were full of virulent anticommunist rhetoric. When Beauvoir went to a hairdresser in the neighborhood, the girl who washed her hair said accusingly, "Why are you all communists in France?"[59]

At the beginning of August she and Algren moved to Miller, on Lake Michigan, where Algren had rented a cottage. They slept in separate rooms. Beauvoir struggled with despair. What was she doing there? Would she ever again experience passion? She took corydrane, an amphetamine mixed with aspirin, in order to be able to work on her new novel, the one that would eventually be called *The Mandarins.* A few months before, when she had been in Paris longing for Algren's body, he (the author of *Never Come Morning*) had asked her what the title was. "Never Come Woman," she had quipped.

The summer passed. They swam in the lake. One afternoon Beauvoir nearly drowned. This dramatic incident briefly revived their old passion. In the evenings, they walked along the beach and wondered whether the world was about to end in nuclear war. Beauvoir tried to calm herself by thinking of Sartre. "The novelty and romance and happiness of my life are with you, my little companion of 20 years," she wrote to him. As for Vanetti and her "avarice," she was glad that Sartre had for once managed to be firm.

She was counting the hours until her return. "You'll see what a beautiful life we'll have from now on, as soon as we're back together," she told Sartre. As she was writing her letter, the moon was veiled by an orange dawn. She felt sure they were about to begin a happy old age.

NINE

CRYSTAL BLUE EYES

January 1951 – December 1954

Sartre had changed, it was true. He had always worked hard, but now, with the help of corydrane, he had turned himself into a work machine. Gone were the evenings he and Beauvoir had once enjoyed at the cinema; gone were their strolls together through Paris. He did not have time.

Corydrane, a stimulant or "upper," was fairly widely used in the 1950s. But whereas journalists would take a tablet or a half-tablet to get them going, Sartre took four. Most people took them with water; Sartre crunched them. They tasted bad, very bitter, and whether or not it was masochism, Sartre liked to give himself a hard time. On top of the corydrane, he smoked two packets of unfiltered Boyards a day and consumed vast quantities of coffee and tea. In the evening, he drank half a bottle of whiskey, then took four or five sleeping pills to knock himself out.

Increasingly, he felt that writing was a futile, self-indulgent pursuit in a world where children were starving and injustice was everywhere. He no longer read the novels Beauvoir enjoyed; he did not care anymore about fine sentences. He was convinced that politics mattered; literature did not.

He took corydrane to stave off his anxiety about the utter irrelevance of what he was doing. Under the influence of the drug, instead of writhing in anguish, he wrote at white heat. For hours at a stretch he produced page after page, hardly able to keep up with his pen, borne away by a feeling of his own power.

He had temporarily put aside a huge philosophical tome he called *Ethics*. His essay on Genet, begun as a preface, had grown into a thick book, something between philosophy and literature, a monumental portrait that would leave readers admiring and uncomfortable. ("Who can swallow such a thing?" Cocteau would ask in his journal, noting Sartre's "will to be the center of attention in literature, and render everything else insipid."[1]) He had begun a book on Italy, a country he loved with a passion. His intention, as usual, was to talk about "everything" (history, politics, social problems, the church, art, architecture, and tourism), and was enjoying writing it, but guilt got the better of him. Politics was calling; the project struck him as an indulgence and was permanently shelved. His writing on his favorite cities—Venice, Capri, Rome, and Naples—published posthumously, shows Sartre at his most sensuous and poetic. He spent pages describing the plashing sound gondolas make.[2]

At the beginning of 1951, he put several projects aside to write a play. His secretary, Jean Cau, observed that Sartre did not seem to enjoy writing plays nearly as much as other things, and that each time he embarked on one, it caused a major trauma in the Sartrean entourage. So why did he do it? He had initially written a part for Olga; these days it was for Wanda. "Others offered jewellery; he offered plays," writes Cau.[3]

Wanda loved the stage, and showed genuine talent. She was currently involved with a young man, but for Sartre she remained part of the family, part of the brood of women, including his mother, who needed his support and protection. He saw her regularly. When he went away, he wrote her affectionate, humorous letters. Financially, she was entirely dependent on him.

The writing of *The Devil and the Good Lord* proved a nightmare. Sartre worked obsessively, but did not meet the deadline and kept adding scenes. Rehearsals began, and Sartre had still not finished it. Simone Berriau, the director of the Théâtre Antoine, was furious with him. She wanted cuts, not additions. Sartre refused to oblige. The tears, screams, and anger were reported in the press. When the curtain rose the first night, June 7, 1951, the play, which had finally been reduced to four hours, was already the talk of the Paris theater season. Wanda, under her stage name, Marie Olivier, played alongside Pierre Brasseur and Maria Casarès, two of the best known actors in France. All three were praised. The play was a triumph.

The family had to be tactful about toasting Wanda's success. Olga, who was generally considered a far better actress than her younger sister, had suffered a major humiliation. After her tuberculosis, she had been impatient to resume her career and had taken on small roles with success. But she also wanted to be in the new production of *The Flies*. She had been the original Electra, and she did not want to see anyone else in the part Sartre had written for her. Her doctor firmly advised against her taking on such a demanding role too soon. Olga insisted. Shortly before the opening night, it was reported in the press that the director, Raymond Hermantier, did not think Olga was up to it, but that Sartre had ordered him to keep her.

In fact, Olga had not regained her powers. Her old fire was not there. Her breath let her down, and her voice was still not strong. The critics flayed her. Olga was devastated. To the chagrin of the family, she vowed never to step onto a stage again. She would keep to her word, and for the rest of her life she felt like a failure.

Boris Vian was going around telling people that Sartre had stolen his wife. Boris now wanted a divorce. Michelle was terrified. She did not want to be caught up in a scandal. And if she were declared an adulteress, Boris might gain custody of their children.

When she and Sartre went out together, Michelle disguised herself with sunglasses and hats. When they traveled, they were obliged to take separate rooms. "It was like a detective novel," Michelle Vian recalls. "A messy, sordid business."[4] In Capri, she was alarmed when a press photographer sprang in front of them and started clicking his camera. In Rome, a private detective came up to them: "We are looking for Monsieur Sartre, who is accompanied by Madame Vian." It took Sartre a considerable wad of notes to pay him off.

Sartre told Michelle not to worry; he would look after her and the children. "It feels sensuous to give you money," he said.[5] He hired a top lawyer to represent her. The cat-and-mouse games continued until the divorce came through, in September 1952, with Boris declared the guilty party.

Beauvoir felt bleak. Sartre had never seemed farther away from her. He was reading enormously, mostly about Marxism, pushing his thinking to the limits, as he liked to do. He called it "breaking the bones in my head."[6] With great enthusiasm, he would tell her to read this or that book, but Beauvoir already had more than enough to read, and she was not particularly interested in politics. She had no illusions that she could change the world that way.

She was having immense difficulties with *The Mandarins.* Sartre had pointed out the weaknesses in the first draft, and she was not at all sure she could remedy them. At times it seemed so difficult to pull the threads together that she wondered whether she should give up and start something else. Sartre's dismissive attitude toward fiction did not help.

In September 1951, she flew back to Chicago. She and Algren had decided to see each other on a different basis. They spent a peaceful month at the cottage on Lake Michigan. When they said good-bye, Beauvoir said how good it was that they had managed to retain their friendship. "It's not friendship," Algren retorted, "I could never give you less than love."[7] Beauvoir sobbed all the way to New York, where she wrote to him from her hotel: "I feel utterly in your hands, absolutely defenseless, and for once I shall beg: keep me in your heart or chase me away, but don't let me cling to love to find out suddenly it is there no more."[8] Algren wrote an angry letter back, telling her it was over.

Beauvoir had made quite a bit of money from *The Second Sex,* and had treated herself to a record player, a huge apparatus that Boris Vian helped her choose. She and Sartre spent one or two evenings a week at the Rue de la Bûcherie listening to jazz and contemporary classical music—Schönberg, Webern, and Bartók. (The records were 78s in those days, and lasted only five minutes.) In November, Beauvoir bought a car. "A woman cannot live without some passion," she wrote to Algren. "As love is forbidden, I decided to give my dirty heart to something not so piggish as a man: and I gave to myself a nice beautiful black car."[9]

an-Paul and his mother,
ane-Marie Sartre (née Schweitzer).
itions Gallimard

Hélène and Simone de Beauvoir with
their mother, Françoise, at Meyrignac.
Sandro Agénor

René Maheu, at eighteen, in Toulouse. *Jean and Isabelle Maheu*

Jean-Paul Sartre, 1939, shortly before war broke out. *Gisèle Freund, Nina Beskow Agency*

Olga Kosakiewicz, 1942–43, rehearsing for *The Flies*. (Studio Harcourt
photo.) *Sylvie Le Bon de Beauvoir*

cques-Laurent
ost, around 1938.
lvie Le Bon de
auvoir

Beauvoir and Bianca Bienenfeld, Lycée
Molière, 1938. *Bianca Bienenfeld Lamblin*

Sartre with Nathalie Sorokine, 1941 or 1942. *Éditions Gallimard*

Simone de Beauvoir in her room at the Hotel Louisiane, 1946.
Les films de l'équinoxe; fonds photographique Denise Bellon

Marie Olivier (Wanda) and Michel Vitold, rehearsing for Sartre's play
The Victors, 1946. *Roger-Viollet*

At the bar of the Pont-Royal, near Gallimard, in 1947. From left: Dolores Vanetti, Jacques-Laurent Bost, Jean Cau, Jean Genet, and Sartre. *Jacques de Poitier, Scoop, Paris Match*

Sartre, Boris Vian, Michelle Vian, and Beauvoir at the Café Procope, around 1948. *Yves Manciet/Rapho*

Simone de Beauvoir, Chicago, 1950. Nelson Algren's friend, Chicago
photographer Art Shay, had driven Beauvoir to a friend of his who had
a bathroom. He writes: "She had taken her bath. It was while she
fussed at the sink afterward that I had the sudden impulse. She knew
I took it, because she heard the click of my trusty wartime Leica
Model F. 'Naughty man,' she said." *Art Shay*

Algren at the railroad yards in Chicago on a rainy day, 1950. *Art Shay*

Sartre at his desk, 42 Rue Bonaparte, overlooking the Place Saint-Germain, around 1950. *Gérard Géry, Scoop, Paris Match*

Beauvoir and Claude Lanzmann, Paris, winter 1952–53. *Collection Particulière/Jazz Editions*

Sartre, Evelyne Rey, and Serge Reggiani at the Théatre de la Renaissance, after a performance of *The Condemned of Altona,* May 1960. *Agence Bernand*

Sartre and Arlette Elkaïm outside the Coupole in Montparnasse, on March 20 1965, two days after her legal adoption by Sartre.
France Soir

Sartre, Beauvoir, and Lena Zonina, arriving at Vilnius Airport, Lithuania, summer 1965. *Antanas Sutkus*

Celebrating Sartre's seventieth birthday at Sylvie Le Bon's, June 1975.
Sylvie Le Bon de Beauvoir

Beauvoir, Sartre, and Sylvie Le Bon, at Tomiko Asabuki's house in
Versailles, 1977. *Sylvie Le Bon de Beauvoir*

Beauvoir at her tiny worktable in the Rue Schoelcher, 1978.
Janine Niepce/Rapho

She found it unbearable to think that her love life had ended. Sartre was ensconced with Michelle. Bost (unbeknownst to Olga) was having a sizzling affair with the writer Marguerite Duras. And all Beauvoir had to dream about, as she lay in her "virgin bed," was her "nice shining car."[10]

At forty-four, she was convinced that she had been "relegated to the land of shades."[11] It felt like an amputation. How could she accept the idea that she would never again lie in a man's arms? She told herself she had to, for the sake of dignity. "I hate the idea of aging women with aged bodies clinging to love."[12]

In *The Second Sex,* she had already described the plight of aging women, in strong language. The tragedy, as she saw it, was that women lost their sexual desirability long before they lost their sexual desire. No sooner had they attained their full erotic development than they were observing the first signs of aging in the mirror. "Long before the eventual mutilation, woman is haunted by the horror of growing old."[13]

In January 1952, Beauvoir's typist, a woman her own age, died of breast cancer. Soon afterward, Beauvoir noticed a lump in one of her own breasts. She panicked. Her doctor said he thought it was nothing, but she should come back in six weeks. By then, in mid-March, the lump was bigger, and she was getting stabs of pain in her right breast. The doctor rolled the lump between his fingers and said she needed to have a biopsy. If it turned out to be a malignant tumor, did she agree to have her breast removed?

I repeated to Sartre, in a strangled voice, what the doctor said. His way of consoling me shows what clouds were lowering on our horizon: if the worst came to the worst, I could count on twelve or so more years of life; twelve years from then the atomic bomb would have disposed of us all.

On the evening before the operation, a nurse shaved her armpit. "In case they have to take everything off," she said. When Beauvoir came to, after surgery, a voice was telling her that all was well. She floated off again, this time "rocked by angels."[14]

•　　•　　•

The cold-war conflict had intensified. The Americans were bombing North Korea and pressuring the French government to continue its war in Indochina. Sartre was convinced that the world's main aggressors were the Americans, and that the Soviets genuinely wanted peace. Moreover, he had come to the conclusion that in France the Communist Party was the only group that truly cared about the workers. In Rome, in May 1952, he heard the news that the French government had brutally repressed a communist demonstration in Paris, and arrested the communist leader Jacques Duclos, on trumped-up charges. Sartre was beside himself with fury. He would refer to this episode as his "conversion" to communism. "When I came back hurriedly to Paris, I had to write or I would suffocate," he said later.[15]

Beauvoir had never seen Sartre sit down at his desk in such a mood of urgency. "In two weeks, he's spent five nights without sleep, and the other nights he only sleeps four or five hours," she wrote to Poupette.[16] At the very time when most Western intellectuals were distancing themselves from Stalinism, Sartre was writing *The Communists and Peace,* a spirited defense of the Communist Party. For the next four years, he became what was known as a "fellow traveler"—someone who sympathized with the Communist Party without being an actual member. As he saw it, workers should join the party to defend their interests, but intellectuals needed to retain their independence.

In the spring of 1952, Beauvoir found herself looking forward more than usual to Sunday afternoons, when the *Temps modernes* people crowded into Sartre's study in the Rue Bonaparte. Eager to make the journal more political, Sartre had invited some young Marxists onto the editorial board—men who, like him, were close to the party but not in it. His secretary, Jean Cau, had suggested his friend Claude Lanzmann. Beauvoir liked Lanzmann immediately, and enjoyed his input at the meetings. "He would say the most extreme things in a completely offhand tone," she writes, "and the way his mind worked reminded me of Sartre. His mock-simple humor greatly enlivened these sessions."[17]

It was not his mind alone that Beauvoir found appealing.

Lanzmann was a handsome twenty-seven-year-old (the same age as Cau), with dark hair and crystal blue eyes. Beauvoir was feeling wistful. When Cau confided in her that Lanzmann thought her beautiful, she thought Cau was joking. After that, she noticed Lanzmann looking at her during meetings.

At the end of July, Bost and Olga gave a party in their apartment, on the floor below Beauvoir's, on the Rue de la Bûcherie. The group was splitting up for the summer. Bost and Jean Cau had been commissioned to co-write a travel guide on Brazil, and were about to fly to Rio. Sartre and Beauvoir were setting off for two months in Italy. Claude Lanzmann was making his first visit to Israel.

They drank a lot of whiskey that evening. Lanzmann gazed drunkenly at Beauvoir. For the first time, she made a point of talking to him. The next morning the phone rang in her apartment. "Can I take you to a movie?" Beauvoir felt a pang of excitement. "Which one?" she asked. Lanzmann's voice was soft: "Whichever one you like."[18]

Beauvoir stalled nervously. She had a lot to do before leaving Paris. Lanzmann pressed her, and she agreed to a drink the following afternoon. To her astonishment, when she put the receiver down, she burst into tears.

They talked the whole afternoon, into the evening, and arranged to meet for dinner the next day. Lanzmann was flirtatious. Beauvoir protested that she was seventeen years older than he. Lanzmann said he did not think of her as old. On the second night he stayed in her apartment on the Rue de la Bûcherie. And the next night as well. When Beauvoir set off for Milan in her little Simca Aronde, Lanzmann waved to her from the footpath. Beauvoir, who was famous in the family for her navigating skills, got lost in the suburbs trying to find the Route Nationale 7. She was glad to have a long drive ahead of her, "to remember and dream."

Two days later, her head was still in the clouds when she picked up two English girls who were hitchhiking. It was raining and the road was slippery, and she had only just commented to them that she must be very careful when the car skidded off the road, tearing a milestone out of its socket. The milestone saved their lives. After Beauvoir dropped the girls at their destination, she stopped at a station for gas, then drove off with her bag on the roof of the car. When she realized that the bag was not on the seat beside her, she stopped the car and ran back along the road in a panic. A cyclist came racing up, holding her bag at arm's length. "I'm losing my head," Beauvoir thought to herself.

Sartre had taken the train to Milan, and they met at the Café della Scala, on the famous square. Sartre had never been in a car alone with her before, and Beauvoir worried that he would be impatient with her clumsiness. He was the other extreme. On the open roads he urged her on recklessly: "Pass him, go on, pass him."[19]

It was an unusually hot summer. Beauvoir wanted to visit museums, art galleries, and churches. All Sartre wanted to do was work. They compromised. In the mornings they went sightseeing, and after lunch they returned to their rooms, which were by then suffocatingly hot. While everyone else was taking a siesta, they threw themselves into their work. Sartre was working with feverish intensity on *The Communists and Peace.* Beauvoir was grappling with *The Mandarins.*

Sartre's closeness to the communists worried Beauvoir at first. Wouldn't it involve major concessions? She and Sartre firmly believed that intellectuals had a responsibility to tell the truth, and that this meant remaining independent. Lanzmann and the other new members of the *Temps modernes* took a different view: they were pleased when Sartre spoke out in favor of the party. Beauvoir writes: "I was put in the position of having to challenge my most spontaneous reactions, in other words, my oldest prejudices."[20]

If Beauvoir was finally persuaded by Sartre's rapprochement with the French Communist Party (the most Stalinist of all the communist parties in Western Europe), other friends were not. Merleau-Ponty, who had once been to the left of Sartre, now accused him of "ultra Bolshevism." They had a row, and Merleau-Ponty, who had given his soul to the journal for years, resigned from *Les Temps modernes.* Beauvoir defended Sartre in an essay called "Merleau-Ponty and Pseudo-Sartrianism."

The talk of Paris that summer was the public altercation between Sartre and Camus. In his book *The Rebel,* Camus denounced Stalinist totalitarianism and covertly attacked Sartre for sympathizing with it.

As Camus saw it, the "rebel" had an independent mind, whereas the "revolutionary" was an authoritarian character who invariably rationalized killing. Camus argued that violence is always unjustifiable, even as a means to an end.

At meetings of *Les Temps modernes* there had been heated discussions over Camus's book. Nobody liked it; which of them would review it? Finally, Francis Jeanson, one of the young Marxists who had recently joined the team, wrote a review that was a great deal more savage than Sartre would have liked. But he ran it without changes.

Camus felt betrayed. He replied with a seventeen-page open letter, addressed not to Jeanson but to "Monsieur le Directeur." Camus was weary of being told by armchair intellectuals how he should think, he said. In his view, by embracing Stalinism, Sartre had signed up for servitude and submission.

Sartre responded with a twenty-page diatribe. "My dear Camus," he began, "our friendship was not easy, but I will miss it":

> Your combination of dreary conceit and vulnerability always discouraged people from telling you unvarnished truths. The result is that you have become the victim of a dismal self-importance, which hides your inner problems. . . . Sooner or later, someone would have told you this. It might just as well be me.[21]

Camus's letter had been restrained; Sartre's was brutal. For Camus, Robert Gallimard recalls, the rupture with Sartre was like the end of a love story.[22] Beauvoir rallied behind Sartre. "Personally, this break in their relations did not affect me," she would write in her memoirs. "The Camus who had been dear to me had ceased to exist a long while before."[23] Neither Sartre nor Beauvoir ever spoke to Camus again.

Claude Lanzmann received five passionate letters from Beauvoir in Italy, before he sat down, in mid-August, to write a lengthy reply. If he had not already been in love with her, he wrote her, then her letters would have made him fall in love. He had been working ridiculously hard for *France Dimanche*. Then he had been about to write to her when his father turned up and insisted they go fishing, to some place just outside Paris. It had been rather boring, and he had not caught anything.

He was relieved that Beauvoir was not scared by the thought of loving a madman. In the autumn, when they met again, he would explain his "madness" to her. He had booked his boat passage and was leaving for Israel at the end of August. Once there, he would try to write to her every evening. When he said he wanted to reread all her books, she had answered that she wanted to please him just as she was. He wanted her to know that he loved her just as she was. He would always love her, even if from now on she wrote only execrable books. But the fact was, he loved her books, too. In one of her letters, she had promised she would love him until her return. That was not very generous of her. He would do everything in his power to extend the season.[24]

Beauvoir writes that when Lanzmann returned to Paris, two weeks after she did, "our bodies met each other again with joy."[25] Lanzmann was broke after his travels, and Beauvoir soon suggested that he move in with her. They would live together for the next seven years.

At first, the excitement of this "new boy" under her roof made Beauvoir lose her famous concentration. "I was a little dizzy the whole month," she told Algren.[26] In the mornings they worked side by side at the Rue de la Bûcherie; in the afternoons Beauvoir worked at Sartre's. Lanzmann took longer than a month to adjust to his new situation. "For a long time I played at working," he says.[27]

He had been fascinated by Israel, and Beauvoir and Sartre encouraged him to write a book that combined reportage with personal memoir. What had it meant to him to grow up as a Jew in a country that was occupied by the Nazis? What were his feelings and observations as he traveled around a struggling new Israel? Lanzmann was excited by the idea.

The Rue de la Bûcherie apartment was small, and with Lanzmann working there as well, there were soon piles of books all over the floor. The only way they could manage was to eat all their meals out, often at La Bûcherie, the café in the square.

• • •

Lanzmann insisted on using *tu* with Beauvoir. He could not possibly be her lover and address her with the formal *vous,* he said. Years later, Beauvoir told an interviewer:

> I've always found it very difficult to address people in the familiar. I don't know why. I did so with my parents and that should have enabled me to do so with other people too. My best friend Zaza always addressed her girlfriends in the familiar, but she used the polite form with me because I did so with her.... I address nearly everybody in the polite form, apart from one or two people who have forced the familiar on me.[28]

Sartre commented on the phenomenon in an interview with John Gerassi:

> Sartre: The Beaver...doesn't like saying "tu."...So even today we say "vous." We have never said "tu" to each other. Not once. It's funny, isn't it?
>
> John Gerassi: It's very funny. It's quite bizarre.
>
> Sartre: Yes, well, it comes from her, because, when I think about it, I've always, with all the women with whom I have had relationships, used the familiar "tu" form of address. Perhaps not on the first day, but I said "tu" to them. It's the normal thing to do. But not with her. Mind you, don't imagine that it creates the least distance. I have never been closer to a woman than the Beaver. But we have never said "tu."[29]

It was particularly amusing on those rare occasions—such as New Year's Eve—when they met as a group. Sartre said "vous" to Bost, Lanzmann, Beauvoir, and Olga, and "tu" to Wanda and Michelle. Beauvoir said "tu" to Lanzmann, and "vous" to everyone else. Bost and Olga said "vous" to each other, unless they were arguing, in which case it was "tu." In his letters to Olga, Bost sometimes changed in mid-sentence: "Je vous aime. Je t'aime."[30]

• • •

Claude Lanzmann was the archetypal "angry young man." Beauvoir and Sartre were soon referring to him, with affectionate mockery, as "the Little Subject." He was stubborn and willful, and at the same time he was prone to adopt the views of those he admired. When he was sad, he wept. When he was enraged, he was capable of fits of vomiting. "Sartre, most of my friends, myself—all of us were puritans; we kept our reactions under control and externalized our emotions very little," Beauvoir writes. "Lanzmann's spontaneity was foreign to me. And yet it was by his excesses that he seemed near to me."[31]

Lanzmann defined himself first and foremost as a Jew. Nothing was more important to him. He felt proud to be Jewish, and outraged by the anti-Semitism to which his people had been subjected over the centuries. "I want to kill, all the time," he told Beauvoir. Sometimes he would wake from a nightmare shouting, "You're all kapos!"

Despite Beauvoir's encouragement, Lanzmann eventually had to abandon his book. "He lacked the necessary perspective to write about himself," she writes. "He began very well, but then came up against obstacles within himself."[32]

Lanzmann no doubt attributed his "madness" to his difficult past. The eldest of three children, he was twelve when his parents separated. The children had witnessed violent domestic scenes. Their mother, Paulette, left for Paris, abandoning the three children to their father, who was then living in Brioude, a little town in the Massif Central. When Claude was fourteen, the war broke out. For long periods during the Occupation, the children did not know whether their mother was alive or dead.

Like their father, Claude and Jacques Lanzmann were both active in the Resistance. After the Liberation, the brothers went to Paris, while Evelyne, their young sister, stayed with their father and stepmother in Brioude. Claude attended the Lycée Louis-le-Grand, where he prepared for the entrance exam to the Ecole Normale, and made friends with his fellow students Jean Cau and Gilles Deleuze. Jacques studied art.

Claude Lanzmann says that it was in Paris, after the war, where he discovered the extent of French complicity with the Jewish genocide. He grappled with strong emotions. How could he stay in France among these people? While in high school in 1943, he had been hugely excited by

Sartre's *Being and Nothingness.* In 1946, Sartre's new book, *Portrait of the Anti-Semite,* marked him even more deeply. This man Sartre, who was not a Jew, appeared to understand Jews from the inside. His essay was also a brilliant analysis and denunciation of anti-Semitism. "It was because of that book that I stayed in France," Lanzmann says today.[33]

On the weekends, Claude and Jacques spent considerable time in the small two-room apartment crammed with antique furniture, rare books, and surrealist art, where their mother Paulette lived with her second husband, the Jewish Yugoslav poet Monny de Boully. Once the young men were inside the door, the generous Boully would press gifts on them. Paulette would push a plate of food in front of them, draw up a chair beside them, and ply them with questions.

Throughout the war, the Boullys had been in hiding—camping in friends' cellars and attics, and constantly changing abodes. They often told the story of their closest scrape with death. One day, in June 1943, they ventured out to have lunch with their close friend Max Jacob, the poet. Passing Gestapo agents took one look at Paulette, who had a pronounced Semitic nose, and arrested them both. After a long interrogation, two officers took Boully away to examine his penis. In his terror, his penis had shrunk to the size of a peanut and was hidden in skin. He was in fact circumcised, but the officers, who were not medical men, let him go. The Boullys were miraculously saved. Max Jacob was not so fortunate. He died a year later, in Drancy.[34]

On Saturday evenings, the Boullys held a salon in their cluttered apartment in the Rue Alexandre-Cabanel. Painters, writers, and intellectuals, including Cocteau, Aragon, and Paul Eluard, came to drink and talk in that cozy, smoky place. Food remained scarce in the postwar years, but the hospitable Paulette always managed to provide something to eat. Claude and Jacques Lanzmann were nearly always there with their friends. "We were formidably narcissistic young men," Olivier Todd remembers. "We had the view that if you knew someone important, you were important too."[35]

Paulette, who was hugely ambitious for her children, particularly her eldest son, was known by all and sundry as "The Mother." She had a pronounced stutter. According to Serge Rezvani, a young artist friend of Jacques Lanzmann's, this gave her a fascination she knew how to manipulate:

Her eyes, highlighted by a thick black line, seized your gaze and never released it. An immense convulsion shook her and her heavily painted heart-shaped mouth proffered that eternal first syllable, which she almost never got beyond. Monny tried to finish for her, but she kept trying to speak and to capture your attention, she put her hand on your cheek so you could not turn your head. Her intense desire for contact was exhausting. How many times, after talking to The Mother, have I felt my legs as soft as if I'd just run for miles![36]

At the age of sixteen, Jacques and Claude's sister, Evelyne, came to Paris and lived in the maid's room upstairs in the Boully home, under the roof. Claude had visited Brioude with his philosopher friend Gilles Deleuze in tow. Claude idolized Deleuze, and in no time Deleuze had become Evelyne's new god. She moved to Paris to be near him. They were briefly lovers. When he rejected her, she stopped eating and began to waste away. After some months of this, her mother and stepfather gave the handsome young Rezvani some money and implored him to take her out and cheer her up.

In the time-worn Jewish tradition, the Boullys were matchmakers. As Serge Rezvani describes it, he and Evelyne were put under intense pressure. Although they were not in love, they found themselves marrying. Evelyne was eighteen; Rezvani was nineteen.

Claude Lanzmann and his friends were always hatching wild schemes to make money. In her memoirs, Simone de Beauvoir writes with amusement that as a twenty-year-old senior at the Lycée Louis-le-Grand, Claude Lanzmann "rented a cassock and went around knocking on rich people's doors and collecting money."[37] Rezvani writes that Claude took the train to Deauville and stood at the door of a casino, hoping to charm some cash out of inebriated winners, and that he used to joke about marrying some "rich old biddy."[38] Jacques Lanzmann admits that all three Lanzmann children used to steal from Monny de Boully, who was already very generous toward them.[39] Jacques remembers Claude writing to Cocteau pretending he had a lung disease and requesting money for treatment. Cocteau wrote back recommending a doctor and kindly offered to pay the bill. Nothing came of it.[40]

Jean Cau came up with the idea of writing to famous writers and asking to become their secretary. He sent off a dozen or so letters. To the astonishment of his friends, he got a reply, just one. In the spring of 1946, when the new existentialist craze was at its height and Jean-Paul Sartre was as famous as a film star, Jean Cau, at the age of twenty-one, became his secretary.

Lanzmann had to make do with the more modest job of rewriter at the conservative tabloid *France Dimanche*. It paid well and had the virtue of leaving him time for serious writing, but Lanzmann chafed with frustration. He felt he was just marking time.

Jean Cau was in Sartre's employ for six years before he was able to organize a lucky break for Lanzmann, and have him invited onto the editorial board of *Les Temps modernes*. A few weeks later, in a euphoric mood, the two friends had a wager. Which of them would be able to seduce Simone de Beauvoir?

"He won," Jean Cau told Olivier Todd. "So much the better for me."[41]

If the affair with Simone de Beauvoir was begun as an opportunistic bet, those who knew him well agree that Lanzmann was quickly caught up in his own game. His brother, Jacques, and his future wife, Judith Magre, do not have the slightest doubt that Claude loved Simone de Beauvoir. "He may not have been *in love*," says Judith Magre, "I can't say. But I know he *loved* the Beaver. It would always remain a very, very deep attachment."[42]

At the age of twenty-seven, Lanzmann, had entered a new world. Jean-Paul Sartre and Simone de Beauvoir were internationally famous, with a sexy whiff of scandal about them. Whenever they walked into a café or restaurant, people recognized them. "Imagine what it was like for me to meet Sartre after the war, having discovered him during the war," Lanzmann says. "He was a rocket, he dazzled with life and intelligence. . . . He made ideas look easy. He was never abstract."

Lanzmann admits that there were dangers for Sartre's young acolytes. "Sartre's word was like the word of an evangelist. . . . He used to severely demolish people. And that induced a certain laziness of judgment in others. . . . It was enough that Sartre said: 'He's a bastard' or 'he's a dog.' We didn't make the effort to look beyond that."[43]

Lanzmann does not feel that Beauvoir had the same crushing effect. On the contrary, she spectacularly opened up his horizons. She was forty-four, in the prime of life, and full of vitality. With her, he discovered the pleasure of travel, setting off in a car with maps and guidebooks, and exploring new places. He was astounded by her appetite for the world. He had never seen anyone work as hard as she did, and had never known anyone with such a capacity for happiness. When she said she would do something, she did it. "She was the most reliable person you could possibly imagine."

Beauvoir loved him deeply—Lanzmann calls her *"une grande amoureuse"*—and yet she never curtailed his liberty. From the beginning, Beauvoir insisted that he go out with other women as well, and he did. "You could tell her everything," he says. "She almost never made moral judgments. Well, not with those she loved. Her first reaction was to force herself to understand, and to put herself in the shoes of the other person."

It was a shock for Lanzmann to discover Beauvoir's vulnerability. "I saw her sobbing so many times," he remembers. "Suddenly a storm of emotion would come over her. She would almost suffocate with sobbing. It was frightening." He accepts her own explanation, that she could not come to terms with the idea of mortality.

Claude Lanzmann was used to his mother interrogating people. Nevertheless he was astounded by Beauvoir and Sartre's "tell everything" policy. Beauvoir expected the same of him, and Lanzmann was not always in the mood. Occasionally he would snap at her, "This is impossible!" He preferred things to come out in their own time, he says, maybe a couple of hours later, after a glass of wine or whiskey.[44]

For the Easter vacation in 1953 they went to Saint-Tropez with Sartre and Michelle. Beauvoir and Lanzmann stayed in the Hôtel de l'Aïoli, along with Sartre. Michelle and her two children stayed nearby, in a house on the square. (Boris Vian had leased the house for ten years, and he allowed Michelle to go there with the children.) At night, Michelle was unable to leave the children, and the two men took turns eating with Beauvoir. There were no tourists in the town that week, Lanzmann recalls, and only two restaurants were open, next door to each other on the port:

Simone de Beauvoir has always had a loud voice, and while she dined with Sartre in restaurant X, I was the only customer in restaurant Y. And I heard Beauvoir tell Sartre everything— because they told each other everything, that was the rule. I heard Beauvoir tell Sartre everything she had done with me during the day, where we had been walking, what I had said, which book I had been reading, which book she had been reading.... When I met her again, after dinner, she told me everything that Sartre had said, which I had just heard. And when it was my turn, when I dined with Beauvoir, and Sartre was all alone in his corner, in his restaurant, reading a book or the paper, it was the same thing.

After dinner, the three of them would meet at the Aïoli, for drinks by the wood fire. Just before midnight, Sartre would disappear to phone Michelle and Wanda. Every day, wherever he was, even if he was exhausted, Sartre called his women at around midnight. Lanzmann would sometimes overhear bits of his conversation. "It was more or less the same talk for each one," he recalls. " 'My little darling,' he called them. But the intonation was a bit different in each case."

The women were jealous, says Lanzmann, and Sartre kept them in almost total ignorance of each other. "If one lies, one has to lie well.... One needs accomplices. Simone de Beauvoir was an accomplice. And I sometimes found myself being one too."[45]

Beauvoir was in love again. Lanzmann brought passion back into her life, with all its joys and anxieties. She had not thought a man would desire her again. (She told Algren that she saw Lanzmann as "rather a kind of incestuous son than a lover.... he asks for a motherly tenderness rather than something else."[46]) She had the joy of an intelligent, stimulating, energetic companion. They went to films together, they discussed books, they read each other's work, and they were always venturing out somewhere new—on long trips, weekend trips, and evening outings. "When time was short, we would content ourselves with going out to dine in the countryside near Paris, happy to smell the greenery, to see the lights flowering along the highways, to feel the city's breath as we drove back."[47]

At first, she was anxious. Algren had not been able to love on her terms. Would Lanzmann be able to? She soon realized that Sartre was an additional draw for Lanzmann. She also worried about her relationship with Sartre. Were they drifting apart? "Of course we would always remain intimate friends, but would our destinies, hitherto intertwined, eventually separate?"[48]

Together, she and Sartre negotiated the new waters. She did not want to give up the two months' vacation she had every year with Sartre, but neither did she want to leave Lanzmann for that long. Sartre agreed that Lanzmann could join them for two weeks of that time. And during the five weeks that Sartre was traveling, first with Michelle (three weeks) then with Wanda (two weeks), Beauvoir would go abroad with Lanzmann.

In February 1953, Jacques Lanzmann, the adventurous, red-haired, twenty-six-year-old middle sibling, returned from a two-year sojourn in South America. For two years he had been almost completely out of contact with his family.

From the airport he made his way to his mother's apartment. That's where he heard the astonishing news that Claude was living with Simone de Beauvoir, and that Evelyne, who had divorced Rezvani, was on tour in the provinces, acting in a Chekhov play under the stage name of Evelyne Rey. "Wait until you see her," said Monny.

Jacques scarcely recognized his sister. Never had he seen anyone change so dramatically. As an adolescent, Evelyne had been thin and bony, with thick dark brown bangs, a prominent nose (like her mother), and crystal blue eyes (like her father and brothers). By the time she was married, at eighteen, she had rounded out and become a beautiful strong-faced brunette. Now, at twenty-three, she had transformed herself into a Barbie doll. She had the body of a pinup girl, and she accentuated it with clinging clothes and high heels. Her hair had become platinum blond. And she sported a small turned-up nose. "It was the fashion," says Jacques Lanzmann. "It was horrible."[49]

The problem—even Evelyne seemed to think this—was that her new appearance did not fit her personality. A highly intelligent, politically committed, intense, tormented woman, she had made herself into a sex symbol. As Beauvoir puts it, tactfully: "Evelyne was ... so pretty that people were amazed by her intelligence."[50]

Sartre had heard a great deal about Claude Lanzmann's sexy younger sister. He asked to meet her. Claude Lanzmann arranged a dinner. He remembers saying to Beauvoir, "Here we go. This will surely lead to an affair."[51]

It was the spring of 1953, and *No Exit* was playing at the Théâtre de l'Athénée, with Evelyne in the role of the seductive young narcissist Estelle. The critic from *Le Monde* raved: "We can no longer imagine another Estelle than Evelyne Rey ... the quintessence of the eternal feminine."[52] After the play, the four of them went out to eat. Evelyne was radiant, and Sartre was enchanted.

Beauvoir recalls: "Sartre said to me: 'Do you think that I could perhaps, I don't know, send her some flowers?' ... He wanted to have another affair. I said to him, yes, go for it, you can only try. ... The desire for an affair, that's something he never lost."[53]

In his memoir, *Le Testament amoureux,* Serge Rezvani claims that Claude Lanzmann acted as a "procurer" for his sister. Jacques Lanzmann says, "Yes, Claude regularly served as a 'Madame' for Evelyne."[54] Several people, notably Bianca Bienenfeld and Nelson Algren, have said the same about Beauvoir, meaning that she set Sartre up with her young women friends, knowing exactly what would happen.

Evelyne was yet another of Sartre's fragile young women. She was six when her mother abandoned the family. During her adolescence her brothers were away—at school in Clermont-Ferrand, and then in Paris—and she lived alone with her Jewish father and Catholic step-mother in the countryside near Brioude. Her father thought she might be safer if she converted to Catholicism. But he had not expected her to embrace God with such passion. For a time she

became quite messianic, with dreams of becoming a nun and convert-
ing the blacks in Africa. She would always remain something of a
mystic. Love, for her, meant adoration.

The love affair with Gilles Deleuze had been disastrous. She had
become so thin and weepy after he jilted her that the family genuinely
feared she would die. The marriage with Serge Rezvani had not made
her happy either.[55] Like her siblings, Evelyne was driven by ambition,
while at the same time plagued by feelings of inadequacy. One day
Rezvani had suggested she take up acting. Excited by the idea, she
enrolled for classes with the famous drama teacher René Simon. He
told her that with that Semitic nose of hers she would go precisely
nowhere. "Fix it!" he ordered her imperiously. Rezvani remembers
evening after evening in which Evelyne would stand in front of the
mirror, curse her appearance, and weep.

To his dismay, Evelyne began to turn herself into a New Look
model. She acquired vampish gestures, wore elbow-length black
gloves, and smoked with a long cigarette holder. Rezvani could not
help thinking that rather than actually being one, she was acting the
part of a femme fatale.

The marriage ended in 1950. For several months the two of them
did not see each other. When they met again, at the *Deux Magots,*
Rezvani hardly recognized the smiling woman who came toward him,
with her small, upturned nose. He was horrified. He thought she had
"banalized" her beauty.

In June 1953, Sartre and Beauvoir, accompanied by their lovers, met
up for a few days in Venice. The couples stayed in different hotels.
On Saturday, June 20, Beauvoir and Lanzmann spent the morning
walking on the Lido beach, then took a *vaporetto* back to the Piazza
Roma, where they had arranged to meet Sartre and Michelle for a late
lunch. As they disembarked, they caught sight of a newspaper with
the large headline: I ROSENBERG SONO STATI ASSASSINATI. The
worldwide demonstrations and nine appeals to the U.S. Supreme
court had not saved Ethel and Julius Rosenberg. The previous
evening, just before sundown (the start of the Sabbath), the two,

accused without evidence of transmitting the secret of the A-bomb to the Soviets, had been strapped into the electric chair and put to death.

Sartre's face, when they saw him, was rigid. Lunch was canceled. Sartre went straight back to his hotel and phoned the Parisian paper *Libération,* promising them an article by midnight.[56] The four met up that evening at ten P.M., in the Café Florian, in Piazza San Marco. Sartre handed his article to Beauvoir and Lanzmann. They read it and both had the same reaction. It was no good. In his fury, Sartre was ranting, and had lost his punch.

Sartre sat up all night rewriting the article, and phoned it through to Paris the next morning. The family had rarely seen him so angry and upset. "So much for 'American leadership of the free world,' " he wrote. "Your free world is not ours."[57]

Beauvoir wrote to Nelson Algren the next day, from the room she shared with Lanzmann at the Hotel Luna. Algren had been active on the "Save the Rosenbergs" committee, and she was sure he would feel as she did. "Even right wing people agree on one point: this is the biggest mistake made by USA in the Cold War," she wrote.[58] She had been profoundly moved by the letters Ethel and Julius Rosenberg had written each other from their prison cells. Gallimard had published them in translation, she told Algren, and the proceeds were going to the Rosenbergs' two young sons.

Algren wrote back in July. He was in one of his bitter moods. The Rosenbergs died for a lie, he said. The Soviet Union was no workers' democracy, and only second-rate people believed it was. He had not been moved by the Rosenbergs' letters from prison. Nor by the television coverage. He still kept seeing that "little fat fool of a woman in a shapeless green dressing gown walking up to that electric chair." He had read Sartre's comments in a newspaper, and he thought Sartre was wrong. The United States was not yet a fascist country, even though executing the Rosenbergs was a fascist act. He still believed there was more hope in the United States than in the USSR. Sartre should not disown the United States too soon.[59]

She was interested in what he had to say about the Rosenbergs, Beauvoir replied. It was true that in the Soviet Union the former Stalinist leader Beria had just been arrested for spying. A strange business. She supposed Algren was right: it was difficult to have much confidence in the Soviet Union.

Beauvoir was conciliatory with the men she loved.

From Venice, Beauvoir and Lanzmann drove to Trieste, where they discovered, to their surprise, that it was not difficult to obtain visas for Tito's Yugoslavia. "We're fantastically excited," Beauvoir wrote to Sartre.[60] They stacked the car with provisions and spare oil, and ventured into communist territory. Lanzmann had already been to East Germany, but this was Beauvoir's first experience of life behind the iron curtain. They found Yugoslavia poverty-stricken, but they were impressed by the atmosphere of solidarity among the people.

Beauvoir then spent several weeks in Amsterdam with Sartre and was looking forward to meeting Lanzmann in Basel when she heard the news that he had had a car accident and was in a hospital in Cahors, in the southwest of France. She set off in the car immediately. Sartre took the train to Paris. He was going to join them in a week.

A few days later, Beauvoir wrote to Sartre from Cahors. Lanzmann had been in severe pain, but he was getting better and was back on his feet:

> It's bright sunshine and I'm in a dentist's waiting room with no paper, which explains why I'm writing on these scraps. In an hour's time it will be midday, my tooth will be fixed and the car too, and we'll leave Cahors. We'll drive gently round the region until Wednesday.
>
> Here I am again. I have my tooth and am just leaving. Listen, I'd like to show you the Lascaux caves. So, instead of coming to Cahors, get out at Brive. The train leaves at 8.50 and arrives at 14.39. I'll be at the station to meet the first and second trains— or at the Poste Restante, if so instructed. We could also arrange to meet at the Truffe Noire hotel, 21 Bld Anatole-France, and you can also wire me there on Wednesday.

She closed with careful instructions. While Sartre was in Paris, would he please transfer his Italian royalties to his French bank account, ring the secretary at *Les Temps modernes,* and call at the Rue de la Bûcherie apartment to pick up mail, a work folder, shirts, socks, and underpants for Lanzmann? "Till Wednesday, o little yourself. A big hug and lots of kisses. Your charming Beaver."

Later that week, the three of them spent a morning looking around the Gothic cathedral in Albi, northeast of Toulouse. After lunch, Lanzmann and Beauvoir explored the town while Sartre spent the afternoon sitting in the hotel garden, under an arbor, writing an immensely long letter to Evelyne Lanzmann. He read it to them that evening. "It was a magnificent letter," Claude Lanzmann recalls, "a very *literary* letter. An account of his day and Albi's red cathedral. He spoke about himself, about her. He said he wished she were there."[61]

Sartre had begun a tempestuous affair with Evelyne. A replay of the quasi-incestuous tangles between Beauvoir, Bost, and the Kosakiewicz sisters? Sartre's secretary, Jean Cau, joked that if Sartre and Beauvoir had a daughter, Jacques Lanzmann would be sleeping with *her.*

In his autobiographical narrative *Words,* which he drafted the following year, Sartre comments on his incest fantasy:

> As a brother, I would have been incestuous. I used to dream about it. Origin? A cover-up for forbidden emotions? It may well be. I had an older sister, my mother, and I wanted a younger one. . . . I made the serious mistake of often looking among women for this sister who had never turned up. . . . Echoes of this fantasy can be found in my writings. . . . What attracted me in this family link was not so much the temptation to love as the prohibition against making love; I liked incest, with its mixture of fire and ice, enjoyment and frustration, so long as it remained platonic.[62]

There was nothing platonic about this relationship. "Evelyne was one of the women Sartre was most attached to," Beauvoir would tell

John Gerassi in 1973. "He was extremely jealous. . . . When he did not get letters, he was very moody, . . . he became very dark."

"With Evelyne, I saw him anguished like an adolescent," Claude Lanzmann says of Sartre. "When he hadn't heard from her one day, he got up at least ten times from the table to phone."[63]

Evelyne was a tall woman, like Sartre's mother. Sartre admitted to Beauvoir that this made him self-conscious in public. "I thought other people looked upon me as a figure of fun, being the lover of such a tall girl. . . . But sensually I liked it very much."[64]

Evelyne was aware that she was not the only woman in Sartre's life, but he assured her that he was no longer sleeping with any of them. He insisted, nevertheless, that Michelle Vian must not hear of their affair. She was very jealous, he said, and he did not want to hurt her.

Evelyne would have liked to proclaim to the world Sartre's love for her. It was hurtful that she could not go out with him publicly, travel on vacation with him, or talk about their affair except to close friends. Over time, she would come to resent this.

For her part, Michelle had no idea about Evelyne. To be sure, Sartre was intensely preoccupied with his work, but he still made love to her, and his letters were as passionate as ever. "I kiss you everywhere," he wrote to Michelle. "I adore you, my sweetheart, I miss you."[65]

Thirty years later, a Sartre scholar interviewed Michelle Vian at length. When he unwittingly mentioned Sartre's affair with Evelyne, presuming she knew about it, Michelle could not believe her ears.[66]

Evelyne—along with Wanda and Michelle—became another of Sartre's "mistresses." He kept her handsomely. When they first met, Evelyne was living in a hotel in Montmartre. Sartre installed her in a two-bedroom apartment at 26 Rue Jacob, five minutes from where he lived with his mother, on the Rue Bonaparte.

Jacques Lanzmann, who was broke after his travels in South America, moved in with his sister. "I have always lived above my means," he writes in his memoirs. "Luckily, Sartre was there to mop up Evelyne's financial messes. And luckily, Evelyne was there to mop up mine."[67] Evelyne and Claude both handed Jacques money, indirectly from Sartre and Beauvoir. Sometimes the gift was more direct.

When Jacques's girlfriend went to Switzerland for an abortion, it was Sartre who paid.

Jacques Lanzmann was writing a book about his experiences in South America. Beauvoir recognized that he had considerable talent, and helped in every way she could. She handed him money regularly, and published an extract from his book in *Les Temps modernes*. When he finished the book, it was she who edited the manuscript, with her usual care and skill. *Le Rat d'Amérique*, published in 1955, was nominated for the Prix Goncourt.

Meanwhile, Sartre had written a fourth play for Wanda: *Kean*, adapted from a melodrama by Alexandre Dumas. It was a resounding success.[68] Sartre promised Evelyne he would write a play for *her*, too.

Beauvoir was seriously worried about Sartre. He had been working far too hard all year and was suffering from high blood pressure. His doctor prescribed a long rest in the country, but Sartre ignored him and went on working at his usual frenetic pace. He took no exercise. He occasionally went on diets. ("Most of my life I've tried to lose weight so as to give the impression of a thin little man instead of a fat little man," he said. "Besides, fatness was something I thought of as surrender and contingency."[69]) But Sartre enjoyed eating. His favorite food was the rich Alsatian cuisine his mother had cooked in his childhood—cabbage, pork, and all kinds of sausages filled with fat. He hated vegetables and fruit. He loved cakes, chocolate, and sugar-drenched desserts. And he never touched lobsters, oysters, or any kind of shellfish.

The worst was the corydrane. He had started crunching as many as twenty tablets a day. Beauvoir and Lanzmann kept telling him, "You're mad. You're killing yourself." Sartre would say he did not care; he wanted to switch on the sun in his head.[70]

At the end of May 1954, he left for three weeks in the USSR. It was his first trip there; he'd been invited by the Soviet Writers Union. Before he left, he stayed up for several nights, writing a preface to a book of Cartier-Bresson's photographs of China. On the way, he stopped in Berlin to participate in a Peace Movement meeting. He wrote his speech on the plane.

In the USSR he gave talks, attended meetings, met official groups, and spoke on the radio. He was whirled around on sightseeing tours across the country. There were endless official receptions and banquets, with a staggeringly heavy consumption of vodka. Always the little tough guy, Sartre was determined to keep up with his large Slavic hosts. At the end of yet another meal in which he had already drunk too much, the writer Simonov presented him with a drinking horn full of wine. "Empty or full, you shall take it with you," he challenged Sartre.

"No letter from you," Beauvoir wrote to Sartre at the beginning of June. The French newspapers sported photos of him in Red Square and on the banks of the Moskowa. Beauvoir had been reading books about the USSR, but she would have preferred a letter. ("L's waiting avidly for one, because of the stamp—I promised to make him a present of it.") Evelyne, who had been in the hospital, had received Sartre's flowers but was "suffering acutely from the lack of letters," and Beauvoir had done her best to console her. She had also given Wanda her money and made arrangements for Michelle to get hers. "I had your mother on the phone this morning... she seemed in good form. Your whole little world is doing fine in fact.... I kiss you with all my soul, my dear, sweet little beloved."[71]

After a short visit to London, Beauvoir and Lanzmann returned to the Rue de la Bûcherie to find an urgent note from Bost under their door: "Come and see me at once." They rushed downstairs, to Bost and Olga's apartment. Sartre's secretary, Jean Cau, had phoned Bost to say that Sartre was in a hospital in Moscow, with high blood pressure. Beauvoir panicked. The whole group went to see Jean Cau, who assured them that it was nothing serious. But Beauvoir remained uneasy. They decided to go to the Soviet embassy and ask the cultural attaché to phone Moscow.

At the embassy, they were told they could phone the USSR themselves. All they had to do was to pick up the receiver and ask for Moscow. Beauvoir writes:

The image of the Iron Curtain was still so firmly fixed in our minds at the time that we had some difficulty believing them. We went back to the Rue de la Bûcherie, I asked for Moscow, for the hospital, for Sartre. At the end of three minutes, I was stupefied to hear his voice. "How are you?" I asked anxiously. "I'm very well, thank you," he answered in polite tones. "How can you be well if you're in the hospital?" "How do you know I'm in the hospital?" He seemed mystified. I explained. He admitted that he'd had a sudden attack of high blood pressure, but it was over and he was returning to Paris.[72]

Sartre spent ten days in the hospital in all, and returned to Paris exhausted. For months afterward he was depressed, with no energy, and close to a nervous breakdown.

Years later, he would claim that he was too sick to think clearly when he insisted in an article in *Libération* that there was complete freedom of expression in the USSR. The statement was so palpably false that even Ilya Ehrenburg, the Soviet writer who had been responsible for Sartre's invitation to Moscow, rebuked him for his rosy reporting.

In *The Mandarins,* Anne Dubreuilh, musing about her husband, the Sartre-like Robert Dubreuilh, finds herself thinking the unthinkable:

"There was a time when he would have spoken out," I said to myself. There was a time when he was completely forthright, would let neither Russia nor the Communist Party get away with anything.

In 1975, Sartre would admit that he had lied after his first visit to the USSR:

Actually, "lied" might be too strong a word: I wrote an article— which Cau finished because I was ill—where I said a number of friendly things about the USSR which I did not believe. I did it partly because I considered that it is not polite to pour shit on your hosts as soon as you are back home, and partly because I didn't really know where I stood in relation to both the USSR and my own ideas.[73]

Until the Soviet invasion of Hungary in 1956, Sartre never criticized the USSR in public statements.

Sartre went to Rome, with Michelle, to convalesce. He slept a great deal. To Beauvoir he wrote that he did not seem capable of rubbing two ideas together. At the end of August, when they made a trip to Germany and Austria, Beauvoir was shocked by his apathy:

> The first evening, in his hotel room in Strasbourg, he stayed for a long while just sitting in his chair, hands on his knees, back bent, eyes blank. We had dinner in a restaurant in La Petite France. "Literature is a lot of horseshit," he told me. . . . Fatigue was making him see everything in the worst possible light; writing was such an effort for him that he could no longer see any meaning in it.[74]

In Rome, Sartre had started work on an autobiography, the book that would become *Words*. If he felt the urge to look back on his childhood, it was to explore what he now saw as his "neurosis." Applying the method he called "existential psychoanalysis" to himself, he showed that he had used his freedom to rebel against his family, who had wanted to confine him in a cotton-wool world of bourgeois illusions. As Sartre saw it, he had rejected religion, but his roots "sucked up its juices," and what he did was to replace one form of blindness with another.

He replaced religion with literature. For almost fifty years, his reality had been words. He had been convinced that writing would bring him salvation and glory. Well, he had changed. In *Words* he described himself as a man who was "waking up, cured of a long, bittersweet madness, who cannot get away from it, who cannot recall his old ways without laughing and who no longer has any idea what to do with his life."

There is no doubt that Sartre's corydrane habit was covering up a chronic depression. It was something no love affair could shake off. Beauvoir was one of the few to understand just how vulnerable he was behind his public façade. Sartre was forever questioning himself and his motives: he was worried about his place in posterity and anguished about the inefficacy of his actions.

With the help of immense doses of corydrane, Sartre managed for the most part to maintain his delusions of grandeur. Throughout the fifties and sixties, he set out, time and again, to write *everything* about a subject. In his book on Genet—and later, Flaubert—he professed to be able to grasp a person in his or her *totality*. For Sartre it was all or nothing. If his writing could not change the world, then it was not worthwhile.

In reality, he had not been cured of his bittersweet madness, and he knew it. Ironically, he was taking unusual pains with *The Words*. The narrative in which Sartre expressed his profound disillusion with literature was to be his most beautifully crafted work. It was the book that would win him the Nobel Prize.

Beauvoir had completely rewritten *The Mandarins*. Never had she worked so hard on a book. She had begun it in 1949, and finished the first draft in 1951. After four years of writing and rewriting, the typed manuscript was huge: twelve hundred pages. Beauvoir was exhausted when she handed it in, in May 1954.

For weeks before its publication, in October 1954, Beauvoir was nervous. She had written about Sartre, Camus, and Koestler with the thinnest of fictional disguises. She had portrayed well-known political feuds. Anne Dubreuilh's affair with the Chicago writer Lewis Brogan was closely based on her affair with Nelson Algren, and Beauvoir had dedicated the book to him. She had never revealed more about her own life, her lost illusions, her vulnerabilities. What were readers going to make of it? She was sure the communists and anticommunists would hate it with equal ferocity.

To her astonishment, the reviews were mostly very positive. The original print run of eleven thousand proved far too small. Forty thousand copies were sold in the first month. Beauvoir learned that the book was a serious contender for France's most respected fiction award, the Prix Goncourt.

Two days before the jury's announcement, a group of journalists positioned themselves in a café on the corner of Beauvoir's street. On Sunday, December 5, she and Lanzmann eluded the whole bunch of them by slipping out a back door and taking a taxi to a friend's apartment. The following morning they listened nervously to the radio. The news came through at midday. Beauvoir was the winner.

She did not go to the Goncourt lunch and thank the judges. Nor did she go to the Gallimard cocktail party and allow the press to take photos. Instead, she and Lanzmann quietly made their way to Michelle Vian's for a celebration lunch with Sartre, Olga, and Bost. Sartre ceremoniously presented her with a book on the Goncourt brothers, the two literary men who had founded the prize in 1903.

Beauvoir posed for a couple of press photos only. She was photographed with her mother, inside Françoise de Beauvoir's apartment, and on the landing outside. It made Beauvoir happy that her mother could for once be proud of her, without reserve. Beauvoir agreed to one interview only, in the communist newspaper *Humanité Dimanche*. She wanted to make the point that the book was not intended to be anticommunist.

Beauvoir was already internationally famous. On both sides of the Atlantic she was well known as the companion of the infamous Jean-Paul Sartre. *The Second Sex* had been published in the United States a couple of years earlier, to great acclaim and none of the sour chauvinism that had greeted the book in France. But now Beauvoir had shown the world that she was not merely a brilliant polemicist. She was also a first-class fiction writer.

"Everybody praises the 'American love story,'" she wrote to Nelson Algren.[75] She hoped he would be granted a passport one of these days, so that he could come and see his friends in Paris. They missed him.

TEN

EXILES AT HOME

August 1955 – February 1962

Beauvoir and Lanzmann were tired of the tiny studio in the Rue de la Bûcherie that leaked every time it rained. The atmosphere in the street had changed since the outbreak of hostilities in Algeria the previous November. There were no more knife brawls. These days, when they looked into the Arab-run Café des Amis, across the road, they saw neatly dressed men in leather jackets sitting in front of glasses of milk. The Arab districts in Paris were now dominated by Islamic militants, who forbade the sale of alcohol.

With her Goncourt prize money, Beauvoir bought an artist's studio in a cream-colored 1920s building on the Rue Schoelcher, a narrow street that skirted the Montparnasse Cemetery. It was in the heart of Montparnasse, a few blocks away from the Dôme and the Coupole, and twenty minutes from Sartre in the Rue Bonaparte, and yet it was quiet. "Nobody on the other side of the street except dead people," she told Algren.[1] She and Lanzmann moved in mid-August of 1955.

The studio was at street level, with a very high ceiling. A spiral staircase in one corner led up to a small bedroom and bathroom. A huge window, facing northwest, filled the space with sun and sky. It was a small, modest place, but by the time Beauvoir installed her writing desk in the corner by the window, bought two yellow divans and two purple armchairs, and arranged her books, paintings, masks, travel souvenirs, and Giacometti lamps, she was convinced she had one of the nicest homes in Paris.

She liked the sense of permanence. As she unpacked her things, she mused that she was living five minutes from the apartment where she was born, and that this was no doubt the place where her friends would come to sort through her affairs after her death.

She loved to watch the evening sky turn pink and golden over the cemetery. And she cherished the moment, at around five in the morning, when she'd linger briefly at the upstairs window, breathing in the dawn and the promise of gathering heat, before going back to bed.

She did not even have time to buy a refrigerator, let alone put ice and whiskey in it, before she and Sartre left for China at the beginning of September. As always, she took with her a vast array of reading material about the country they were visiting. They stayed a month in Peking ("a big quiet peasant town"[2]), then traveled around the country. They were impressed by the victories Mao's communist government had made over malnutrition, epidemics, and infant mortality, and profoundly moved by the way the people worked with their bare hands—no machines—to build houses, schools, and dams.

But the trip was tiring. Never had they been confronted with such a radically foreign culture. Living conditions were Spartan, and conversations were often awkward. Apart from two or three French literature specialists, no one had heard of them.

On their way back, they stopped in Moscow and plunged into a busy week of sightseeing, talks, and interviews. Beauvoir could see why Sartre had ended up in the hospital the year before. Near the end of their stay they were invited to attend a critics' congress:

> Simonov asked Sartre to participate in one of the afternoon sessions; beforehand we would lunch with him and some of his friends from Georgia. "Excellent! But I won't drink," Sartre said. They agreed to that. All the same, there were four bottles of different kinds of vodka on the restaurant table, and ten bottles of wine as well. "Just sample the vodkas," Simonov said, and

went on, inexorably, to fill our glasses four times. . . . My own head was on fire, and I was full of admiration when Sartre managed to get up and talk quite sanely about the role of the critic.[3]

On their last day in Moscow, Sartre was still going strong. Beauvoir, worn out, spent the day in bed reading a novel about the Russian Revolution and reveling in her solitude.

By the fall of 1955, the Algerian War was blazing. Sartre and Beauvoir were sickened by the "great tide of chauvinism and racism" that had flooded the French press since the outbreak of hostilities the previous November.[4] The signs were clear enough that the colonial era was coming to an end. Morocco and Tunisia were about to gain their independence from France. It was time to get out of Algeria, too. But the majority of French people did not see things that way.

The defeat of the French army at Dien Bien Phu in May 1954 had finally made France withdraw from Indochina. But humiliation in Indochina had made the French government even more determined not to give up Algeria.

Les Temps modernes declared its support for Algerian independence, a stance that most of their countrymen bitterly resented. For the next seven years, while the Algerian War became more and more ugly, Sartre and Beauvoir were regularly denounced as "anti-French." In cafés and restaurants, the anti-Arab talk at neighboring tables made them cringe. At the cinema, they had to watch newsreels that celebrated French military operations in Algeria. They felt like exiles in their own country.

Back from China, Sartre wrote a film script, *The Salem Witches,* adapted from Arthur Miller's play *The Crucible,* an allegory about the anticommunist witch hunt in the United States. (The movie would star Yves Montand and Simone Signoret.) And he began a new project, which he had been mulling over for years: on Gustave Flaubert. He had a love-hate relationship with Flaubert, the man and the writer. As an adolescent, Sartre had read and reread *Madame Bovary,* and knew whole passages by heart. He was intrigued by the way Flaubert portrayed somewhat negative characters, with whom one nevertheless sympathized. During the war, Sartre had read Flaubert's correspondence with a similar uneasy fascination. Flaubert's conception of literature, with his endless painful search for *"le mot juste"* and his refusal of any type of political *engagement,* was the exact opposite of Sartre's own. So why Flaubert? "You have to knock heads with what challenges you," Sartre told people.[5] Sartre loved to immerse himself in another person's world, turning it temporarily into his own. It was a form of traveling outside himself.

His aim was to use existentialist, Marxist, and Freudian methods to explain what Sartre called Flaubert's "neurosis." He had written similar studies of Baudelaire and Jean Genet, but over the years Flaubert would become an all-consuming obsession for him. There was a wealth of material on Flaubert (his correspondence alone ran to fifteen thick volumes), and Sartre was convinced that if he studied the evidence carefully enough, he could come to a perfect understanding of the man. He disagreed with the basic tenet of psychoanalysis—that the unconscious makes us ultimately unknowable. "The fundamental project in my 'Flaubert' is to show that at bottom . . . every human being is perfectly capable of being understood if the appropriate methods are used and the necessary documents are available."[6]

Beauvoir had decided to write a book about China. *The Mandarins* had drained her emotionally and spiritually; she did not want to write another novel straight away. Her book on China, *The Long March,* would involve a great deal of research, but hard work had never intimidated her. She saw it as a chance to learn more about China, while at the same time challenging the anticommunist prejudices of her Western readers. A travel book would date fast; she had to write it quickly. That year she worked as much as ten hours a day:

I worked at home in the morning and at Sartre's during the afternoon: sometimes I would sit at my worktable in either place for four hours at a stretch without once lifting my head. Sometimes too Sartre would get quite worried because my face turned red: I felt I was on the verge of an attack of congestion and threw myself on his divan for a few moments.[7]

She did not speak Chinese, she had not been in the country long, and this time she had had no "local youth" to explain things. She was very aware of these limitations, and was pleasantly surprised by the good reviews the book received. Claude Roy, a specialist on China, wrote in *Libération* that he read the book with a pleasure that never subsided. "It's always refreshing and pleasant to travel in the company of an intelligent, sensitive and attentive writer . . . Simone de Beauvoir saw what everyone has seen, but she understood many things that no one has fathomed so well."[8]

The Mandarins came out in the United States in May 1956. The dedication to Nelson Algren left American readers in no doubt as to the real-life model for Lewis Brogan, the Chicago writer depicted in the novel. Algren had not minded Beauvoir's travel book, *America Day by Day,* published in the United States three years before—where he had been easily recognizable as "NA." In fact, he had been rather flattered by it. But this novel showed him, so to speak, in his pajamas.

It did not help that while Beauvoir was flying high with success, Algren was at an all-time low. He had thought he would make his fortune when Hollywood bought the film rights for *The Man with the Golden Arm,* but in the end he had not made a cent out of it, and the movie had been cut so drastically by Hollywood's zealously anticommunist censors that it no longer carried any punch at all. In desperation, Algren had churned out another book, and his publishers rejected it. He had divorced his wife for the second time and gambled away the last vestiges of his money. There was nothing he would have liked to do more than to run away to Paris for a time, but the State Department was not issuing passports to anyone who had ever had an affiliation with the Communist Party. When he was asked to swear that he never had, Algren lied. Then realized, too late, that he could be indicted for perjury.

If *The Mandarins* was receiving a lot of attention in the United States, it was partly due to the American love story. Algren resented this. "A good female novelist ought to have enough to write about without digging up her own private garden," he ranted to a reporter. "For me, it was just a routine relationship, and she's blown it up."[9]

When the comment appeared beside his photograph in *Time* magazine, Algren felt embarrassed about sounding so sour. He tried to make a long-distance call to Paris to explain, but when Lanzmann picked up the phone, Algren hung up and wrote Beauvoir a letter instead. He had not been himself when he barked at the newspaper men, he told her, and had said dismissive things to show off. He had been hurt by the passage where Anne Dubreuilh declared that her love for Brogan was dead.

Beauvoir said she understood, and their friendship survived. Once again, Algren's letters were full of nostalgia for the past. He missed her, he said. He realized he had spent the happiest days of his life with his little French frog. One day, he had gone back to see his old street in Chicago. "It came back to me what a Wabansia miracle had happened there." He kept thinking of moments on their travels, like the evening in Rome when they rode home in a horse and carriage, over the cobbles, in the rain. He was doing too much remembering, he said.

Early one morning, in July 1956, Sartre and Michelle met Beauvoir and Lanzmann at the Coupole. They were about to travel as a foursome to Greece and Yugoslavia. "I gazed, with incredulous gaiety bubbling up inside me, at our shiny cars parked at the kerb," writes Beauvoir, "and pictured them as they would look in ten days, sweeping into Athens covered with dust."[10]

Beauvoir had traded in her Aronde for a larger Ford Versailles. Sartre had bought Michelle a secondhand two-door red Peugeot. Michelle had become a good driver. She often drove her friend André Reweliotty and his jazz musicians from gig to gig late at night.

The four made their way via Venice to Belgrade. For the most part, the two couples kept to their own cars. But since Sartre did not drive, this meant that Michelle had no rest. At one point, when the cars stopped for petrol, Lanzmann suggested a swap. "You must be tired," he said to Michelle. "I'll drive for a bit, if you like." Lanzmann clambered in behind the wheel, and Sartre got into the other car with Beauvoir.

Lanzmann fancied Michelle. In February 1955 they had driven

from Paris to Marseille together, taking turns at the wheel, and afterward he sent her a postcard complaining that "the wretched [*les damnés*] had no other possibilities than to move from the left side to the right."[11] This time, somewhere near Belgrade, he pulled off the road so they could admire the view, and put his arm around Michelle and tried to kiss her. She smiled and pushed him away. She could never quite warm to Lanzmann, she says. She found him insufferably vain and arrogant. And she was well aware of his reputation as a womanizer.

The two couples generally spent their time separately, but met up for either lunch or dinner as a foursome. According to Michelle, the three "intellectuals" were never short of something to say, but she herself said little. Beauvoir was perfectly nice to her and was always singing her praises to the others, but Michelle sensed that Beauvoir did not really like her.

Michelle called her "Beaver." They all did. Nevertheless, for her, Beauvoir was like a mother-in-law—indulgent on the surface, but distant, and intimidating.[12]

Sartre and Beauvoir had acquired a new routine, which they kept up for the rest of their lives: September and October in Rome. After spending five weeks with their other companions, this was *their* time. They took adjoining hotel rooms in the center of the city, and worked. They loved the ancient city, with its old squares and stone fountains. Most of all they loved the beauty of the Roman nights. They avoided the intellectuals' cafés—like Rosati, on the Piazza del Popolo, where people came up and asked for autographs, and journalists for interviews. They usually ate on the Piazza Navona, not far from the Spanish Steps and the Trevi fountain, and lingered in the square till midnight, talking over drinks, with the splash of the fountains in the background. Their Italian friends—writers, artists, film and theater people—were all communist sympathizers, and seeing them in the evenings was part of the pleasure of Rome.

Beauvoir would knock on Sartre's door at eight in the morning, and they would dress and go down to the square to read the newspapers, French and Italian, over breakfast. Sartre would order as many as three double espressos. At ten A.M. they'd return to their rooms to work until two. Lunch was a light meal, no alcohol. They liked to finish up with a gelato, then go for a walk. At five P.M. they were back at their desks for three or four more hours of work.

On October 24, 1956, they walked up to a press kiosk in the Piazza Colonna to buy their morning papers, and read that Soviet tanks had entered Budapest, killing hundreds of Hungarians and wounding thousands. For Sartre, the news was like a body blow. How could the USSR go against its promise of non-intervention? Why taint itself in the eyes of the world with this crime?

That evening they had dinner with communist friends on Via Veneto. A guitarist strummed old Roman songs. Sartre and his artist friend Renato Guttoso were almost weeping into their whiskeys as they went over and over the events, trying to understand what it all meant. Guttoso could not bear the thought of the lonely wilderness he would face if he left the party. And Sartre dreaded breaking the bond he had so carefully built up with the communists over the last few years. He had made so many enemies by standing up for communism, and now he risked losing his few allies. The group was briefly distracted when their actress friend Anna Magnani sat at their table and sang mournful songs, accompanied by the guitarist. Then she disappeared into the night, and they resumed their tortured discussions.

Sartre had a difficult decision to make. Since 1952 he had been the most famous fellow traveler in Europe. In *The Communists and Peace,* he had argued that Soviet foreign policy was defensive, whereas American foreign policy was entirely aggressive, and bent on destroying the Soviet Union. He was heavily invested in the Peace Movement, a worldwide organization whose headquarters were in Moscow. He believed in peace; he believed in socialism; he had wanted so much to believe in the Soviet Union. Furthermore, he knew that if he condemned the USSR, the American propaganda services would have a field day.

He spoke out. "I condemn the Russian aggression completely and unreservedly," he said in an interview in the conservative French magazine *L'Express.* He added that he was breaking "regretfully but completely" with those of his Soviet friends who had failed to denounce, or were unable to denounce, the massacre in Hungary. As for the French Communist Party, who had tried to justify the Soviets' bloody coup, their excuses were "the outcome of thirty years of lying and ossification."

He added that the United States was not innocent either. "America's responsibility in the present events is undeniable. . . . The Marshall Plan, to begin with. Its avowed aim was to prevent the construction of socialism in the 'satellites.' "[13]

Beauvoir joined Sartre in protesting the Soviet aggression. She was pleased that Sartre had taken a strong stand. No one knew better than she did what it cost him.

In the midst of these turbulent weeks, Evelyne Rey broke up with Sartre. They had been lovers for three years. She had found another man: a lawyer who was short, witty, and ugly, and who, all her friends agreed, could almost have been Sartre's brother. At least her affair with him was not clandestine. She was tired of remaining hidden in the background with Sartre. Beauvoir and Michelle Vian had a public role in Sartre's life. Why couldn't she?

Sartre told Evelyne he would never abandon her. He would continue to look after her financially. They would see each other three times a week, and he promised to write a play for her soon.

In the winter of 1956, Beauvoir began the project she had first thought of writing ten years earlier—her childhood memoirs. In 1946, Sartre had suggested that she first explore what it meant to be a woman, and that had led to *The Second Sex*. She had gone to the United States, met Algren, and written about her trip, then struggled for years with *The Mandarins*. She had gone to China and written about that. In those ten years, she had become the most famous woman writer in the world. Now she would write her memoirs from a very different vantage point. She would look back on her life as a dramatic success story. Above all, she was far more confident about her relationship with Sartre than she had been in 1946.

In 1946, Sartre's passion for Vanetti had Beauvoir worried that she was about to be replaced. Since then, she and Sartre had gone their own ways more than ever, and yet they had survived. Indeed, they had invented their coupledom anew. She could look back at their life together with a gratifying sense of achievement.

Memoirs of a Dutiful Daughter would take her eighteen months. Beauvoir had never enjoyed writing more. She discussed their childhood with her sister Poupette and mulled over memories with friends. She read through old diaries and went to the Bibliothèque Nationale to consult newspapers from the period. She reread the books that had influenced her as a young girl.

There were many discussions with Sartre. What did he think? Did she dare talk openly about her parents? The tensions in her family? Her father was dead, but her mother would be hurt. Could she write frankly about Zaza, her conflict with her mother, her romance with Merleau-Ponty, Zaza's death? They agreed that in some cases she should use pseudonyms. Merleau-Ponty became "Jean Pradelle." René Maheu became "André Herbaud." Even so, the men would recognize themselves instantly, of course. And so would everyone who knew them. The project was fraught with difficulties.

Beauvoir began the narrative with her birth in January 1908, and ended it in 1929, the year she met Sartre, the year Zaza died, the year that had changed her life.

Shortly before he left on his summer vacation in 1956, Sartre received a letter from a nineteen-year-old French Algerian girl. Arlette Elkaïm was a philosophy student who was hoping to get into the Ecole Normale Supérieure for women in Sèvres, near Versailles. She told Sartre she had read *Nausea* and *Being and Nothingness* and was interested in phenomenology. She was writing a dissertation on injustice. Could she possibly come and discuss it with him?

Sartre asked for a copy of her dissertation. After they corresponded for a few weeks, it became obvious to him that the girl was seeking help beyond her studies. They met in November, when Sartre was back from Rome.

Elkaïm was originally from Constantine, in Algeria. She had arrived in France in September 1954, two months before the Algerian War broke out. Her mother was an Arab: her father was a Sephardic Jew, a

French government functionary who identified with the French colonizers. Elkaïm felt both Algerian and French, she was not at all sure how she felt about the Algerian Arabs demanding their independence.

When Elkaïm was fourteen, her mother had committed suicide. Elkaïm partly blamed her father. He was authoritarian, she told Sartre, and tyrannical. Elkaïm really did not know what she was doing in France, except that she wanted to get away from her father and stepmother. She didn't have any friends, and didn't know what she wanted to do with her life.

Sartre slotted her into his schedule on Sundays, for two hours in the afternoon. "I had a lot of personal problems at the time, and if he hadn't been there, I don't know how things would have turned out," Elkaïm recalls. "I lived off that meeting for the rest of the week."[14]

They sat opposite each other in Sartre's study—she in the leather armchair, he on his hard-backed upright (a Schweitzer family heirloom)—and Sartre asked probing questions. He treated it like a psychoanalytical session, except that he played an active role himself, and made comments and observations. When she was silent, he waited. He let her cry when she needed to. At the end of the session he told her he cared a great deal about her, and they would continue their conversation the following week.

"He did it with gaiety and perseverance, sometimes with a bit of violence," Elkaïm says. "He shook me up, tried to get me to look at the world, and even enjoy it. Today I realize I had a belated education from him—even if I had to struggle sometimes not to see the world with his eyes."[15]

They were briefly lovers, but Sartre ended that aspect of their relationship after two or three months. The soft-eyed Elkaïm made him think of a doe. She brought out fatherly feelings in him rather than anything else.

In July 1957, Elkaïm failed her exams, and decided not to sit them again. Sartre thought she might have some talent for journalism and sent her to see a friend of his at the *Nouvel Observateur*. Nothing came of it. "I was like a little mouse," Elkaïm says. "I couldn't take myself seriously. I despised myself all the more because I had things to say, but couldn't say them."[16] She became financially dependent on Sartre.

Looking back later, after she had become his legally adopted daughter, Elkaïm thought she had probably asked too much of Sartre in those early years. She was hopelessly passive, she said. Sartre was busy with his own work, and always in a hurry. He was fatherly and caring, but not quite fatherly enough to realize that she needed to move out from his orbit. She only ever saw him by himself. He never introduced her to the members of the family. She saw him at fixed times: there was no spontaneity in their meetings whatsoever. What did she expect from him? She really did not know.

It was impossible for Jean Cau, Sartre's secretary, not to be aware of the lies Sartre told his women. Sartre would phone two girlfriends in a row, telling the second a quite different story from the first. Cau recalls an occasion when Sartre put down the phone and sighed:

> "It's difficult, sometimes."
> "Sure is," I say. "I wonder how you manage. Tough situation."
> "That's the word exactly, Cau. There are situations which I call *rotten*. Try as one might to resolve them, it's impossible to get out of them externally intact."
> "Yes, yes. I see. But what about internally? How do you manage that?"
> "In some cases, you're obliged to resort to a temporary moral code."

Cau was impressed by this notion of a temporary morality. It was like opening an umbrella in a storm, he thought to himself. The dilemma for the Sartrean subject, Cau mused, is that he is not alone in the world, and he does not create *the situation* (an important Sartrean concept) that is rotten. Of course he is *free* to confront it in this or that way, but the *Other* sticks to him and bogs him down. What do you do if you are Sartre and you find yourself persecuted by the Other? You resort to a temporary moral code! That way, you wriggle out of the situation, and the huge moral edifice you have constructed remains intact.[17]

Cau and Sartre fell out in the summer of 1957, and they parted ways. Cau, a "prolo-made-good," who had always had a conservative edge to him, had become an outright political reactionary.

But as a secretary, Cau had made himself indispensable. These days the demands made on Sartre were overwhelming. Every day he received dozens of letters soliciting his help. Would he give money, write an article, be on a committee to help militants, political prisoners, or refugees? Would he write a preface for a friend's book, sign a manifesto, attend a meeting, speak at a reunion, read a manuscript?

Sartre replaced Cau with another young man: Claude Faux, a lawyer, who was close to the communists. In 1961, Faux would marry Gisèle Halimi, a radical lawyer, who was receiving death threats for her defense of FLN *(Front de Libération Nationale)* militants. She became Sartre's personal lawyer, fighting cases of copyright infringement and piracy for him. Sartre himself never cared about these things, Halimi writes in her memoirs. They infuriated *her,* but he saw them as trifles. All he wanted was time, time to get on with his work.[18]

Looking back, Beauvoir called 1958 "that excruciating year."[19] It was a crisis year, both for her and for Sartre.

In January, Beauvoir turned fifty, which she hated. She and Lanzmann went skiing for two weeks, but he was busy writing an article for *Les Temps modernes,* and rarely ventured out onto the slopes. She skied alone. Impatient with her lack of progress in the sport, she told herself it was her age.

The Algerian War had intensified. Paris, full of men swaggering around in French military uniforms, felt once again like an occupied city. It was impossible not to notice the police harassment of Arabs in the streets. *Les Temps modernes* published reports of barbaric torture perpetrated by the French military on Arab resistance fighters.

Sartre seemed almost crazed by his political rage. He was working with a kind of desperation, buoyed up by vast quantities of corydrane, scarcely bothering to reread what he had written, and never taking the time to cut or trim. By the end of the day he was so speedy that he was mixing up his words, and when he drank, the alcohol went straight to his head. On those evenings when they were together in her apartment. Beauvoir tried in vain to restrain him:

> "That's enough," I'd say to him; but for him it was not enough; against my will I would hand him a second glass; then he'd ask for a third; two years before he'd have needed a great deal more; but now he lost control of his movements and his speech very quickly, and I would say again: "That's enough." Two or three times I flew into violent tempers. I smashed a glass on the tiled floor of the kitchen. But I found it too exhausting to quarrel with him. And I knew he needed something to help him relax, in other words something to destroy himself a little.[20]

In his frenzy to produce, Sartre was continually putting things aside to work on something else. He had shelved Flaubert, he had shelved his autobiography, *Words,* and he had abandoned his book on Italy. His book-length essay *Search for a Method* situated existentialism in relation to Marxism. As soon as he had finished that, he began a much longer and densely complex essay, *Critique of Dialectical Reason.* Sartre now argued that individuals had very little power in modern society: they could only regain their freedom by means of group revolutionary action.

In the spring of 1958 he put aside the *Critique* to write a play. Wanda was out of work again. Evelyne, ever since he had known her, had been begging him to write a part for her. Sartre wanted to write about a French soldier who had been in Algeria and had colluded with torture, then returns home as a hero, to face his family and their questions. Since he knew the censors would never allow him to write about the Algerian War, Sartre decided to set the play in postwar Germany, and make his protagonist a Nazi. He promised Simone Berriau, director of the Théâtre Antoine, that it would be ready in time for the 1958 fall season.

The growing crisis in Algeria was threatening to spill over into France, which was on the edge of civil war. The president of the Fourth Republic called upon the wartime Resistance hero General de Gaulle to come out of retirement to deal with the crisis. De Gaulle was made prime minister on June 1. He ordered the drafting of a new constitution, which would give him far-reaching powers when he became president the following year. It was to be put to the people's vote in a public referendum on September 28.

Sartre and Beauvoir went down to Italy in mid-June, earlier than usual, convinced that De Gaulle was about to rule France as a dictator. It was stiflingly hot in Rome. Sartre poured his anger and disillusionment into his play *The Condemned of Altona,* about the use of torture by the military. But his fury got in the way of the drama. When Beauvoir read a draft, she was appalled.

She was trying to write the second volume of her memoirs, but was not in the mood. For the first time in six years she was not spending the summer with Lanzmann. He was traveling in China and North Korea with a team of journalists. She could sense that he was drifting away from her. Her journal entries during those weeks in Rome were filled with anxiety. "Sartre is working on his play: and I'm trying to interest myself in my past.... I've got to kill time somehow.... Didn't sleep much.... I'm so tense I've been taking sarpagan.... After the tension, depression.... I'm too down to write.... I slept badly and woke up with my nerves in knots.... I am always seized by panic just before I wake up.... Tonight, once more, life sinks its teeth into my heart."[21]

Memoirs of a Dutiful Daughter were going to be published in October, and Beauvoir was nervous. "I do feel uneasy—almost remorseful—when I think of all the people I've brought into it and who'll be furious."[22] The volume she was currently writing was even more delicate. How much could she say about her relationship with Sartre? She could not talk about her nine-year affair with Bost, because of Olga. Could she write about the trio with Olga? She had no desire to discuss Sartre's wartime relationship with Wanda. "Why are there some things I want so much to say," she asked herself, "and others I want to bury?"[23]

In mid-August, Michelle arrived in Rome to spend a month with Sartre. Beauvoir returned to Paris alone, to an empty apartment.

All summer, Sartre had been upset by the lack of letters from Michelle Vian. He had written to his "darling little carp" (from the French expression "as mute as a carp") and protested that he had

experienced too many "hellish silences" that year. "Ring me. Pick up
the phone," he implored Michelle. He added in English: "Have a
heart."[24]

Michelle Vian says today that she, too, was having a personal crisis
that summer. For almost ten years, she had divided her life between
two men. Neither of them knew that she slept with the other. It was
tearing her apart, making her ill. She arrived in Rome desperately
needing attention. Sartre was obsessed by his play. Michelle cried a
lot, knowing there was nothing Sartre hated more than tears. She
talked of killing herself. Sartre was cold.

"I felt I had no future," says Michelle, "and I blamed André
Reweliotty and Sartre. André was so temperamental, melodramatic,
and Russian—always shouting at his fellow musicians and banging his
fists against the wall. And Sartre was so indifferent. I knew he didn't
want to be with me anymore. I knew he didn't need me. That whole
summer in Rome, he said he didn't have time to go to lunch. He
didn't want to go to museums. He told me to go out by myself. All he
wanted to do was work."[25]

Behind Sartre's back, Michelle wrote dramatic letters to Reweliotty,
telling him she was contemplating suicide. One day, she and Sartre were
in their hotel room—Sartre was cleaning his teeth—when there was a
knock at the door. Michelle said: "Come in!" And there stood André
Reweliotty. He had been on tour in Venice, playing with his friend
Sidney Bechet, the New Orleans jazz clarinetist. When he got Michelle's
last letter, Reweliotty had hurried to Rome to see her.

That afternoon, Sartre discovered the truth. For the last nine
years—indeed, from the beginning of their relationship—Michelle
had been unfaithful to him. That evening, Michelle disappeared with
Reweliotty.[26]

Sartre was left by himself in Rome, feeling distraught. He had not
been faithful himself over the years, but that did not stop him from
being morally enraged by Michelle's lies. He knew, of course, that she
and Reweliotty had been lovers before he came along. He also knew
that Michelle spent a lot of time with Reweliotty at his country
house, and that when Reweliotty and his band played in provincial
towns, Michelle signed the contracts, arranged their itineraries,
booked the hotels, and did the night-time driving when the musi-

cians were tired. But he had always believed Michelle when she said that she and Reweliotty were simply friends. He had never thought—he had not allowed himself to envisage the hypothesis—that they had continued to be lovers.

Evelyne had often told him to wake up. But Evelyne had every reason to dislike Michelle, and so Sartre had never attached much importance to Evelyne's suspicions. It is true that even Bost had conjectured that Michelle probably slept with Reweliotty. But Sartre would not hear of it. To him, Michelle was the embodiment of innocence.

Sartre remained in Rome a few more days, struggling to write an article—the second of a series of three—that he had promised to *L'Express* about De Gaulle and the forthcoming referendum. He had called the first "The Pretender." He called this one "The Constitution of Contempt." And then, on the evening of September 14, he caught the night train back to Paris.

Beauvoir was at the Gare de Lyon early the next morning to meet him. It was raining. Sartre was emotionally exhausted, and so was she. They spent the day talking.

Sartre was about to start work on his third article for *L'Express,* but he had developed a liver infection. "He was so worn out, so feverish and weak-headed on Sunday afternoon that it looked as though it would be impossible for him to write it," Beauvoir wrote in her journal. "He worked for twenty-eight hours at a stretch, without sleep and almost without a break."[27]

Sartre collapsed, and Beauvoir spent a whole evening editing his piece. She could hardly read his handwriting, and his spelling was appalling. She had to rewrite bits and make judicious cuts and links. "An ungrateful task, and pretty tiring when it's got to be done fast," she observed. Eventually she thought the article "very good indeed." Sartre called it "The Frogs Who Wanted a King."

Lanzmann was back from Korea but absorbed in an article on China, and busy with the "no" campaign for the forthcoming referendum.[28] Beauvoir hardly saw him. "I don't know if it's exhaustion or irritation," she noted in her journal, "but my constant state of tension, which I feel especially in the back of the neck, the eyes, the ears, the temples, makes work difficult."[29]

In the referendum on September 28, the vote was a resounding "yes." Beauvoir wept. "It's a sinister defeat . . . a repudiation by eighty per cent of the French people of all that we had believed in and wanted for France. . . . It's rather dreadful to be against a whole country, your own country."[30]

Sartre was viscerally affected. He had vertigo, he had difficulty walking, and he stumbled over his words. But he refused to see a doctor. He had a play to write, he said. The deadline had passed. In early October, at lunch with Simone Berriau, the director of the Théâtre Antoine where the play was to be performed, Sartre carefully put his glass down an inch from the table. The glass fell and shattered. Simone Berriau was shocked. She finally managed to persuade Sartre to let her make an appointment with a doctor. Beauvoir was grateful to her.

The doctor said that Sartre's left ventricle was tired, and that he needed a good rest. Sartre went on working. Behind his back, Beauvoir went to see the doctor, who told her that Sartre had narrowly missed having a heart attack. "He is a very emotional man. He has overworked himself intellectually, but even more so emotionally. . . . Let him work a bit if he insists, but he mustn't try racing against the clock. If he does, I don't give him six months."[31]

Beauvoir then went to see Simone Berriau, who agreed to put off *The Condemned of Altona* for a year, till the following fall. Sartre did not even have the energy to be angry about Beauvoir's interference. He greeted her news with an indifferent smile. But from that day on, he worked more slowly.

At first, Lanzmann tried to hide his new affair from Beauvoir. But she knew. One night, he returned at midnight to the Rue Schoelcher and found her sitting on her bed crying. "Tell me the truth," she said.

He told her. He had fallen in love. The other woman was thirty-five, beautiful, rich, aristocratic. She had two children, her husband had died in a plane accident, and she lived in a sumptuous apartment on the Quai aux Fleurs, overlooking the Seine.

"The Beaver was immediately, as always, constructive and under-standing," Lanzmann recalls. "Her idea was, 'Ok, we'll share you.' Three days with one, three days with the other. But it didn't work. Most women can't do that. They want to conquer and destroy."[32]

The affair ended after six months, when Lanzmann discovered that his new love had lied to him about her age. (She was actually forty-five.) After that, Lanzmann and Beauvoir began to reconstruct their relationship, transforming it into a friendship. In the summer of 1959, they spent ten days together in Menton, on the Côte d' Azur. Both were relieved to be able to maintain a close bond.

The Condemned of Altona, Sartre's ninth play, opened on September 23, 1959—a year later than planned. There had been the usual traumatic scenes during rehearsals. The play was once again too long, and as usual, Sartre hated to make cuts. The lead parts were demanding, and the pro-ducer did not consider Evelyne and Wanda up to it, but Sartre insisted. Wanda had at least had a chance to prove herself in the past, but Evelyne was just twenty-nine, and this was her first major part. Everyone in the theater world knew she had been Sartre's mistress and that she owed the role to him. The pressure on her was intense.

The Nazi soldier, stiff and unbending in his SS uniform, was bril-liantly acted by the Italian-born actor Serge Reggiani. He was praised to the skies. Wanda and Evelyne were damned with faint praise.

Sartre was criticized for tedious passages, and some critics chose not to see the obvious allusions to the Algerian War. But many deemed it his finest play.

Now that he no longer saw Michelle Vian, Sartre was spending more time with Arlette Elkaïm. Previously they had met for two hours on a Sunday afternoon. Now he allotted her two evenings a week. And Michelle's annual three weeks of vacation with Sartre went to Elkaïm.

In September 1959, a few days after the premiere of *The Condemned of Altona,* Sartre and Elkaïm flew to Ireland, where they stayed with the American film director John Huston on his large estate near Galway.

Huston wanted to discuss the Freud screenplay Sartre was writing for
him. Elkaïm, who spoke some English, acted as interpreter.

Huston wrote later:

> Sartre was a little barrel of a man, and as ugly as a human being
> can be. His face was both bloated and pitted, his teeth were yel-
> lowed and he was wall-eyed. . . . There was no such thing as a
> conversation with him; he talked incessantly, and there was no
> interrupting him. You'd wait for him to catch his breath, but he
> wouldn't. The words came out in an absolute torrent.[33]

Sartre thought Huston equally impossible to talk to. He wrote
Beauvoir two long letters about the madness he encountered in that
"huge barracks of a place," surrounded by green fields, cows, and horses.

In Ireland, Elkaïm began to see for the first time that all was not
well with Sartre. Until then, her admiration had blinded her.
"Corydrane was a very negative aspect of our relationship," she would
tell John Gerassi in 1973. "The Beaver knew him so much better, and
she says what she thinks. I was only too liable to be passive. After a
while, I began to have my own thoughts at last. . . . Sartre was taking
loads of corydrane. His tongue would be black with the stuff. It alienated me. But I didn't revolt; I would have been scared to." Instead,
she fell into a depression, which she had to hide from Sartre because
he could not deal with it.[34]

In his letters, Sartre tried, not very convincingly, to reassure
Beauvoir that he was being abstemious:

> I'm not drinking (except one little dry martini, sometimes 2.
> No scotch. Except for the first two nights). . . . I'll be back on
> *Thursday* at 11:30. . . . I'll drop Arlette at her place and come right
> over to you. I've told no one else my arrival time. . . . If I write to
> Evelyne before then to make a date, it will be for late afternoon.
> Tell her you don't know.
>
>   Warmest greetings, my sweet, I send you a great big kiss. I've
> talked only about myself, but that was to entertain you. Till
> Thursday, little Beaver.

These days, Sartre's nervous tension was such that he could not sit still. He kept shuffling his feet, to the point that he wore out a piece of carpet in Beauvoir's apartment. She covered it with a patch. His elbows were so busy that with their perpetual movement he made the arms of her chairs threadbare. For years he had not been able to sleep without earplugs and four or five strong sleeping pills.

In the early evening of January 4, 1960, the phone rang in Beauvoir's apartment. It was Lanzmann, telling her that Camus had been killed in a car accident. Camus was forty-six, six years younger than Beauvoir. She was aghast:

> I put down the receiver, my throat tight, my lips trembling. "I'm not going to start crying," I said to myself, "he didn't mean anything to me any more." I stood there, leaning against the window, watching night come down over Saint-Germain-des-Prés, incapable of calming myself or of giving way to real grief. Sartre was upset as well, and we spent the whole evening with Bost talking about Camus. Before getting to bed I swallowed some belladénal pills . . . I ought to have gone to sleep; I remained completely wide awake. I got up, threw on the first clothes I found, and set out walking through the night.[35]

Camus had edited *Combat* during the Resistance; he had danced at the "family's" *fiestas;* he had sent Sartre and Bost to America. Camus and Sartre had fallen out over Stalinism. More recently, the Sartre clan despised Camus for what they saw as his sympathy to the French in the Algerian War.[36] But as a person, they *missed* him.

In a poignant tribute to Camus, Sartre played down their rupture. "A quarrel is nothing—even should you never see each other again. . . . That did not prevent me from thinking of him."[37]

At seventy, Sartre would remember Camus more fondly than ever: "There was a side of him that smacked of the little Algerian tough guy, very much a hooligan, very funny. . . . His language was very racy—so was mine, for that matter—we told filthy stories one after

another, and his wife and Simone de Beauvoir pretended to be
shocked. . . . He was probably the last good friend I had."[38]

Nelson Algren arrived in Paris in February 1960. Beauvoir, who was
spending five weeks in Cuba with Sartre, had left him the key to her
apartment and instructed Olga, Bost, and Michelle to look after him.

Algren was shocked by how ravaged Olga looked these days, but he
enjoyed flirting with Michelle. "The Golden Zazou had lost some of
her sheen," he would write in his memoir *Who Lost an American?*, "but
was still the Michelle who cared for people."[39] Michelle had been
re-admitted into the family after she attempted suicide. She had
been desperate without Sartre.

After Sartre and Beauvoir returned to Paris, Michelle and Algren
continued to go out together some evenings. "Simone de Beauvoir
organized our dates," Michelle says. "We danced to 'Night and Day,'
and Algren tried to hold me tighter. In a taxi, as we passed the Palais
de Chaillot, he took my hand and put it between his legs." When she
told this to Sartre the next day, Sartre, aroused by the story, made love
to her—the first time in two years. After that, their physical relationship was back on.

Michelle was overjoyed that Sartre still desired her, but she no
longer had any illusions that he would give her much of his time.
They saw each other once a week for two hours. Michelle loved
André Reweliotty, but she loved Sartre more. She was forty-two, and
decided that it would fill the void in her life if she had a child by
Sartre. "He didn't mind," she says. "He wouldn't have looked after it,
of course, but he was as happy to give babies as anything else."[40]

As fate would have it, Michelle, who had always become pregnant
so easily when she did not want to, could no longer conceive. She
consulted an obstetrician (Dr. Lagroua Weill-Hallé) and discovered
that she had blocked fallopian tubes. She underwent an operation,
but still nothing happened. In the past, she had become pregnant
three times by Sartre, and had had three abortions. It appeared that
the last abortion had left her sterile.[41]

•   •   •

Beauvoir and Sartre had come back very enthusiastic about Cuba. They were there for what Sartre called "the honeymoon of the Revolution."[42] There was a festive atmosphere on the island, the streets were full of people dancing, and the two writers had been fêted wherever they went. They even spent three days traveling around the island with Fidel Castro. Press photographs disseminated throughout the world showed Sartre and Beauvoir standing next to the handsome young Castro, who towered over them both; in another photo they were plowing through the water in a fast motorboat, with Castro standing at the helm; in a third they sat talking to the heavy-booted revolutionaries Castro and Che Guevara, all three men smoking thick Cuban cigars.

Back in Paris, Sartre wrote a series of articles about Cuba ("Hurricane over the Sugar Cane"), while Beauvoir devoted time to Algren. They had not seen each other for eight years, and were nervous at first. They soon relaxed. Algren wore the same old corduroy trousers and worn jacket. "Despite the years of separation and the stormy summers of 1950 and '51, we felt as close as during the best days of 1949," Beauvoir writes in her memoirs.[43]

She and Algren spent cozy days in the Rue Schoelcher. Algren got up first and squeezed orange juice for them both. He installed his electric typewriter on the small desk Lanzmann had once used. They worked together in the mornings, and in the afternoons Beauvoir continued to work at Sartre's. They traveled to Marseille, Spain, Istanbul, Greece, Crete. Occasionally, it seems, they made love.

In August, Beauvoir flew to Brazil with Sartre, leaving Algren once again in her apartment. He stayed on a few more weeks. From Rio, Beauvoir wrote tender letters to her "subversive beast of my heart, my faraway love." She loved him "more than ever and forever," she said.[44] Algren wrote three short letters, and then there was silence. When Beauvoir returned to Paris in November, she hoped to find a pile of letters from him. There was not one. He had left her some photos of their time in Istanbul, a book, some magazines, a nut bar, and a poem on her desk. But he had gone. She missed him.

Beauvoir had not enjoyed the Brazil trip. She was upset by the silence from Algren. She would have liked to go on walks with Sartre, just the two of them. Instead, Sartre gave lectures on colonialism and the Algerian War, and there were endless meetings, interviews, press conferences, and dinners. Wherever they went, Sartre was greeted as a hero, particularly by young people. But he was suffering from shingles, caused by overwork and depression.

Then Beauvoir became ill. In a godforsaken little town on the Amazon River she developed a high fever. She and Sartre were scared of her dying in that place, and took a plane at four in the morning back to Recife. By the time they arrived, Beauvoir felt half dead. She was in the hospital for a week with suspected typhoid fever. While she lay in bed sweating, Sartre tried to seduce Christina, a twenty-five-year-old Brazilian journalist, a virgin, with flaming red hair. As soon as she felt strong enough, Beauvoir (whose English was not up to her usual standard) wrote to Algren, half amused, half despairing:

> The girl . . . believes in God, and when she understood Sartre should not have hated to sleep with her, she thought he was the Devil himself. They quarrelled. Sartre had a hell of a life in this dreary hostile town with me in the hospital and the half friendly, half scared red-headed girl; he drunk a little heavily and at night, to sleep, he swallowed heavy doses of gardenal. The result was that when he get up at morning, he could not stand on his legs; he went banging against the walls and walked in zig-zag all long. When coming to the hospital he looked groggy—that enraged me but I could do nothing. The girl drank too, when I had recovered we spent a crazy night, she broke glasses in her naked hands and bled abundantly, saying she should kill herself, because she loved and hated Sartre and we were going away the next day. I slept in her bed, holding her wrist to prevent her to jump by the window. . . . She will come to Paris and Sartre says maybe he will marry her! What of the Algerian one then? Well, that is the future.[45]

Beauvoir did not hear from Algren, but there were plenty of worried letters and phone calls from Paris. Before they left, Sartre and Beauvoir had been among 121 French intellectuals to sign the "Manifesto of the 121," demanding independence for Algeria and amnesty for all French soldiers who refused to take up arms against the Algerian people. An inflammatory petition, it advocated insubordination. Among the other well-known names were André Breton, Marguerite Duras, Michel Leiris, Alain Robbe-Grillet, Nathalie Sarraute, and Simone Signoret. And at the *Temps modernes,* Bost, Lanzmann, Pouillon, and Pontalis had all signed.

The other thing that was happening while they were away was the trial of Francis Jeanson, a militant member of the *Temps modernes* committee, who had worked for the Algerian National Liberation Front, the FLN. At the trial, which was making front-page news, one of Jeanson's defense lawyers read out a letter from Sartre: "If Jeanson had asked me to carry a suitcase or to give sanctuary to Algerian militants and I could have done it without putting them in danger, I would have done it without hesitation."[46] The letter caused an outcry. Sartre was widely accused of treason.

Near the end of October, when Beauvoir and Sartre were about to come home, Lanzmann phoned to say that under no circumstances should they land in Paris. There had been death threats made against Sartre. Five thousand war veterans had paraded down the Champs-Elysées shouting, "Shoot Sartre!" Thirty of the 121 signatories had already been charged. Some had been fired from their jobs. And all were threatened with five years in prison. The atmosphere in the country was so tense that Sartre risked being assassinated or thrown in jail as soon as he got back. Beauvoir was also in danger. The ultra-right-wing nationalists knew they could get at Sartre by threatening her. And she had incurred wrath in her own right with her spirited defense, published in *Le Monde,* of Djamila Boupacha, an Algerian Muslim and member of the FLN whom French soldiers had viciously tortured, including raping her with a broken bottle.[47]

At the insistence of their friends, Sartre and Beauvoir changed their flight to Barcelona. They were met there by Bost and Pouillon. Lanzmann joined them just outside Paris. They drove into the city by the back roads.

The next few months were a very strange time. Sartre and Beauvoir were living together, and because of the death threats, they were scarcely able to go out. They ate ham, sausages, and lots of canned food. When Bost visited, he cooked them a decent meal. The Brazilian girl wrote passionate letters, but Sartre decided he would not marry her after all. Beauvoir's *The Prime of Life* came out in November, to huge acclaim. The critics agreed that Beauvoir's most exciting writing was about her own life.

Sartre called a press conference in Beauvoir's apartment to protest the charges against thirty of the signatories of the manifesto. "If those individuals are found guilty, then we all are. If not, let them withdraw the case."[48]

In the end, the charges were withdrawn. The government was not prepared to press charges against Sartre. "You do not imprison Voltaire," De Gaulle said, meaning Sartre. And so the others could not be punished either.

Sartre's name had protected them from prison, but he could not prevent his friends losing their jobs. In a gesture that reminded them of McCarthyist America, those who were employed by the state— teachers, radio and television people—were blacklisted and fired. Jean Pouillon, who worked for the National Assembly, was suspended for six months without a salary.

The end of the Algerian War was in sight: De Gaulle was talking about independence. The backlash from right-wing French national-ists was brutal. In July 1961, Sartre's apartment on the Rue Bonaparte was hit by a plastic explosive. The damage was not too bad, but Sartre moved his mother to a hotel on the Boulevard Raspail, and he himself camped out at Beauvoir's place. In October, some thirty thousand Algerians demonstrated against an eight-thirty P.M. curfew imposed on Muslims in Paris. It was a peaceful march until the French police swooped down on them, shooting, clubbing, and throwing them into the Seine. At least two hundred Algerians were killed. The main-stream press covered up the atrocity. *Les Temps modernes* told the truth about these and other horrors.

It was in a state of fury about colonialism and its crimes that Sartre sat down to write a preface for Frantz Fanon's book *The Wretched of the Earth*. He and Fanon had met in Rome the previous summer, and though Fanon was dying of leukemia, he had talked to Sartre with feverish urgency for three days and nights, scarcely stopping to sleep. A black psychiatrist originally from Martinique, Fanon was involved with the FLN. In his book he argued that violence was a "cleansing force" for the third world, which restored pride and self-respect to the natives who had been colonized.

Sartre agreed. The oppressed had to answer violence with violence, he wrote in his preface. It was the only way they would attain their liberation. Fanon's book, with Sartre's famous preface, would become a "little red book" for third-world revolutionaries.

In January 1962, a second plastic explosive destroyed the apartment on the Rue Bonaparte. Neither Sartre nor his mother was there, but the contents of the flat were wrecked, and many of Sartre's papers were lost. His mother was now permanently installed in a hotel. Sartre rented a tenth-floor studio five minutes away, in a modern building at 222 Boulevard Raspail. He had almost no furniture, and worked at a white Formica table, with books all over the floor. All he salvaged from his mother's apartment was the wooden chair that had belonged to his great-grandfather. "This chair is the only thing I care about," he told his friend Liliane Siegel, "except my books, of course." Siegel looked at the chair dubiously. "I like it to be uncomfortable," Sartre said. "I don't like seats that corrupt."[49]

The first time Siegel turned up there for her weekly appointment on Tuesday afternoons, she was horrified by Sartre's ugly new surroundings. Liliane Siegel was the latest beautiful, troubled Jewish woman Sartre was saving with his existential psychoanalysis. ("He was particularly good at getting people to talk," she writes. "He detected the slightest pretence, the smallest lie, he interpreted silences, observed facial expressions, went through everything with a finetooth comb. He made no concessions, harked back to a phrase, demanded fuller information. . . . He wanted to know all or nothing."[50]) Liliane had come to depend heavily on their meetings. She had a practical bent, and could drive a car, and she liked to help Sartre whenever she could. She bought two wooden desks at a flea market—

one for Sartre, one for Beauvoir—and some bookshelves and lamps. Her son delivered and installed them.

In June 1962, just as Algeria was finally gaining its independence, Sartre and Beauvoir flew to Moscow. They were completely disillusioned with France and the thousands of deaths it had caused by clinging to colonialism. They were angry with the American government, which had implemented an economic embargo of Cuba. "It seems your dirty Kennedy is going to make serious troubles for Castro," Beauvoir had written to Algren at the time of the Bay of Pigs crisis. "I hate this grinning boy and his grinning wife."[51]

Beauvoir and Sartre climbed up the steps of the plane, desperately hoping to see new signs of freedom in the Soviet Union.

ELEVEN

WHITE NIGHTS, VODKA, AND TEARS

June 1962—November 1966

After his vehement denunciation of the Soviet invasion of Hungary in 1956, Sartre must have been surprised to receive an invitation from the Soviet Writers Union. But under Nikita Khrushchev, the USSR was undergoing what it called a "thaw."[1] Khrushchev had condemned the abuses and purges of the Stalin regime. He was aware that Soviet culture could not remain forever in a deep freeze, and had embarked on a "de-Stalinization" policy, which involved an easing of censorship. The writer Ilya Ehrenburg (who was not in the party but was close to the communist nomenclature) was pushing Khrushchev to open up the cultural exchange between East and West. And as Ehrenburg would have pointed out, Jean-Paul Sartre—the most prominent intellectual in France, an active militant for world peace, a man of the left but not in the Communist Party—was the perfect man to court.

Sartre and Beauvoir flew to Moscow on June 1, 1962. Lena Zonina, a guide and interpreter from the Soviet Writers Union, was at the airport to meet them, and at their full disposal during their three-week sojourn. Zonina was a literary critic and translator, and unlike the other Russians they would meet, she knew their work well. She was hoping to translate some of it.[2]

Sartre and Beauvoir had the impression that the Soviet Union was coming out of the Dark Ages. For the first time, Russians were hearing jazz, dancing to rock and roll, and reading translations of writers like Faulkner, Hemingway, Sartre, and Camus. Khrushchev had even permitted the journal *Novy Mir* to publish *One Day in the Life of Ivan Denisovich,* a novel by the unknown writer Alexander Solzhenitsyn, who had nearly died in a Siberian forced-labor camp. Never before had a book portraying life in the gulag been published in the Soviet Union.

This time, instead of the solemn banquets to which Sartre had been subjected in 1954, Sartre and Beauvoir were invited to people's homes, where they could talk fairly freely to other writers and intellectuals. Wherever they went, Lena Zonina was by their side. A highlight was their visit to Leningrad, a city they thought as enchanting as Rome. They walked with the crowd by the Neva River, and stood in front of the Winter Palace, thinking about the violent revolution that had taken place in that magnificent setting—scenes that were etched in their minds by photographs and old films. "The 'White Nights of St Petersburg'; in Norway, in Finland, I had thought I knew what they were like," Beauvoir would write, "but the magic of the night-time sun needs this ghost-haunted, petrified décor from the past to complete its spell."[3]

Despite the atmosphere of relative freedom, it was easy to remain insulated from everyday life in the Soviet Union. The Peking Hotel in Moscow, where Sartre and Beauvoir were staying, was a world of its own, a palace for foreigners. They disliked eating there, and preferred Zonina to take them to local restaurants, which meant standing in line with the Muscovites. Some evenings she took them to the Writers Club.

Zonina, they were relieved to discover, was no Stalinist. She had been. Her real name was "Lenina," reflecting her parents' commitment to the revolution. It embarrassed her. She preferred "Lena."[4] Until the end of the Second World War, her family deeply admired Stalin. And then came more Jewish purges. In 1949, her father, Alexander Zonin, a writer, was arrested as a "rootless cosmopolitan" (code for Jewish intellectual) and sent to a camp in Kazakhstan. As the daughter of an "enemy of the people," Zonina was not allowed to continue her university studies.

Because she wrote French well, Ilya Ehrenburg employed her as his secretary. It took courage, for which she would always be grateful to him. Ehrenburg's own position was highly precarious. Like her, he was Jewish, and having lived for almost twenty years in Paris, he had a strong rapport with Western intellectuals. He was fortunate to have survived this long, and he knew it.

When her father was released from the camp in 1955, Zonina went back to the University of Moscow to pursue postgraduate studies in French. That had led to her present job—in the International Commission, the most prestigious section of the Writers Union.

At thirty-eight—twice married and divorced—Zonina lived with her mother and her two-year-old daughter, Macha, in a dilapidated apartment building in the center of Moscow. While Lena was at work, her mother looked after little Macha. The women shared the shopping, which involved endless waiting in line, then climbing up five flights of rickety stairs with shopping bags.

Zonina struggled constantly with fatigue. Shortly after Macha's birth, she had developed severe diabetes. She had to follow a draconian diet and give herself three injections a day. Allergic to the pig insulin produced in the Soviet Union, she relied on friends in the French embassy to bring her insulin from the West. And even though she carried bread in her handbag in case of a hypoglycemic attack, one day, in a Moscow restaurant, Sartre and Beauvoir saw her keel over in front of their eyes.

"There was nothing lukewarm about Lena," Beauvoir would write in her memoirs. "She had a passionate feeling for truth and justice. But she never indulged in dogmatism or priggishness; she was gay, ironical, and sometimes very funny. . . . There was a bond between us that is hard to define—an understanding, an instant communication. . . . It was a great pleasure, walking about with her or sitting in her flat, talking and drinking vodka."[5]

For her part, Lena admired Sartre's and Beauvoir's writing, their political commitment, and their independence as a couple. She had been more than a little intimidated as she waited for them at the airport, but in no time she felt at ease in their company and found herself joking and laughing with them, and telling them about her life.

• • •

Two weeks after returning to Paris, Sartre flew to Moscow again, this time on his own. From July 10 to 16, 1962, he took part in the World Peace Congress in Moscow. Lena Zonina was once again his official interpreter. Because the sessions started early in the mornings, she, too, was accommodated in the hotel.

As soon as he got back to Paris, Sartre wrote her the first of many passionate letters. He had never remembered the number of a hotel room before, he wrote, but he would not forget number 606 until he was senile. For six nights, her room had been their mutual home. He loved her. He missed her presence. He missed her somber voice, her breasts, her soft skin. He missed her thick black hair, her naked shoulders, her smile.[6]

How tender and brave her smile had been at the airport, he wrote. He had climbed into the plane feeling as if he had had a tooth yanked out. Settling back in his seat, exhausted with pain, he had wiped away tears. The plane took twenty minutes to climb through the clouds. Then everything was blue—a hard, metallic blue—and he lit his first cigarette. Throughout the three-and-a-half-hour trip, he could not sleep. Lena would not let him sleep. He would start to doze, then a vivid memory would jerk him awake.

"Ma femme," he called her. In Moscow, he had felt as if they were married. They had turned up at people's houses together and they had left together. In the conference sessions, he was conscious of her beautiful heavy body next to his. Had she noticed that their hips or thighs were nearly always touching? He loved it when she asked him to light her cigarette and their fingers touched.

She had been so busy, running everywhere, organizing things. Did she remember answering the phone that morning, her toothbrush still in her mouth? He had felt so happy, free, and calm with her in Moscow.

She had looked after him, protected him. It made him feel almost feminine. In order for him to be understood, she had to be at his side. His French words had made love with her Russian words in the air. Back in Paris, he could not get used to speaking to people without an intermediary.

Theirs was a forbidden love, he told her, like Romeo and Juliet. Separated by three thousand kilometers and an iron curtain, their access to each other depended on cold-war politics. They would not see each other for six months, and it was going to be hard. Would Zonina decide that six months was too long? She had told him that she had always been the one to end her relationships with men. It made him anxious.

She would never suffer because of him, he assured her. He would rather gouge out his eyes than cause her pain. He hoped he could rely on her, and that the only danger to their love would be external. They had to be able to give each other all their trust and confidence.

Because of the Soviet censors, Sartre and Zonina did not send letters through the mail. They had to wait until a trusted confidant traveled between Paris and Moscow—most often Ilya Ehrenburg or a friend from the French embassy in Moscow. It sometimes took weeks. Sartre, who liked to write to Zonina every day, ended up sending letters that were forty or more pages long. He would put the letter inside a packet containing articles or a manuscript, ostensibly sent by Beauvoir, who wrote on the envelope.

Sartre had shown himself susceptible to Slavic charm over the years. But Lena Zonina was very different. Unlike the Kosakiewicz sisters or Nathalie Sorokine, she was no "White Russian." Her family had not fled the 1917 revolution. And she was Jewish. To Sartre, she represented so many things: Slavic exoticism, the communist revolution, anti-Semitic persecution. The hardship of her life made him feel guilty, he told her. He thought of her tramping up five flights of stairs, and felt bad every time he stepped into his elevator.

Zonina protested that Sartre was in love with a fantasy. She did not want to symbolize Mother Russia. She wanted to be his lover, not his *Soviet* lover.

She was no fantasy, Sartre assured her. She was his refuge. He needed her in order to be happy. He needed her in order to feel himself. There were only two people in his life he truly cared about: the Beaver and his little Lentchka.

●   ●   ●

Was Lena Zonina a KGB agent, paid to get close to Sartre and inform
on him? The suggestion has been floated around from time to time.[7]
Sartre himself was aware of the rumor and laughed at it.[8] But what *did*
it mean that Sartre, who was always so careful to preserve his political
independence, had fallen in love with an official representative of the
Soviet government?

The Writers Union was a large organization with some six thousand members, established by the Central Committee of the
Communist Party. Its senior officers were Communist Party members, some of whom were in the KGB. The interpreters who worked
in the International Commission enjoyed certain privileges, like
travel, though when they traveled to the West, they were obliged to
leave close family members behind, in case they entertained any ideas
about defecting. Whenever they spoke to foreigners, they were
required to submit detailed reports.

Jean-Paul Sartre was no nuclear scientist; he had no trade secrets
that interested the Russians. His value was as a propaganda tool.
"The importance of his visit cannot be exaggerated," Zonina noted in
her first report. "His influence on the avant-garde intelligentsia in
the West is immense at the moment."[9]

Lena Zonina's position would have been impossible if she had
fallen in love with a Western intellectual who was overtly critical of
the USSR. But she hadn't. During the years in which they were
lovers, 1962–1966, Sartre fell into line with Soviet propaganda
almost completely. On his visits to the USSR, he made it clear to
everyone he met that he was there because he wanted to appreciate
the *positive* things. Like them, he was committed to world peace, he
said.[10] And he was eager to foster cultural ties between East and
West. In his preface to Lena Zonina's Russian translation of *Words,* he
even wrote that for Frenchmen of his generation, "The great event in
our lives was your revolution."[11]

Lena Zonina was considerably more critical of the Soviet government than Sartre was. She had remained loyal to Ilya Ehrenburg, who
signed protest petitions, kept his distance from the apparatchiks at
the Writers Union, and dared to express positive views about two

men who were much reviled in party circles—Pasternak and Solzhenitsyn. In the circle Zonina mixed in, everyone was critical of the government—at least in the privacy of their own homes.

Indeed, most Soviet intellectuals were liberal thinkers, and they were disappointed that Sartre, despite his position of influence, said nothing to challenge the Soviet government. "They found him rather naïve, a bit dishonest, even," says Gilbert Dagron, who was the cultural attaché at the French embassy in Moscow at the time, and a close friend of Lena Zonina. "He saw things, but did not say them." Sartre was always afraid that the conservative press would use any criticism he made of the Soviet Union as propaganda for the American side. Dagron talked to Sartre for an hour in Sartre's room at the Peking Hotel. Sartre commented that certain things were "scandalous," and Dagron urged him to write about them. "I can't," Sartre said. "The *Figaro* would praise me."[12]

Did the KGB know about Zonina's love affair with Sartre? It is inconceivable that it did not. Foreign guests were under constant surveillance. As Beauvoir points out in her memoirs, there were always supervisors in the corridors of their Intourist hotels.

Were the authorities worried by the affair? It brought Sartre to the USSR far more often than he would otherwise have come, which made the USSR look good. If the aim of the Soviet authorities was to impress Sartre with the freedom of the Soviet Union and the warmth of Soviet hospitality, they could not have done better. And with Sartre came Simone de Beauvoir. Her memoirs were best sellers in the West, and at a Moscow press conference in June 1962 she promised to convey her positive impressions of the USSR in the next volume.[13]

Zonina and Sartre had no illusions that the authorities did not know about their affair.[14] Lena was no doubt questioned about it. She would have had to act as if Sartre did not know that the authorities knew. Sartre himself had to act as if he did not know that they knew. For Sartre, who was always fascinated by the masks people wear and the roles they play, this intricate spying game would have been intriguing.

A handful of Zonina's reports to the Writers Union have been published in the French journal *Commentaire*. They are thoroughly innocuous. She wrote, for example, that Sartre's first trip had been difficult to organize, as they had to take into account his "extreme impatience towards any sign of what he calls 'propaganda.' " She explained that Sartre and Beauvoir had wanted to spend the day sightseeing in Rostov with the writer Yefim Dorosh; the authorities did not allow this, and in a fury Sartre insisted on being driven back to Moscow. For Sartre's future visits, Zonina had this advice: "His program has to be planned in such a way that he has the impression of meeting only those people whom he wants to meet. . . . In short, he needs to be given the impression that it is he who has determined his program." One could imagine Sartre dictating this to Zonina with a grin on his face.

Alone with Sartre and Beauvoir, Lena would often express impatience with Sartre's rose-colored view of communism. To her, he was an idealistic Western intellectual, full of illusions. "He doesn't *want* to understand," she would say to friends after he left.[15]

Sartre and Beauvoir were in Rome in mid-August 1962 when the Italian writer Carlo Levi, just back from Moscow, handed Sartre a letter from Zonina. Sartre told Zonina that he took the letter with a show of indifference and put it in the lower pocket of his jacket, where he stroked it voluptuously with his finger.

It was reassuring to know that she loved him on July 17 and 19, he wrote back, but could he be sure she loved him *now?* A whole month had elapsed since she had written that letter. He worried that she might not be missing him enough, or that she might be missing him too much. He could not bear it if she decided their love was too difficult.

He and Beauvoir were staying on the outskirts of Rome, in a modern district on a hill, he wrote. They much preferred old Rome, but they wanted to avoid the heat and pollution. Beauvoir had almost finished *Force of Circumstance,* the third volume of her memoirs, and he was reading it in the evenings. He thought it very good—even better than the second volume, which, in turn, had been better than the first. The stumbling point was the politics, which bored Beauvoir almost as much as it bored him. She had some revision to do. They estimated it would take her another six months. Beauvoir did not mind. She loved writing her memoirs. In the evenings, over drinks, they talked until late into the night. Sartre liked it best when they talked about Zonina.

"The Beaver . . . is the Truth," he explained. "That's useful to me for she tells me you love me." She had also declared that Zonina was the only one of Sartre's women to be worthy of him, and that if anything ever happened to *her,* Beauvoir, he should dump the others and put himself in Zonina's hands.

He had changed in the Soviet Union, Sartre told Zonina. She had changed him. Through her, he had recovered his tenderness. Through her, he had recovered his youth. She had given him back his old fire.

Was she eating at the Writers Club that night? Was she making eyes at other men? Remember, she had promised to tell him if she was ever unfaithful to him. He worried that her diabetes might be worse and that he would not even know about it. He could not wait to see her. He loved her. In letters he would tell her as much as possible about his daily existence. He wanted her to be able to picture the people in his life.

Bost was also in Rome that summer, Sartre wrote. They were working together on the Freud scenario for a John Huston film.[16] Olga had just joined Bost, and already they were arguing. They were both good people and yet as a couple they broke each other's hearts. Olga was deeply unhappy, and that made Bost feel guilty. Olga looked far older than her years. No doubt it was the vestiges of her tuberculosis, as well as her lifelong obsession with slimming. Her pale eyes made no impression on her face anymore. Her hair, formerly full and blond, was dyed auburn and dried out from too much washing. Since her tuberculosis, she and Bost had lived together like sister and brother. These days Bost was in love with another woman, an American who lived in Paris.[17] Olga guessed but did not know who it was. She had always been horribly jealous.

•   •   •

Sartre was back in Paris, writing to Zonina from his tenth-floor apartment. Her photo was on the wall in front of his desk. He had taken up his essay on Flaubert again, which he had put aside for the last seven years. He was horrified by it, he told her. Under the effect of corydrane, he had written page after page and had thought himself a genius. Now it read like the writings of a madman. But he wanted to finish this book. Flaubert still fascinated him.

Apart from work, he was engaged in his usual "medical round," he told Zonina. This was how he referred to the women in his life. Wanda was forty-four and had become a recluse. She was "drunk with unhappiness and hatred." She had acted in his plays without the least success. He did not think she acted badly—nor well, either—but nobody other than he had ever employed her. The problem was, she liked to act but she did not like the public, and they felt it. He saw her for two hours, three times a week. To pass the time, he helped her make sense of her gas bill and her taxes and so on. But she hated explanations. "Shut up, shut up!" she would shout at him. "Let me speak!"

Evelyne, too, was an actress with no engagements, he told Zonina. He wrote a part for her in *The Condemned of Altona,* but she was bad, and the critics said so. In the end, Sartre realized he had not done her a favor. Evelyne was very intelligent but had no self-esteem, and she was always seeking validation in violent passions that never lasted. Each time there was a rupture there would be another deluge of tears from her, on Sartre's divan. When her last man left her, she attempted suicide. Sartre saw her three times a week, an hour and a half each time.

Arlette Elkaïm was also intelligent, but she was lazy and constantly sick. She had a boyfriend, André Puig, an aspiring writer, who was seeing another woman, and this made her unhappy.[18]

But it was Michelle Vian who worried him most at the moment. She had suffered a terrible blow. For years she had lived with the jazz clarinetist André Reweliotty. That summer, at the end of July, they had been heading off on vacation in his burgundy-colored convertible. Reweliotty was driving too fast, and the car skidded off the highway. Michelle was ejected onto the grass bank and was scarcely hurt at all. Reweliotty was trapped by the steering wheel. For two hours, until the ambulance came, Michelle sat cradling his head, trying to stop the blood coming out of his mouth. After two days in a coma, he died.

Michelle had spent the rest of the summer alone in her apartment in Paris. She was an insomniac at the best of times; now she dreaded the nights more than ever. In her nightmares she kept seeing herself back on that highway. She and Reweliotty had loved each other. She had been the manager of his jazz group. Her life was going to be very empty now. Sartre would try to see her more often in the next few months.

He assured Zonina that he no longer had a shadow of a feeling for Michelle. They had an old, old friendship, that was all. He respected the way she struggled against her madness. And at the moment he felt deep sympathy for her.

Zonina wrote a morose letter back. Sartre and Beauvoir seemed to have had such a sociable time in Rome. And these stories about Sartre's other women unsettled Zonina. It seemed to her it would not take him long to find a new one.

They had not had a particularly sociable time in Rome, Sartre replied. His head had been full of thoughts of her. There was no reason in the world for her to be envious of any of his women. As for any new woman, there wouldn't be one. If he courted someone else, it would mean he did not love her anymore. And that was out of the question.

In December 1962, Sartre and Beauvoir flew to Moscow to spend Christmas with Zonina. Since Sartre's relationship with Lena was officially a secret, it was Beauvoir's presence as his traveling companion that made it possible for him to be alone with Lena. Over the next four years, Sartre would make nine trips to the USSR, with Beauvoir as his ever-obliging chaperone.

This time they were experiencing the Russian winter. Before leaving Paris, they bought boots and fur hats for themselves, and books, medicine, woolens, stockings, blouses, and perfume for Zonina. Sartre also gave her a ring.

Moscow was freezing but sunny. Some people made their way around the city on skis. In the evenings, the trees in the city squares sparkled with Christmas lights. On Christmas Eve, Beauvoir writes, they were invited to a party in the foyer of a theater near Mayakovsky Square:

> When we got there, fat young women were arriving: they hurried to the cloak-room, shed their fur coats, boots and thick wool skirts, and reappeared, slim and elegant in light evening dresses and slippers. . . . As we had our supper at a little table we watched the couples dancing; they danced modern dances, and danced them very well, to the sound of excellent recorded jazz. . . . We thought it a good sign that they were allowed to wear these elegant clothes and to listen to this Western music.[19]

They returned to Leningrad. In the summer Beauvoir had found that city quite magical. This time, in the depth of winter, she thought it dreary. The sun did not rise until ten, then it cast a faint light on the gray streets before vanishing at three in the afternoon. She spent a great deal of time alone in her room.

When he got back to Paris, Sartre wrote to Zonina: "Leningrad, you know, is the strongest and most beautiful memory in my life." He had loved the brief hours of light between dawn and dusk, and their room, which they had almost never left. He had not been so happy since his twenties. He noticed that she had not cried in the car on the way to the airport, as he had. But she had looked very sad.

"There has been one undoubted success in my life: my relationship with Sartre," Beauvoir wrote in *Force of Circumstance*. "In more than thirty years, we have only once gone to sleep at night disunited."

In the epilogue to the third volume of her memoirs. Beauvoir attempted to sum up her life. She also wanted to dispel some "stupid misconceptions." Sartre had not written her books, as some people suggested. It was not true that all her convictions were put into her head by Sartre. If she had chosen Sartre—and she *had* chosen him—it was because he led her along paths she wanted to take. Yes, Sartre had helped her, a great deal. She had also helped him.

Beauvoir was in a defiant mood when she wrote that epilogue in March 1963. And she was sad. She was fifty-five, and felt she had crossed a frontier.

She had written about her trip with Sartre to the Soviet Union in the summer of 1962. She mentioned their friendship with Lena Zonina. She did not say—she could not, for obvious reasons—that while she herself was trying to come to terms with the celibacy imposed on her by aging, Sartre was courting the beautiful Lena in front of her eyes. But she did not hide the piercing sense of loss she felt when she contemplated her future:

> While I was able to look at my face without displeasure I gave it no thought, it could look after itself. The wheel eventually stops. I loathe my appearance now: the eyebrows slipping down towards the eyes, the bags underneath, the excessive fullness of the cheeks, and that air of sadness around the mouth that wrinkles always bring. . . . Yes, the moment has come to say: Never again! . . . Never again shall I collapse, drunk with fatigue, into the smell of hay. Never again shall I slide down through the solitary morning snows. Never again a man. . . .
>
> The only thing that can happen now at the same time new and important is misfortune. Either I shall see Sartre dead, or I shall die before him. It is appalling not to be there to console someone for the pain you cause by leaving him. It is appalling that he should abandon you and then not speak to you again. Unless I am blessed by a most improbable piece of good fortune, one of these fates is to be mine. Sometimes I want to finish it all quickly so as to shorten the dread of waiting.

She ended her epilogue with some of the most beautiful moments in her life: "the dunes of El-Oued, Wabansia Avenue, the dawns in Provence, . . . Castro talking to five hundred thousand Cubans, . . . the white nights of Leningrad, the bells of the Liberation, an orange moon over the Piraeus, a red sun rising over the desert, Torcello, Rome, all the things I've talked about, others I have left unspoken." She thought of the young girl she once was, who anticipated her future with a beating heart. In the meantime, she had learned the truth about the human condition—the hunger, oppression, violence, and injustice. Not so far ahead of her was death and the abyss. "The promises have all been kept. And yet, turning an incredulous gaze towards that young and credulous girl, I realize with stupor how much I was gypped."

The rhetorical flourish of her conclusion would be widely misunderstood. Her readers seemed to feel personally invested in Beauvoir's happiness and success. They did not see that she meant this both as a political statement and as a comment on the inevitable anguish of the existential void. To them, it was an admission of personal failure, something they could not bear from the writer who had become, for them, the very symbol of a fulfilled, independent woman.

For a couple of years now, Sartre's account at Gallimard had been in the red. He had started books and not finished them, and had written numerous political articles that brought no income. Now he needed to publish a book fast. In the spring of 1963, he took his autobiographical narrative, *Words,* out of a drawer. He had written most of it in 1954.

When he looked at what he had written, he thought it quite good. He decided that it did not matter if he had gone no further than the age of ten. As an exploration of why he had embraced the myth of the sanctity of literature, the narrative could stand as it was. For several months he reworked sentences that were already the most polished he had ever written. "I wanted to be literary in order to show the error of being literary," he told Beauvoir.[20] He dedicated the book "To Madame Z." To Lena Zonina he wrote: "It's for you, my wife, Madame Z(artre)."

The critics would hail *Words* as Sartre's return to literature. Everyone agreed that it was his most moving and beautifully written book. Sartre was amused by the irony, but pleased—not least, he told Zonina, because this made it the best present he could give her.

In the summer of 1963, Sartre and Beauvoir spent six weeks in the Soviet Union, traveling with Zonina through the Crimea, Georgia, and Armenia. The countryside was magnificent, but food shortages were worse and shopping queues longer than ever. The cultural thaw had proved a savage disappointment. The government had tentatively opened the doors of the Soviet house to Western influences, the Russian people had embraced those influences too eagerly, and the doors had been hastily slammed shut again. Khrushchev's position among the Stalinist jostlers for power was precarious, and he was now defending Stalin and attacking abstract art, jazz, and anything else that came from the West. He no longer tolerated criticism of the postrevolutionary era. And in a long speech he made that spring, he singled out Ilya Ehrenburg for particular criticism.[21]

It was on this trip that Sartre suggested marriage to Zonina. He had discussed the idea with Beauvoir. With Soviet freedom fast evaporating, there was a danger that he and Zonina would no longer be able to see each other. She would have far better medical care in France. They both knew that if Sartre asked for permission for Zonina and her daughter to leave, the Soviet government would almost certainly feel obliged to consent.

Zonina asked for time to think about it. As she pointed out to Sartre, it was a wrenching decision for her to make. If she left the Soviet Union, she would never be allowed to go back. She loved French culture, but was intensely wary of the West, and she despised the ruthlessness of capitalism. She would never be allowed to bring her mother with her, and how could she leave her behind? She would not easily find work in France, and she would never agree to be one more of Sartre's dependent women. She did not think she could do it.

After their long sojourn in the Soviet Union, Sartre and Beauvoir went, as usual, to Rome. They stayed in their favorite lodgings, the Minerva, a rundown hotel located in an ancient palace right in the center of the city.

Sartre was writing an essay on the problems of revolution in the third world. Beauvoir, having handed in *Force of Circumstance,* was mostly reading that summer. Sometimes they took the car and went away for a few days—to Sienna, Venice, or Florence.

As soon as they returned to Rome after a short absence, they would hurry over to the Poste Restante. Sartre was hoping for a letter from Zonina. For weeks there had been silence. He worried that she might be ill, or that she did not love him anymore. At night he tormented himself. If he had to choose between the two explanations, which would he choose?

In early October, a letter finally arrived from Moscow. Sartre read it in the Piazza della Minerva, in front of their hotel. "Your hands are trembling," Beauvoir said to him. It was true. His legs were trembling, too.

"It does not just depend on us," Zonina wrote to Sartre. "The more I read the Beaver's memoirs, the more I understand that I could never decide to change things. And this kills something in me. You know that I feel friendship for the Beaver. I respect her, I admire the relationship you have. . . . But you and the Beaver together have created a remarkable and dazzling thing which is so dangerous for those people who get close to you."[22]

He was thinking about their siestas on the Black Sea, Sartre wrote back. Their lovemaking. Did Zonina realize that he and Beauvoir never spent an evening alone together without talking about her?

At the end of October, the day before Sartre and Beauvoir were due to return to Paris, Bost phoned to say that Beauvoir's mother had fallen and broken her femur bone.

November 1963 was a long, sad month. Simone and Poupette took turns beside their mother's bed. Françoise de Beauvoir was seventy-seven and had been fragile and in pain with arthritis for some years. Now her surgeon discovered a massive cancerous tumor. The night after the operation, Poupette stayed at the hospital and Simone went home to spend the evening with Sartre at the Rue Schoelcher:

We played some Bartók. Suddenly, at eleven, an outburst of tears that almost degenerated into hysteria. . . . This time my despair escaped from my control: someone other than myself was weeping in me. I talked to Sartre about my mother's mouth as I had seen it that morning and about everything I had inter-preted in it—greediness refused, an almost servile humility, hope, distress, loneliness—the loneliness of her death and of her life—that did not want to admit its existence. And he told me that my own mouth was not obeying me any more: I had put Maman's mouth on my own face and in spite of myself, I copied its movement. Her whole person, her whole being, was concen-trated there, and compassion wrung my heart.[23]

In those few weeks, Beauvoir felt closer to her mother than at any time since her childhood. Françoise was gentle and thoughtful; she even apologized to the nurses for taking up their time. At times, on her dying mother's face, Beauvoir saw the smile of the young woman in love she had seen when she was five. Françoise treasured every last drop of life. At the end, when she slept nearly all the time, Françoise mourned: "But these are days that I lose."[24]

It was Sartre who suggested that Beauvoir write about the tragic adventure she and Poupette were undergoing with their mother. Beauvoir was scandalized, but tempted.

When her mother died in early December, Beauvoir could think of little else. She found that writing about it helped her deal with her grief. *A Very Easy Death* was the most tender book she would ever write. She dedicated it to her sister, Poupette.

Words was published in January 1964, and Sartre, once again, had money in his bank account. He was fifty-nine. One day, in the bar of the Pont-Royal, Robert Gallimard, his publisher, asked him about his plans for his literary estate. Sartre had never thought about it:

"At my death everything will go to the Beaver."
    "Have you married Simone de Beauvoir?"
    "No, of course not. You know that."
    "Have you made a will?"
    "No."
    "Then everything will go to your family. To the Schweitzers."[25]

It made no sense for Sartre to appoint Beauvoir as his literary heir and executrix: they were almost the same age. Sartre thought of Arlette Elkaïm. She was the youngest member of the family. He had always liked the fact that she seemed less interested in money than his other women. If anything, Elkaïm was too thrifty; she protested when he spent money on her. These days he saw her as a daughter. She was as jealous as the other women about Zonina's forthcoming visit to Paris, but she was the only one who aroused Sartre's sympathy. "She's really the daughter whose father is re-marrying," he told Zonina. He decided to adopt her legally.

Beauvoir had no great liking for Elkaïm, who had always been envious of her. And she was privately contemptuous of Elkaïm's financial dependence on Sartre. ("Would you have agreed to be supported yourself, when you were twenty?" Beauvoir once asked Sartre. "No one has ever blamed Van Gogh for having been more or less supported by his brother. Because he painted, because he really had reasons for accepting. . . . But the people who settle down in that kind of life. . . . Don't you find that it warps your relations with those people? Giving them money, for life, without any reciprocity?"[26])

Beauvoir always tried to see things from Sartre's point of view, and she accepted his decision. She could see that he was determined. But she worried about the other women. They would never be able to accept this, she told Sartre. She hoped it would not destroy them.

In mid-October 1964, the *Figaro Littéraire* reported that the Swedish Academy favored Jean-Paul Sartre for that year's Nobel Prize in Literature. The journalist observed wryly that Sartre's "controversial political past would not be held too much against him."

Sartre and Beauvoir talked it over. The risk was clear. If Sartre accepted, he would be seen as capitulating to the bourgeoisie, the bad boy who had finally fallen into line. The money was a small fortune. There was a lot Sartre could do with 250,000 Swedish kroner, both for good causes (he thought of the antiapartheid committee in London) and for his dependents. (He wanted to buy Wanda an apartment, for example.) They decided to ask some younger people what they thought.

The *Temps modernes* committee was elated by the news. They were unanimous: Sartre should accept. Beauvoir was not at all convinced. She asked a twenty-three-year-old female friend who was an active member of the Socialist Party, and the verdict was quite different. The young woman wrote an impassioned letter to Sartre, telling him that she and her militant friends agreed: Sartre would not be Sartre if he took the prize. She reminded him that the Nobel had been awarded to Boris Pasternak in order to embarrass the USSR.

Sartre and Beauvoir were strongly affected by this reaction. It was true that in 1958, Pasternak had been awarded the prize for *Doctor Zhivago,* a novel that was too critical of postrevolutionary Russia to find a publisher in the USSR, but had been published in the West to great acclaim. Communists the world over had been disgusted by what they saw as the perversity of the Nobel jury's decision.

Sartre fired off a letter to the Swedish Academy. He apologized for being so presumptuous as to write to them before the vote was taken, and assured the Academy of his profound respect, but he wanted to ask the members, for reasons that were personal as well as objective, not to include him among the possible prize recipients. He was hereby informing them that if he were awarded the prize, he would not accept it.

The news came over the wire services on Monday, October 19, around midday: Sartre had been named for the Nobel Prize in Literature. In Paris, the journalists set off like a pack of hounds. One of them finally ran Sartre down at the Oriental, a hotel at Denfert-Rochereau, where he was having lunch with Beauvoir. The young man burst in and announced: "You've won the Nobel Prize!"

Sartre put down his knife and fork. He would await confirmation, he said, but if the prize were offered to him, he would turn it down. Why? "I have nothing to say. I reserve my explanations for the Swedish press." Sartre returned to his lentils and lamb. The evening headlines read: "Sartre refuses."[27]

For days, the literary world was abuzz. Would the Swedish Academy nevertheless award Sartre the prize? Why was he refusing it? Was this yet another instance of what Sartre liked to call his "aesthetic of opposition"? Was he sulking because Camus had been awarded the prize five years earlier? Was he afraid Simone de Beauvoir would be envious if he accepted? More serious journalists pointed out that Sartre had always hated elitism, and that none of his books showed this more clearly than *Words*. The last sentence reiterated his desire to be "a whole man, made of all men, worth all of them, and any one of them worth him."

The Swedish committee held to its decision. Sartre was formally announced as the winner on October 24, 1964. The evening before, Sartre went to Beauvoir's apartment to hide from the press. His mother, whose hotel was a little farther up the Boulevard Raspail from Sartre's apartment, rang to say there was a crowd of reporters in front of his building. A small group of journalists doggedly rang Beauvoir's doorbell. At two in the morning, Sartre finally went out and made a brief statement.

"The writer must refuse to allow himself to be transformed into an institution," he declared in an explanation published in *Le Monde*. He would have been glad to accept the prize during the Algerian War, after he had signed the "Manifesto of the 121," he said, because it would have honored the freedom they were fighting for. But nobody had offered it to him then. He feared that his acceptance would be taken in right-wing circles as a sign that he had been forgiven for the sins of his controversial political past.

He went on to say that though this was perhaps not at all the intention of the Swedish Academy, the Nobel Prize *looked* as if it were a distinction reserved for writers of the West or rebels from the East. He added: "It is regrettable that the prize was given to Pasternak before being given to Sholokhov, and that the only Soviet work to be crowned so far is one that is not published—in fact, it's forbidden—in its own country."

In November, Sartre wrote to Zonina. He had not heard from her. He did not even know what she thought about his decision. Until now he had taken for granted that she would understand him and agree with him. But now he was hesitating. How *had* she reacted?

Zonina came to Paris in December 1964. Sartre had been worried about her visit. His apartment was Spartan. Would she be comfortable there? He planned to have her sleep on his narrow divan, with him on a folding bed by her side. Beauvoir insisted they should have her Rue Schoelcher apartment. She moved to Sartre's place.

Sartre had thought Zonina would be impressed by his decision to turn down the Nobel Prize. She wasn't. She deplored these accommodating gestures he kept making towards the Stalinists, she told him.[28] In the last few weeks, Khrushchev had been forced out of power, and there were going to be further restrictions on liberties in the USSR. It was a dark time for the Russian people. The Soviet intellectuals fervently wished that Sartre had taken the opportunity to speak out, rather than playing up to the communists as he had. And why on earth had Sartre claimed that Sholokhov deserved the prize more than Pasternak? Didn't he realize that Sholokhov was a Stalinist lackey? In Russia, her dissident friends were laughing at him.

In the end, Sartre said they should not argue anymore about what they were saying in the USSR. The fact is, he was also concerned with reactions in the West.[29]

There were other strained conversations. Sartre had to break the news to Zonina that he was going to adopt Elkaïm. Despite her reservations, Zonina could hardly doubt Sartre's love. If he had won the Nobel Prize, it was for *Words,* the book he had dedicated to her, which she had translated into Russian, and which had been a best seller these last few months in the USSR. And if he had refused the Nobel Prize, Zonina could see that his decision was largely an expression of solidarity with her homeland, Russia, and partly, at some level, with her.

Zonina stayed for three weeks. Sartre and Beauvoir both went to the airport to see her off. The three of them wondered how on earth she would get through Soviet customs with the presents she was taking back.

"I love you more than ever," Sartre wrote to Zonina the next day. He had spent the night at Beauvoir's apartment on the Rue Schoelcher, and it was still full of memories of Zonina. He and Beauvoir had talked till one-thirty A.M. "About you," he told Zonina. He had gone upstairs to sleep. Beauvoir had slept downstairs on the sofa, as usual. At three in the morning she had woken up and, noticing light under Sartre's door, had come upstairs to enjoin him to sleep. She had found him on the floor, his head on a detective novel, his glasses beside him. Apparently he had murmured, "Lena darling," and without opening his eyes, had slipped into bed and gone straight back to sleep.

On March 18, 1965, Arlette Elkaïm, at the age of twenty-eight, became Sartre's legal daughter. Beauvoir and Sylvie Le Bon were the official witnesses at the signing ceremony. Arlette was being given legal and moral rights that Sartre had never given to any other woman. She was now officially called Arlette Elkaïm Sartre. After Sartre's death, she would become his heir and the manager of his literary estate. Along with Gallimard, she would inherit the money that came in over the years from Sartre's royalties, copyright permissions, and translations. One day, she would be a very wealthy woman.

The news made the front page of France Soir, with a large photograph of Sartre and his "Jewish-Algerian daughter." Readers were shocked. Sartre a *father?* Had he not declared in *Words:* "There are no good fathers. . . . It is not the men who are at fault but the paternal bond which is rotten?"[30] Sartre's friends and acquaintances, none of whom had been forewarned, were hurt and bewildered. They felt abandoned, left out of a family secret. As for Wanda, Michelle, and Evelyne, they were beside themselves with grief and rage.

A few months earlier, when he first tried to broach the subject with his women, Sartre had promised each in turn that he would not adopt Arlette without that woman's consent. He made the same promise to Liliane Siegel, whom he had been psychoanalyzing for the past five years. Siegel recalls that Sartre kept asking her: "Have you changed your mind yet?" She had not. Nor had the others.

That evening, when the news burst over Paris, Wanda started breaking the furniture in her apartment. Evelyne wept. "You didn't have the right to do that to me," she told Sartre. "You told me you would never do anything to hurt me. Well, you have hurt me." Michelle had threatened to kill herself if Sartre went ahead with the adoption. She did not carry out her threat, but she felt utterly betrayed.[31] Liliane Siegel, who was never a lover of Sartre's (though he had pressured her) found herself unable to finish the yoga class she was teaching that evening. She went home and sobbed. Finally, when she was able to speak, she phoned Beauvoir:

"Liliane, what is it? Talk to me. Get a grip on yourself."

"He said . . . he said, Beaver, that he'd never do it without my consent!"

"Ah, so you know. He wanted to tell you himself . . ."

"But he promised, Beaver . . ."

"Come on, calm down, you know very well that it doesn't mean a thing to him."

"He'd promised, Beaver."

. . .

"Are you alone?"

"Yes."

"It's late, Liliane, take a sleeping pill, you can talk about it with him tomorrow. Are you listening to me, Liliane?"

"Yes."

"Then do as I say. Take care, my dear."[32]

Sartre told both Beauvoir and Zonina that the reaction of the other women left him cold. He saw envy and material interest behind their sobs and complaints, he said.

Soviet intellectuals kept wishing that Sartre would take more advantage of his influence, which, since his rejection of the Nobel Prize, was greater than ever before. When Sartre and Beauvoir returned to the Soviet Union in July 1965, Zonina and her friends were outraged by the Brodsky trial. Joseph Brodsky, a young Jewish poet, had been condemned to five years of forced labor in a remote state farm, accused of "social parasitism." Although he earned his living as a translator, he did not belong to the Writers Union, or any other state organization, so this was "parasitism." At Ehrenburg's urging, Sartre, for the first time since he had started regularly coming to the USSR in 1962, made an intervention. He wrote to the president of the Supreme Soviet, asking for Brodsky to be pardoned. His letter was so courteous that it verged on sycophantic: "Mr. President, If I take the liberty of addressing you, it's because I am a friend of your great country. . . . I know perfectly well that what the western enemies of peaceful coexistence are already calling 'the Brodsky affair' is a regrettable exception."[33]

Zonina was more forthright in the report she wrote the Soviet Writers Union about Sartre's visit. "The arguments of [Brodsky's] accusers are so absurd and incredible that the friends of the USSR, including Sartre, have trouble defending our country."[34]

After their month with Zonina, Sartre traveled for three weeks with Arlette, then two weeks with Wanda. Beauvoir went on vacation with a new friend, Sylvie Le Bon.

In the spring of 1960, Sylvie Le Bon, a seventeen-year-old baccalaureate student from Rennes, had written Beauvoir an admiring letter. A few months later, Le Bon came on a visit to Paris, and Beauvoir took her out to dinner. The girl was clearly extremely bright and had a lively, attractive face, but she was painfully shy, nervous, and fidgety. She wanted to study philosophy at the Ecole Normale. Beauvoir encouraged her. When they parted, Beauvoir bought her a bunch of newspapers and magazines from a press kiosk, telling her it was important to know something about politics.

Over the next three years they met from time to time. They drew closer after Françoise de Beauvoir's death, in November 1963. Beauvoir found Le Bon a great comfort. By that time, Le Bon was living at the Ecole Normale for women on the Boulevard Jourdan (near the Cité Universitaire, where Sartre had once lived), and doing brilliantly in her studies. She and her girlfriends were often in trouble with the authorities for their unruly behavior, and Beauvoir enjoyed hearing about these wild doings. The two women liked to discuss books and films. By 1964 they were seeing each other regularly.

Le Bon was flattered to be sought out by the most famous woman writer in France. As for Beauvoir, with the twenty-one-year-old Le Bon as a companion, there were moments when she felt almost young again. The pages she would write about Le Bon in *All Said and Done* were as warm as any she ever wrote:

The better I knew Sylvie, the more akin I felt to her. She too was an intellectual and she too was passionately in love with life. And she was like me in many other ways: with thirty-three years of difference I recognized my qualities and my faults in her. She had one very rare gift: she knew how to listen. Her observations, her smiles, her silences, made one feel like talking. . . . I told her about my past in detail, and day by day I keep her in touch with my life. . . . I loved her enthusiasms and her anger, her gravity, her gaiety, her horror of the commonplace, her uncalculating generosity.

That summer, in August 1965, the two women went to Corsica. Le Bon had done extremely well in her *agrégation,* and they had reason to celebrate. Le Bon calls it their "honeymoon."

After their travels with others, Beauvoir and Sartre spent six weeks together in Rome. They were besieged by desperate phone calls from Paris. Rehearsals were in progress for a new production of *The Condemned of Altona.* Six years after the original production, Serge Reggiani was again playing Frantz. The lead female roles had again gone to Evelyne and Wanda. Sartre had insisted on this.

According to the phone calls, the rehearsals were going badly, very badly. The producer, François Périer, and Serge Reggiani both told Sartre the same thing: Wanda had not been up to it six years ago, and now, after all the drugs she had taken, she was an embarrassment to the rest of the cast. She spent her time in the dressing room, she had not learned her lines properly, and she did not have her heart in it. Sartre was firm: "You play it with Wanda or you don't play it." There were tearful phone calls from Evelyne, who threatened to drop out of the play if Sartre did not do something about Wanda. Sartre lectured Evelyne about family loyalty.

The production was a disaster. Both the women, Evelyne and Wanda, were flayed by the press. One critic after another complained that they were inaudible and acted mechanically. It was as if Serge Reggiani were alone onstage, they said. "I have never seen an actress

so completely without talent," one critic said of Wanda. He described
Evelyne Rey as a "magnificent block of ice."[35]

On October 12, dreading the domestic scenes that awaited him,
Sartre said good-bye to Beauvoir in Naples. He was taking the
overnight train back to Paris; Beauvoir was driving back alone in her car.
They arranged to meet in the evening of the fourteenth, at seven P.M., at
her place.

Sartre's train got to Paris on the morning of the thirteenth, and he
launched straight into what he called his "official duties," which
meant seeing the women, one after the other. That night he went to
bed early, exhausted. On the fourteenth, he got up and read through
his correspondence, and was at his mother's in time for lunch.

He and his mother were at the table when Lanzmann rang. It had
been announced on the news that Beauvoir had had an accident, and
was in a hospital in Joigny. That afternoon, Lanzmann and Sartre
drove down the motorway at a hundred miles an hour. They found
Beauvoir in a private room, fussed over by nurses, with four broken
ribs, a swollen face, and a massive bruise over her left eye, where she
had had stitches. She told them, with the febrile excitement of someone in shock, that she had rounded a bend too fast and found herself
in front of a huge truck, and that the driver had saved her life by
swerving to the left. The front of her sturdy Peugeot 404 was
smashed in. The police had told her there were lots of accidents on
that curve. She had not at first realized she was hurt. When she was
helped out of the car, all she could think of was how she would get to
Paris by seven that evening. And then the ambulance men had
arrived and made her lie on a stretcher, and she saw that she was
bleeding and felt the pain.

Lanzmann returned to Paris, and Sartre stayed the night in a
nearby hotel. The next day, he accompanied Beauvoir back to the Rue
Schoelcher in an ambulance. She was in pain, unable to undress herself. Sartre helped her upstairs and assured her he would stay with her
until she could walk again. "What good are you to me," she said,
"since with your earplugs and sleeping pills I need to shake you to
wake you up?" He promised to compromise and not use his earplugs.

She was in bed for three weeks. Sartre, Lanzmann, and Le Bon
took turns looking after her. A nurse came for an hour every day to

help. "The hardest thing is to keep people away," Sartre told Lena. "Her apartment is literally invaded by flowers."

Zonina came back to Paris in mid-November 1965, for three weeks. It had not been easy getting a travel visa from the Soviet government. Sartre had had to write letters stating that Zonina was his translator and she had been invited by the *Temps modernes*. She stayed in a hotel on the Boulevard Raspail, close to Sartre's apartment. This time, Sartre did not tell the other women about her visit.

In December, Sartre and Beauvoir accompanied Zonina to St.-Raphael, a resort town on the Riviera, where Zonina was speaking at a conference. Sartre told the women he was with Beauvoir. *France Soir* reported that Sartre and Beauvoir had been seen walking around St.-Raphael with their Russian friend and interpreter Madame Zonina. As soon as Sartre was back in Paris, Michelle was on the phone:

"I knew you were with your Russian girlfriend."
"Ah, the *France Soir* article. It's quite wrong."
"How can it be?"
"Zonina gave a talk at St-Raphael, but it was last year. . . . You know what newspapers are like."

When Sartre went to see Elkaïm at their usual hour, he found a note on the door: "I'm not here. No point in ringing the bell. The dog won't stop barking." Sartre tore up the note, dropped the pieces on the doormat, and went to have a coffee. When he came back the shreds of paper had disappeared, so he knew Elkaïm was in. He rang the bell, setting off a racket of barking. Finally Elkaïm opened the door. For a long time she listened coldly while he gave his excuses. Then she went to the bathroom, and he heard her vomiting.

Sartre reminded her of their agreement. He had fully assumed his paternal role, he said, but she should not confuse it with another role. Her only demands of him should be filial. Elkaïm told him she did not like to be lied to.

In the end, she accompanied him as far as his mother's hotel. It appeared, Sartre told Zonina, that they were more or less reconciled.

•   •   •

From May 2 to June 6, 1966, Sartre and Beauvoir were back in the
Soviet Union. "What are you doing here in the midst of all this?"
Ehrenburg asked them.[36] He and Zonina and their friends could talk
of little other than the disastrous trial and deportation of two young
writers, Yuly Daniel and Andrei Sinyavsky, who as a result of publishing anti-Soviet works in the West, under pen names, had been sen-
tenced to years in hard labor camps. On Ehrenburg's initiative, a
petition was sent around calling for the writers' immediate release.
Zonina was one of sixty-two out of six thousand members of the
Soviet Writers Union who dared to sign. "It called for a great deal of
courage," Beauvoir writes. "Putting one's name to this petition meant
taking the risk of never being sent abroad again, of losing one's job
and of remaining unpublished for ever."[37]

It was the beginning of the dissident movement. Intellectuals were
now furtively passing self-published, forbidden literature—samizdat—
among themselves. But it was a depressing, frightening time. Sartre
and Beauvoir returned with Zonina to Yalta and Odessa, then took
the train to the Ukraine. They were constantly running up against
prohibitions. Foreigners could not travel here; foreigners were not
allowed to go there. It was absurd and immensely frustrating.

In 1965, the year after Sartre refused the Nobel Prize, the Swedish
Academy had awarded it to the Soviet writer Sholokhov. When
Zonina tried to arrange a meeting between Sartre and Solzhenitsyn
in the summer of 1966, she was told that Solzhenitsyn had no desire
to meet him. Solzhenitsyn was apparently enraged by Sartre's comment that Sholokhov deserved the Nobel Prize more than Pasternak.
The comment had no doubt influenced the Academy.

"Our trip was perfect happiness," Sartre wrote to Zonina when he
got back to Paris. "There was nothing gay about it, however. Your
health, your moments of fatigue, . . . the depressing atmosphere of
Moscow, the 'affair,' and all the serious things—painful things—we
said to each other."[38]

Zonina, as usual, was more blunt. She was angry about events in
the Soviet Union, she told Sartre, and had resigned from the Writers
Union in disgust. She felt very unhappy, and above all, terribly tired.

Sartre did not understand her life. How could he, since he did not know its daily detail? He had disappointed her. She had loved him for his liberty, but she had come to realize that he was not free. He did not say what he believed. He did not do what he wanted to do.

Sartre was crushed, unable to work for a week. "Everything you said was so true in its hardness that I could only accept it," he wrote back. It did not help, he said, that he was growing old. He had become less free as he grew older. There were so many accumulated obligations. His only real freedom was *her,* Lena, and the love he had for her.

Beauvoir's story "Misunderstanding in Moscow," discarded during her lifetime and published after her death, sheds interesting light on her feelings in the summer of 1966, as she traveled around the Soviet Union with Sartre and Zonina.[39] Even the fictional transformations are revealing. The Sartre character is called André; the Zonina character is called Macha, the name of Zonina's real-life daughter. In the story Macha is not André's lover, but his daughter. And yet they act like lovers.

The story is set at the time of writing, in June 1966. André and Nicole are a French couple in their early sixties. Both are painfully conscious that they are aging. André is a well-known and politically committed intellectual, and in Paris he is in constant demand. Nicole is a retired schoolteacher. They have always told each other everything, at least in theory.

They have come to Moscow to see André's daughter, Macha. She was brought up by her mother, and André saw very little of her while she was growing up, but in the last five years they have discovered each other with joy.

Macha is waiting for them at the airport. "A beautiful young woman," Nicole thinks to herself. They wait an interminable time for the baggage to arrive. Nicole had forgotten; nothing happens fast in this country. Macha drives slowly (like everyone else in Moscow) to the Peking Hotel. André says how excited he is to be there again. Nicole is already missing Paris.

They get out of the car and breathe in the familiar smell of diesel fumes. The price of their hotel room has tripled in the last three years. At least the plumbing works, Nicole thinks to herself. And for the first time there are curtains covering the windows.

André has often said how pleased he is that the two women—"the two people he loves most in the world"—get on so well. Nicole, it is true, feels real friendship for Macha. But from the time they arrive, she also feels twinges of other things.

She feels old, for a start, and tells herself that it must be the contrast with Macha, who is so fresh and vigorous. And she can't help it: she's bored with Moscow. The city is uglier each time they see it. "It's a pity that changes are almost always for the worse," she muses, "whether places or people."

Each time they visit the USSR, Macha acts as their guide and interpreter. She is the one who has to negotiate their itinerary with the Intourist authorities. She is the one who knows this country, its contradictions, and its frightful red tape. But it means they are in her hands. And sometimes Nicole would prefer not to have Macha decide everything—right down to the square they sit in to have lunch, the one Macha insists has the best view of the church.

Macha is admirably independent, Nicole reflects. She is submissive to no man. And yet she enjoys her femininity—far more so than she, Nicole, has ever done. Perhaps it is because Macha lives in a country where women do not suffer from an inferiority complex.

Nicole longs to be alone with André. On their previous visits to the Soviet Union, Macha had her own work to attend to as well. On this trip, she is with them all the time. André appears to like it. Nicole keeps wondering: doesn't he ever want to be alone with me? They never have a chance to talk, just the two of them. It is making her morose.

Sometimes she finds herself forgetting that Macha is André's daughter. There is a complicity between them, a freshness and tenderness. The two of them say "tu" to each other, and both say "vous" to Nicole. It hurts Nicole to see André use the same words and winning smiles with Macha that he once used with her. She is fed up with the interminable discussions between André and Macha about Soviet culture. And she can sense Macha's impatience with André's

questions and comments. " 'You are too abstract,' Macha kept telling him."

The vacation lumbers past. In less than a week they will return to
Paris. Nicole is looking forward to their departure. Then André ruins
everything.

He smiled at her. "You wanted to go and see a dacha. Well, it's
arranged," he told her.

"Oh, Macha *is* good."

"It's the dacha of a friend of hers, about thirty kilometers
away. Youri will drive us there, not this Sunday but the next."

"The next? But we're leaving on Tuesday."

"No, Nicole. You know we decided to extend our trip by ten
days."

"You've decided that, without even telling me!" Nicole said.

Suddenly there was red smoke in her head, a red fog in front
of her eyes, something red was screaming in her throat. He
doesn't give a damn about me! He didn't say a word!

Did he really believe he had told her? she wonders. He was drinking a lot, far too much, and was often drunk. But, in fact, Nicole is
sure he is lying. It would not be the first time. He lied about empty
bottles, and sometimes he pretended he had seen a doctor when he
hadn't. When she caught him, he laughed. "It would have been too
long to explain, so I took a shortcut." But this time, she can hardly
contain her fury.

The fact that he had lied was not the worst: he lied out of cowardice, like a child afraid of reprimand. The worst was that he
had made this decision with Macha without taking her into
account in the least. . . . In three weeks he had never once tried
to wangle a tête-à-tête with her; all his smiles, all his tenderness
went towards Macha.

Nicole is unable to hide her rage. She threatens to go back to Paris
early. "If you want to," André says. In front of Macha, they keep up a

polite façade all day. In the evening, André drinks four glasses of vodka. There's something senile about his attempts to converse with Macha in Russian, Nicole thinks to herself. Macha was giggling at his accent; the two were as thick as thieves. Nicole is beginning to wonder whether her past life with André was quite simply a mirage. So many women lied to themselves about their lives. Perhaps she did, too.

She drinks too much and goes to bed feeling sad and lost. When she wakes up, her head is heavy. She opens her eyes. There's André, sitting in an armchair at the end of her bed, watching her. Her lips tremble. He is speaking to her, in that caressing voice she liked so much. We can never be quite sure about our memories, he says. He comes toward her, puts his arms around her shoulders, kisses her on the temple, and tells her that even if he did forget to tell her, there is no reason to be so upset. She clings to him, her cheek on his jacket, and cries. What a relief! It is so tiring to hate someone you love.

In the corridor she takes his arm. They are reconciled. It was a misunderstanding.

Three months later, in mid-September 1966, Beauvoir and Sartre flew to Tokyo together. Seventeen hours of flight. A new country, a new adventure.

Sartre had more readers in Japan than in any other country. Beauvoir's *The Second Sex,* translated into Japanese in 1965, was a best seller. Nevertheless, they were by no means prepared for the reception awaiting them. There were more than a hundred journalists at the airport, blinding them with their flash bulbs. A vast crowd of mostly young people called out their names and tried to catch hold of their hands and arms as they passed. Their interpreter, Tomiko Asabuki, guided them into a room where they were bombarded with questions from the press.

For a month they traveled around the country, gave lectures, and met left-wing intellectuals. Sartre spoke at a huge meeting to protest the Vietnam War. Beauvoir, as usual, ploughed through a small library of books about Japan. Sartre, as usual, preferred to try to understand the culture by getting to know one person intimately. During their stay, the tiny, attentive, adoring Tomiko Asabuki became his lover.[40] "In almost every journey we've made or that you've made, there's been a woman who turned out to be the incarnation of the country for you," Beauvoir observed.[41]

On their way back, they stopped for five days in Moscow to see Zonina. It was Sartre's eleventh trip to the Soviet Union. He did not want to know it, but he knew, and Zonina knew. Their love affair was over.

TWELVE

TRAGIC ENDINGS, NEW BEGINNINGS

November 1966–May 1971

Her suicide created shock waves in the French Left Bank intelligentsia. Evelyne Rey, formerly Evelyne Lanzmann, killed herself on November 18, 1966. She was thirty-six. "All those who knew her loved her," declared the obituary in the *Nouvel Observateur,* "because she was bursting with life and because she loved everything."[1]

There was nothing ambiguous about Evelyne's death. She took an overdose of barbiturates and made sure no one would find her until the pills had done their job. She left several farewell letters on her table—to her brother Claude and to Sartre, among others—in which she scrupulously tried to relieve them of remorse. "I am suffering and it's no one's fault. My relationship with myself has gone off track."[2]

Evelyne's acting career had not been a success. "In a way she didn't have acting in her blood," her brother Claude Lanzmann says. "She was afraid of the audience."[3] Her best role was as Estelle, in Sartre's play *No Exit* (a part Sartre had originally written for Wanda), and she had been thrilled when O.R.T.F., French Radio and Television, broadcast a television adaptation of the play in October 1965. Tragically, her one really major role, the one Sartre had written for her—Johanna, in *The Condemned of Altona*—had proved too difficult for her. The "magnificent block of ice" remark had stung. On the whole, the theater had brought her a lot of heartache and humiliation.

Her love life had been equally disastrous. She was beautiful, and men were readily attracted to her, but the men she loved were usually married, and in any event not committed to her. Her affair with Sartre had been clandestine. Of course, Sartre had been loyal to her in his way and had continued to see her three times a week, an hour and a half each time, and to support her financially. But she knew he was disappointed in her as an actress.

Recently, both Sartre and Evelyne's brother Claude had been pressing her to give up acting and take up journalism. "That would be to accept my defeat as an actress," she had protested.[4] The final straw was when her body failed her. In March 1966 she had been about to leave on tour with *Altona* when she contracted pleurisy. For weeks she was in the hospital, in a great deal of pain. When she came out, only one of her lungs functioned, and the slightest exertion left her breathless.

From then on, she was tired and depressed, anxious about her career, and frightened about her health. In the late autumn, feeling slightly stronger, she went to Tunisia to participate in a documentary about Tunisian women. She came back exhausted, but seemed proud of the work she had done. While there, she had taken up with a former lover, a well-known television producer who had plans for her to play a leading role in his forthcoming television show.[5] But she was not in love with him, and she was tired of acting. One morning in November, in the cold predawn hours, she chose death.

Sartre reacted to the news with violent abdominal cramps. "There is, of course, the guilt," he told Zonina three months later. "We all feel that. It weighs on us. Life wasn't easy for her, and finally, I wasn't easy on her either, despite appearances." Since Evelyne's death, he felt no joy in anything, he added, and no desire to do anything, except to plod on with Flaubert.

"To tell the truth, of all the deaths that occurred among people I knew during these last years, only one really moved me very deeply, and that was Evelyne's," Beauvoir would write in *All Said and Done*. "But I have no wish to speak of it."

In truth, Beauvoir would have liked to talk about it, but couldn't.

She had promised Sartre she would not mention his passion for Evelyne, because of Michelle. She discussed the problem with Claude Lanzmann. Should she talk about Evelyne without talking about Evelyne's relationship with Sartre? Lanzmann said no; that would completely falsify Evelyne's life. But when *Force of Circumstance* came out, Evelyne was very hurt. She had been a close member of the family for years, and once again she had been left out of the public picture. Beauvoir had talked at length about Claude, but scarcely mentioned *her*. She seemed doomed to be hidden in the background.

When Evelyne killed herself, she and Sartre had not been lovers for ten years. Nevertheless, Beauvoir felt sure that the unsatisfactory relationship with Sartre had played a role in Evelyne's suicide. She told John Gerassi:

> To understand Evelyne you need to understand what her rather complicated relationship with Sartre was like, and perhaps this relationship was at the root of her suicide, though I don't think so. Already because of Michelle, it was a mess. Sartre gave her a lot—his time, his energy, his presence, his tenderness—really, he gave her a lot. . . . But it stopped at a clandestine relationship. Everyone knew about it, but it was nevertheless not public. . . . Evelyne did not like that.[6]

Ten years after that conversation with Gerassi, Beauvoir's biographer, Deirdre Bair, asked Beauvoir about Evelyne's suicide. Beauvoir became agitated and spoke with obvious distress. "It was this very, very, great, great friendship she had for Sartre that scarred her enormously," Beauvoir said in such a low voice that Bair could hardly hear her. "I should have written about her . . . I saw her a lot and liked her very much. I owed that to her."[7]

Jacques Lanzmann is convinced that her men friends *used* Evelyne. She was known both for her beauty and for being the lover of famous men, and this made her something of a trophy. After Sartre there were many boyfriends. "They could join hands," he says bitterly. "They had her hide."[8]

Evelyne's former husband, Serge Rezvani, writes that though Evelyne's death was a brutal shock to her family and friends, no one wanted to see the real tragedy behind it. "Today I can say that Evelyne was the consenting victim of a misogynous frivolousness which, until 1968, characterized the Left Bank intelligentsia."[9]

Rezvani received a lot of flak for that sentence. The Left Bank critics did not like it at all.

In the early sixties, the second and third volumes of Beauvoir's memoirs aroused a febrile new interest in the Sartre-Beauvoir couple. *The Prime of Life* (1960) and *Force of Circumstance* (1963) were runaway successes. There were photos of Beauvoir and Sartre in all the magazines. The Sartre-Beauvoir legend was firmly in place.

Beauvoir's memoirs, the *story* of her life, inevitably had repercussions in her actual life. She received letters, many letters. Some readers were grateful; others were enraged.[10] Some wished she had said more; many wished she had said less. There were frequent complaints about distortions and misrepresentation. Sartre's other women were angry about being left in the background, as if they hardly featured in Sartre's life.

To anyone who knew the Sartrean clan, it was clear that Beauvoir was taking control of the public image. She was telling the story *her* way. It is not that she skimmed over all the anguished episodes in her past; she did not. Much of it was scrupulously honest. But the act of writing gave her immense power. She was publicly stating her position of primacy among Sartre's women. She could leave Wanda out of the story. She could put in a withering comment here and there about Olga, Dolores, or anyone else who had once caused her torment. Above all, the tone and viewpoint of her narrative created the *effect* of control. She was looking back on her past from a position of triumph.

"Everything changes when you tell about life," the narrator in Sartre's novel *Nausea* muses. "It's a change no one notices: the proof is that people talk about true stories. As if there could possibly be true stories; things happen one way and we tell about them in the opposite sense. You seem to start at the beginning: 'It was a fine autumn evening in 1922. . . .' And in reality you have started at the end."

Wanda hated Beauvoir's memoirs. She was jealous of the fuss surrounding them. She resented this idealized portrait, as she saw it, of the Sartre-Beauvoir relationship. To her, the books were full of lies. Beauvoir had hardly mentioned Wanda's role in Sartre's life during the war. Worse, the books made Wanda wonder about Sartre. To her, he had always systematically denied his closeness to Beauvoir.

Like her sister, Wanda had always been prone to wild rages, but after their mother's death, in the early 1960s, Wanda developed paranoia. She thought everyone was plotting against her, and her hatred grew violent. Her mental state was not helped by drugs. For the past decade she had been rivaling Sartre with her intake of amphetamines and barbiturates. These days she was taking cocaine as well. There were sinister scrapes with drug dealers. Once, she fell in the street and did not know where she lived. The police picked her up and took her to a hospital. Finally, they contacted Sartre.

These days, Wanda hated her sister, Olga, but there was no one she hated as much as Beauvoir. Whenever she came across Beauvoir's photograph in the press, she would cover it with furious scribbling. She stuck pins in a voodoo doll, trying to will Beauvoir to an early death. After *Force of Circumstance* came out, Wanda obtained a gun—a "lady's revolver," which could kill from close range—and told Sartre she had every intention of committing murder.

It was Sylvie Le Bon who took action. She formed a small "commando unit," she says, with two girlfriends from the Ecole Normale. They rang Wanda's bell on the Rue du Dragon and announced over the intercom that they were journalists from *Elle* magazine, hoping to be able to interview the famous actress Marie Olivier. Wanda let them in. While her girlfriends pounced on Wanda and held her captive, Le Bon went through Wanda's drawers, looking both for the gun and for letters from Sartre. (Beauvoir was afraid Wanda would destroy the letters she had received from Sartre over the years.) Le Bon found the gun, but not the letters.[11] The women left Wanda bruised and terrified.

Beauvoir told Le Bon off in no uncertain terms. "I told her I intended to take the gun from Wanda. She did not try to stop me," Le Bon says today. "It was the mid-sixties. They were radical times. I was a little terrorist." She smiles. "It's true, we were rather crazy. I'm not proud of this episode."[12]

•   •   •

Nelson Algren was the only person who vented his fury publicly about Beauvoir's memoirs. *America Day by Day* and *The Mandarins* had already stretched his tolerance. "To publicize a relationship existing between two people is to destroy it," he told an interviewer. "See, the big thing about sexual love is it lets you become her and lets her become you, but when you share the relationship with everyone who can afford a book, you reduce it. It no longer has meaning. It's good for the book trade, I guess, but you certainly lose interest in the other party."[13]

That was before he read *Force of Circumstance*. The English translation came out in the United States in the spring of 1965. As a prepublication appetizer, extracts were published in the November and December 1964 issues of *Harper's* magazine. The two installments were called "The Question of Fidelity." The editors picked out those morsels that would most interest American readers: namely, Beauvoir's account of her and Sartre's "American affairs"—Sartre's with Vanetti and hers with Algren. Dolores Vanetti was given the thinnest of disguises as "M." Algren was called by his name. He was out in the open, swinging in the breeze.

The November issue had a candy pink cover featuring two blue eyes. Beauvoir's? On a wintry Chicago evening, Algren opened the magazine at the cover story. He read how excited Sartre had been to go to America after the Liberation. He read about Sartre's affair with "M." in New York. Then he read about Beauvoir's own trip to America:

> I became attached to Nelson Algren toward the end of my stay. Although I related this affair—very approximately—in *The Mandarins,* I return to it, not out of any taste for gossip, but in order to examine more closely a problem that in *The Prime of Life,* the second volume of my autobiography, I took to be too easily resolved: Is there any possible reconciliation between fidelity and freedom? And if so, at what price? . . .
>
> There are many couples who conclude more or less the same

pact as that of Sartre and myself: to maintain throughout all deviations from the main path a "certain fidelity." "I have been faithful to thee, Cynara! in my fashion." Such an undertaking has its risks. . . .

If the two allies allow themselves only passing sexual liaisons, then there is no difficulty, but it also means that the freedom they allow themselves is not worthy of the name. Sartre and I have been more ambitious; it has been our wish to experience "contingent loves": but there is one question we have deliberately avoided: How would the third person feel about the arrangement?

In the December installment, subtitled "An American Rendezvous," Algren was treated to details he himself had never been told:

"When you get to Chicago, go and see Nelson Algren for me," a young intellectual told me when I was in New York in 1947. I have given a faithful account of my first meeting with him in my book *America Day by Day* . . . but I did not mention the rapport that immediately sprang up between us. . . . I called him before I left for the railroad station; they had to take the telephone away from me by force. . . .

The weeks passed; Sartre asked me in one of his letters to postpone my departure because M. was staying another ten days in Paris. Suddenly that made me feel the nostalgia I described Anne as feeling in my novel *The Mandarins*: I'd had enough of being a tourist; I wanted to walk about on the arm of a man who, temporarily, would be mine. I called Algren. . . .

People would often talk about him to me; they said he was unstable, moody, even neurotic; I liked being the only one who understood him.

Algren reviewed Beauvoir's memoirs in the magazine *Ramparts*:

"When you get to Paris, see Simone de Beauvoir," a pseudo-intellectual once urged me. People claimed she was surprisingly sententious, humorless and tyrannical for a good writer. I liked being the only one to know she wasn't a good writer. As soon as I reached the Deux Magots I phoned the native quarter.[14]

He reviewed the book again in *Harper's*. His piece was called "The Question of Simone de Beauvoir." The following extracts give the gist:

No chronicler of our lives since Theodore Dreiser has combined so steadfast a passion for human justice with a dullness so asphyxiating as Mme. de Beauvoir. While other writers reproach the reader gently, she flattens his nose against the blackboard, gooses him with a twelve-inch ruler, and warns him if he doesn't start acting grown-up she's going to hold her breath till he does. . . .

When Madame is right she is very *very* right. And when she's wrong she's preposterous. . . .

Mme. de Beauvoir's world, that she reports with such infinite accuracy, is a reflected vision; no one ever lived behind that looking-glass. Which is why all the characters of her novels, although drawn directly from life, have no life on the printed page. . . .

Not one to risk her own freedom, Mme. de Beauvoir sensed she could trust Jean-Paul Sartre to be faithless. That was a shrewd move right there. . . . "Sartre and I have been more ambitious; it has been our wish to experience 'contingent loves.' " . . .

Put cats in the coffee and mice in the tea—
And welcome Queen Alice with thirty-three!

Anybody who can experience love contingently has a mind that has recently snapped. How can love be *contingent*? Contingent upon *what*? . . . Procurers are more honest than philosophers. They name this *How-about-a-quickie-kid* gambit as "chippying." . . .

Mme. de Beauvoir's early determination "to write sacrificial essays in which the author strips himself bare without excuses" she has since employed with such earnestness and skill that practically everybody has now been sacrificed excepting herself. . . .

Saigon, they say, will fall one day. With a terrible rush and a horrible roar, nation upon nation will fall into riot, totter to anarchy, and plunge at last into endless night. Beaches whereon waters once met the land, and the sky came down to meet both, will shrink from the sea's irradiated touch. Then a low dread pall of greenish-gray will enwrap and enwind earth, forest, sky-scraper, and sky in an endless orbit through endless space through endless time, in a silence without end.

Except for one small hoarse human voice burbling up from the ancestral ocean's depths—"In this matter man's sexuality may be modified. Sartre needs peace and quiet. The dead are better adapted to the earth than the living. Bost is on the cin-ema Vigilance Committee. I want to go skiing. Merleau-Ponty"—

Will she ever quit talking?[15]

In the summer of 1966, *Zeitgeist,* a small literary magazine in the Midwest, published a poem by Algren called "Goodbye Lilies, Hello Spring." He dedicated it to Simone de Beauvoir.[16]

I was like Héloise You were Abélard
On the paperback shelves it'll sell by the yard—
Avoid, avoid that shadowy plot
And the old fraud below it who can't shut her mouth—
O wasn't it magical O wasn't it tragical
Love like ours will never die out
(Providing I tell it the way it was not)—

The last of the three stanzas reads:

Down in some basement below the bin
Where baby-rats drown when water creeps in
Straight down upside-down in the slag and the guck
Stuff the yammering humbug straight down in the muck.

Let her yack on forever way way down there
Then slam the door and jump up the stair—
Open the window and let in some air
Each April should teach us how to swing:
Saying Goodbye Lilies
Hello
Spring.

In May 1981, Nelson Algren was seventy-two. He had moved to Sag Harbor, Long Island. He had just been elected to the prestigious American Academy of Arts and Letters, and a journalist, W. J. Weatherby, came to his cottage to interview him.

In the course of the conversation, Weatherby asked Algren about Beauvoir. Algren had not had any communication with Beauvoir for almost twenty years, but it did not take him long to become worked up. "I've been in whorehouses all over the world and the woman there always closes the door, whether it's in Korea or India," he said. "But this woman flung the door open and called in the public and the press. . . . I don't have any malice against her, but I think it was an appalling thing to do."[17] Algren had previously mentioned seeing a doctor about a heaviness in his chest. Weatherby thought it wise to change the subject.

The following evening, Algren was due to have a party in his cottage, to celebrate his new award. The first guest to arrive found Algren's dead body lying on the floor. He had died of a massive heart attack.

In France, too, the newspapers reported his death. Poupette rang Simone to offer her condolences. Beauvoir was cold. "Aren't you sorry?" Poupette asked. "Don't you feel anything for him?"

"Why should I?" her elder sister answered. "What did he feel for me that he could have written those horrible things?"[18]

But she did not take off Algren's ring. She would wear it to her grave.

Sartre was under a lot of pressure, emotionally and politically, and was drinking heavily. In February 1967, three months after Evelyne's

suicide, he and Beauvoir made a trip to the Middle East—first to
Egypt, then to Israel. The *Temps modernes* was doing a special issue on
the Israeli-Arab conflict, with Claude Lanzmann coordinating the
Israel section and Ali el Samman, a young Egyptian journalist who
was studying in Paris, the Arab section. The four of them traveled
around Egypt together, seeing the sights, visiting Palestinian refugee
camps, and talking to left-wing intellectuals. They even met
President Nasser.

On their last night in Cairo, they were given a lavish farewell dinner in a sixteenth-century Arab palace, with a floor show that
included belly dancing and a whirling dervish. When Beauvoir went
to bed it was after midnight, and the men were still going strong.
Sartre, according to Claude Lanzmann, was by this time "dead
drunk":

> He drank because there was a woman he wanted to seduce. He
> was very nervous, tense and aggressive. If you asked the Beaver,
> she would probably say we'd just got back from Gaza and he had
> seen refugees. It's true, but not the whole truth. There was this
> woman and he had to leave her. It was the day before we were
> flying out. We were with an Egyptian fellow who had been our
> guide—a journalist, a very nice, funny guy, Ali. And in this hotel
> room, stuffed with microphones, Sartre said: "You're a homo,
> Ali, you're a dirty homo."
>
> The guy did not know what had hit him. He laughed at first, a
> forced laugh. I said, "Sartre, stop it. You're nuts." Sartre said
> "You fuck off, Lanzmann." And then he called me a homo, too.
> And finally I said to Ali, "Listen, we're going to have to put him
> to bed." We had to pick him up, undress him, and so on.
>
> The next morning, at 8 or 9, there was a press conference, the
> big one before we left. I went to wake the Beaver in her room,
> and told her Sartre wouldn't be able to do it. Sartre had blood-
> shot eyes, but he did it. He has an iron constitution. . . . But he's
> aggressive, this guy. . . . and macho. When he's in a bar with a
> woman at 3 am and there are guys who piss him off, he speaks
> their language, like a gangster. I've seen him intimidate tough
> men.[19]

After Egypt, Sartre and Beauvoir spent two weeks in Israel. Claude Lanzmann flew home after three days, and Elkaïm flew in to Tel Aviv. Sartre thought it important for his adoptive Jewish daughter to see Israel.[20]

The Arab-Israeli issue went to press at the end of May. In his introduction, Sartre said how divided he and his friends felt in this conflict. They had lived through World War II and been horrified by anti-Semitism in Europe. During the Algerian War, they had sided with the Arab freedom fighters in their struggle against colonialism. "We are living this conflict as if it were our personal tragedy."

A few days later, on June 5, 1967, Israel bombed Egypt. By the end of the Six-Day War, as it came to be known, Israel had captured the Sinai Peninsula, East Jerusalem, the Golan Heights, the Gaza Strip, and the West Bank. French intellectuals were once again divided. Had Israel acted in self-defense, as it claimed, or had it been the aggressor? It was like the Dreyfus affair, Sartre wrote to Zonina. Everyone had strong opinions, and he himself risked falling out with his best friends.

The Arab-Israeli conflict was one of the few subjects on which Sartre and Beauvoir slightly diverged. They both firmly believed that the Jews had the right to a nation and that the Palestinians had a right to Palestine. But Sartre was dismayed by the policies of the Israeli government, who seemed determined to make negotiation with the Palestinians impossible. Beauvoir, convinced that the Palestinian leaders would not be content until they had destroyed Israel, was more sympathetic to Israel. "I was not in complete agreement with any single one of my friends," she writes, "and with some of them I was in total conflict."[21]

The Six-Day War caused a wariness between Sartre and Claude Lanzmann that would never entirely disappear. Lanzmann was passionately pro-Israel; Sartre was sharply critical of Israeli expansionism. Lanzmann, who had once been so impressed by Sartre's book on anti-Semitism, was now calling Sartre an "anti-Semite." Sartre told Lanzmann he was an "imperialist."[22]

But Lanzmann could not bear to fall out with Sartre. Nor could Bost. Sartre had once thrown Bost out of Beauvoir's apartment because Bost had sided with Jean Cau in an argument. On that occasion, Sartre ended up running after him, and they made up over a drink.

In their old age, Beauvoir remarked to Sartre: "Bost would have done anything not to remain on bad terms with you. And there's someone else who did a great deal not to break with you when there were disagreements, and that is Lanzmann."[23]

After Sartre's death, Jean Cau wrote:

> Sartre does not get angry. He expels people. There is no other choice.... If the Other takes a distance from Sartre, it can only lead to rupture.... And Sartre's entourage loudly approves of the exclusion. Out of servility? Not at all. His entourage breathes the Sartrean air. It's comprised of planets orbiting, as if nature intended it, around their night star. (A planet is not servile.) No, on the contrary, between Sartre and his satellites there reigns an atmosphere of cordiality, complicity, coded language, and humor. The relationship is not that of a master pontificating to his disciples ... but rather that of a "great guy" professor with students who are utterly disrespectful of his function (Sartre himself invites this disrespect), but fanatical about his person.[24]

Few had the privilege of observing Sartre close up, in his own home, as Cau did for eleven years. Cau's insights came from years of intimacy, followed by exclusion.

Sartre and Beauvoir had been outraged when the Americans began bombing North Vietnam in February 1965. Two years later, they participated in the Russell Tribunal, established by Bertrand Russell (who was ninety-four at the time) to arouse world opinion against American atrocities in Vietnam.

In May 1967, the tribunal met in Stockholm. The discussions lasted ten days. In November, the group met again, this time in Copenhagen. There were horrific reports from witnesses, including John Gerassi, the son of Stépha and Fernando—who had been in Vietnam collecting evidence—and Gisèle Halimi, Sartre and Beauvoir's lawyer friend.

The days were grueling, but the evenings were sociable. Sartre and Beauvoir met old friends from around the world. At some of the meetings, Claude Lanzmann stood in for Sartre. Bost was reporting for the *Nouvel Observateur.* Sylvie Le Bon came for the weekend, and she and Beauvoir hired a car and explored the region. Arlette Elkaïm participated in the capacity of Sartre's secretary.[25] Beauvoir and Sartre particularly liked Vladimir Dedijer, the Yugoslavian intellectual and militant, who presided over some of the meetings. Elkaïm, no doubt influenced by their affection for him, had an affair with him.

Sylvie Le Bon was teaching philosophy at the very school in Rouen— the Lycée Jeanne d'Arc—where Beauvoir had once taught. The minute her classes were over, Le Bon would take the first train back to Paris. In Rouen, she stayed in the Hôtel La Rochefoucauld, near the station, where Beauvoir had lived for two years. She took her morning coffee and croissant in Beauvoir's old haunt, the Métropole. "All this gave me a certain feeling of being reincarnated," Beauvoir would write in *All Said and Done.*[26]

Friends were struck by Le Bon's resemblance to Beauvoir. "Sylvie . . . expressed herself a bit like the Beaver—an unaffected, rather staccato way of talking—and seemed to echo her thoughts. She wore her hair in a chignon like the Beaver and there was something similar about her profile," Gisèle Halimi writes. "And she had the same friendly disposition."[27]

In *All Said and Done,* Beauvoir would write about her relationship with Sylvie in much the same way she had described her relationship with Lanzmann:

I was wrong in 1962 when I thought nothing significant would happen to me any more, apart from calamities; now once again a piece of great good fortune was offered to me. . . . There is no one who could have appreciated more than I what I have received from her. . . . She is as thoroughly interwoven in my life as I am in hers. . . . We read the same books, we see shows together, and we go for long drives in the car. There is such an interchange between us that I lose the sense of my age: she draws me forwards into her future, and there are times when the present recovers a dimension that it had lost.

Both women have always denied that it was a sexual relationship. Throughout her life, Beauvoir insisted, in public, that she had never had a sexual relationship with a woman. She would sometimes skirt around the question, saying that she thought all women were to some degree homosexual in their tastes, since women were more attractive, softer, their skin was nicer, and they were often more charming than men. "I have had some very important friendships with women, of course, some very close relationships, sometimes close in a physical sense," she said, "but they never aroused erotic passion on my part."[28] Her letters to Sartre, published posthumously, would indicate the opposite.

Sylvie Le Bon talks about this subject with the same vagueness and ambiguity. She says it was love, not friendship, that she and Beauvoir felt for each other. They were "intimate." Their relationship was "carnal but not sexual." She claims they were both primarily male-oriented. Echoing Beauvoir, Le Bon speaks as if lesbian lovemaking were simply not the real thing. She balks at the word *couple*. They were not a couple, she says, because from the beginning, Beauvoir encouraged her to have relationships with other people, and she did.

Looking back, Le Bon thinks she was too young to understand certain things, but that Beauvoir wanted her to be independent and not make demands Beauvoir could not satisfy. "The Beaver often used to tell me that she had been very cautious with me," Le Bon says. "She felt she had made mistakes in the past."

By the time she met Le Bon, Beauvoir was painfully conscious of her own aging body. In 1968, she published *The Woman Destroyed,* three novellas that explore the theme of the older woman coming to terms with no longer being sexually desirable. After that, she began research for an exhaustive essay on old age.

Le Bon remembers an emotionally charged turning point. They were traveling together in the North of Scotland in 1969, and feeling very close one evening. Le Bon wanted more. Beauvoir told her gently, "Any man would love to have you in his bed. But I am, quite literally, like an impotent man." Sylvie wonders what would have happened if she had taken the initiative. Perhaps Beauvoir simply needed reassurance? But she was young at the time, Le Bon says, and she took everything Beauvoir said at face value.

After that, they felt freer together, Le Bon says. What had to be said had been said, and they could be intimate at certain moments, without making any demands on each other.[29]

Sartre liked to describe himself as "the district nurse."[30] "You're lucky," he told his psychoanalyst friend Jean-Bertrand Pontalis. "Sick people come to your rooms, and they pay you. In my case, I'm the one who does the rounds, and I pay them."[31]

Sartre's schedule varied little over the years. He got up at eight-thirty. After breakfast in a local café, he worked from nine-thirty till one P.M. He had lunch with Michelle, Arlette, or Beauvoir, usually at the Coupole or the Palette, on the Boulevard du Montparnasse, then went back to work from four-thirty till eight-thirty P.M., with Beauvoir working beside him. On Monday and Thursday evenings he ate at Arlette's apartment; afterward they talked or watched television, and he slept there—he upstairs, she downstairs. Tuesday and Saturday evenings were at Beauvoir's, and he slept at her place. He spent Wednesday evenings with Michelle, then went home. Friday evenings he was at Wanda's till eleven P.M., then went home.

The weekends were equally rigidly organized: Saturday lunch with Arlette, Saturday evening with Beauvoir, Sunday breakfast with Arlette; Sunday lunch with his mother at her hotel (roast pork and mashed potatoes), and the evening with Michelle. After Anne-Marie Mancy died, in 1969 (he seemed to deal surprisingly easily with her death), Sartre had Sunday lunch with Beauvoir and Le Bon at the Coupole.

Complain as he might about the demands made on him, Sartre *chose* to prop himself up with this schedule. It gave him a sense of stability. His women shielded him from the world. They provided a diversion from work. They made him feel loved and needed. Sartre needed to have company. One night, when for once he found himself on his own—he would normally have been with Arlette, but she was away—he let himself into Arlette's apartment to watch television.

When André Puig, Arlette's boyfriend, came in around midnight, he found Sartre lying on the floor dead drunk. It took Puig half an hour to help Sartre to his feet.

Beauvoir spent a lifetime observing how easy it was for women to drive Sartre into a corner. "That guilty conscience of his," she said.[32] Sartre felt beholden to his women for loving him. He often wondered to what extent he was responsible for their unhappiness, their failure to find fulfillment. Why was Wanda, who had once read Stendhal and Tolstoy with pleasure, no longer capable of reading even detective novels? "Madness always leaves one feeling guilty," he told Lena. He knew there had been mistakes made somewhere, by someone.

He professed to hate the jealous scenes to which he was constantly subjected, but Sartre did more than most men to provoke them. His women all lived within ten minutes of him;[33] they rarely saw one another, and none of them knew the truth about his life. Arlette had no idea that after going for three weeks' vacation every year with *her,* Sartre went away with Wanda for two or three weeks. Wanda did not know that Sartre still saw Michelle. When he slept at Beauvoir's, he told Wanda he was sleeping at home. His letters to Wanda were filled with outrageous inventions. He'd be late back to Paris, he once told her. He was locked up in a castle in Austria. When he went off with other women, his alibi, nearly always, was Beauvoir. "I told you from the beginning I'd have to spend time with Simone de Beauvoir," he would say in an impatient voice to any woman who complained.

In September 1966, Sartre was in Japan, where he was having an affair with his Japanese interpreter, Tomiko Asabuki. "I want to fuck you," he wrote to Michelle. "I often think about it." By this time, Michelle Vian was beginning to wake up to Sartre's fabrications. "Before you lied well, but now you lie badly," she complained. "I don't want the whole truth. I just don't want to say 'How is the Beaver?' when you are with someone else."[34]

Every so often, there was a leak. When John Gerassi interviewed Wanda in 1973, he remarked that Michelle was very jealous. There was a long silence. Finally Wanda said in a small, incredulous voice, "I sometimes ask Sartre about Michelle. He tells me he never sees her!" Gerassi, realizing his mistake, hastened to cover up for Sartre: "That's true *now.* But you know, I meant a time in the past. He must have seen her then."[35]

In his letters to Zonina, Sartre recounted with amusement the lies he told his other women. At the same time, he assured Zonina that he was faithful to her and that she had nothing to be jealous about. He felt "vigilant friendship" for Wanda and Michelle, he said, and paternal feelings for Arlette. In reality, throughout his five-year affair with Zonina, Sartre continued to have a sexual relationship with Michelle, and possibly also with Wanda.

Although things between them had been at a low ebb for some time, Lena did not break off permanently with Sartre until the spring of 1967. She was hurt that Sartre had decided to spend three weeks in Spain that summer, instead of coming to the USSR as usual. Sartre explained that Beauvoir wanted to be with him a little longer that year. It was hard for Beauvoir in the USSR, he said, where she practically never saw him alone. "This is the least I can do for her, who twice a year acts as our chaperone without protesting, out of friendship for you and me."

He told Michelle the same story. He was going to spend July in Spain with Beauvoir, he said. It was *France Soir,* once again, who gave him away. Michelle, an avid reader of the gossip columns, came across a photo of him in Barcelona with Arlette. When he got back, she pointed it out to him.

"That's not Arlette," Sartre said.[36]

"For me, the most striking thing when I think about Sartre, it's how this man always tried to make a clean sweep of everything he was— *tabula rasa*—and start again at zero . . . as if he were nothing or no one," says Claude Lanzmann.[37]

May 1968 marked an important turning point for Sartre. At the age of sixty-three, he underwent another transformation. Once again this involved a radical refusal of his earlier self. Throughout his life, the only identity Sartre had assumed whole-heartedly was that of the intellectual, the committed intellectual, who took political stands on important issues. Now he started to disparage himself as a "classical intellectual" who considered himself apart from the masses, as opposed to a "new intellectual" who was part of the masses and engaged in street action. As a first step toward becoming the latter, he changed the way he dressed. He stopped wearing suits and ties. From now on, even when he gave public talks, he wore casual shirts and sweaters.

Immediately after the first serious clashes between students and police in Paris, Sartre and Beauvoir published a brief statement in *Le Monde* giving their support to the students.[38] In the next weeks, Sartre threw his weight behind what was now being called the "student revolution." He did not give advice; he took the view that this was a moment for young people to speak, and that he had a great deal to learn from them. Indeed, it was he who interviewed the student leader, Daniel Cohn-Bendit, in the *Nouvel Observateur,* rather than the other way around. Whereas the mainstream press dismissed Cohn-Bendit as a flaming-haired rabble-rouser, Sartre gave him a platform.

What Sartre found refreshing about May 1968 was that the students were asking not for power, but for freedom. They wanted a different type of society, a fundamental change in human relations. Their slogans gave free rein to the imagination. They were wary of institutional power structures and wanted universities to be less rigid and stultified. Sartre wholeheartedly agreed. The only way to learn, Sartre said, was to question what one was taught. This included questioning one's teachers. "A man is nothing if he isn't a contester."[39]

In August 1968, Soviet tanks entered Czechoslovakia. For the second time in twelve years, the USSR was being an outright aggressor. In Rome, Sartre gave an interview, calling the Soviets "war criminals." At the end of November, he and Beauvoir made a trip to Prague to show their solidarity with the Czechs.

Sartre wrote to Zonina that he would not be coming back to the Soviet Union. He and Beauvoir were breaking completely with the Soviet government. This meant he would not see Zonina, unless she came to Paris. "I want you to know that whatever you think about our relationship, this is terrible for me."[40]

Over the next few years, Sartre and Beauvoir's Russian friends were no longer permitted to travel; many of them lost their jobs, and struggled to scrape together a living. Neither Sartre nor Beauvoir would ever see Moscow again.

•   •   •

The *Temps modernes* committee now met in Beauvoir's apartment, every two weeks, at ten-thirty on Wednesday mornings. Half a dozen young people had joined the group in 1968, among them several women, including Sylvie Le Bon. They generally gossiped for an hour—about films, books, and people—then set to work.

Some of the former members had left because of intellectual clashes with Sartre.[41] The remaining old-timers were Jacques-Laurent Bost and Jean Pouillon, who had been there since the beginning, André Gorz, an Austrian Jewish political scientist who had joined the team in the late 1940s, and Claude Lanzmann, who had been there since 1952. (These days, he was making *Shoah*, a film on the Holocaust, and was often away.) Beauvoir still conscientiously read through the submissions. And she and her feminist friends ran a column called "Everyday Sexism."

Sartre rarely turned up. Beauvoir would chide him: "Sartre, that makes three times that you haven't come. This time you must."[42] Under pressure, he would come and give his opinion on things. But he no longer cared much about the journal. It was almost thirty years old. For him, it had become an institution.

These days, Sartre was more excited by the young revolutionaries in the Maoist movement. The French Maoist newspaper, *La Cause du peuple*, had been repeatedly seized by the government, on the grounds that the articles were an incitement to illegal violence. Its editors had been arrested, charged with provoking crimes against national security. A Maoist leader, Pierre Victor, approached Sartre. Would he be prepared to assume temporary editorship of the paper, to prevent its being banned? Sartre had always felt strongly about freedom of the press. He agreed that the newspaper was one of the few organs in which workers were able to speak out. In April 1970, he became its editor in chief.

In June, Sartre and Beauvoir distributed copies of *La Cause du peuple* among the bustle of the street market on the Rue Daguerre, near Denfert-Rochereau. As further protection, they had signed most of the articles in that issue with their own names. The police did not bother them, but they did arrest two Maoists who were distributing the paper the same day in another area. A week later, Sartre and Beauvoir repeated the performance. This time they were arrested, along with sixteen others. As soon as they arrived at the police station, the two of them, but not the other sixteen, were released.

"There are two standards . . . for the distributors of *La Cause du peuple*," Sartre declared. He explained that he had distributed the papers not because he had any desire to go to prison, but because he believed in a free press and wanted to show the double standard and cowardice of the so-called justice system.

The trial of those arrested took place on September 11. "If they are guilty, I am even more so," Sartre said. In October he and Beauvoir distributed the newspaper again. No one bothered them, and after that the paper was not confiscated again. Sartre and Beauvoir had braved possible legal reprisal to protect the liberty of the left-wing press in France.

In November, Sartre visited the Renault factory in Paris. The newspapers printed a photo of him standing on a barrel with a microphone, talking to the workers. Even his friends at the *Temps modernes* considered that Sartre was making himself look foolish. These street actions were backfiring on him, they said. The media was trivializing him. Sartre was not deterred.

He was seeing a lot of Pierre Victor and his Maoist militant friends. Sartre insisted "I am not a Maoist." He had no time for Mao's *Little Red Book,* and he did not put his faith in the Chinese Cultural Revolution—or in any other revolution, for that matter. But he felt close to the Maoists. He liked their rejection of elitism, hierarchies, and leaders. He liked the Maoist idea that the intellectual should listen to the masses and work with them, rather than attempt to lead them. He agreed that proletarian violence was simply "counterviolence"—a necessary response to the violence that was capitalist oppression.

It seemed to Sartre that young men like Pierre Victor represented the "new intellectual." They spoke street language, and used *tu* with everyone they met, including Sartre. They were physically tough, and dressed like thugs, in black leather jackets and heavy boots. At the same time, Sartre thought he saw in them a new kind of sensitivity—a softness he had previously associated with femininity.

Pierre Victor was twenty-nine, long-haired, and good-looking. "I like him, I'm very fond of him," Sartre told Beauvoir. "I know he's not to everybody's taste, but I think he's intelligent."[43] Beauvoir was surprised to see Sartre, for the first time in years, spending a great deal of time with a male. "I find the adult male deeply disgusting," Sartre admitted to her. "What I really like is a young man, insofar as a young man is not entirely different from a young woman. It's not that I'm a pederast, but the fact is that at present young men and young women are not so very different in their clothes, their way of talking, and their way of behaving."[44]

Pierre Victor liked to challenge Sartre. They would argue about something, and Victor would say: "Haven't you learnt anything, then, from 1968?" Sartre would consider himself reprimanded.

Victor tried to persuade Sartre to give up his interminable work on Flaubert. The first two volumes were coming out soon. Why didn't Sartre stop at that? The book was written in difficult language and not at all accessible to the common reader. Why didn't Sartre write a novel for the common people? Or a revolutionary treatise?

Sartre said he could not do that. Flaubert interested him. Sartre was too old to change his ways and put his intellectual work to the service of the masses. The best he could do was to make himself available for political tasks he considered important.

The Maoists became Sartre's new secret life. With Pierre Victor, he went to workers' homes to talk about their working conditions. He attended meetings of immigrant workers. And sometimes he would join Victor and his friends for an evening meal in Victor's commune in the suburbs.

Through Pierre Victor, Sartre entered yet another world. He was embarking on another adventure, another beginning.

Simone de Beauvoir did not share Sartre's enthusiasm for the Maoists. She found them dogmatic and did not approve of their violence and police-baiting. It was Michelle Vian who followed Sartre down the Maoist path. Her son, Patrick, had been very involved in the 1968 student demonstrations. "I was in all the major demonstrations," Michelle Vian says. "Near the front. Often walking beside

Sartre."[45] In January 1971, Michelle and a small group of leftists protested conditions in Paris's Santé prison with a hunger strike. They occupied Saint Bernard's Chapel in the Montparnasse railway station, without eating a thing, for twenty-one days. Sartre visited them often, and encouraged them.

Arlette Elkaïm says she grew much closer to Sartre after 1968. Her adoption by him three years earlier had given her a new status, but it was the student revolution that really changed their relationship. Sartre's respect for youth culture gave her a new validity. He was no longer so impatient with her unstructured way of thinking. They started to discuss things. Sometimes they shouted at each other. At times Sartre called her a reactionary. But he listened to her more than he used to.[46]

For three years in a row, Arlette brought a boyfriend along on her annual vacation with Sartre. It was Vladimir Dedijer, the Yugoslavian militant. Since Dedijer was a married man, Sartre provided a cover for Arlette, just as Beauvoir had done for him with Zonina. Sartre complained to Arlette that threesomes were a bore, but he put up with it.

For the first time in their lives, Sartre and Beauvoir were involved in entirely different political battles. When they met to talk in the evenings, they reported to each other on two disparate worlds. Sartre was plunged in Maoism, Beauvoir in feminism. While Sartre was painfully conscious of his marginal status in the contemporary anti-humanist intellectual climate, Beauvoir had become a leading icon of the international women's movement.

The first women's liberation groups were founded in France in the summer of 1970. Abortion was still illegal in Catholic France. When two young women got in touch with Beauvoir and suggested a manifesto in which well-known women would declare they had had an abortion, she immediately said, "It's an excellent idea."

For the next few months, a group of women activists met in Beauvoir's apartment on Sunday afternoons to organize the campaign. One of the younger members of the group, Claudine Monteil, recalls that she would turn up just before five, and Beauvoir would open the door with the words, "Ah! You're on time!" Beauvoir would sit on the yellow sofa that faced the clock. The other women sat around in a circle—on the other yellow sofa, or in the purple armchairs, or on the rug.

Beauvoir's manner was frank to the point of brutality, says Monteil, but she treated everyone as an equal, and she listened carefully. Around 6:45 P.M. Beauvoir would start to look at the clock, and speak even faster than usual. That was the sign that they had to wrap up the discussion. At 6:55 P.M., on the dot, the women were propelled out the door.[47]

The campaign was a triumph. Due in large measure to the influence of Simone de Beauvoir, the organizers managed to collect 343 signatures. The "Manifesto of the 343" was published on April 5, 1971, in the *Nouvel Observateur*. The statement was brief: Every year a million women in France underwent abortions, and though the procedure was simple under medical supervision, these abortions were dangerous because they were clandestine. The women declared that each one of them had aborted. (In actual fact, many of them, including Beauvoir, never had.[48]) The signatories demanded the right to free contraception and safe legal abortion.

Well-known signatories included Colette Audry, Dominique Desanti, Marguerite Duras, Gisèle Halimi, Simone Signoret, Catherine Deneuve, and Jeanne Moreau. Among the women in the Sartre-Beauvoir circle, Olga Kosakiewicz, Arlette Elkaïm, Michelle Vian, Hélène de Beauvoir, and Liliane Siegel signed.[49]

The manifesto caused a major scandal. For the first time that taboo word *abortion* was being pronounced on French radio and television. Conservatives referred to "the 343 sluts." The women were pleased. They had set the wheels in motion. In fact, it was a triumph. Four years later, in 1975, abortion would become legal in France.

Every summer, as soon as Le Bon finished teaching, she and Beauvoir set off on their travels for five weeks. Sartre would go on vacation first with Arlette, then with Wanda.

From mid-August, Beauvoir and Sartre were in Rome for two months. This was *their* time—the only time in the year when Beauvoir had Sartre more or less to herself. But Le Bon did not want to be apart from Beauvoir for so long. She wanted to be in Rome until school started again. "We'll see how it goes," Beauvoir said.

In the first years, Sylvie stayed at the Albergo del Sole, in the Piazza della Rotonda, ten minutes away from Beauvoir, who shared an air-conditioned top-floor suite with Sartre at the Albergo Nazionale, in the Piazza Montecitorio. Le Bon never saw Beauvoir alone. ("Of course not. This was the Beaver's time with Sartre!") But she was invited to join Beauvoir and Sartre two or three times a week for meals.

By the early seventies, Le Bon had passed the test. Sartre was not bored in her company. Beauvoir suggested she move to their hotel. After that, Le Bon joined them for one meal a day—lunch or dinner, alternately.

"The evenings were the really special time," says Le Bon. "The evenings were long, leisurely, and gay. We laughed a lot." Sartre and Beauvoir were careful whom they spent their evenings with, Le Bon says. As they grew older, they liked more than ever to spend their precious time with intimate friends.

Beauvoir continued to encourage Le Bon to lead her own life, to have her own lovers. Le Bon did not find this easy. In 1968, there was a romance with Bost, whom Le Bon thought inordinately handsome. "At first I didn't want to," Le Bon says. "Simone de Beauvoir said: 'Why not? You must experience everything.' No, she wasn't jealous. She was happy for us both."[50]

When Le Bon had a friend or lover with her in Rome, her friend tended to resent Le Bon's reverential attitude toward Sartre and Beauvoir, and the way everyone's time was measured out in carefully preestablished doses. "The problems came from others," Le Bon says. "Never from the Beaver."[51]

For several years in a row, Sartre and Beauvoir attempted an Easter vacation in Saint-Paul-de-Vence, in the south of France, as a foursome. It had worked in the past, with Claude Lanzmann and

Michelle Vian. Surely it could work with Elkaïm and Le Bon? Sartre and Elkaïm took the train down; Beauvoir and Le Bon drove. Sartre and Elkaïm had two rooms in the hotel annex; Beauvoir and Le Bon shared a cottage at the bottom of the garden. The lunch and dinner arrangements were organized as usual. Once a day the four ate together—either lunch or dinner. Otherwise they ate in pairs. Neither Le Bon nor Elkaïm was at all happy when they found themselves, just the two of them, across the table from each other.

Elkaïm was only six years older than Le Bon, but to Le Bon she seemed like an old woman. "She was always cold or tired or sick. She didn't care about good food. She didn't drink; alcohol made her ill. She was incredibly passive. She never had anything to say. My god, she was a bore!"

Tolerance was not Le Bon's strong suit, and with Beauvoir she did not hold herself back. The minute they were together, she would explode: "Arlette is impossible!"

Beauvoir would try to calm her down. "Personal hatred is degrading," she would tell Le Bon. "And it gets us nowhere at all."[52]

"After the second sex comes the third age," the critics joked. Beauvoir had started work on *The Coming of Age,* her book on old age, in June 1967. For months she rose early and took a taxi to the Bibliothèque Nationale, to make sure she got a seat when the library opened at nine A.M. (She refused to have a seat reserved for her. Why special privileges for her?) Just as she had done for her essay on women twenty years before, she studied the biological, ethnological, and historical data on old age. The second half of the essay was devoted to the lived experience. She visited homes for the aged. She read what writers had written in their memoirs about their old age.

The book came out in January 1970. For weeks it was at the top of the best-seller lists. The reviewers declared it a rich and lucid book that read like a novel. They pointed out that Beauvoir had again tackled a social taboo. Once again she had broken the conspiracy of silence.

The book was translated into English in 1972, and given a spiteful review in the *Los Angeles Times.* "Reckless generalizations," the reviewer said. "Having already served, unwittingly, as the sociologist behind much of the hearsay in *America Day by Day,* I wonder who's feeding her airy persiflage now. I hope it isn't Sartre."[53]

The reviewer was a rather jaundiced writer from Chicago called Nelson Algren.

Sartre had been working on Flaubert for more than ten years. It was a major publishing event when two thick volumes called *The Family Idiot* appeared in bookstore windows in May 1971. Apart from his essays and interviews (brought out over the years in successive volumes collectively called *Situations*), there had been no new book by Sartre in seven years—not since *Words,* in 1963. His name was often in the newspapers, and he was frequently seen on television newsreels, but that was all.

The first two volumes came to more than two thousand pages and merely covered the first thirty-six years of Flaubert's life. This was just a beginning, Sartre said. He was revising the third volume. After that, he would embark on a fourth, which would explain *Madame Bovary.*

"Sartre's awe-inspiring book is without a doubt the most extraordinary work ever composed by one writer about another," John Weightman would write in the *New York Review of Books.* "I have been reading it for a month in varying moods of exasperation, humility, exultation, and despair.... So far he has only got to the foothills of the subject. To deal with it completely he will have to digest the universe."[54]

Sartre told Beauvoir how happy he felt when his copies of the book arrived from Gallimard. It gave him as much pleasure, he said, as the publication of his very first book, *Nausea.*

THIRTEEN

THE FAREWELL CEREMONY

May 1971–April 1986

Throughout her life, Beauvoir would suddenly be gripped by suffocating anxiety and despair, frightening crises in which she would be racked by sobs and which she explained as a fear of death and the metaphysical void. "For a few hours I would be ravaged by a kind of tornado that stripped me bare," she writes. "When the sky cleared again I could never be certain whether I was waking from a nightmare or relapsing into some long sky-blue fantasy, a permanent dream world."[1] She preferred not to dwell on the anxieties that lurk so palpably beneath the surface of her writing: her fear of solitude, abandonment, and the loss of love.[2] But she openly admitted to being haunted by what she saw as the worst nightmare of all: Sartre's death.

The one book she would write after Sartre's death, the only book she ever wrote that he did not read, *Adieux: A Farewell to Sartre,* was a poignant portrayal of Sartre's physical decline. He had abused his body recklessly, and it began to take its toll early on. In 1954, when he was hospitalized in Moscow with high blood pressure, Beauvoir was filled with foreboding. Sartre was forty-nine. Four years later, at the age of fifty-three, he narrowly avoided a heart attack. By his early sixties, he was having severe dizzy spells. Apparently there were problems with the blood circulation in the left hemisphere of his brain.

His doctors urged him to smoke and drink less. Sartre ignored their warnings.

On Tuesday, May 18, 1971, Sartre arrived at the Rue Schoelcher looking dreadful. His right arm was partially paralyzed, his mouth was twisted, and he was slurring his words. Beauvoir tried hard not let her panic show. Sartre said he had woken up like that, at Elkaïm's. He had not seen a doctor, and that evening he insisted on drinking four or five glasses of whiskey as usual. By midnight he could not pronounce his words at all, and was scarcely able to stagger upstairs to bed. Beauvoir spent a sleepless night tossing on the downstairs divan.

The next day the doctor confirmed her fears that Sartre had had a slight stroke. He forbade Sartre to walk. Le Bon drove them back to the Rue Schoelcher and stayed a while. Sartre's cigarette kept dropping from his lips. Le Bon kept picking it up and handing it to him. Sartre put it back between his lips, and it fell again. Conversation was impossible. Beauvoir put on Verdi's *Requiem*. "It's most appropriate," Sartre said.

He remained in that state for ten days. He could not play the piano with Elkaïm, he could not write, and he did not seem to have the slightest interest in anything. Beauvoir had always found it painful to part from Sartre when he went off at the beginning of July, first with Elkaïm for three weeks, then with Wanda for two. That summer, she found their separation wrenching:

We had lunch together at La Coupole, where Sylvie was to come for me at four o'clock. I stood up three minutes before the hour. He gave me an indefinable smile and said, "So this is the farewell ceremony!" I touched his shoulder without replying. The smile and the words stayed with me for a great while. I gave the word farewell the ultimate meaning it was to have some years later.[3]

The two women drove down to Italy for their vacation. For the first few days, Beauvoir kept asking herself what she was doing there. Every night, for the entire five weeks, she wept herself to sleep. Sartre was sixty-six that summer; she was sixty-three. And already she feared the worst.

Telegrams assured her that Sartre was fine. Only later did she find out that he had suffered an even worse crisis in mid-July, in Berne. Elkaïm had not informed her. Since then, he had improved again. In Naples he had gone with Wanda for quite long walks.

This was to be the pattern for the next nine years. There would be a crisis, and Beauvoir would be gripped by terror. Then Sartre would recover, and she would allow herself to hope. It was exhausting.

In mid-August, they settled into their sixth-floor suite at the Hotel Nazionale in Rome. Sartre was correcting the third volume of *The Family Idiot*. Beauvoir was polishing *All Said and Done,* the fourth and final volume of her memoirs. When they got back to Paris, he read her manuscript carefully and offered helpful criticism, as usual.

In February and March 1972, Sartre, Beauvoir, and the *Temps modernes* team sat around for two weekends—first in Beauvoir's apartment, then in Sartre's studio—and talked about Sartre's past while the cameras whirred. Michel Contat and Alexandre Astruc were making a documentary on Sartre.

Between sessions, Jean Pouillon told Contat sadly, "He should have been filmed in 1950. Now you only have a pale notion of how brilliant he could be."[4] Nevertheless, when the film, *Sartre,* was finally released, in 1976, after a series of budget problems, the French public was captivated. It was like sitting in on a family reunion, the reviewers said. Sartre looked like the eternal postgraduate student in his rollneck black pullover, and he had not lost his considerable charm.

One critic, Gilles Lapouge, said he was particularly moved by Jacques-Laurent Bost, who spoke about his former teacher with great tenderness, and Simone de Beauvoir, "very beautiful, who sometimes, out of a stray memory, a mere nothing, made strange sparks burst forth."[5]

During the next two years there were more dizzy spells. Sartre suffered from incontinence. His legs hurt, and he could no longer walk far. In the fall of 1972, the dentist removed all his remaining teeth and fitted him with a plate. Sartre drank too much, but always, throughout his trials, he continued to work.

He had begun work on volume four of Flaubert. He wrote about the oppression of the Basques in Franco's Spain. He spoke out for the rights of immigrant workers and political prisoners. He denounced political repression in Cuba. Beauvoir joined him in signing an appeal demanding that not only Russian Jews but all Russian citizens be granted permission to leave the USSR, if they so wanted.

With his Maoist friends, Sartre helped found a new revolutionary daily, *Libération.* It was an ambitious project—a truly democratic venture, born of 1968—and he abandoned his *Flaubert* for six months to throw himself into it. He contributed money, wrote articles, and attended meetings. For a year, until he had to give up for health reasons, he was the official editor in chief. It was due to Sartre's prestige that the newspaper had the political freedom to take flight and become one of the most important left-wing papers in France. Sartre was delighted by its success.[6]

All Said and Done, dedicated to Sylvie Le Bon, was published in September 1972. For the first time Beauvoir had no project in mind. The women's movement kept her busy, and she found the distraction a godsend. She became the president of Choisir and the League of Women's Rights, groups that informed women of their rights, advocated free contraception and the legalization of abortion, and provided free defense for women in court. Beauvoir wrote prefaces, gave interviews, and met with feminists from around the world. Her main writing was her daily journal, in which she obsessively chronicled Sartre's deterioration.

Fortunately, she had Le Bon. "Joy of my Life," Beauvoir called her.[7] Five years earlier, she had written to Le Bon from Japan: "My Sylvie, I am delighted to be returning to Paris, because of Paris and because I want to work, but most of all to see you again. It is a great happiness for me to know that you exist, a happiness that stays with me constantly."[8]

Le Bon had finally landed a teaching job in Paris. She was thirty now, and her father persuaded her that it was time to give up her hotel life and invest in her own place. She bought a quiet courtyard apartment on the Avenue du Maine, twenty minutes from Beauvoir. It was a rare day when the women did not see each other.

Whereas Sartre saw his women strictly one at a time, Beauvoir had always enjoyed sharing her companions with Sartre. They spent Saturday evenings with Le Bon, mostly in Beauvoir's apartment. Occasionally the three of them went to the opera, which Le Bon loved. (They kept Sartre's one smart suit at Beauvoir's place for these outings.) On Sundays they had lunch at the Coupole. Every summer, Le Bon spent time with them in Rome. Sartre liked Le Bon to be with them. He was more cheerful when she was there.

At moments, there was a slight whiff of the old trios. There had been some sort of sexual encounter between Le Bon and Sartre in Rome in 1968. Sartre had let his hands wander. Le Bon had invited it. "I pretended I was drunk. For me, Sartre was the great writer. I was in awe of him." Beauvoir did not seem to mind when Le Bon told her about it afterward.[9]

One Sunday, Beauvoir and Sartre were invited by their friend Tomiko Asabuki, their former Japanese interpreter, to lunch at her house in Versailles. Le Bon went too. They ate stuffed duck and drank excellent wines, and on the way back in the car, Le Bon "made ardent declarations to Sartre." He was, Beauvoir writes, "delighted."[10]

There were stormy scenes, too, which Beauvoir does not mention in *Adieux.* These usually occurred on Saturday evenings on the Rue Schoelcher, when they had had too much to drink. Sartre would complain about one or another of his helpless women. Le Bon would retort that he was paternalistic and macho, that he suffered from a "God complex," and that he *made* these women helpless. They were always either sick or tired, she railed. From what? Doing nothing? For a man who never wanted a family, you have the worst of family life!

Sartre said he knew it, but he preferred to be a fool than a jerk. These women depended on him. He had obligations to them. He had no respect for men who left their women in the lurch.

"But that's such an old-fashioned way of thinking!"

"Well, I'm old-fashioned. And now I'm too old to change."[11]

It was the height of the women's movement. Le Bon, along with Beauvoir, was spending considerable time discussing sexual politics in various women's groups. In interviews, Beauvoir would assert that economic independence was the fundamental prerequisite for female independence. And here was Sartre supporting three women who spent most of their time, it seemed to Le Bon, giving him a hard time.

The subject that was most likely to cause Le Bon to explode was Arlette Elkaïm. She was Sartre's most expensive commodity. He had already bought her an artist's studio on the Rue Delambre, two minutes from the Dôme. But Elkaïm was asthmatic and she liked to escape from the city's pollution as often as possible, and so Sartre bought her a house in the south of France, as well. "I saw red," says Le Bon. "Arlette never had a job. She was completely parasitical on Sartre. She was always saying she did not want his money, and she kept taking it from him. And there was Sartre, who by the end of the month could not even afford a pair of shoes for himself. The whole thing drove me mad."

There were occasions when Le Bon stormed out in a fury, slamming the door behind her. The next day she would apologize, embarrassed. "Yes, your behavior was odious," Beauvoir would agree. And Le Bon was forgiven.

These days, Le Bon is full of remorse about those outbursts. "I was brutal back then. I said exactly what I thought, no holds barred. It did not make life easier for the Beaver, who was in the middle, and worried sick about Sartre's health."[12]

In March 1973—when he was sixty-eight—Sartre had another stroke. He no longer recognized his friends, no longer knew where he was. The doctor said it was asphyxia of the brain, and pressed him again to give up his heavy drinking and smoking. Sartre made a vague effort, then went back to it.

In July, he spent three weeks with Elkaïm in her house in the village of Junas, near Nîmes. For hours he sat on the balcony, gazing ahead of him. He could barely make out the contour of the houses, he told her. At the end of the month, Beauvoir and Le Bon, who had been traveling in the south of France, went to fetch him in the car and take him to Venice, where (without Elkaïm's knowing it) he was to spend two weeks with Wanda. Beauvoir was shocked to see him walk-ing with small, faltering steps.

Beauvoir and Le Bon stayed on a few days in Venice, meeting Sartre at nine-thirty A.M., behind Wanda's back, for breakfast in the Piazza San Marco. Beauvoir was reassured to hear that Wanda was giving him his medicines carefully, and taking him on little walks. "Then one morning I left him," she writes. "I did not want Sylvie to get bored with Venice, which she was beginning to know by heart."[13] They left him their addresses, and wished him *bon courage* in putting up with Wanda. Sartre said he would miss them. And the two women set off for Florence.

Later, Beauvoir would tell her biographer, Deirdre Bair, that she felt a "double-edged guilt" in those years.[14] She had Le Bon to con-sider as well as Sartre, and she worried about imposing a tired old man on a vigorous young woman. Le Bon liked to explore new places. So did she. But if she enjoyed herself with Le Bon, she would feel bad about Sartre.

In mid-August, Beauvoir and Le Bon went to meet Sartre at Rome's Fiumicino Airport. He was almost blind. In Venice, the sun had hurt his eyes, he said. He had scarcely been able to see the city he loved so much. Beauvoir took him to a specialist, who said that Sartre had suffered hemorrhages behind his left eye (his only good eye), but that his sight would surely improve in time. For months Sartre clung to that hope.

They were a threesome in Rome that year. Beauvoir read to Sartre every morning. He slept in the afternoons, and Beauvoir and Le Bon went for a walk or read side by side in the shade. The most painful moments were meals. Sartre was pre-diabetic and had put on a lot of weight, and it worried Beauvoir to see him tuck in to huge quantities of pasta and ice cream. And then there was his messy eating. Sartre, who had spent his life being so self-conscious about imposing his body on others that he hated even to ask directions in the street, had no idea what embarrassment he was inflicting on his table companions. He could no longer see the food on his plate or at the end of his fork, and he had almost no sensation around his mouth. Afraid of vexing him, Beauvoir, could not keep telling him to wipe his face with his napkin.

Olga and Bost came to Rome for a few days and were horrified to find Sartre looking like a doddering old man. He could not stand being fussed over. He hated people taking him by the arm, as if he were a blind man. At most, he allowed friends to steer him by lightly touching his elbow. They had to pretend that nothing had changed. It was heart-rending.

The tables had turned. It was no longer Sartre who was doing the medical round. Now his women were doing it. At the age of sixty-eight, Sartre had become totally dependent on others. His legs hurt if he walked the slightest distance. He could make out lights and colors, but could no longer recognize objects, and certainly could not read or write. His life as a writer was completely destroyed.

It was decided that Sartre should move into a two-bedroom apartment, so that Beauvoir and Elkaïm could take turns sleeping over. The ever-practical Liliane Siegel found an apartment in a modern high-rise, at 22 Boulevard Edgar Quinet, on the other side of the Montparnasse Cemetery from Beauvoir. They installed Sartre there in October 1973. The apartment was again on the tenth floor, with a superb view over Paris. Sartre could not see it, though he could vaguely appreciate the evening sunsets. He never felt at home there. "This apartment is the place where I don't work anymore," he told Beauvoir.[15] During the week, when it was her watch, he preferred to sleep at the Rue Schoelcher. At weekends, he stayed at Elkaïm's.

Sartre battled with depression. He had always looked toward the future. What was left for him now? The whole point of his life was writing. "I think *with my eyes*," he had written to Beauvoir when he had eye troubles during the Second World War. "If I cannot *focus* them, I cannot focus my thoughts."[16]

In a group, Sartre would sometimes sit and say nothing. Lena Zonina made another visit to Paris at the end of the year, and Sartre had been looking forward to seeing her again. But at their first lunch together—Beauvoir and Le Bon were also there—the atmosphere was dismal. Le Bon tried hard to provide some animation. Sartre hardly said a thing.

One morning in Venice, during Easter 1974, Beauvoir was reading to Sartre in his hotel room. Outside, the sunshine looked inviting, and they decided to go down to the hotel's terrace, beside the water. When Beauvoir went to take the book they had been reading, Sartre said plaintively, "*Before,* when I was more intelligent, we didn't read. We talked."

Beauvoir was hurt to the quick, and they spent the rest of the morning talking. But privately she had to admit to herself that conversations with Sartre were no longer the same:

> Sartre . . . had in fact retained his intelligence; he made remarks about what we read and discussed the books. But he would let the conversation drop quite soon; he did not ask questions nor did he offer fresh ideas. Not many things interested him on any level. But by way of compensation he grew very set in his ways, making it a rule to keep to given sequences, replacing real pleasure in things by obstinate adherence to a pattern.[17]

In Rome that summer, they talked into a tape recorder, with Beauvoir asking Sartre questions about his past. "At present nothing interests me," Sartre told her. Beauvoir gently prodded answers out of him. They told themselves it would provide an oral sequel to *Words*.[18] In the afternoons and evenings, they took short walks. Beauvoir read him two thick books: Solzhenitsyn's *Gulag Archipelago* and Joachim Fest's biography of Hitler.

By the end of that summer, Sartre was facing up to the fact that he would never see again. He told himself that he could still hear and speak. He would get friends to read to him, and he would try to think aloud, with a tape recorder.

He asked Pierre Victor—who was always saying that the "new intellectual" should work in collaboration—to be his "secretary." He meant a kind of intellectual collaborator, somebody with whom and against whom he could think, now that he no longer had access to the printed word. Victor hesitated. Liliane Siegel rang him up and told him he *must.* It was agreed. Sartre would keep on André Puig to do the daily administrative work. Pierre Victor would come for three hours every morning, except the Sabbath, to read to Sartre and discuss ideas with him.

Elkaïm phoned Beauvoir in a panic. She did not trust Pierre Victor, she said. He had an aggressive, overpowering personality, and she was afraid he would become "Sartre's Schoenmann." She was referring to Ralph Schoenmann, the authoritarian secretary-general of the Russell Tribunal, who had made himself a laughingstock at the Stockholm and Copenhagen meetings by constantly claiming to speak on behalf of the absent Bertrand Russell, too old and fragile to be there himself.

Beauvoir did not like Pierre Victor much either. But Sartre seemed happy at the idea of working with him. She was pleased for Sartre, and relieved to have some time for herself. It was tiring to read aloud to Sartre every morning. What could be the problem with paying Pierre Victor to be Sartre's eyes for three hours a day, and to bring back some joy and stimulation to his life? Later, she would terribly regret her attitude.

In November 1974, Sartre signed a contract with French national television to write ten programs on his relationship to twentieth-century French history. For nine months, Beauvoir and Pierre Victor read relevant books and documents to Sartre. And then, in August 1975, the contract was canceled, ostensibly for budget reasons. At a press conference, Sartre, Beauvoir, and Victor spoke of "indirect censorship."

All that remained for Sartre now, in the way of work, was the book he and Pierre Victor were planning, based on their tape-recorded discussions. The provisional title was *Power and Liberty*. They knew they did not think the same way. Like most of his contemporaries, Victor was more interested in Deleuze and Foucault these days, and in the new intellectual fashion known as structuralism. The point of their collaboration, as they saw it, was to think in opposition to each other, to think dialectically.

Victor was convinced the book was going to be important. To some extent, Sartre let himself be carried along by his young friend's enthusiasm. But he was aware of the problems. "You have ideas that are not mine and that will make me go in certain directions that I used not to take," he told Victor. As he saw it, this would be "a work set apart" from the rest of his work, "not belonging to the whole."[19]

Beauvoir and the old-timers at *Les Temps modernes* were grateful that Pierre Victor was keeping Sartre intellectually stimulated. They admired Sartre's fighting spirit. But privately, Jean Pouillon recalls, they looked upon this new project as "the delusion of an old man who refused to give up."[20]

Pierre Victor was not his real name, and he sometimes disguised himself with a false beard and sunglasses as well. Benny Lévy, alias Pierre Victor, was born in Cairo to a Sephardic Jewish family who left Egypt during the 1957 Suez crisis, when Victor was eleven. The Algerian War was blazing, and Victor found it difficult to work out his relationship with France. At the age of fifteen, he read Sartre and was bowled over. "For me, the French language was Sartre," Victor said later.[21] He was bright, and by the age of twenty, he was studying at the Ecole Normale Supérieure. But he had never managed to obtain residence papers, which meant he could be thrown out of the country at any time. As a Maoist militant who came in frequent contact with the police, he hid behind a false identity.

Beauvoir was convinced, even in hindsight, that Pierre Victor took on the job of Sartre's secretary out of a genuine and deep affection for Sartre. As usual, Sartre gave more than he received. Victor was rewarded for his three hours a day with a salary that was generous even for a full-time job. What's more, Sartre wrote to President Giscard d'Estaing on Victor's behalf, and managed to get him French citizenship.

As Pierre Victor saw it, his task was to keep the little flame in Sartre alive:

I often felt like quitting. I would arrive, ring the bell, and at times, he wouldn't even hear me. He'd be there, alone, dozing in his armchair, and, through the door, I could hear the music of France Musique coming from the radio that Simone de Beauvoir had left on for him, so that he wouldn't feel too lonely or too bored. It was a constant struggle against death. At times, I had the impression I was there to fend off sleep, lack of interest, or, more simply, torpor. . . . What I was really involved in was a sort of resuscitation.[22]

Sartre and Victor quickly abandoned the fourth volume of Flaubert, and spent their time discussing history and philosophy instead. Victor was charismatic, fiery, and inclined to be hectoring. Elkaïm, hovering in the background, was sometimes alarmed. "He would come up with a very crucial, complex question at the moment Sartre was about to give in to his fatigue," she remembers. "At other times, he would start reading to him very loudly, with extraordinary zest and passion, as if in a state of exaltation: It was quite scary."[23]

When he felt up to it, Sartre enjoyed himself. At other moments, Victor's haranguing voice simply tired him. "Pierre would quite like to absorb me," he told Liliane Siegel. "Some days he baits me, we have a row, sometimes that amuses me and I stand up to him, but at other times it bores me so I give in."[24]

To commemorate Sartre's seventieth birthday, in June 1975, *Le Nouvel Observateur* published an interview with him. Michel Contat asked Sartre about politics, books, his relationship to music, friends, and money. Sartre agreed he had made a lot of money in his life, and still had plenty coming in from royalties, foreign contracts, interviews, and his teacher's pension, but he always spent it faster than he made it. "There are people who are financially dependent on me," he explained. (He did not say that he was paying salaries to Puig and Victor, monthly allowances to Wanda, Michelle, and Arlette, supporting a new girlfriend, Hélène, paying his cleaning woman, and helping out the local beggar.) "At the moment there's nothing left, and for the first time I'm wondering how I'm going to manage."[25]

"There are several women in my life," he said. "Although in a sense Simone de Beauvoir is the only one, really there are several." Nevertheless, he mentioned only Arlette Elkaïm and Michelle Vian by name, referring to Elkaïm as "my adopted daughter," and Michelle as "the wife of Boris Vian."

He made it clear that his intellectual relationship with Simone de Beauvoir had meant everything to him:

I have been able to formulate ideas to Simone de Beauvoir before they were really concrete.... I have presented all my ideas to her when they were in the process of being formed.

Because she was at the same level of philosophical knowledge as you?

Not only that, but also because she was the only one at my level of knowledge of myself, of what I wanted to do. For this reason she was the perfect person to talk to, the kind one rarely has. It is my unique good fortune....

Still, you have had occasion to defend yourself against Simone de Beauvoir's criticisms, haven't you?

Oh, often! In fact we have even insulted one another.... But I knew that she would be the one who was right, in the end. That's not to say that I accepted all her criticisms, but I did accept most of them.

Are you just as hard on her as she is on you?

Absolutely. As hard as possible. There is no point in not criticizing very severely when you have the good fortune to love the person you are criticizing.

The interview was the summation of a life. There were things Sartre wanted to say, and he knew this might be his last chance to say them. He had dedicated books to other women; he had been photographed with them in the press. But at the age of seventy, he was making a public declaration of his love and his gratitude to Simone de Beauvoir.

Sartre's women were middle-aged now. In 1975, the year Sartre turned seventy, Wanda was fifty-eight, Michelle Vian was fifty-five, and Arlette Elkaïm was almost forty. Behind their backs, Sartre had embarked on a last romantic attachment with a young woman. Hélène Lassithiotakis, a dark-haired Greek woman in her early twenties, had rung his doorbell sometime in 1972. "Do you remember me? We met in Athens at one of your lectures."

Sartre paid for her to come to Paris for a year and study philosophy. He saw a lot of her. "When I'm with her, I feel as though I were
thirty-five," he told Beauvoir.[26] Near the end of that year, Lassithiotakis had a psychotic episode in the street. Le Bon drove her to Saint
Anne's psychiatric hospital. "The Beaver and I used to joke with
Sartre about all his mad women," Le Bon says. "We told him: 'It's *you*
who drive them nuts!' "[27]

Sartre was blind by then, but it did not stop him from making several
visits to Athens, accompanied by Beauvoir or Pierre Victor. And
Lassithiotakis made trips to Paris. "Because of the medicines she took
she had gained over twenty pounds," Beauvoir writes. "Furthermore,
she was as silent now as she had been talkative before her illness. But she
was still beautiful and Sartre liked being with her."[28]

The affair lasted five years. In 1977, Sartre called it off, telling
Beauvoir that Lassithiotakis was too self-seeking. But just as he had
with his other women, he continued to see her as a friend.

In March 1977, Sartre did the unthinkable. He had bad pains in his
left leg. His doctor had told him that if he did not give up smoking he
would have to have first his toes amputated, then his feet, then his
legs. Sartre said he would think it over. Two days later, he decided to
stop. He handed his cigarettes and lighters to Le Bon. (Beauvoir
rarely smoked anymore.) He never went back to smoking, and did
not seem to find the deprivation burdensome. He even encouraged
friends to smoke in front of him.

But he would not give up alcohol, and this became an aspect of the
power struggle among the women. He told Beauvoir he was restricting
himself to one glass of whiskey a night. Meanwhile, Michelle smuggled in
whiskey bottles, which Sartre hid at the back of his bookcase. He would
put on a soft voice, Michelle Vian says, like a naughty boy defying his
mother: "You know, I don't tell the Beaver everything."

When Beauvoir saw him with an obvious hangover, there were
scenes. "It infuriated Beauvoir," says Michelle Vian. "She was his
mama. She was the only one allowed to give him his bottle."[29]

For a time Michelle spent Saturday nights at Sartre's place. When his doctor made a home visit and found Sartre's blood pressure way up again, he took Liliane Siegel aside—it was her turn with Sartre— and asked whether he had been drinking. Siegel told him that Sartre regularly drank half a bottle of whiskey on his Saturday nights with Michelle. The news reached Beauvoir's ears. "I telephoned Michelle," she writes, "telling her why she was no longer to come to Sartre's on Saturdays."[30]

There was another incident, which Beauvoir does not mention in *Adieux*. Liliane Siegel's cleaning woman used to go around to Sartre's apartment once a week. It was not a pleasant job. Sartre had never been fussy about cleanliness, and now he could not see. One day the young woman, who was Portuguese and devoutly Catholic, announced that she would not be going back. On questioning it came out that she had heard a woman having an orgasm in Sartre's bedroom. She was terribly embarrassed, and had left in a hurry.

Siegel knew Sartre's schedule. She rang Beauvoir, and told her. Beauvoir made another phone call to Michelle Vian. The conversation, Michelle recalls, was awkward:

"Michelle, we're friends, aren't we?"
"Yes."
"You know Sartre is very tired. He mustn't drink. He mustn't smoke. He mustn't be excited. He mustn't have relations. It's not good for him. You see what I mean?"

The next time they saw each other, Sartre explained to Michelle, "It's not so bad. . . . My prostate isn't in good condition. If I want to . . ." He added: "I don't tell everything to the Beaver, you know."[31] According to Michelle Vian, they continued to make love (not intercourse) until near the end of Sartre's life.

Sartre was furious with Siegel. "You make me sick. You're a filthy sneak," he shouted. "I never want to see you again."[32]

Olivier Todd once asked Sartre how he coped with all his women, some of whom were notoriously jealous.

I lie to them, Sartre said. It is easier, and more decent.
    Do you lie to all of them?
    He smiles.
    To all of them.
    Even to the Beaver?
    Particularly to the Beaver.[33]

Sartre might have meant this as a lighthearted retort, but it was
another betrayal. When Todd's book was published, a year after Sartre's death, Beauvoir was hurt and angry—with Todd, rather than
Sartre.[34] In *Adieux,* published a few months later, she retaliated.
"Sartre . . . did not like [Todd] at all and had only a very superficial
relationship with him, which is the contrary of what Todd tries to
insinuate in his book."[35]

Arlette Elkaïm disliked Beauvoir, but most of all she resented
Michelle. "The Beaver does not disturb anything—though I'm sure
she'd be disturbed if I upset her vacation with Sartre—but Michelle is
in the way," Elkaïm grumbled to John Gerassi in 1973.

Elkaïm admitted she was "rather exclusive," and that she had been
"very very jealous" of Sartre at times. What was strange, she said, was
that she had the distinct impression that he *liked* her jealousy. ("He is a
bit sadistic. It amuses him.") But Sartre hid many things, Elkaïm said,
and it was impossible to know what he was feeling. She thought he
was probably anxious about dying, but whenever she chided him
about drinking too much, he would drink more, to show he didn't
give a damn. Sartre did not like being told what to do.[36]

Elkaïm spent most mornings at Sartre's apartment, along with
Sartre's secretary, André Puig, and Pierre Victor. Sartre and Victor
would work, and Elkaïm occasionally interrupted with tea or medicine. She had dropped her wariness about Pierre Victor. They had a
lot in common: they both came from North Africa, they were both
Jewish, and both of them cared a great deal about Sartre. She and
Victor were even learning Hebrew together.

•   •   •

Pierre Victor had discovered Jewish theology. He would turn up in the mornings keen to discuss Emmanuel Levinas and messianism. "What next? Maybe he'll decided to become a rabbi!" Sartre joked to Elkaïm.[37]

In February 1978, Sartre went with Victor and Elkaïm on a four-day trip to Jerusalem. (It was Victor's first time there.) Beauvoir was worried about Sartre traveling, but she heard later that they had taken Sartre to the plane in a wheelchair, and stayed in a luxury hotel, and that their friend Eli Ben Gal drove them everywhere. Sartre enjoyed himself.

But when they got back, there was an ugly episode, a foreshadowing of what was to come. Pierre Victor penned a hasty article on the peace movement in Israel, and asked Sartre to co-sign it. Victor sent it to the *Nouvel Observateur*. Shortly afterward, Beauvoir received an urgent phone call from Bost: "It's horribly bad. Here at the paper everyone is appalled. Do persuade Sartre to withdraw it." Beauvoir read the article, found it very weak, and managed to persuade Sartre to drop it. He did not appear to have much invested in it.

Sartre did not mention the incident to Victor, who did not find out about the article's being withdrawn till the next *Temps modernes* meeting. Victor had started to attend meetings, usually in place of Sartre. Beauvoir, assuming he knew, said something about it. Victor stormed out, shouting about censorship and calling his older colleagues "putrefied corpses."[38] It was the last they saw of him at the *Temps modernes*.

Victor had declared open war on those he referred to disdainfully as "the Sartreans." Elkaïm was on his side. Throughout her life, whatever the difficulties, Beauvoir had always made a great effort to be on good terms with the people Sartre loved. For her, this new turn of events was devastating. She could only wonder about Sartre's own loyalties. What did he say to his two young friends about *her*? Did he defend her to them? Or did he indulge their complaints, and even abet them?

In March 1979, Pierre Victor organized an Israeli-Palestinian conference in Paris, under the aegis of *Les Temps modernes*. Sartre went along with the idea. From the beginning, the "Sartreans" were skeptical.

The most prominent participant was Edward Said, the Palestinian intellectual and activist, who came from New York for the occasion. For Said, Sartre was "one of the great intellectual heroes of the twentieth century." Said had accepted his invitation eagerly, and looked forward to the meeting of minds.

Years later, Said would write about those extraordinary few days. He was shocked to see that Sartre hardly seemed to know what was going on, and was completely dependent on the little entourage that fluttered around him:

Sartre's presence, what there was of it, was strangely passive, unimpressive, affectless. He said absolutely nothing for hours on end. At lunch he sat across from me, looking disconsolate and remaining totally uncommunicative, egg and mayonnaise streaming haplessly down his face.

The discussion was dominated by Pierre Victor, whom Said observed to be a "deeply religious Jew" and "part-thinker, part-hustler."

Early on, I sensed that he was a law unto himself, thanks no doubt to his privileged relationship with Sartre (with whom he occasionally had whispered exchanges) and to what seemed to be a sublime self-confidence.

After a second day of "turgid and unrewarding discussions," Said interrupted, saying he had come from New York to hear Sartre. Victor looked irritated. There were whisperings. Finally Victor announced, "Sartre will speak tomorrow."

The next day, the group was handed two pages of text allegedly written by Sartre, which were full of "banal platitudes," and were totally uncritical of Israel's policies toward the Palestinians. Said knew the pages could only have been written by Victor.

Edward Said returned to the United States bewildered and disillusioned. "I was quite shattered to discover that this intellectual hero had succumbed in his late years to such a reactionary mentor."[39]

•   •   •

On Sartre's seventy-fourth birthday, on June 21, 1979, the romance novelist Françoise Sagan sent Sartre a love letter, which she asked his permission to publish. She admired him both as a writer and a man, she wrote. He had written the best books of his generation; he had defended the weak and the oppressed; he was the soul of generosity. "Making love and offering love, a seducer always ready to be seduced, you have far outstripped all your friends with your vitality, intelligence and brilliance."[40] Sartre was pleased, of course, and after that, he and Sagan saw each other regularly. He took her to gourmet restaurants, and she cut up his meat and held his hand. She became another of his whiskey smugglers, another woman who intensely resented Beauvoir.[41] Sartre called Sagan "naughty Lili."

"Do you realize, child, that not counting the Beaver and Sylvie, there are nine women in my life at the moment!" Sartre boasted to his friend Liliane Siegel.[42] Realizing his bottomless need for female attention, Siegel introduced him to others. He would ask her whether they were beautiful, then take them out to lunch and grope them outrageously. Siegel was once invited along on one of these occasions. She was shocked when the other woman started "pawing" Sartre and telling him the "smutty details" of her sex life, in language Siegel found pornographic.[43] Sartre, she had to admit, was enjoying himself.

"The last five years of Sartre's life were terrible for Beauvoir," says Sylvie Le Bon. "She couldn't stand Sartre being blind. She could be stoic for herself, but not for him. She *acted* stoic in front of him." The worst moments were when Sartre was on vacation with Arlette or Wanda. Beauvoir went away with Le Bon, who had to look on while Beauvoir took extravagant doses of Valium and drank far too much whiskey. In the evenings, she would often fall to pieces and weep. On occasion her legs gave way and she collapsed.[44]

Le Bon watched over Beauvoir, trying surreptitiously to water down her whiskey. Le Bon had become a devoted nurse. After school, she drove Beauvoir and Sartre to doctors and ran errands for them both.

Claude Lanzmann lived five minutes away from Beauvoir, on the Rue Boulard. Whenever he was in Paris, he saw her twice a week, but he was often away, working on his nine-and-a-half-hour documentary film, *Shoah*. Beauvoir had lent him a considerable sum to help get it off the ground. (The film would be launched in 1985. Beauvoir wrote a moving preface to the published text.)

Bost and Olga lived on the Boulevard Edgar Quinet, across the road from Sartre, but Olga spent most of her time in Laigle. In separate interviews, Sartre and Beauvoir both told John Gerassi that Bost had become something of a bore these days, and that when they spent the evening with him, Bost usually got drunk. He was depressed, they said, and painfully aware that he had not lived up to his talent. (Everyone in Paris intellectual circles thought this of Bost, and surmised that he had been crushed by Sartre.) Beauvoir added that Bost found Sartre's decline hard to bear and was dreading the thought of Sartre's death.

At the beginning of March 1980, Beauvoir heard that extracts from Sartre's discussions with Pierre Victor were about to appear in the *Nouvel Observateur,* in three successive issues. It was an important moment for Sartre. After years of silence, he would be back in the public arena.

Over the years Beauvoir had occasionally asked to see the transcript of their dialogue (it had grown to some eight hundred pages), but Sartre and Elkaïm had both been evasive. Now Sartre let Beauvoir read the forthcoming extracts. She read them in Sartre's apartment, while Sartre sat in his armchair gazing blankly ahead of him. She was appalled.

For the first time in print, Pierre Victor had used his real name. The "Benny Lévy" Beauvoir encountered in these discussions was aggressive and sarcastic, more an interrogator than an interviewer. It was as if he had deliberately set out to trip Sartre up. He interrupted Sartre, corrected him, trotted out things Sartre had said to him in private, posed leading questions, and mocked him. Sometimes Sartre appeared to agree, simply because Lévy did not give him time to explain:

BL: You said to me once, "I've talked about despair, but that's bunk. I talked about it because other people were talking about it, because it was fashionable. Everyone was reading Kierkegaard then."

J-P S: That's right.

Lévy, who now looked upon his militant past as "militant stupidity," seemed determined to make Sartre see his lifetime of political engagement in the same way. Throughout their discussions, Lévy constantly used the word *failure*. Did Sartre now look upon his decision to write as a failure? What about his fellow traveling with the communists? Did Sartre, looking back, see himself as a "sinister scoundrel, a dimwit, a sucker, or a basically good person?"

J-P S: I'd say, a person who's not bad. . . . When he gave in to Party demands, he turned into a dimwit or a sucker. But he was also capable of not giving in, and then he was not so bad. It was just the Party that made the whole thing unbearable.

BL: Let's talk plainly. Was that person a failure, was he one of the group of failures that has undermined the left's thinking over the past forty years?

J-P S: I think so, yes.

BL: What do you think today of this aspect of your activities?

J-P S: I was a fellow traveler for a very short period. . . . Around 1954 I went to the USSR, and almost immediately afterward, because of the Hungarian uprising, I broke with the Party. That's my total experience as a fellow traveler. Four years. What's more, to me it was secondary, since I was doing something else at the time.

BL: Do I detect a trace of doublethink here? . . . Let's talk about the intellectual's need to cling onto something. How did this need finally lead you and many others to cling onto the Stalinist rock?

J-P S: It wasn't Stalinism. Stalinism died with Stalin. The term "Stalinism" is used today to designate absolutely anything.

BL: How is it that some intellectuals needed something to cling to—needed to find a prop, a basis, in that trash?

J-P S: Because it was a question of finding a future for society. . . .
I didn't think I could change the world all by myself . . . but I did
discern social forces that were trying to move forward, and I
believed my place was among them.

In the last of the three interviews, Benny Lévy dragged Sartre
through the mud for declaring in *Portrait of the Anti-Semite* that there
was no such thing as Jewish history. Somehow he got Sartre, a lifelong
friend to secular Jews, to accept Lévy's premise that the "real Jew" was
a religious Jew. There followed a long discussion of messianism.

Overall, Sartre defended himself better than Beauvoir seemed to
think. As she saw it, Lévy had manipulated a tired old man. He had
trivialized Sartre's entire thinking, his entire past. Beauvoir read the
text through tears, and when she finished, she threw it across the
room. She pleaded with Sartre to stop the interviews' publication.

Sartre was surprised. He had expected some criticism, but not this.
He was blind; he depended on Benny Lévy, and he knew about Lévy's
hot temper. He was caught between two powerful forces, and he was
going to have to betray one of them. "You know, Beaver, I am still alive
and thinking," he told her. "You must allow me to continue to do so."[45]

To Beauvoir, it was a double betrayal—of Sartre, and by Sartre. "She
cried," Denise Pouillon recalls. "She could not stop crying. Floods of
tears. We cried inside ourselves. Her suffering was terrible."[46]

Claude Lanzmann and Bost rang Jean Daniel, the editor of the
Nouvel Observateur, trying to persuade him to stop publication of the
Lévy interviews. Jean Daniel hesitated. But then came a phone call
from Sartre himself. His voice was loud and clear. He wanted the
interview to be published in its entirety, he said. If Jean Daniel
did not go ahead and publish it, Sartre would send it elsewhere. He
knew his friends had phoned Daniel, but they were wrong to
have done that. "The itinerary of my thought eludes them all," he said,
"including Simone de Beauvoir."[47] (In fact, there was one exception
among the Sartreans: André Gorz was not against the publication, and
believed it represented a genuine evolution in Sartre's thinking.)

The interviews were published over three weeks, on March 10, 17,
and 24, 1980. The public did not know what to make of them. Could
this really be Jean-Paul Sartre talking about messianism? Was he in

full possession of his faculties? And who was this imperious young man, Benny Lévy?

The second of the three issues had appeared, and relations between Sartre and Beauvoir remained strained. On Wednesday, March 19, they spent the evening with Bost, in Sartre's apartment. After Bost left, Beauvoir stayed there, sleeping in the second bedroom. The following morning, when she went to wake Sartre at nine A.M., she found him sitting on the edge of his bed gasping for breath. He'd been there since five A.M., unable to speak, let alone call out. Beauvoir rushed to the phone to call his doctor. There was no dial tone. It turned out that Puig had not paid the bill. There was no money in the coffers. The service had been cut off.

Beauvoir scrambled into her clothes and rushed down to the concierge's ground-floor apartment to phone. The doctor came quickly, took one look at Sartre, and came back downstairs and phoned for an ambulance. The ambulance arrived, and Beauvoir stood by while Sartre was given emergency treatment that lasted almost an hour. Then holding an oxygen mask over his head, they took him down in the elevator on a stretcher, and put him in the ambulance.

Beauvoir went back up to the apartment. She showered, dressed, and went to lunch, as scheduled, with Jean and Denise Pouillon. Little did she know that she would never enter Sartre's apartment again.

After lunch, she asked Jean Pouillon to accompany her to the hospital. "I'm rather frightened," she told him. Sartre had been taken to the Broussais Hospital, nearby. She found him in the intensive care unit. He was breathing normally now, and told her he felt fine.

After a few days, there appeared to be a ray of hope. Sartre was transported to the cardiology ward. The doctors said he had a pulmonary edema, caused by hypertension or cardiac insufficiency.

The group settled into a new routine. Elkaïm spent mornings and evenings at the hospital; Beauvoir was there in the afternoons. The others arranged their visits accordingly. Bost and Claude Lanzmann came to see Sartre in the afternoon, during Beauvoir's shift. Michelle

Vian, Wanda, and Benny Lévy came while Elkaïm was there. Sartre's women read to him in relays. Detective novels.

Sartre was tired, and hardly spoke. He had nasty-looking bedsores. His kidneys were no longer functional. But he was still lucid. One afternoon, he asked Beauvoir anxiously, "How are we going to manage the funeral expenses?"[48]

He was soon back in the intensive care ward. On April 13, when Beauvoir hovered near his bed, Sartre took her by the wrist. His eyes were closed. "I love you very much, my dear Beaver," he said. The next day, his eyes still closed, he made a little pout and offered her his lips. Beauvoir kissed him on the mouth and cheeks. These were not words Sartre usually said. This was not a gesture he usually made. She understood.

On Tuesday, April 15, Beauvoir rang the hospital at ten A.M., as usual. The nurse sounded hesitant. Beauvoir hurried over. Sartre was in a coma, but he was breathing quite strongly. She spent the day by his bedside. At six P.M., Elkaïm took over. Three hours later the phone rang in the Rue Schoelcher. "It's over," Elkaïm said.

Beauvoir returned to the hospital with Le Bon. She found Sartre looking much the same, except that he was no longer breathing. From his bedside, she rang Bost, Claude Lanzmann, Jean Pouillon, and André Gorz. They came straight away. The authorities said they could stay with the body for several hours—until five in the morning, if they were quiet and did not disturb the other patients.

Beauvoir, already heavily sedated with Valium, asked Sylvie to go out and buy some whiskey. Pouillon did not want Le Bon to leave Beauvoir, and he went instead. Elkaïm went home. For the next few hours, the group drank, reminisced, and sobbed. Sartre had left no instructions. They knew he wanted to be cremated, and he had once stipulated that he did not want to be beside his mother and stepfather, at the Père Lachaise Cemetery. It was obvious to his friends that Sartre's final resting place had to be the Montparnasse Cemetery. He had lived within the shadows of its walls for most of his life.

In the early hours of the morning, Beauvoir wanted to be left alone with Sartre, and the others left. She pulled back the sheet and went to lie down beside him. "No, don't do that!" an orderly shouted at her. A nurse explained: "It's the gangrene, Madame." Beauvoir had not realized that Sartre's bedsores were gangrenous. The nurse let Beauvoir lie on top of the sheet, beside Sartre. She was so drugged she even fell asleep for a short time. At five in the morning, the orderlies came and took Sartre away.

Sartre's death made front-page news around the world. The tributes mourned the passing of a great man. "Sartre inhabited his century like Voltaire and Hugo inhabited theirs," said *Libération*. "The world is a poorer place than it was yesterday," said *Le Figaro*. "What we will keep is the example of an indefatigible combat for the dignity of man, for freedom, justice and peace," said *Le Matin de Paris*. Beauvoir was flooded with letters and telegrams.

For the next few days, she retreated to Le Bon's apartment. In her own, she could not face the phone, which never stopped ringing. She left it to Claude Lanzmann, Bost, and Le Bon to make the funeral arrangements.

President Giscard d'Estaing came in person to the hospital and spent an hour beside Sartre's coffin. He understood that Sartre, a man who had always rejected official honors, would not want a national burial, he told Sartre's friends, but the government would like to pay the costs of his funeral. The Sartreans thanked him, but refused.

The Paris sky was leaden on Saturday, April 19, 1980. It looked as if there would be rain. In the late morning, Beauvoir went to the hospital with Le Bon and Poupette, to see Sartre for the last time. His coffin in the hospital morgue was still open. He was dressed in a suit and tie. They were the only clothes of his Beauvoir kept in her apartment, for those occasions when they went with Le Bon to the opera. To the mourners who filed past the coffin Beauvoir kept saying softly, "He didn't suffer." She asked Bernard Pingaud, from the *Temps modernes,* to take some photos. Just before two P.M., the undertakers closed the casket. Beauvoir kissed Sartre good-bye, on the lips.

An immense crowd had gathered in front of the hospital. At 2:15 P.M., the heavy gates swung open. People craned forward. The first vehicle through the gates was a minibus—covered in a mountain of red roses, white arum lilies, and wreaths—transporting those friends who were unable to walk the three-kilometer route. Next came the hearse, with the coffin in the back, draped in black. Claude Lanzmann sat next to the driver. Simone de Beauvoir, Poupette, Le Bon, and Elkaïm sat behind.

The streets of Montparnasse and Saint-Germain were packed. The crowd, estimated to be fifty thousand, was mostly young people. Many carried flowers—a carnation, jonquils, a branch of lilac—which they waved as the hearse passed. Journalists knocked on the hearse windows, with their lenses pressed to the glass. "This is the last of the 1968 demonstrations," Claude Lanzmann said.

Beauvoir had Valium tablets in her handbag, and she was chewing them as if they were throat lozenges. She was barely aware of what was going on around her. She told herself this was exactly the funeral Sartre had wanted, and he would never know about it.

The procession reached Denfert-Rochereau. People had climbed onto the famous lion statue. A young man was sitting on the lion's head. The hearse turned down the Boulevard Raspail, past the Rue Schoelcher on the left, past Sartre's old apartment at number 222, past the Dôme, the Coupole, and Rotonde at the Vavin intersection. It turned up the Rue du Départ, then left onto the Boulevard Edgar Quinet, past number 29, where Sartre had spent his final years. They traveled extremely slowly, because of the crowd. At four-thirty P.M., they entered the main entrance of the cemetery.

Once inside the gates, the cars could hardly move forward. There were people everywhere. Sartre's friends had refused a police presence—Sartre would not have wanted that—but it meant that no one was holding back the crowd.

The hearse pulled up by the grave. The men carried the coffin through the crowd and lowered it, without ceremony, into the hole. When a frail little figure in black trousers, a raincoat, and a sunset-colored turban climbed out of the back seat, there was a burst of applause. People pressed forward. Lanzmann and Bost went ahead, clearing a path through the crowd. Le Bon and Poupette helped Beauvoir to the side of the grave.

The jostling was such that a young Belgian philosopher fell in the hole, on top of the coffin.[49] One of the men from the funeral parlor had to climb in and help him out. Some younger people tried to hold back the crowd to protect Beauvoir. Clothes were torn. People wept. Beauvoir looked as if she were about to faint. Someone hurried off to fetch something for her to sit on. The guard at the gate supplied an office chair. For ten minutes—it seemed like an eternity—Beauvoir sat beside the grave staring down at the coffin—indifferent to the cold drizzle, the clamor, and the clicking cameras—clutching a rose, weeping her heart out. No one who saw it would forget the sight. It was on the evening news.

One of the funeral men made a sign, and there was a flurry of activity. The crowd was too dense for people to walk up to the grave, and so their flowers and bouquets were passed overhead, from hand to hand, and those standing close tossed them onto the coffin.

The men picked up their shovels. Beauvoir was helped to her feet. This was it, the final separation, after fifty-one years. She dropped her rose onto the coffin and staggered toward the exit, supported by friends. On the way she collapsed onto a tombstone. She would scarcely remember the short car ride to Lanzmann's place. She would scarcely remember the next month of her life.

Sartre's official plot was not ready, and he had been buried in a temporary grave. Five days later, his remains were disinterred and taken to the Père Lachaise Cemetery to be cremated. Then the ashes were returned to the Montparnasse Cemetery. Sartre's permanent resting place was beneath a simple sand-colored tombstone, separated by a tall, ivy-covered wall from the Boulevard Edgar Quinet, where he had last lived.

A small group of friends attended the cremation; Beauvoir was too weak. She was at Le Bon's, and that morning she had been unable to get out of bed. When Lanzmann and Le Bon came back after the ceremony, they found her sitting on the floor beside her bed, delirious. They rushed her to the Cochin Hospital. For a week she was mostly unconscious. For the second time in her life she had reacted to a crisis by developing pneumonia. It was as if her lungs could not work without Sartre being there. She could no longer breathe.

Her condition was so bad that the doctors predicted she would never fully recover. When she went home, a month later, she still could not walk.

" 'The doe' ... transformed herself into a vulture," Sartre's friend Georges Michel would write in disgust.[50] The day after Sartre's cremation, Elkaïm, helped by Benny Lévy, emptied Sartre's apartment. They took his papers, books, and few possessions to Elkaïm's place. As for Sartre's furniture, Benny Lévy took it to his communal house on the outskirts of Paris.

Elkaïm would find herself paying a fine to the taxation department for removing Sartre's affairs before they could be officially assessed, but as Sartre's adopted daughter, all the legal rights were hers. Beauvoir had none.

"Everyone knew why she did it," Beauvoir told Deirdre Bair afterward. "I was the only other person who had a key, and she was afraid of my legitimate claim to many things there."[51] Sartre had not made a will. On Beauvoir's behalf, Le Bon and Lanzmann asked Elkaïm for certain mementos—the Schweitzer family chair Sartre had loved, a Picasso drawing, a painting by Riberolle, which she felt had been given to her as well as to Sartre. "Let her ask me for them if she wants them that much," Elkaïm told them. Beauvoir preferred to let them go.

Beauvoir had already suggested to Le Bon that she adopt her legally. Le Bon had resisted the idea. She did not want in any way to be compared with Elkaïm. She also knew the public would say that she and Beauvoir were simply imitating Sartre. But Beauvoir now pressed her more urgently. The situation was difficult. Beauvoir's legal heir was her sister, Poupette. French law was strict, and Beauvoir's doctors were only legally entitled to discuss Beauvoir's condition with her family—in other words, with Poupette. Poupette and her husband, Lionel de Roulet, lived in Goxwiller, in Alsace, and Beauvoir was terrified that the doctors might force her to go and live with them. Beauvoir had never much liked Roulet, a career diplomat and a political moderate. And behind Poupette's back, Beauvoir had been quite scathing, over the years, about her sister—her lack of talent, as Beauvoir saw it, and her delusions about this.[52] In any event, Poupette was merely two years younger than she was. Beauvoir needed a younger heir and literary executor.

Le Bon could see that the adoption would give Beauvoir peace of mind, and she agreed. Although she did not use the name until after Beauvoir's death, she became Sylvie Le Bon de Beauvoir.

"After Sartre died, Sylvie was everything to Beauvoir," Liliane Siegel says. "If Sylvie hadn't been there, I know Beauvoir would not have lived long."[53]

When Beauvoir could gather her strength, she sat down to write *Adieux: A Farewell to Sartre.* She began by addressing Sartre: "This is the first of my books—the only one no doubt—that you will not have read before it is printed."

Beauvoir had always dealt with turmoil and grief by writing about it. This book, based on her journals from the last ten years, depicted her protracted farewell to the man she had loved. She did not resort to sentimentality. She portrayed Sartre's physical deterioration with her usual concern to tell the truth, however brutal. Many readers, including Arlette Elkaïm, Michelle Vian, and Lena Zonina, considered the book in bad taste. Others were moved by the love, anguish, and sorrow straining beneath the narrative surface, and Beauvoir's struggle not to mention her sense of betrayal.[54]

Beauvoir was fair to Benny Lévy (whom she still called Pierre Victor), though she made no bones about her dislike of him. Elkaïm was pushed to the background of her narrative. The only comment Beauvoir made that was actually negative was where she talked about the alliance Elkaïm and Victor had formed.

> Victor had changed a great deal since Sartre first met him. Like many other former Maoists he had turned toward God—the God of Israel, since he was a Jew. His view of the world had become spiritualistic and even religious. . . . Victor was supported by Arlette, who knew nothing whatsoever about Sartre's philosophical works and who sympathized with Victor's new tendencies—they were learning Hebrew together. Sartre was confronted with this alliance, and he lacked the perspective that only a thoughtful, solitary reading could have given him; so he gave way.[55]

Amid the general critical uproar after the book's publication in 1981, *Libération* published an open letter to Simone de Beauvoir from Arlette Elkaïm Sartre:

> Sartre is well and truly dead then, in your eyes, it seems, since you take advantage of it so harshly and resolutely trample on the faces of people whom he loved, with the aim of discrediting the interviews he did, the year he died, with Benny Lévy...
>
> Before his death, Sartre was quite alive: he virtually no longer saw anything, his organism was deteriorating, but he heard and understood, and you treated him as a dead man who inconveniently enough, appeared in public—this last comparison is not mine but his.[56]

Beauvoir did not reply. Two years later, she published the letters Sartre had written her over the years. "Anyone who reads his letters to me will know what I meant to him," she told friends.[57] To protect a handful of people, she censored some of the harsh comments Sartre had made about others, but in the interest of truth-telling, she deposited the originals in the Bibliothèque Nationale.

Robert Gallimard knew the letters would create a scandal, and they did—particularly those passages where Sartre clinically described taking a girlfriend's virginity. The shock would be even greater when Beauvoir's letters to Sartre were published in 1990, after her death, without any censorship whatsoever on the part of Sylvie Le Bon. The scathing comments about others (including Beauvoir's sister, Poupette) were left intact, and so were the details of her lesbian relationships. With each new publication, readers shook their heads in wonder. Was this the famous Sartrean pact of transparency? This voyeurism and exhibitionism, this lying to others? Many remarked that the complicity between Sartre and Beauvoir resembled the scheming Viscount of Valmont and the Marquise de Merteuil in *Les Liaisons dangereuses.*

At the same time, there was something refreshing about this couple close up. Here were Sartre and Beauvoir frolicking around on paper with the sheer voluptuous pleasure of telling each other every detail of their lives. Here was Sartre, an ugly little man who owned a few clothes, a pipe, and a fountain pen, and who seemed to care only about thinking, writing, and loving. Here was Beauvoir, who dared to live as freely as Sartre, whose intelligence shone as brightly as his own, and whose passion for life was inexhaustible.

Beauvoir died on April 14, 1986, six years after Sartre almost to the day. Like him, she died of pulmonary edema. Over five thousand people followed her hearse through the streets of Montparnasse. Her ashes were buried beside Sartre's.

There are always fresh bouquets of flowers on their tomb in the Montparnasse Cemetery. Their books have been translated into dozens of languages. A vast industry has grown up around them, with shelves of biographies, monographs, and memoirs, as well as innumerable articles, conferences, and university courses on their work and their lives. Tourists haunt the cafés—now the most fashionable drinking places on the Left Bank—where the couple used to write during the war, eager to work in the warmth, surrounded by the bustle of life.

The Hôtel Mistral, on the Rue de Cels, has a large plaque in front, stating that Sartre and Beauvoir lived there on several occasions during the war. Under Sartre's name is a quotation from a letter he wrote Beauvoir: "There is one thing that hasn't changed and cannot change: that is that no matter what happens and what I become, I will become it with you." Under Beauvoir's name there's a passage from her memoirs: "I was cheating when I used to say that we were only one person. Between two individuals, harmony is never a given; it must be constantly conquered."

The Place Saint-Germain, the cobbled square in the heart of Saint-Germain-des-Prés, with the Deux Magots in one corner and Sartre's old apartment at 42 Rue Bonaparte in another, has been renamed the Place Sartre-Beauvoir.

NOTES

PREFACE

1. Jacques-Pierre Amette, "Simone de Beauvoir: Ces lettres qui ébranlent un mythe," *Le Point,* April 15, 2004.
2. Michel Contat, "Sartre/Beauvoir, légende et réalité d'un couple," in *Literature and Its Cults,* ed. Péter Dávidházi and Judit Karafiáth (Budapest: Argumentum, 1994), pp. 1542–43.

CHAPTER ONE: NINETEEN TWENTY-NINE

1. Hélène de Beauvoir, *Souvenirs* (Paris: Librairie Séguier, 1987), p. 90.
2. "Mon petit poulet," "mon poulot," "ma poulotte," or "ma poulette" are terms of endearment in French, and mean "my little chicken." "Poulou" is an amusing variation.
3. Sartre interview with John Gerassi [hereafter Gerassi interview with Sartre], December 18, 1970, Beinecke Library, Yale, and with Catherine Chaîne, *Le Nouvel Observateur,* Jan./Feb. 1977. Jan. 31, pp. 74–87 and Feb. 7, pp. 64–82.
4. Sartre [hereafter S] to Simone Jollivet, undated letter, 1926, in *Witness to My Life: The Letters of Jean-Paul Sartre to Simone de Beauvoir, 1926–1939* [hereafter *Witness*], trans. Lee Fahnestock and Norman MacAfee (New York: Charles Scribner's Sons, 1992), p. 21.
5. Raymond Aron, *Mémoires* (Paris: Julliard, 1983), p. 32. Aron was shocked, at times, by the harshness of the pranks Sartre thought up.
6. Paul Nizan, *Aden Arabie* (Paris: Rieder, 1931).
7. Sartre's foreword to the 1960 edition of *Aden Arabie.*
8. Simone de B [hereafter S de B], *Memoirs of a Dutiful Daughter* [hereafter *MDD*], trans. James Kirkup (Cleveland: World Publishing Co, 1959), pp. 310–13.
9. *MDD,* p. 311.
10. Beauvoir quotes this passage from her journal in *MDD,* p. 311.

11. "Little Man" is the hero of Kipling's *The Jungle Book*—the boy who grew up in the jungle and is finally brought back to civilization by the sight of a beautiful young woman.

12. *MDD*, pp. 312–13.

13. Beauvoir's journal (unpublished) [hereafter Beauvoir's journal], May 3, 1929, Beauvoir papers, Bibliothèque Nationale, manuscript room, microfilm 6538–6539.

14. *MDD*, p. 325. (Trans. modified.)

15. *MDD*, pp. 336–37.

16. Beauvoir's journal.

17. Henriette Nizan and Marie-José Jaubert, *Libres Mémoires* (Paris: Robert Laffont, 1989).

18. *MDD*, p. 160.

19. *MDD*, pp. 339–40.

20. Zaza's journal, July 14, 1929, *Zaza: Correspondance et Carnets d'Elisabeth Lacoin (1914–1929)* [hereafter *Zaza*] (Paris: Seuil, 1991), pp. 304 and 367.

21. *MDD*, p. 194.

22. Unpublished journal, May 6, 1927, quoted in Margaret A. Simons, *Beauvoir and the Second Sex: Feminism, Race, and the Origins of Existentialism* (Lanham, Md.: Rowman and Littlefield, 1999), p. 195.

23. An Ecole Normale Supérieure for women had been established at Sèvres, just outside Paris, in 1881, but it was not nearly as prestigious as the male institution in the heart of the Latin Quarter, and did not include philosophy in its curriculum.

24. Simone de Beauvoir, *Adieux: A Farewell to Sartre* [hereafter *Adieux*], trans. Patrick O'Brian (New York: Pantheon, 1984), pp. 294–95.

25. Marron to S, November 4, 1927, Sotheby's catalogue, *Collection Littéraire*, Paris, June 26, 2002.

26. "Sartre et les femmes," interview with Catherine Chaîne, *Le Nouvel Observateur*, January 31, 1977, pp. 74–87.

27. Simone de Beauvoir, *The Prime of Life* [hereafter *PL*], trans. Peter Green (New York: World Publishing, 1962), p. 77.

28. S to Jollivet, undated, 1926, in *Witness*, p. 19.

29. S to Jollivet, April 1926, in *Witness*, p. 9.

30. Ingrid Galster, "Cinquante ans après *Le Deuxième Sèxe:* Beauvoir en débats," *Lendemains* 94 (1999).

31. Toril Moi makes these points in *Simone de Beauvoir: The Making of an Intellectual Woman* (London and Cambridge, Mass.: Blackwell, 1994).

32. *PL*, p. 12. (Trans. modified.)

33. Hélène de Beauvoir, *Souvenirs*, recueillis par Marcelle Routier (Paris: Séguier, 1987), p. 94.

34. Beauvoir's journal, September 2–4, 1929.

CHAPTER TWO: THE PACT

1. Beauvoir's journal, September 10, 1929.
2. *PL,* p. 73.
3. *PL,* p. 39.
4. Sartre, *The War Diaries, November 1939–March 1940,* trans. Quintin Hoare (New York: Pantheon, 1984), p. 75.
5. Zaza to her father, August 27, 1929, in *Zaza,* p. 355.
6. Zaza to S de B, August 28, 1929, in *Zaza,* p. 359.
7. Deirdre Bair, *Simone de Beauvoir: A Biography* (New York: Simon and Schuster, 1990), p. 147.
8. *MDD,* p. 294.
9. Merleau-Ponty to S de B, undated (probably early 1959), Sylvie Le Bon de Beauvoir private archives.
10. In 1928, Germaine Marron's parents hired private detectives to investigate Sartre. They came snooping around the Ecole Normale. It seems that whatever it was they found out, the Marrons did not find it encouraging.
11. Bair, *Simone de Beauvoir,* p. 152. In 1958, when Beauvoir asked Sartre's mother, who also lived in La Rochelle back then, whether she knew about the affair, Mme Mancy said that everyone in town knew about it.
12. S de B to S, January 6, 1930.
13. S to S de B, undated, in *Witness,* p. 32.
14. Beauvoir's journal, 1929–31. Some of this journal is quoted in Margaret A. Simons's article "Lesbian Connections: Simone de Beauvoir and Feminism," *Signs* 18, no. 1 (Autumn 1992): 148.
15. S de B, "Conversations with Jean-Paul Sartre" (1974), in *Adieux,* p. 159.
16. *PL,* pp. 72–73. (Trans. modified.)
17. Simone de Beauvoir, *The Second Sex,* trans. H. M. Parshley (New York: Knopf, 1953), p. 653.
18. *PL,* pp. 70–74.
19. Ibid., p. 47.
20. Ibid., p. 40. I have replaced the fictional pseudonyms, Mme. Lemaire and Pagniez, with their real names, and slightly modified the published translation.
21. *PL,* p. 82.
22. Gerassi interview with Sartre, February 26, 1971.
23. S to Simone Jollivet, undated, 1926, in *Witness,* pp. 16–17.
24. Beauvoir copied Maheu's letter for Sartre, January 6, 1930, *Letters to Sartre, 1940–1963* [hereafter *Letters to Sartre*], trans. Quintin Hoare (New York: Arcade Publishing, 1991), p. 4.
25. *PL,* p. 20.
26. Ibid., p. 63.
27. Ibid., p. 65.
28. Bair, *Simone de Beauvoir,* p. 172.

29. *PL,* p. 89.

30. As a child, Sartre had once gone to Switzerland with his grandparents.

31. *PL,* p. 99.

32. Ibid., p. 104.

33. Ibid., 109.

34. Lycée Montgrand files at the Archives de Marseille. Suzanne Tuffreau was born in 1895, which made her thirty-five years old when Beauvoir met her. A married woman, she had been teaching English at the Lycée Montgrand since July 1927.

35. *PL,* p. 114.

36. Ibid., p. 115.

37. Ibid., p. 119.

38. Bair, *Simone de Beauvoir,* p. 176.

39. *PL,* p. 133. Since the correspondence between Beauvoir and Sartre during the Marseille period was lost or destroyed (except for one published letter from Sartre, dated October 9, 1931), there is no documentary evidence to hold up against Beauvoir's memoirs.

CHAPTER THREE: OLGA KOSAKIEWICZ

1. *PL,* p. 143.

2. Annie Cohen-Solal, *Sartre: A Life* (1985) (New York: Random House, 1987), p. 79.

3. Gerassi interview with Sartre, March 26, 1971.

4. Colette Audry, "Portrait de l'écrivain jeune femme," *Biblio* (November 1962).

5. Colette Audry interview with Deirdre Bair, March 5, 1986, Bair, *Simone de Beauvoir,* p. 183.

6. The affair is known about in Sartre circles. Raymond Queneau mentions it in his *Journeaux 1914–1965* (Paris: Gallimard, 1996), July 24, 1951, p. 767.

7. Gerassi interview with Sartre, March 26, 1971.

8. Sartre, *War Diaries,* p. 285. (Trans. modified.)

9. Ibid., p. 62.

10. In *PL,* Beauvoir writes ambiguously: "There was no feeling of jealousy on my part. Yet this was the first time since we had known one another that Sartre had taken a serious interest in another woman; and jealousy is far from being an emotion of which I am incapable" (p. 220).

11. *PL,* p. 220.

12. Ibid., p. 188.

13. Ibid., pp. 189–90; p. 94.

14. In 1944, after the Liberation, the town of Laigle changed its name to L'Aigle.

15. S de B to Olga Kosakiewicz, July 1934 (undated), Sylvie Le Bon de Beauvoir archives.

16. Ibid., July 1934.

17. Beauvoir said this to Sartre later (January 24, 1940; *Letters,* p. 269).

18. Sartre, *War Diaries*, p. 123.

19. Ibid., p. 87.

20. Sartre, *War Diaries*, p. 76. It was a quotation from the Swiss writer Rodolphe Töpffer.

21. Marie Ville told this to Beauvoir. Simone de Beauvoir, *Journal de guerre: Septembre 1939–janvier 1941* (Paris: Gallimard, 1990), p. 91.

22. Sartre, *War Diaries*, p. 77.

23. Both of them wrote about that afternoon: S de B, *PL*, p. 249, and Sartre, *War Diaries*, p. 77.

24. *PL*, p. 252.

25. Ibid., p. 253.

26. Sartre, *War Diaries*, p. 274.

27. John Gerassi interview with Olga Kosakiewicz, May 9, 1973. Gerassi collection, Beinecke Library, Yale University.

28. Sartre, *War Diaries*, p. 76.

29. Ibid., p. 77.

30. On her marriage certificate (in the *mairie* of the sixth arrondissement) Olga's birthdate is given as November 6, 1917. Sylvie Le Bon de Beauvoir confirms that this is wrong. Without a birth certificate (it was in the U.S.S.R.), it was easy for Olga to fudge the truth. She wanted to make herself look younger than Bost, who was born on May 6, 1916.

31. *PL*, p. 273.

32. S de B to Olga, September 6, 1935, Sylvie Le Bon de Beauvoir archives.

33. *PL*, p. 281.

34. Beauvoir wrote to Olga: "I know that often you do not realize your worth," September 6, 1935.

35. Madame Kosakiewicz to S de B, August 11, 1935, Sylvie Le Bon de Beauvoir archives.

36. *PL*, p. 292.

37. Olga Kosakiewicz Bost, phone interview with Deirdre Bair, 1982, Bair, *Simone de Beauvoir*, p. 200.

38. Bair, *Simone de Beauvoir*, p. 194.

39. Sartre, *War Diaries*, pp. 61–62. The irony is that Sartre had spent years working on his own character, trying to control emotions he considered weak. At the age of twenty-one, he told Simone Jollivet, "I was born with a personality to match my face: foolishly, stupidly emotional, cowardly, self-indulgent. My sentimentality can make me teary-eyed about the least little thing" (undated letter, 1926, *Witness*, p. 4).

40. Sartre gives this longing to Mathieu, in *The Age of Reason*, trans. Eric Sutton (New York: Knopf, 1947), p. 73, but he often expressed this longing himself.

41. Sartre, *War Diaries*, p. 78.

42. *PL*, p. 313.

43. Ibid.

44. Sartre to S de B, April 1937, in *Witness*, p. 79.

45. *PL*, p. 141.

46. S de B to Olga, October 1, 1935.

47. Sartre to S de B, May 3, 1937, in *Witness*, p. 100.

48. *PL*, p. 343.

49. *Adieux*, p. 159.

50. Sartre's mad protagonist in his short story "Erostratus" was inspired by Zuorno.

51. Sartre, *War Diaries*, p. 4.

52. *PL*, p. 353.

53. John Gerassi interview with Wanda Kosakiewicz, March 23, 1973. Gerassi collection, Beinecke Library, Yale University.

54. Mouloudji comments that Wanda was a formidable walker and would trudge for hours, with the steady rhythm of an alpine hunter. Marcel Mouloudji, *La Fleur de l'âge* (Paris: Grasset, 1991).

55. Sartre portrays this taxi scene in *The Age of Reason*. It's one of the instances where "Ivich" is based on Wanda as much as on Olga. "He leaned towards her; . . . he laid his lips lightly against a cold, closed mouth; he was feeling defiant; Ivich was silent. Lifting his head, he saw her eyes, and his passionate joy vanished. He thought: 'A married man messing about with a young girl in a taxi,' and his arm dropped, dead and flaccid; Ivich's body straightened with a mechanical jerk, like a pendulum swinging back to equilibrium. 'Now I've done it,' said Mathieu to himself, 'she'll never forgive me.' He sat huddled in his seat, wishing he might disintegrate."

56. S to Wanda Kosakiewicz, undated. [February 1937], Sylvie Le Bon de Beauvoir archives.

57. *PL*, p. 353.

58. Gerassi interview with Sartre, October 27, 1972.

CHAPTER FOUR: THE PROSPECT OF WAR

1. Sartre, *War Diaries*, p. 78.

2. Influential friends of Sartre, Charles Dullin and Pierre Bost (Jacques-Laurent Bost's elder brother, and a reader at Gallimard), had asked Gaston Gallimard himself to look at Sartre's rejected manuscript. Gallimard declared it "splendid" and "inspired."

3. *PL*, p. 377.

4. *PL*, p. 372.

5. A selection of Sartre's letters to Wanda from Greece were published in *Les Temps modernes*, Oct.–Dec. 1990, nos. 531–33, pp. 1292–1429.

6. *PL*, p. 380.

7. Sartre, *War Diaries*, pp. 248–49.

8. Ibid., p. 122.

9. S to S de B, September 1937, in *Witness*, p. 142.

10. Bair, *Simone de Beauvoir*, p. 197.

11. Quoted in *Nouvelle Revue Française,* January 1970, p. 78.

12. Bianca Lamblin, *A Disgraceful Affair,* trans. Julie Plovnick (Boston: Northeastern University Press, 1996), p. 19.

13. S de B to Bost, November 28, 1938, *Correspondance Croisée, 1937–1940* (Paris: Gallimard, 2004), p. 136.

14. Lamblin, *A Disgraceful Affair,* p. 20.

15. Ibid., p. 25.

16. S to S de B, July 14, 1938, in *Witness,* p. 155. (Trans. modified.)

17. S to S de B, Wednesday, July [20] 1938, in *Witness,* p. 164. Beauvoir cut several graphic passages from the published version.

18. Sartre, *War Diaries,* p. 285. The character in Sartre's short story "The Childhood of a Leader," a young man who is obsessed with seduction, has the same problem with his facial muscles when he is bent on conquest. "The corners of his mouth hurt because he had smiled so much."

19. S to S de B, May 1937, *Witness,* p. 110. (Trans. modified.)

20. Sartre, *War Diaries,* p. 269.

21. Sartre, *War Diaries,* p. 269, and *Adieux,* p. 311. In a *Playboy* interview in May 1965, Sartre told Madeline Gobeil: "Feminine ugliness is offensive to me. I admit this and I'm ashamed of it." (*The Writings of Jean-Paul Sartre,* vol. 1, *A Biographical Life,* comp. Michel Contat and Michel Rybalka [Evanston, Ill.: Northwestern University Press, 1974], p. 466.)

22. Sartre, *War Diaries,* p. 267.

23. S to S de B, Sunday, July 1938, in *Witness,* p. 166.

24. S to Wanda Kosakiewicz, undated [1938], Sylvie Le Bon de Beauvoir archives.

25. S de B to S, July 15, 1938, in *Letters,* p. 16.

26. S de B to S, July 27, 1938, in *Letters,* p. 21. (Trans. modified.)

27. S de B to Bost, August 22, 1938, in *Correspondance,* p. 57.

28. Bost to S de B, August 3, 1938, in *Correspondance,* p. 47.

29. Bost to S de B, August 6, 1938, in *Correspondance,* p. 50.

30. S de B to Bost, September 2, 1938, in *Correspondance,* p. 69.

31. The novellas *When Things of the Spirit Come First (Quand prime le spirituel)* would eventually be published in 1979. Despite their immaturity, they are lively and engaging, with ironic wit and pungent observations. Sartre found numerous passages good.

32. S de B quotes his comment in a letter to Bost, December 22, 1938, *Correspondance,* p. 162.

33. *PL,* p. 380.

34. *She Came to Stay,* trans. Yvonne Moyse and Roger Senhouse (New York and Cleveland: World Publishing, 1954), p. 341.

35. Ibid., p. 368.

36. Reviewers also talked about the semipornographic aspect of the book. Its publication was another occasion on which Beauvoir was given a hard time by her parents. "My father has read your book," she told Sartre. "He's outraged by the

obscenities, and by the fact that you dedicated the book to Kos, whom he suspects of being your mistress." S de B to S, January 3, 1940, *Letters*, p. 240.

37. Lamblin, *A Disgraceful Affair*, p. 39.
38. Ibid., pp. 42–43.
39. My interview with Bianca Bienenfeld Lamblin, June 29, 2002, Paris.
40. S to Bienenfeld, July 1939 (undated), in *Witness*, p. 190.
41. S de B to Bost, February 5, 1939, in *Correspondance*, p. 233.
42. S de B to Bost, November 11, 1938, in *Correspondance*, p. 106.
43. S de B to Bost, November 27, 1938, in *Correspondance*, p. 133.
44. Bost to S de B, May 25, 1939, in *Correspondance*, pp. 375–76.
45. S de B to Bost, June 4, 1939, in *Correspondance*, p. 386.
46. S de B to Bost, June 8, 1939, in *Correspondance*, pp. 396–97.
47. S to S de B, late July 1939, in *Witness*, p. 200.
48. Bost to S de B, August 19, 1939, in *Correspondance*, p. 414.
49. S to Wanda, September 21, 1939, Sylvie le Bon de Beauvoir archives.

CHAPTER FIVE: WAR
1. *PL,* p. 446.
2. S to S de B, September 9, 1939, in *Witness*, p. 240.
3. S to S de B, September 4, 1939, in *Witness*, p. 232.
4. S to S de B, September 7, 1939, in *Witness*, p. 236.
5. S to S de B, September 12, 1939, in *Witness*, pp. 241–42.
6. S to S de B, October 2, 1939, in *Witness*, p. 275.
7. October 10 and 11, 1939, *Carnets de la drôle de guerre, Sept 1939–Mars 1940* (Paris: Gallimard, 1995), pp. 116–21. (This new French edition includes the first notebook, Sept.–Oct. 1939, which turned up in June 1991. It is not included in the earlier English edition.)
8. S to S de B, September 26, 1939, in *Witness*, p. 265.
9. This is my comment, not his. Wanda had left school before her baccalaureate, and her letters are full of mistakes.
10. November 26, 1939, Sartre, *War Diaries*, p. 47.
11. Sartre, *War Diaries*, p. 63.
12. S to S de B, December 1, 1939, in *Witness*, p. 377.
13. S to S de B, November 24, 1939, in *Witness*, p. 361. (Trans. modified.)
14. Sartre, *Being and Nothingness*, tr. Hazel Barnes (New York: Philosophical Library, 1956), pp. 489–91.
15. S de B to S, October 7, 1939, in *Letters*, p. 102.
16. S de B to S, November 18, 1939, in *Letters*, p. 173.
17. Sylvie Le Bon de Beauvoir's archives contain several letters from Olga to Simone de Beauvoir, full of anxieties.
18. S de B to S, October 25, 1939, in *Letters*, p. 140. (Trans. modified.)
19. S to S de B, September 13, 1939, in *Witness*, p. 247.

20. S de B to S, November 6 and 10, 1939, in *Letters,* pp. 148–54.

21. S to S de B, November 6, 7, 8, 1939, in *Witness,* pp. 326–31.

22. S de B to S, December 11, 1939, in *Letters,* p. 206.

23. S to S de B, December 23, 1939, in *Witness,* p. 424.

24. Bost to S de B, October 25, 1939, in *Correspondance,* p. 608. Because of frequent power outages, hairdressers had difficulty setting and perming women's hair, and "turbans" came into fashion as a way of lifting the hair off the face. Beauvoir was told the style suited her. She would continue to wear turbans throughout her life, long after the fashion had changed.

25. S de B to S, December 17, 1939, in *Letters,* p. 218. (Trans. modified.)

26. S de B to S, December 14, 1939, in *Letters,* p. 211.

27. S de B to S, December 21, 1939, in *Letters,* p. 223. (Trans. modified.)

28. S de B to S, January 14, 1940, in *Letters,* p. 255.

29. S de B, *Journal de Guerre,* February 2, 1940, pp. 266–67.

30. S to S de B, February 24, 1940, in *Quiet Moments in a War: The Letters of Jean-Paul Sartre to Simone de Beauvoir, 1926–1939,* trans. Lee Fahnestock and Norman MacAfee (New York: Charles Scribner's Sons, 1992), p. 75.

31. S to S de B, February 15, 1940, in *Quiet Moments,* pp. 54–55.

32. Bost to S de B, January 6, 1940, in *Correspondance,* p. 884.

33. S de B to S, February 18, 1940, in *Letters,* p. 276. (Trans. modified.)

34. Ibid.

35. Marcel Mouloudji, *Le Petit Invité* (Paris: Balland, 1989).

36. S quotes Wanda's letter to S de B, February 23, 1940, in *Quiet Moments,* p. 71.

37. S enclosed a copy of his letter to Colette in his letter to S de B, February 23, 1940, in *Quiet Moments,* p. 73.

38. S to S de B, February 24, 1940, in *Quiet Moments,* p. 75.

39. S to S de B, February 29, 1940, in *Quiet Moments,* pp. 87–89.

40. S to S de B, March 1, 1940, in *Quiet Moments,* pp. 89–90.

41. S de B to S, February 27, 1940, in *Letters,* p. 279.

42. S de B to S, March 4, 1940, in *Letters,* p. 285.

43. At the end of March 1940, while Sartre was with Wanda, Beauvoir visited Bost at the front, in the Meuse region, getting them both into trouble with the authorities.

44. Beauvoir makes this point in *PL,* p. 508.

45. Sartre reproached Wanda for not telling him about Olga's affair. He asked her if Olga had told Bost. Wanda replied that of course Olga had not. Did Sartre really expect Olga to tell Bost, who was far away and who had told her that he had only his relationship with Olga to cling to? This "purely physical affair" was not worth such a bloodbath. Sartre wrote back that her attitude was "charming." He wondered if Wanda, too, would have a "purely physical affair" while he was on the front line, and not tell him. (Sartre to Wanda, May 26, 1940, Sylvie Le Bon de Beauvoir archives.)

46. S to S de B, May 3, 1940, original letter in Bibliothèque Nationale, Paris. Beauvoir deleted this whole discussion from the published version.

47. S to S de B, May 8, 1940, original letter in Bibliothèque Nationale, Paris. Beauvoir deleted this passage from the published correspondence. Michel Contat sums up these two letters in *Literature and Its Cults,* pp. 153–54.

48. Niko Papatakis, the filmmaker, born in 1918, is best known for his controversial 1963 film *Les Abysses,* which made allegorical reference to the Algerian War. Sartre wrote a blurb supporting it, which Papatakis used in his press release. Papatakis's memoirs, *Tous les désespoirs sont permis,* were published by Fayard in 2003.

49. My interview with Niko Papatakis, Café de Flore, October 30, 2003.

50. S to S de B, May 12, 1940, in *Quiet Moments,* p. 180.

51. S to Wanda, May 11, 1940 (Sylvie Le Bon de Beauvoir archives) and May 17, 1940. (This one letter to Wanda is among Sartre's letters to Beauvoir at the Bibliothèque Nationale, Paris.)

52. S to S de B, May 29, 1940, Bibliothèque Nationale, Paris. (Some sections were cut from the published version.)

53. Beauvoir describes this journey, giving her own experience to Hélène, in her novel *The Blood of Others.*

54. S to S de B, July 8, 1940, in *Quiet Moments,* p. 233.

55. *Adieux,* p. 389.

56. Papatakis knew nothing about Olga's pregnancy until after the event. It was very unpleasant, he writes, to find himself gossiped about at the Flore, subjected to public obloquy for having failed in his responsibilities. Niko Papatakis, *Tous les désespoirs sont permis,* pp. 260–61.

57. Beauvoir wrote to Sartre about "two sinister weeks due to a sickness of Olga's, with whom I was alone in Paris." She could not permit herself to be more explicit. S de B to S, October 17, 1940, *Letters to Sartre,* p. 342. (Trans. modified.)

58. S to S de B, July 23, 1940, in *Quiet Moments,* p. 236.

59. S to S de B, July 28, 1940, in *Quiet Moments,* p. 237.

60. S to S de B, July 29, 1940, in *Quiet Moments,* p. 239.

61. S de B to S, March 14, 1941, in *Letters,* p. 372.

62. *PL,* p. 521.

63. Ibid., p. 574.

64. Nathalie Sorokine's mother would describe the situation, and her daughter's difficult character, in the official complaint she made to the Board of Education in March 1942. Ingrid Galster, "Juin 43: Beauvoir est exclue de l'université. Retour sur une affaire classée," *Contemporary French Civilization* (winter/spring 2001).

65. The hotel, which was at the corner of the Rue Berthe, has been replaced by an apartment building. The artist studios were named the Bâteau Lavoir.

66. S de B to S, March 14, 1941, *Letters,* p. 372.

67. S de B to S, January 20, 1941 and February 21, 1941, in *Letters,* p. 367 and pp. 371–72.

68. *PL,* p. 576.
69. Ibid.

CHAPTER SIX: OCCUPIED PARIS

1. *PL,* p. 581.
2. My interview with Dominique Desanti, Paris, August 27, 2003.
3. Beauvoir writes that Socialisme et Liberté was disbanded in October 1941. Dominique Desanti and Simone Debout Devouassoux, both members of the group, independently stated to me that the group continued until May or June 1942.
4. Dominique Desanti, "Sartre: Une leçon à une débutante en 1942," in Ingrid Galster, *La Naissance du "Phénomène Sartre," Raisons d'un succès (1938–1945)* (Paris: Seuil, 2001).
5. S to S de B, undated, 1941, *Quiet Moments,* p. 251. Beauvoir changed the name "Wanda" to "Tania" in the published letters.
6. Bair, *Simone de Beauvoir,* p. 231.
7. S de B, *A Very Easy Death* (New York: Random House, 1965), p. 36. (Trans. modified.)
8. Ibid., p. 36.
9. In Beauvoir's novel *The Blood of Others* (1945), Blomart, the Sartre character, tells the jealous young Hélène, "Listen, you know I'm not the least bit in love with Madeleine. Personally, I'd end our physical relations without the least regret."
10. *Adieux,* p. 312.
11. S de B to Nelson Algren, August 8, 1948, *A Transatlantic Love Affair* (New York: New Press, 1998), p. 208.
12. Sartre interviewed by Beauvoir, summer 1974, in *Adieux,* p. 302 and p. 314.
13. *PL,* p. 606.
14. Ibid., p. 609.
15. Gerassi interview with Olga Kosakiewicz, May 9, 1973. Beinecke Library, Yale University.
16. Gerassi interview with Wanda Kosakiewicz, March 23, 1973. Beinecke Library, Yale University.
17. *PL,* p. 574.
18. Sorokine's mother wrote this in her report to the Ministry of Education. Sylvie Le Bon de Beauvoir confirms that Sorokine slept with both Sartre and Bost. Beauvoir and Bost told her this independently.
19. Mouloudji paints an amusing portrait of Sorokine in the second volume of his memoirs, *La Fleur de l'âge,* p. 26ff. He writes that Sorokine was an aggressive seductress and an inveterate thief. She pursued him vigorously, and they spent the night in a hotel, for which he paid. The next morning she went off with the sheets, blanket, and pillow. He was embarrassed.
20. Galster, "Juin 43," pp. 139–41, and Gibert Joseph, *Une Si Douce Occupation, Simone de Beauvoir et Jean-Paul Sartre 1940–1944,* Paris: Albin Michel, 1991.

21. Galster, "Juin 43," p. 147.

22. What Madame Sorokine did not know was that in 1939, Bianca Bienenfeld's mother had also threatened Beauvoir with exposure to the Ministry of Education.

23. In April 1942, the same rector had tried to get Sartre suspended, but failed. Gibert Joseph, *Une Si Douce Occupation,* pp. 218–21.

24. Beauvoir wrote this on June 25, 1944, after Bourla's death, in unpublished notes: Sylvie Le Bon archives.

25. *PL,* p. 626.

26. Today this is a very chic hotel, in the heart of the tourist area.

27. Sartre, "Paris sous l'Occupation," *La France Libre* (London), no. 49, Nov. 15, 1944, pp. 9–18, reprint. *Situations, III* (Paris: Gallimard, 1949).

28. S to Barrault, July 9, 1942 in Ingrid Galster, *Sartre, Vichy et les intellectuels* (Paris: Harmattan, 2001), pp. 41–44.

29. *PL,* p. 649.

30. Ibid. A hostile press campaign had the play removed from the theater. As well as for Sartre and Olga, it was a blow for Charles Dullin, to whom Sartre, in his gratitude, had dedicated the play.

31. My interview with Dominique Desanti, Paris, August 27, 2003. Sartre asked permission from the resistant writers group, the CNE (the National Committee of Writers), to put on *The Flies.* They gave permission willingly and praised the message of the play in their newspaper, *Les Lettres Françaises.*

32. *PL,* p. 674.

33. Ibid., p. 673.

34. S to S de B, Monday, February 1946, in *Quiet Moments,* p. 275. (Trans. modified.)

35. Raymond Queneau, *Journaux 1914–1965* (Paris: Gallimard, 1996), p. 769.

36. Leiris, August 28, 1943, *Journal de Michel Leiris, 1922–1989* (Paris: Gallimard, 1992), p. 384.

37. *A Very Easy Death,* p. 68.

38. *PL,* p. 674.

39. Sartre dedicated the play "To That Lady," the term he and Guille used for Madame Morel.

40. Arthur and Cynthia Koestler, *Stranger on the Square* (London: Hutchinson, 1984), p. 67.

41. My interview with Robert Gallimard, Lourmarin, October 15, 2003.

42. S to S de B, early 1944, *Quiet Moments,* p. 264.

43. *PL,* p. 689.

44. Ibid., p. 670. S de B inhabited room 36, on the corner of the Rue de Seine and the Rue de Buci.

45. Bost recalls the incident in the film *Simone de Beauvoir,* by Josée Dayan et Malka Ribowska (Paris: Gallimard, 1979).

46. *PL,* p. 691.

47. Mouloudji, *La Fleur de l'âge,* p. 138ff.

48. Raymond Queneau, Monday, April 17, 1944, *Journaux 1914–1965*, p. 569. (The passage is wrongly placed in 1945 in the published journal; Queneau wrote April 17, but not the year. In fact, April 17 fell on a Monday in 1944. And all other accounts point to this event's occurring in 1944.)

49. *PL*, p. 698.

50. Gibert Joseph, *Une Si Douce Occupation*, chap. 13.

51. Bost to Beauvoir, April 1944, unpublished letter, Sylvie Le Bon de Beauvoir archives.

52. Sartre to Lena Zonina, October 3, 1962, Macha Zonina private archives.

53. "A Walker in Insurgent Paris" consisted of seven articles, published between August 27 and Sept. 2, 1944, written through Sartre's eyes, in first-person reportage.

54. S de B, *Force of Circumstance* [hereafter *FC*], trans. Richard Howard (New York: Viking, 1968), p. 18.

55. *PL*, p. 723.

CHAPTER SEVEN: FAME

1. Cohen-Solal, *Sartre: A Life*, p. 223.

2. *Adieux*, p. 227.

3. *FC*, p. 25.

4. *Adieux*, p. 236.

5. Sartre, *Situations, III* (Paris: Gallimard, 1947), p. 113–15.

6. Nizan and Jaubert, *Libres Mémoires*, p. 365.

7. Sartre, "Individualisme et Conformisme aux Etats-Unis," *Le Figaro*, March 29, 30, 31, 1945, reprinted in *Situations, III*.

8. Camus was dismayed that Sartre gave his best essays to the conservative *Figaro*, and filed rather bland pieces to *Combat*.

9. Dolores Vanetti Ehrenreich interviewed by Annie Cohen-Solal, May 4, 1983, *Sartre: A Life*, p. 237.

10. Cohen-Solal, *Sartre: A Life*, p. 237.

11. Gerassi interview with Sartre, December 31, 1971.

12. Sartre, "President Roosevelt tells French Journalists of his Love for Our Country," *Le Figaro*, March 11 and 12, 1945.

13. Sartre, "Ce que j'ai appris du problème noir," *Le Figaro*, June 16, 1945 (my trans.).

14. *Adieux*, p. 306.

15. *FC*, p. 34.

16. *Useless Mouths* portrays an interesting moral dilemma. A community is under siege. Food is in short supply, and most important, the warriors need to be fed. What is the community's responsibility toward the women, children, and old people? Should they be thrown in the moat?

17. "He was a very exciting teacher," Nadine Chaveau says. "All the girls fell in love with him." Chaveau would become Maheu's lifelong mistress, and the mother

of his second son. "He always had affairs," she says. "It was like a game with him." My interview with Nadine Chaveau, Paris, October 5, 2003.

18. Jean Maheu private archives. Maheu did not tell his girlfriend, Nadine Chaveau, about his affair with Beauvoir. Beauvoir told Sartre about Maheu, but apparently kept quiet about the affair with Vitold. (Bair, *Simone de Beauvoir,* p. 302.)

19. FC, p. 41.

20. Bair, *Simone de Beauvoir,* p. 302.

21. Whether or not he admitted this at the time to Beauvoir and Sartre, Bost told Sylvie Le Bon de Beauvoir, in later years, that he went to bed with Dolores Vanetti. His more serious affair, while he was in New York, was with Vanetti's best friend, the artist Jacqueline Breton Lamba, who was strikingly beautiful. (My interview with Le Bon de Beauvoir, November 22, 2003.)

22. Sartre, "Self-Portrait at Seventy," interview with Michel Contat, *Nouvel Observateur,* June and July 1975.

23. FC, p. 46.

24. The play was a fiasco, heavily criticized for its tedious moralizing, and it closed after fifty performances. Some reviewers praised Olga's performance, but nevertheless, she took the play's failure as a personal disaster.

25. Sartre had been planning a journal ever since he came back from the German prison camp. But he had been obliged to wait. During the war, there was censorship and a paper shortage. After Liberation, Gallimard offered financial support. The editorial committee was formed in September 1944.

26. This and the following quotations are taken from *Existentialism,* tr. Bernard Frechtman (New York: Philosophical Library, 1947).

27. *L'Ecume des Jours* (Paris: Gallimard, 1947) has been variously translated as *The Froth of Passing Days, Foam of the Daze, Froth on the Daydream,* and *Mood Indigo.* Boris Vian dedicated the novel to his wife, Michelle. She would become one of Sartre's great loves.

28. *Adieux,* p. 305.

29. S de B to S, December 19, 1945, in *Letters,* p. 392. The skiing holiday never took place, but there seems little doubt that Beauvoir would have liked an affair with Camus.

30. S de B to S, December 15, 1945, in *Letters,* p. 391.

31. S de B to S, February 13, 1946, in *Letters,* pp. 403–404. Sartre did write to Beauvoir in Tunisia, but since she left for Tunis a month later than she had originally anticipated, the letters were sent back to Paris. He, too, was slightly worried. In New York, a month went past before he received a letter from her. He surmised that Tunisia was not "particularly favored by the postal system" (S to S de B, February 1946, in *Quiet Moments,* p. 274).

32. FC, p. 68.

33. FC, p. 69.

34. My interview with J.-B. Pontalis, Paris, January 14, 2004.

35. Nizan and Jaubert, *Libres Mémoires,* p. 384.

36. S to S de B, December 31, 1945, in *Quiet Moments*, pp. 269–71.
37. *Time*, January 28, 1946.
38. "Talk of the Town," *New Yorker*, March 16, 1946.
39. She quotes her journal in *FC*, p. 88.
40. *FC*, p. 78. (Trans. modified.) Sartre had written in *Being and Nothingness*, "Who would be content with a love given as pure loyalty to a sworn oath?"
41. *All Said and Done* [hereafter *ASAD*], trans. Patrick O'Brian (New York: Paragon House, 1993), p. 91.
42. *ASAD*, p. 92.
43. Jean Cau, *Croquis de mémoire* (Paris: Julliard, 1985), pp. 229–59. Cau remained Sartre's secretary until 1957. This book, published after Sartre's death, surprised everyone by its discretion. In the late 1950s, Cau became an arch reactionary, and he and Sartre fell out bitterly.
44. *New York Herald Tribune*, November 20, 1946 (*The Writings of Jean-Paul Sartre*, vol. 1, p. 139).
45. *FC*, p. 113.
46. S to S de B, Friday, August 1946, in *Quiet Moments*, pp. 277–78. (Trans. modified.)
47. *FC*, p. 114.
48. Ibid., p. 22.
49. Ibid., p. 56.
50. Although Sartre pressed him to, Merleau-Ponty refused to have his name on the cover alongside Sartre's.
51. *FC*, p. 103.
52. Ibid., p. 117.
53. Beauvoir is not the only woman to suggest that Koestler was a sadist. At least one of his biographers describes him as a rapist.
54. Bost and Olga married on October 21, 1946. Sartre and Beauvoir were witnesses.
55. S de B, *America Day by Day* [hereafter *ADD*], (1953), trans. Carol Cosman (Berkeley: University of California Press, 1999).
56. S de B to S, January 25, 1947, in *Letters*, pp. 407–09.

CHAPTER EIGHT: Wabansia Avenue, Jazz, and the Golden Zazou
1. The quoted comments are taken from *ADD* and Beauvoir's correspondence to Sartre.
2. *ADD*, pp. 10–11.
3. S de B to S, January 31, 1947.
4. Ibid. (Trans. modified.)
5. S de B to S, February 11, 1947.
6. Bernard Wolfe and Mezz Mezzrow, *Really the Blues* (New York: Random House, 1946).
7. "The Talk of the Town," *New Yorker*, February 22, 1947.
8. *ADD*, p. 72.

9. H. E. F. Donohue, *Conversations with Nelson Algren* (New York: Hill & Wang, 1964), pp. 180–81.

10. NA to S de B, February 27, 1947, Sylvie le Bon de Beauvoir private archives.

11. S de B to S, February 28, 1947. Unfortunately, nothing came of it.

12. Ivan Moffat to S de B, March 19, 1947, Sylvie le Bon de Beauvoir private archives.

13. Bair, *Simone de Beauvoir*, pp. 377–78.

14. *Daily Princetonian*, April 22–24, 1947, quoted in Claude Francis et Fernande Gontier, *Les Ecrits de Simone de Beauvoir, Textes inédits ou retrouvés* (Paris: Gallimard, 1979), p. 147.

15. The book was retranslated by Carol Cosman and reprinted by the University of California Press in 1999, with a foreword by Douglas Brinkley.

16. *ADD*, pp. 330–34.

17. S de B to S, April 14, 1947.

18. S to S de B, undated [May] 1947, in *Quiet Moments*, p. 279.

19. *The Mandarins*, pp. 332–33.

20. Ibid., p. 351.

21. S de B to NA, May 17, 1947, in Sara Holloway, Vanessa Kling, Kate LeBlanc, and Ellen Gordon Reeves, *A Transatlantic Love Affair* [hereafter *TLA*], notes and translations by Sylvie Le Bon de Beauvoir, (New York: New Press, 1997), p. 15.

22. S de B to NA, June 4, 1947.

23. S de B to NA, July 3, 1947.

24. *FC*, p. 142.

25. When Beauvoir was back in Chicago in the summer of 1950, Algren's friend Art Shay, the well-known Chicago photographer, drove her to a friend's apartment for a bath. She left the bathroom door slightly open, and Shay could not resist the temptation to poke his Leica into the opening. He captured her naked back as she stood in front of the bathroom mirror, pinning up her hair. When she heard the click of his camera, she smiled. "Naughty man," she said. He drove her home, and since Algren was not yet back from playing poker, they sat in the car and had a long conversation about literature, friendship, and fidelity. (Gérard Bonal and Malka Ribowska, *Simone de Beauvoir* [Paris, Seuil/Jazz, 2001], p. 86) and *B & W* magazine, no. 35, February 2005, p. 67.

26. *FC*, p. 171.

27. My interview with Sally Swing Shelley, New York, October 15, 2002.

28. S de B to NA, February 6, 1948.

29. S de B to NA, April 4, 1948.

30. "First Call to International Opinion," November 1947, *The Writings of Jean-Paul Sartre*, vol. 1, compiled by Michel Contat and Michel Rybalka, trans. Richard C. McCleary (Evanston: Northwestern University Press, 1974), p. 205.

31. S de B to NA, April 8, 1948. Sylvie le Bon omitted this letter from the published volume. Deirdre Bair quotes it in *Simone de Beauvoir*, p. 373.

32. S to S de B, May 18, 1948, in *Quiet Moments,* p. 283.

33. *FC,* p. 170.

34. Ibid., p. 173.

35. Beauvoir writes: "During the whole of the month they spent touring the south of France together, he held this piece of capricious coercion against her, he had exchanged his guilt for resentment; it was, for him, a good bargain" (*FC,* p. 172).

36. S de B to NA, July 26, 1948.

37. Sylvie Le Bon, as editor of the collection, quotes Algren's letter in *TLA,* p. 241.

38. S de B to NA, December 3, 1948.

39. S de B to NA, November 1, 1948.

40. Sylvie Le Bon de Beauvoir, "Avant-propos," *Correspondance croisée 1937–1940: Simone de Beauvoir et Jacques-Laurent Bost* (Paris: Gallimard, 2004), p. 12.

41. Beauvoir was inspired by Gunnar Myrdal's book *An American Dilemma,* about the experience of being a Negro in America. Myrdal discusses the mythology of "white" and "black" in similar ways.

42. My interview with Michelle Vian, Apt, south of France, July 11–12, 2002. She told the same story to Michel Rybalka in July 1985.

43. People say that Carole closely resembled André Reweliotty.

44. *FC,* p. 197.

45. Ibid., p. 200–202.

46. S de B to S, July 1950.

47. My interview with Michelle Vian, October 12–14, 2003.

48. My interview with Michelle Vian, July 11 and 12, 2002.

49. S to Michelle Vian, December 1949, Michelle Vian private archives.

50. Michel Rybalka interview with Michelle Vian, Michel Rybalka private archives, July 3–7, 1985.

51. Michel Rybalka interview with Michelle Vian, Rybalka archives, July 3–7 1985.

52. *FC,* p. 229.

53. S de B to NA, May 3, 1950.

54. S de B to NA, May 3, 1950.

55. Michel Rybalka interview with Michelle Vian, July 3–7 1985.

56. Both books were published by Paul Morihien. Beauvoir's *America Day by Day* was republished by Gallimard in 1954.

57. Bost to S de B, August 5, 1950, Sylvie Le Bon de Beauvoir archives.

58. S de B to S, July 1950.

59. *FC,* p. 237.

CHAPTER NINE: CRYSTAL BLUE EYES

1. Jean Cocteau, *Journal: Le Passé défini* (Paris: Gallimard, 1984), p. 302. (Annie Cohen-Solal quotes this in *Sartre,* p. 316.)

2. *La Reine Albemarle ou le dernier touriste* (Paris: Gallimard, 1991). The book has not been translated into English.

3. Jean Cau, *Croquis de mémoire* (Paris: Julliard, 1985), p. 237. (My trans.)

4. My interview with Michelle Vian, Apt, July 11 and 12, 2002.

5. Michel Rybalka interview with Michelle Vian, July 3–7, 1985.

6. *Adieux*, p. 167.

7. Quoted by Sylvie Le Bon de Beauvoir in *TLA*, p. 434.

8. S de B to NA, October 30, 1951.

9. S de B to NA, November 9, 1951.

10. S de B to NA, January 9, 1952.

11. *FC*, p. 291.

12. S de B to NA, March 4, 1952.

13. *The Second Sex* [hereafter *SS*], trans. H.M. Parshley (New York: Alfred A. Knopf, 1953), p. 575.

14. *FC*, p. 269. (Trans. modified.)

15. Sartre, "Merleau-Ponty Alive," *Situations* (New York: George Braziller, 1965). Trans. Benita Eisler and Maria Jolas.

16. *FC*, p. 274.

17. *FC*, p. 264.

18. Ibid., p. 291. (Trans. modified.)

19. Ibid., p. 292.

20. Ibid., p. 302.

21. "Reply to Albert Camus," *Les Temps modernes*, August 1952, reprinted in *Situations*, pp. 71–72.

22. Ronald Aronson, *Camus and Sartre* (Chicago and London: University of Chicago Press, 2004), p. 159.

23. *FC*, p. 272.

24. Claude Lanzmann to S de B, August 18, 1952, Sylvie Le Bon de Beauvoir archives.

25. *FC*, p. 294. Jacques Lanzmann is convinced that Beauvoir and Claude Lanzmann had a strong sexual relationship. He traveled with them to Spain in 1954, he says, and heard loud lovemaking in the next room. "I thought Beauvoir a beautiful woman, beautiful and icy. In bed, I think she was the opposite." My interview with Jacques Lanzmann, Paris, April 22, 2004.

26. S de B to NA, December 9, 1952.

27. My interview with Claude Lanzmann, Cap-Ferret, July 20, 2002.

28. Alice Schwarzer interview with Sartre and Beauvoir, Rome, summer 1972. Schwarzer, *After the Second Sex: Conversations with Simone de Beauvoir*, trans. Marianne Howarth (New York: Pantheon, 1984), p. 59.

29. Gerassi interview with Sartre, March 12, 1971.

30. The Bost-Olga correspondence is in Sylvie Le Bon de Beauvoir's private archives.

31. *FC*, p. 296.

32. Ibid., pp. 295–97.

33. My interview with Claude Lanzmann, July 20, 2002. See also: "Sartre et la génération des années 40," Interview with Claude Lanzmann by Jacques Sabbath and Reine Silbert, *L'Arche,* 26 Sept.–25 Oct., 1971.

34. The details in this paragraph come from Paulette de Boully's preface to a book of Monny de Boully's writing, published posthumously: Monny de Boully, *Au-delà de la mémoire* (Bucharest, Romania: Samuel Tastet, 1991).

35. My interview with Olivier Todd, Paris, July 31, 2002.

36. Serge Rezvani, *Le Testament amoureux* (Paris: Stock, 1981), pp. 100–101. Claude Lanzmann tried to stop the publication of this book. There were legal proceedings. In the end, the publisher suppressed short passages, leaving blank spaces where there had previously been text. Rezvani let me see the original.

37. *FC,* p. 295.

38. Rezvani, *Le Testament amoureux,* pp. 254–55.

39. Jacques Lanzmann, *Le Voleur de hasards* (Paris: Jean-Claude Lattès, 1992).

40. My interview with Jacques Lanzmann, Paris, April 22, 2004.

41. My interview with Olivier Todd, July 31, 2002. Jacques Lanzmann and Judith Magre also told me about this bet.

42. My interview with Judith Magre, Paris, May 7, 2004.

43. "Entretien avec Claude Lanzmann," *Les Temps modernes,* special issue on Sartre, Oct.–Dec. 1990.

44. My interview with Claude Lanzmann, July 20, 2002.

45. "Entretien avec Claude Lanzmann."

46. S de B to NA, February 15, 1954.

47. *FC,* p. 304.

48. Ibid., p. 309.

49. Jacques Lanzmann, *Le Voleur de hasards,* p. 49.

50. *FC,* p. 334.

51. My interview with Claude Lanzmann, July 20, 2002.

52. In fact, he said this of Evelyne a little later, in the spring of 1956, when she acted in another production, directed by Michel Vitold (*Le Monde,* March 31, 1956).

53. John Gerassi interview with Beauvoir, Jan. 30, 1973.

54. My interview with Jacques Lanzmann, April 22, 2004.

55. In *Le Testament amoureux,* Rezvani describes in harrowing terms their marriage and Evelyne's psychological fragility.

56. This was the old *Libération,* not the current newspaper by the same name, established by Sartre.

57. *TM,* July 1953, Sartre's editorial on the Rosenberg case.

58. S de B to NA, June 21, 1953.

59. NA to S de B, July 1953, undated, Sylvie Le Bon de Beauvoir archives.

60. S de B to S, June 1953.

61. My interview with Claude Lanzmann, July 20, 2002.

62. *Words,* trans. Irene Clephane (London: Hamish Hamilton, 1964), p. 36. I have combined a footnote and the text.

63. My interview with Claude Lanzmann, July 20, 2002.

64. *Adieux,* p. 309. Sartre was not talking specifically about Evelyne in this 1974 conversation with Beauvoir, but since Evelyne was his tallest female companion, he presumably was thinking of her.

65. Sartre to Michelle Vian, Sept. 9, 1956, Michelle Vian private archives.

66. This was Michel Rybalka, who taped hours of conversation with Michelle Vian in July 1985.

67. Jacques Lanzmann, *Le Voleur de hasards,* pp. 94–105.

68. Through the character of Kean, an actor, Sartre meditates that the actor's curse is not to know who he really is; the actor "acts himself" every second.

69. *Adieux,* p. 317.

70. "Entretien avec Claude Lanzmann."

71. S de B to S, June 1 and June 8, 1954.

72. FC, p. 318.

73. Sartre added that he had no idea at the time that the forced labor camps had continued to exist after Stalin's death. "Self Portrait at Seventy," *Life/Situations* (New York: Random House, 1977). (Trans. modified.)

74. FC, p. 323.

75. S de B to NA, January 9, 1955.

CHAPTER TEN: EXILES AT HOME

1. S de B to NA, September 1, 1955.

2. S de B to NA, November 3, 1955.

3. FC, p. 348.

4. Ibid., p. 352.

5. Jacqueline Piatier interview with Sartre, "A Long, Bitter, Sweet Madness," *Encounter,* June 1964, pp. 61–63.

6. Michel Contat and Michel Rybalka interview with Sartre, *Le Monde,* May 14, 1971 (*The Writings of Jean-Paul Sartre,* vol. 1, p. 571).

7. FC, p. 358.

8. Claude Roy, *Libération,* June 19, 1957.

9. "People," *Time,* July 2, 1956, p. 33.

10. FC, p. 363.

11. CL to Michelle Vian, February 1955, Michelle Vian archives.

12. My interview with Michelle Vian, Apt, October 13, 2003.

13. "Après Budapest, Sartre parle," *L'Express,* November 9, 1956. What Sartre said about the Marshall Plan is supported by U.S. State Department documents from this time, and was even reported in the U.S. press. On May 9, 1947, a *New York Times* article, "Administration Now Shifts Its Emphasis on Foreign Aid," had this to say about the U.S. Government's change of rhetoric: "The Administration is not happy about the emotional response here and abroad to

the military and ideological aspects of the Truman Doctrine. Consequently, a conscious effort is being made now to emphasize the positive economic problems of reconstructing Europe rather than the military and ideological program of blocking Russian expansion and Soviet communism. The Administration still has the same objective. It has not wavered in its sincere belief that Soviet expansion and infiltration must be stopped."

14. John Gerassi interview with Arlette Elkaïm Sartre, March 5, 1973. Beinecke Library, Yale University.

15. Interview with Arlette Elkaïm Sartre in *L'Express,* April 8–14, 1983.

16. Gerassi interview with Arlette Elkaïm Sartre, March 5, 1973.

17. Cau, *Croquis de mémoire,* pp. 241–42. I am paraphrasing Cau.

18. Gisèle Halimi, *Milk for the Orange Tree* (London: Quartet, 1990).

19. *FC,* p. 466. Trans. modified ["Cette accablante année"].

20. Ibid., p. 398.

21. Beauvoir quotes these extracts from her journal in *FC,* pp. 404–463.

22. *FC,* p. 459.

23. Ibid., p. 443.

24. S to Michelle Vian, July 6, 1958, Michelle Vian archives.

25. My interview with Michelle Vian, July 11 and 12, 2002.

26. Gerassi interview with Sartre, October 27, 1972.

27. *FC,* pp. 455–56.

28. These days, Claude Lanzmann describes De Gaulle as "a great strategist, a great statesman, and a great writer into the bargain," and wonders about the "mad romanticism" with which they were suffused at the time. "We were wrong," he says. "I can't really understand how Sartre, in particular, got De Gaulle so wrong." "Entretien avec Claude Lanzmann," *Temps modernes,* nos. 531–33, Oct.–Dec. 1990.

29. *FC,* p. 456.

30. Ibid., pp. 460–61.

31. Ibid., p. 465.

32. My interviews with Claude Lanzmann, Cap-Ferret, July 20, 2002 and Paris, January 27, 2004.

33. John Huston, *An Open Book* (1959) (New York: Knopf, 1980), p. 295.

34. Gerassi interview with Arlette Elkaïm Sartre, March 5, 1973.

35. *FC,* pp. 496–97. Camus was driving back from the south with Michel Gallimard and Gallimard's wife and daughter. Michel Gallimard, the driver, died five days later, in the hospital. The women, who were sitting in the backseat, survived.

36. Camus, who had grown up in poverty in Algeria, saw the only hope as Franco-Arab reconciliation. He condemned violence on both sides and warned that the FLN was authoritarian and not prepared to compromise. Sartre was also wary of the FLN. However, for him, the only response to the violence of colonialism was violence.

37. "Albert Camus," *Situations,* p. 109.

38. Sartre, "Self-Portrait at Seventy."
39. Nelson Algren, *Who Lost an American?* (New York: Macmillan, 1963), p. 118.
40. My interview with Michelle Vian, July 11 and 12, 2002.
41. I have only Michelle Vian's word to go on that Sartre was prepared to have a child with her. But since all her other statements appear to be correct, and since she gave the physicians' names, I have no reason to disbelieve her. Mme Weill-Hallé became famous for founding family planning in France. Beauvoir wrote a preface to her 1960 book, *La Grand'Peur d'aimer.* The surgeon who Michelle Vian says performed the operation was Dr. Pierre Simon, famous for his writing on "birth without pain."
42. *FC*, p. 503.
43. Ibid., p. 506.
44. S de B to NA, August 26, 1960 and September 23, 1960.
45. S de B to NA, October 29, 1960.
46. Cohen-Solal quotes this statement in *Sartre*, p. 422.
47. Gisèle Halimi, *Djamíla Boupacha* (Paris: Gallimard, 1962).
48. Cohen-Solal, *Sartre*, p. 429.
49. Liliane Siegel, *In the Shadow of Sartre* (London: Collins, 1990), p. 24.
50. Ibid., p. 18.
51. S de B to NA, April 14, 1961.

CHAPTER ELEVEN: WHITE NIGHTS, VODKA, AND TEARS
1. There had been earlier moments of "thaw"—in 1954 and 1959, both short-lived. The term owed its name to Ehrenburg's novel *The Thaw,* published in *Novy Mír* in the spring of 1954.
2. In the next few years, Zonina would translate Sartre's play *The Flies* and Beauvoir's novel *Les Belles Images,* and would co-translate Sartre's autobiography, *Words,* which he dedicated to her, "Madame Z." Sartre's plays *Nekrassov* and *The Respectful Prostitute* had already been put on in Moscow. In the sixties, he had large sums of rubles from Russian translations of his work, but of course he could spend them only in the USSR.
3. *FC*, p. 651.
4. My interview with Macha Zonina, Paris, July 16, 2002.
5. *ASAD*, p. 286.
6. Sartre to Zonina, July 2, 1962, Macha Zonina private archives. The letters rarely contain a date, since they were generally written over several weeks.
7. See Michel Antoine Burnier, *L'Adieu à Sartre* (Paris: Plon, 2000), and Ewa Bérard-Zarzycka, "Sartre et Beauvoir en U.R.S.S.," *Commentaire* 14, no. 53 (Spring 1991). Neither writer claims that Zonina was a KGB agent herself, but they both wonder about the extent of her connection with the KGB.
8. Gerassi interview with Sartre, October 27, 1972.
9. Zonina's report after Sartre's June 1–24 visit is among the Soviet Writers Union files in the Moscow State Archives of Art and Literature. Ewa Bérard-Zarzycka

quotes several of her reports in "Sartre et Beauvoir en U.R.S.S.," in *Commentaire* (my trans.).

10. It is now generally accepted that the Peace Movement, established in Paris in April 1949, and directed from Moscow, was an important vehicle for Soviet propaganda. While preaching peace all around the world, the Soviets were scrambling to build up their own weaponry. In 1975, Sartre told Michel Contat: "I continue to think that during the years of the Cold War the Communists were right. The USSR—in spite of all the mistakes we know it made—was nevertheless being persecuted. It was not yet in a position to hold its own in a war against America, and so it wanted peace" (Sartre, "Self-Portrait at Seventy").

11. Lena Zonina's translation of *Words* was published in *Novy Mir* in late 1964.

12. My interview with Gilbert and Marie-Chantal Dagron, Paris, October 6, 2003.

13. Beauvoir's account of their June 1962 trip, in *Force of Circumstance* (1963) was largely positive. Her report on their later trips to the USSR in *All Said and Done* (1972) was far less so.

14. When John Gerassi asked Sartre, "Did they know about the affair in USSR?" Sartre answered, "I think they knew from the beginning" (interview, October 27, 1972).

15. My interview with Lucia Cathala, Paris, July 24, 2002.

16. Sartre passed in a script that was almost eight hundred pages long. When Huston cut it, Sartre decided it had been mutilated, and withdrew his name altogether from the film.

17. This was Barbara Aptekman.

18. André Puig would become Sartre's new secretary in 1963, an arrangement that lasted until Sartre's death, in 1980. Puig collaborated on *Les Temps modernes*. Sartre would write a long preface to Puig's novel *L'Inachevé* (Gallimard, 1970), which Puig dedicated to Arlette Elkaïm.

19. *ASAD*, p. 287.

20. *Adieux*, p. 214.

21. Ehrenburg's memoirs, which had been appearing in serial form in *Novy Mir*, talked about the "conspiracy of silence" in the 1930s. This was too uncomfortable for Khrushchev. If intellectuals such as Ehrenburg admitted that they had known about Stalin's abuses, Khrushchev, who had been close to Stalin, could hardly claim he did not.

22. Undated letter, courtesy Macha Zonina, quoted by Gonzague de Saint-Bris and Vladimir Fedorovski in *Les Egéries russes* (Paris: Jean-Claude Lattès, 1994), p. 282.

23. S de B, *A Very Easy Death*, p. 31.

24. Ibid., p. 83.

25. Michel-Antoine Burnier, *L'Adieu à Sartre*.

26. *Adieux*, pp. 344–45.

27. Unpublished report by Curtis Cate, quoted by Thomas Molnar in *Yale Literary Magazine* 150, no. 1 (1981).

28. My interview with Macha Zonina, Paris, March 25, 2004. Macha telephoned Irina Kreindlina, Zonina's closest friend, in Moscow to check this with her.

29. Gerassi interview with Sartre, October 27, 1972.

30. *Words,* p. 14.

31. Michelle deplored the fact that Sartre had given Arlette his name. Michelle Vian felt it would have been more appropriate for *her.* My interview with Michelle Vian, October 13, 2003.

32. Siegel, *In the Shadow of Sartre,* pp. 66–67.

33. S to A. I. Mikoyan, August 17, 1965. The letter is printed in Ewa Bérard-Zarzycka's article "Sartre et Beauvoir en U.R.S.S.," *Commentaire* (Spring 1991).

34. Zonina report, July 1–August 5, 1965, in "Sartre et Beauvoir en U.R.S.S."

35. Pierre Macabru, "Reggiani fascine et irrite," *Candide,* September 20–26, 1965.

36. *ASAD,* p. 321.

37. S de B, *ASAD,* p. 320. According to her friend Lucia Cathala, Lena did have difficulties, and soon resigned from the Writers Union. My interview with Lucia Cathala, Paris, July 24, 2002.

38. S to Zonina, June 1966.

39. "Malentendu à Moscou," *Roman 20–50, Revue d'étude du roman du XX siècle* 13 (juin 1992).

40. Tomiko Asabuki, a married woman, does not mention this in her book *Sartre et Beauvoir au Japon en 1966* (Paris: L'Asiathèque, 1996). It is, however, a known fact in Sartre circles, and confirmed by Sylvie Le Bon de Beauvoir.

41. Sartre conversation with Beauvoir, summer 1974, in *Adieux,* p. 303.

CHAPTER TWELVE: TRAGIC ENDINGS, NEW BEGINNINGS

1. *Le Nouvel Observateur,* November 23, 1966.

2. Sartre tells this to Lena in a letter written three months later.

3. My interview with Claude Lanzmann, July 20, 2002.

4. S tells this to Lena Zonina, August 25, 1965.

5. This was Claude Loursais.

6. John Gerassi interview with Simone de Beauvoir, January 30, 1973.

7. Bair, *Simone de Beauvoir,* pp. 462–63.

8. Jacques Lanzmann, *Le Voleur de hasards,* p. 49. Jacques Lanzmann is unable to explain exactly what he means by this, though he talks about "a certain intellectual perversion." He admits that in the final analysis, Evelyne chose her life herself (My interview with Jacques Lanzmann, Paris, April 22, 2004).

9. Rezvani, *Le Testament amoureux.*

10. For example, Judith Magre, Claude Lanzmann's actress wife, hated the portrait of Lanzmann. She thought Beauvoir made him sound like her porter, her case-carrier—young, insignificant, and merely useful to her. Magre had a major row with Beauvoir about it (My interview with Judith Magre, May 7, 2004).

11. When Wanda died in 1989, Le Bon went around to Wanda's apartment with Bost, at the time of the official police inspection. While Bost talked to the

police, diverting them, Le Bon found the bundles of letters from Sartre, and took them. Today they are in Le Bon's possession.

12. My interview with Sylvie Le Bon de Beauvoir, Paris, June 10, 2004.

13. H. E. F. Donohue, *Conversations with Nelson Algren*, p. 269.

14. *Ramparts* 4, no. 6 (October 1965).

15. Nelson Algren, "The Question of Simone de Beauvoir," *Harper's*, May 1965.

16. *Zeitgeist* 1, no. 4 (Summer 1966).

17. W. J. Weatherby, "The Life and Hard Times of Nelson Algren," *Sunday Times*, London, May 17, 1981.

18. Bair, *Simone de Beauvoir*, pp. 502–503.

19. Gerassi interview with Claude Lanzmann, June 5, 1973.

20. Elkaïm had an affair with their guide, Ely Ben-Gal. Sartre encouraged her. He encouraged everyone in his entourage to have affairs. For him, it was part of living to the fullest.

21. *ASAD*, p. 404 ff. Beauvoir explains her point of view in detail in these pages.

22. There was also another cause of tension between them. Shortly before the outbreak of the Six-Day War, Lanzmann had asked Sartre and Beauvoir to sign a petition stating that it was misguided to associate Israel with aggression and imperialism and Palestine with peace and socialism. They signed. As a result, some Arab countries banned Sartre's and Beauvoir's books. Frantz Fanon's widow was so furious with Sartre that she refused to include his preface to *The Wretched of the Earth* in all future editions of the book. Sartre was dismayed that his position of neutrality had been undermined, and held it against Lanzmann for pressing him to sign a petition in the street, without giving him time to think about it.

23. *Adieux*, p. 276. (Trans. modified.)

24. Cau, *Croquis de mémoire*, pp. 282–83, my trans.

25. Arlette Elkaïm helped edit the collection of documents and evidence for publication in *Tribunal Russell: Le Jugement de Stockholm* (Paris: Gallimard, 1967).

26. *ASAD*, pp. 63–64.

27. Halimi, *Milk for the Orange Tree*, p. 315.

28. S de B interview with Alice Schwarzer, 1972, in Alice Schwarzer, *After the Second Sex*.

29. My interview with Sylvie Le Bon de Beauvoir, Paris, April 12, 2004.

30. My interview with Michel Contat, Paris, July 4, 2002.

31. My interview with J.-B. Pontalis, Paris, January 14, 2004.

32. S de B interview with Alice Schwarzer (1982), *After the Second Sex*, p. 110.

33. Sartre had bought apartments for Wanda and Arlette. Michelle had bought hers with money from Boris Vian's literary estate.

34. My interview with Michelle Vian, Apt, July 11–12, 2002.

35. John Gerassi interview with Wanda Kosakiewicz, March 23, 1973.

36. My interview with Michelle Vian, July 11 and 12, 2002.

37. "Entretien avec Claude Lanzmann."

38. Other signatories were Colette Audry, Michel Leiris, and Daniel Guérin.

39. Sartre, "Les Bastilles de Raymond Aron," *Nouvel Observateur,* June 19–25, 1968.

40. S to Zonina, undated letter [late 1968].

41. J.-B. Pontalis and Bernard Pingaud resigned in 1969 after Sartre insisted on publishing a transcript of a dialogue between a psychoanalyst and his patient that, in Sartre's view, showed psychoanalysis as a therapy based not on reciprocity but on violence. Sartre had a major influence on the "antipsychiatry" movement, associated with R. D. Laing and David Cooper.

42. Sartre, "Self-Portrait at Seventy."

43. *Adieux,* p. 280.

44. Ibid., p. 285.

45. My interview with Michelle Vian, October 13, 2003.

46. Gerassi interview with Arlette Elkaïm Sartre, March 5, 1973.

47. Claudine Monteil, *Simone de Beauvoir: Le Mouvement des femmes, mémoires d'une jeune fille rebelle* (Quebec: Alain Stanké, 1995).

48. Sylvie Le Bon says she is one hundred percent sure that Beauvoir never had an abortion.

49. Wanda did not sign. Nor did Sylvie Le Bon. Her job was secure, Le Bon says, but she had students and parents to face, and Beauvoir did not want her to sign.

50. There were too many obstacles, Le Bon says, and the affair did not last long. For almost twenty years, she and Bost were simply friends. After Beauvoir's death, in their mutual grief, they turned to each other again. Olga had died by then. Le Bon inherited Beauvoir's apartment on the Rue Schoelcher, and in the last years of his life, she let Bost live there. Le Bon kept her apartment on the Avenue du Maine.

51. My interview with Sylvie Le Bon de Beauvoir, Paris, June 10, 2004.

52. Ibid., April 12, 2004.

53. Nelson Algren review in the *Los Angeles Times,* June 25, 1972.

54. John Weightman, "Battle of the Century—Sartre vs. Flaubert," *New York Review of Books,* April 6, 1972.

CHAPTER THIRTEEN: THE FAREWELL CEREMONY

1. *PL,* p. 75.

2. Toril Moi gives an insightful analysis of Beauvoir's anguish and displacement strategies in chapter eight ("The Scandal of Loneliness and Separation: The Writing of Depression") of her book, *Simone de Beauvoir: The Making of an Intellectual Woman.*

3. *Adieux,* p. 20.

4. Michel Contat, "Sartre by Himself: An Account, an Explanation, a Defense," *Sartre Alive* (Detroit, Mich.: Wayne State University Press, 1991), p. 353.

5. Gilles Lapouge, *Quinzaine Littéraire,* November 16–30, 1976.

6. The first issue of the new newspaper called *Libération* was in May 1973, by which time Sartre's health had already declined. He resigned as editor in chief in May 1974.

7. S de B to Sylvie Le Bon, undated letter from USSR, 1967, Sylvie Le Bon de Beauvoir archives.

8. S de B to Sylvie Le Bon, Hotel Okura, Japan, October 17, 1966, Sylvie Le Bon de Beauvoir archives.

9. My interview with Sylvie Le Bon de Beauvoir, September 16, 2003.

10. *Adieux*, p. 102.

11. My interview with Sylvie Le Bon de Beauvoir, Feb. 3, 2004.

12. Ibid., April 12, 2004.

13. *Adieux*, p. 53.

14. Bair, *Simone de Beauvoir*, p. 676, note 13.

15. *Adieux*, p. 64.

16. S to S de B, November 18, 1939, in *Witness*, p. 352.

17. *Adieux*, p. 69.

18. Beauvoir would publish these conversations as the second half of *Adieux*.

19. Dialogue between Sartre and Lévy about their collaboration, in *Libération*, January 6, 1977. Beauvoir quotes it in *Adieux*, p. 99.

20. Cohen-Solal, *Sartre*, p. 501.

21. Program on Benny Lévy on *France Culture*, October 25, 2003, after his death.

22. Cohen-Solal, *Sartre*, p. 497.

23. Cohen-Solal, *Sartre*, p. 500.

24. Siegel, *In the Shadow of Sartre*, p. 137.

25. In the last years of his life, Sartre was again in debt to Gallimard, which worried him a great deal. Before he died, he signed over half his rights to his publishers. Gallimard would make a fortune from posthumous sales of his work.

26. *Adieux*, p. 103.

27. My interview with Sylvie Le Bon de Beauvoir, July 17, 2002.

28. *Adieux*, p. 85.

29. My interview with Michelle Vian, October 12–14, 2003.

30. *Adieux*, p. 100.

31. My interview with Michelle Vian, July 11 and 12, 2002.

32. My interview with Liliane Siegel, Paris, July 14, 2002. In her book *In the Shadow of Sartre* (p. 161), Siegel does not give the real reason for Sartre's fury.

33. Olivier Todd, *Un Fils rebelle* (Paris: Grasset, 1981), p. 116.

34. Claude Lanzmann told Todd that these lines hit Beauvoir very hard. My interview with Olivier Todd, July 31, 2002.

35. *Adieux*, p. 30.

36. Gerassi interview with Arlette Elkaïm Sartre, March 5, 1973.

37. Cohen-Solal, *Sartre*, p. 510.

38. *Adieux*, pp. 110–11.

39. Edward Said, "My Encounter with Sartre," *London Review of Books*, June 1, 2000.

40. Françoise Sagan, *Avec mon meilleur souvenir* (Paris: Gallimard, 1984), pp. 147–58.

41. In her book *Avec mon meilleur souvenir*, Sagan covertly criticized Beauvoir for the details in *Adieux*: "I was never horrified or shocked by the way he ate. Of course,

it was all a bit hit-or-miss . . . I take great exception to those who have bewailed these meals. . . . I have naturally been angered by the shameful stories of Sartre's being senile told by people who were close to him."

42. Siegel, *In the Shadow of Sartre,* p. 157.

43. Ibid., p. 159.

44. My interview with Sylvie Le Bon de Beauvoir, July 17, 2002.

45. Bair, *Simone de Beauvoir,* p. 583.

46. My interview with Denise Pouillon, Paris, July 2, 2002.

47. Cohen-Solal, *Sartre,* p. 514.

48. *Adieux,* p. 123.

49. This was Pierre Verstraeten, who had interviewed Sartre on more than one occasion.

50. Georges Michel, *Mes Années Sartre* (Paris: Hachette, 1981), p. 201.

51. Bair, *Simone de Beauvoir,* p. 589.

52. The publication of Beauvoir's letters to Sartre, which Sylvie Le Bon did not in any way censor, was a devastating blow to Poupette. She had spent a lifetime believing that she and Simone were devoted to each other. Now she read the very cruel comments Simone made about her to Sartre. Close friends say that Poupette never recovered from the shock. (Poupette had more than eighty loving letters from Beauvoir, which she wanted to publish, to show the public the other side of the picture. Sylvie Le Bon, Beauvoir's literary executor, who owned the copyright, would not give permission.)

53. My interview with Liliane Siegel, Paris, June 8, 2004.

54. Toril Moi writes of *Adieux:* "Beauvoir's bleak and devitalized prose conveys not only her inability to lift herself out of her sorrow, but also her resolute determination not to mention her conflicts with Sartre. For it is not only Sartre's death that pains Beauvoir, it is also his lack of loyalty to her during their final years, and his cavalier disregard for her feelings in his dealings with other women. The price she pays is an almost complete blockage of affect in her language: on the pages of *Adieux,* her prose is dry as dust. The contrast to *A Very Easy Death* could not be greater: when Beauvoir finally forces herself to confront her long-buried feelings for her mother, she produces the most vibrant, energetic and moving prose she ever wrote" (*Simone de Beauvoir,* p. 251).

55. *Adieux,* pp. 119–120.

56. Arlette Elkaïm Sartre, *Libération,* December 3, 1981, p. 26.

57. Bair, *Simone de Beauvoir,* p. 599.

SELECTED BIBLIOGRAPHY

This bibliography includes only those books, articles, and interviews mentioned in the text.

Simone de Beauvoir

She Came to Stay (Paris, 1943). Translated by Yvonne Moyse and Roger Senhouse (New York: Norton, 1954).

The Blood of Others (Paris, 1945). Translated by Yvonne Moyse and Roger Senhouse (New York: Knopf, 1948).

The Second Sex, 2 vols. (Paris, 1949). Translated by H. M. Parshley (New York: Knopf, 1953).

America Day by Day (Paris, 1948). Translated by Patrick Dudley (New York: Grove Press, 1953); trans. Carol Cosman (Berkeley, Los Angeles & London: University of California Press, 1999).

The Mandarins (Paris, 1954). Translated by Leonard M. Friedman (Cleveland: World Publishing, 1956).

Privilèges. Paris: Gallimard, 1955.

The Long March (Paris, 1957). Translated by Austryn Wainhouse (Cleveland: World Publishing, 1958).

Memoirs of a Dutiful Daughter (Paris, 1958). Translated by James Kirkup (Cleveland and New York: World Publishing, 1959).

The Prime of Life (Paris, 1960). Translated by Peter Green (Cleveland and New York: World Publishing, 1962).

Djamíla Boupacha (with Gisèle Halimi) (Paris 1962). Translated by Peter Green (New York: MacMillan, 1962).

Force of Circumstance (Paris, 1963). Translated by Richard Howard (New York: Putnam, 1964).

A Very Easy Death (Paris, 1964). Translated by Patrick O'Brian (New York: Putnam, 1966).

Woman Destroyed (Paris, 1967). Translated by Patrick O'Brian (New York: Putnam, 1969).

The Coming of Age (Paris, 1970). Translated by Patrick O'Brian (New York: Putnam, 1974).

All Said and Done (Paris, 1972). Translated by Patrick O'Brian (New York: Putnam, 1974).

When Things of the Spirit Come First (Paris, 1979). Translated by Patrick O'Brian (New York: Pantheon, 1982).

Adieux: A Farewell to Sartre (Paris, 1981). Translated by Patrick O'Brian (New York: Putnam, 1984).

Journal de guerre: Septembre 1939–janvier 1941. Edited by Sylvie Le Bon de Beauvoir (Paris: Gallimard, 1990).

Letters to Sartre 1940–1963 (Paris, 1990). Translated by Quintin Hoare (New York: Arcade Publishing, 1991).

A Transatlantic Love Affair: Letters to Nelson Algren (Paris, 1997) (New York: New Press, 1998).

Correspondance croisée: Simone de Beauvoir et Jacques-Laurent Bost, 1937–1940 (Paris: Gallimard, 2004).

Articles and Interviews by/with Beauvoir

"Malentendu à Moscou," *Roman 20–50, Revue d'étude du roman du XX siècle* 13, (juin 1992).

"Jean-Paul Sartre: Strictly Personal." Translated by Malcolm Cowley. *Harper's Bazaar,* January 1946.

"The Talk of the Town," article-interview. *The New Yorker,* February 22, 1947.

"Merleau-Ponty and Pseudo-Sartreanism," (*TM*, June–July 1955). Collected in *Privilèges* (Paris: Gallimard, 1955).

"Le Manifeste des 343. Notre ventre nous appartient." *Le Nouvel Observateur,* avril 5–11, 1971.

Jean-Paul Sartre

Nausea (Paris, 1938). Translated by Lloyd Alexander (New York: New Directions, 1949).

The Wall (Paris, 1939). Translated by Lloyd Alexander (New York: New Directions, 1948).

Being and Nothingness (Paris, 1943). Translated by Hazel E. Barnes (New York: Philosophical Library, 1956).

The Flies (Paris, 1943). Translated by Stuart Gilbert (New York: Knopf, 1947).

No Exit (Paris, 1944). Translated by Lionel Abel (New York: Vintage, 1955).

Portrait of the Anti-Semite (Paris, 1945). Translated by George J. Becker (New York: Schocken, 1948).

The Age of Reason (Paris, 1945). Translated by Eric Sutton (New York: Knopf, 1947).

Existentialism (Paris, 1946). Translated by Bernard Frechtman (New York: Philosophical Library, 1947).

The Devil and the Good Lord (Paris, 1951). Translated by Kitty Black (New York: Knopf, 1960).

Kean (Paris, 1954). Translated by Kitty Black (London: Hamish Hamilton, 1954).

Saint Genet (Paris, 1952). Translated by Bernard Frechtman (New York: George Braziller, 1963).

Search for a Method (Paris, 1957). Translated by Hazel E. Barnes (New York: Knopf, 1963).

The Condemned of Altona (Paris, 1959). Translated by Sylvia and George Leeson (New York: Knopf, 1961).

Critique of Dialectical Reason (Paris, 1960). Translated by Alan Sheridan (London, New Left Books, 1976).

Words (Paris, 1964). Translated by Irene Clephane (London: Hamish Hamilton, 1964).

The Family Idiot, Gustave Flaubert, 1821–1857. vols. 1–2 (Paris, 1971). Translated by Carol Cosman (Chicago: University of Chicago Press, 1981 and 1987).

Situations (translation of *Situations IV,* Paris, 1964). Translated by Benita Eisler and Maria Jolas (New York: George Braziller, 1965).

Life/Situations: Essays Written and Spoken by Jean-Paul Sartre (translation of *Situations X,* Paris, 1975). Translated by Paul Auster and Lydia Davis (New York: Random House, 1977).

Sartre. Texte intégral du film réalisé par Alexandre Astruc et Michel Contat (Paris, Gallimard, 1977).

Witness to My Life: The Letters of Jean-Paul Sartre to Simone de Beauvoir, 1926–1939 (Paris, 1983). Translated by Lee Fahnestock and Norman MacAfee (New York: Charles Scribner's Sons, 1992).

Quiet Moments in a War: The Letters of Jean-Paul Sartre to Simone de Beauvoir, 1940–1963 (Paris, 1983). Translated by Lee Fahnestock and Norman MacAfee (New York: Charles Scribner's Sons, 1993).

The War Diaries: November 1939–March 1940 (Paris, 1983). Translated by Quintin Hoare (New York: Pantheon Books, 1984).

Carnets de la drôle de guerre, sept. 1939–mars 1940 (Paris: Gallimard, 1995). (Contains the first notebook, Sept.–Oct. 1939, which is not included in the earlier English edition.)

La Reine Albemarle ou le dernier touriste (Paris: Gallimard, 1991).

Hope Now: The 1980 Interviews, Jean-Paul Sartre and Benny Lévy (Paris, 1991). Translated by Adrian van den Hoven (Chicago and London: University of Chicago Press, 1996).

Articles and Interviews by/with Sartre

"Individualisme et Conformisme aux Etats-Unis," (1945). *Situations III.*

"Paris sous l'Occupation," (1945). *Situations III.*

"Reply to Albert Camus" (*TM,* August 1952). *Life/Situations.*

"Après Budapest, Sartre parle." *L'Express,* Nov. 9, 1956.

Jacqueline Piatier with Sartre, "A Long, Bitter, Sweet Madness." *Encounter,* June 1964.

"Jean-Paul Sartre: A Candid Conversation with the Charismatic Fountainhead of Existentialism and Rejecter of the Nobel Prize." Interview with Madeleine Gobeil. *Playboy* (Chicago), May 1965.

Sartre, "Les Bastilles de Raymond Aron." *Nouvel Observateur,* June 19–25, 1968.

"Sartre et les femmes." Interview with Catherine Chaîne. *Le Nouvel Observateur,* January 31, 1977, and February 7, 1977.

"Self Portrait at Seventy." Interview with Michel Contat. *Nouvel Observateur,* June and July 1975, reprinted in *Life/Situations.*

"Letters to Wanda," *Les Temps modernes,* Oct.–Dec. 1990, nos. 531–33, pp. 1292–1429.

Secondary Sources

Algren, Nelson. *Who Lost an American?* (New York: MacMillan, 1960).

———. "The Question of Simone de Beauvoir." *Harper's,* May 1965.

Aron, Raymond. *Mémoires* (Paris: Julliard, 1983).

Aronson, Ronald. *Camus and Sartre* (Chicago: University of Chicago Press, 2004).

Asabuki, Tomiko. *Sartre et Beauvoir au Japon en 1966* (Paris: L'Asiathèque, 1996).

Audry, Colette. "Portrait de l'écrivain jeune femme." *Biblio,* November 1962.

Bair, Deirdre. *Simone de Beauvoir: A Biography* (New York: Simon and Schuster, 1990).

Beauvoir, Hélène de. *Souvenirs.* Recueillis par Marcelle Routier (Paris: Séguier, 1987).

Bonal, Gérard, and Malka Ribowska. *Simone de Beauvoir* (Paris: Seuil/Jazz, 2001).

Boully, Monny de. *Au-delà de la mémoire* (Paris: Samuel Tastet, 1991).

Burnier, Michel Antoine. *L'Adieu à Sartre* (Paris: Plon, 2000).

Cau, Jean. *Croquis de mémoire* (Paris: Julliard, 1985).

Cocteau, Jean. *Journal: Le Passé défini* (Paris: Gallimard, 1984).

Cohen-Solal, Annie. *Sartre: A Life* (Paris, 1985; London: Random House, 1987).

Contat, Michel, and Michel Rybalka. *The Writings of Jean-Paul Sartre* (Paris, 1970), vol. 1: *A Bibliographical Life,* translated by Richard C. McCleary (Evanston, Ill.: Northwestern University Press, 1974).

———. "Sartre by Himself: An Account, an Explanation, a Defense." In *Sartre Alive* (Detroit: Wayne State University Press, 1991).

———. "Sartre/Beauvoir, légende et réalité d'un couple." In *Literature and Its Cults.* Edited by Péter Dávidházi and Judit Karafiáth (Budapest: Argumentum, 1994).

Dayan, Josée, et Malka Ribowska. *Simone de Beauvoir.* Texte intégral de la bande sonore du film. *Simone de Beauvoir* (Paris: Gallimard, 1979).

Donohue, H. E. F. *Conversations with Nelson Algren* (New York: Hill and Wang, 1964).

Fanon, Frantz. *The Wretched of the Earth* (Paris, 1961). Translated by Constance Farrington (New York: Grove Press, 1965), with preface by Jean-Paul Sartre.

Francis, Claude, and Fernande Gontier. *Les Ecrits de Simone de Beauvoir* (Paris: Gallimard, 1979).

Galster, Ingrid. "Cinquante ans après *Le Deuxième Sexe:* Beauvoir en débats." *Lendemains* 94 (1999).

———. *La Naissance du "Phénomène Sartre": Raisons d'un succès (1938–1945)* (Paris: Seuil, 2001).

———. *Sartre, Vichy et les intellectuels* (Paris: Harmattan, 2001).

———. "Juin 43: Beauvoir est exclue de l'université retour sur une affaire classée." *Contemporary French Civilization* (winter/spring 2001).

Halimi, Gisèle. *Milk for the Orange Tree* (Paris, 1988; London: Quartet, 1990).

Huston, John. *An Open Book* (New York: Knopf, 1980).

Joseph, Gibert. *Une Si Douce Occupation: Simone de Beauvoir et Jean-Paul Sartre, 1940–1944* (Paris: Albin Michel, 1991).

Koestler, Arthur, and Cynthia Koestler. *Stranger on the Square* (London: Hutchinson, 1984).

Lamblin, Bianca. *A Disgraceful Affair: Simone de Beauvoir, Jean-Paul Sartre, and Bianca Lamblin* (Paris, 1993). Translated by Julie Plovnick (Boston: Northeastern University Press, 1996).

Lanzmann, Claude. "Entretien avec Claude Lanzmann." *Les Temps modernes.* Special issue on Sartre, Oct.–Dec. 1990.

Lanzmann, Jacques. *Le Têtard* (Paris: Robert Laffont, 1976).

———. *Le Voleur de hasards* (Paris: Jean-Claude Lattès, 1992).

Leiris, Michel. *Journal, 1922–1989* (Paris: Gallimard, 1992).

Lévy, Bernard-Henri. *Sartre: The Philosopher of the Twentieth Century* (Paris, 2000; London: Polity Press, 2003).

Mabille, Elisabeth. *Zaza: Correspondance et Carnets d'Elisabeth Lacoin (1914–1929)* (Paris: Seuil, 1991).

Michel, Georges. *Mes Années Sartre* (Paris: Hachette, 1981).

Moi, Toril. *Simone de Beauvoir: The Making of an Intellectual Woman* (London and Cambridge, Mass.: Blackwell, 1994).

Monteil, Claudine. *Simone de Beauvoir, Le Mouvement des Femmes, Mémoires d'une jeune fille rebelle* (Quebec: Alain Stanké, 1995).

Mouloudji, Marcel. *Le Petit Invité* (Paris: Balland, 1989).

———. *La Fleur de l'âge* (Paris: Grasset, 1991).

Nizan, Henriette, and Marie-José Jaubert. *Libres Mémoires* (Paris: Robert Laffont, 1989).

Nizan, Paul. *Aden Arabie* (1931; Maspero, 1960), with foreword (1960) by Sartre.

Papatakis, Niko. *Tous les désespoirs sont permis* (Paris: Fayard, 2003).

Queneau, Raymond. *Journaux, 1914–1965* (Paris: Gallimard, 1996).

Rezvani, Serge. *Le Testament amoureux* (Paris: Stock, 1981).

Sabbath, Jacques, and Reine Silbert. "Sartre et la génération des années 40." Interview with Claude Lanzmann. *L'Arche,* Sept.–Oct. 1971.

Schwarzer, Alice. *After the Second Sex: Conversations with Simone de Beauvoir.* Translated by Marianne Howarth (New York: Pantheon, 1984).

Sagan, Françoise. *Avec mon meilleur souvenir* (Paris: Gallimard, 1984).

Said, Edward. "My Encounter with Sartre." *London Review of Books,* June 1, 2000.

Saint-Bris, Gonzague, and Vladimir Fedorovski. In *Les Egéries russes* (Paris: Jean-Claude Lattès, 1994).

Siegel, Liliane. *In the Shadow of Sartre* (Paris, 1988; Glasgow: William Collins, 1990).

Simons, Margaret A. "Lesbian Connections: Simone de Beauvoir and Feminism." *Signs,* 18, no. 1 (Autumn 1992).

———. *Beauvoir and the Second Sex: Feminism, Race, and the Origins of Existentialism* (Oxford and Maryland: Rowman and Littlefield, 1999).

Todd, Olivier. *Un Fils rebelle* (Paris: Grasset, 1981).

Weatherby, W. J. "The Life and Hard Times of Nelson Algren." *Sunday Times* (London), May 17, 1981.

Bérard-Zarzycka, Ewa. "Sartre et Beauvoir en U.R.S.S." *Commentaire* 14, no. 53 (spring 1991).

A NOTE ON SOURCES

A major source for this book has been Sartre's and Beauvoir's correspondence, published and unpublished. Sartre's letters to Beauvoir (and to some other girlfriends) were compiled by Beauvoir, after Sartre's death. The two-volume *Lettres au Castor et à quelques autres* appeared in French in 1983. In order not to embarrass third parties, Beauvoir left out certain passages and changed some names. However, she deposited the original letters in the Bibliothèque Nationale, where they can be consulted on microfilm in the manuscript room of the old Rue de Richelieu library.

After Beauvoir's death, Sylvie Le Bon de Beauvoir embarked on the daunting task of deciphering Beauvoir's handwriting for future publications. In 1990, she published Beauvoir's letters to Sartre, with no omissions or changes whatsoever. Beauvoir's letters to Nelson Algren, written in English, appeared in 1997. (Algren's literary agent, Candida Donadio, who owned Algren's copyright after Algren's death, would not allow Le Bon to publish Algren's side of the correspondence.) *Correspondance croisée,* the early correspondence between Beauvoir and Jacques-Laurent Bost, appeared in 2004.

As for unpublished sources, Beauvoir's early journals are in the Bibliothèque Nationale. These cover the years 1926–1930, and include interesting entries about her courtship by Maheu and Sartre. And Sylvie Le Bon de Beauvoir has donated dozens of boxes of correspondence (letters *to* Beauvoir) to the Bibliothèque Nationale.

Le Bon de Beauvoir has retained Beauvoir's most intimate correspondence and journals in her personal archives, and she let me see important material that no scholar had seen before: letters to Beauvoir from Nelson Algren, Olga Kosakiewicz, Nathalie Sorokine, Maurice Merleau-Ponty, Ivan Moffat, and Claude Lanzmann; letters from Beauvoir to Olga, from Bost to Olga; some later letters from Bost to Beauvoir; and a journal extract Beauvoir wrote about the death of Jean-Pierre Bourla.

Sylvie Le Bon de Beauvoir says she has not begun to decipher the journal Beauvoir kept in 1958, or the one she kept from 1972 onward, on which she based *Adieux: A Farewell to Sartre*. According to Le Bon, these are so illegible as to be virtually written in code.

Beauvoir's letters to Claude Lanzmann are in Lanzmann's possession, and he tells me he has no plans to publish them. I interviewed him twice, but did not see the letters.

Sartre gave hundreds of interviews, and participated in the 1977 film documentary *Sartre,* but he was discreet about his personal life. That is to say, he was prepared to say things about himself, but did not like to talk about others. Apart from the journal he wrote during the war, he did not share Beauvoir's propensity to write autobiographical material.

Like Beauvoir, Sartre was a prolific letter writer. He said that he would be perfectly happy to see these letters published. However, not much of his correspondence has seen the light of day. The published collections of his letters to Beauvoir, which appeared in English under the titles *Witness to My Life: The Letters of Jean-Paul Sartre to Simone de Beauvoir, 1926–1939,* and *Quiet Moments in a War: The Letters of Jean-Paul Sartre to Simone de Beauvoir, 1940–1963,* also contain a handful of letters to Simone Jollivet, Olga Kosakiewicz, and Bianca Bienenfeld (to whom Beauvoir gave the pseudonym Louise Védrine). A selection of Sartre's letters to Wanda Kosakiewicz from Greece in 1937 was published in a special issue of *Les Temps modernes,* numbers 531–33, Oct.–Dec. 1990.

At this point, most of Sartre's correspondence remains in private hands. I wrote to Sartre's literary executrix, Arlette Elkaïm Sartre, several times, but she never replied. Other researchers have also encountered this wall of silence from her. This is most unfortunate, because not only is Arlette Elkaïm Sartre sitting on a large collection of Sartre papers and correspondence, she also owns the copyright to all Sartre's unpublished writings.

I have been told that Dolores Vanetti Ehrenreich has kept her letters from Sartre, and if Arlette Elkaïm gives her consent, they might possibly be published in the future. Vanetti, who is frail, in her nineties, and living in New York, was gracious to me but would not agree to see me. Apart from a brief interview with Annie Cohen-Solal in the 1980s, Vanetti has systematically refused to talk about her relationship with Sartre.

In the end, I was able to read hundreds of letters that Sartre wrote to other girlfriends, but, sadly, I am not able to quote from them, except for the minimal "fair use" allowed by copyright law. Michelle Vian has kept the thick piles of letters Sartre wrote to her from 1949 onward, and briefly let me peruse them. The letters Sartre wrote to Wanda Kosakiewicz over the years are in Sylvie Le Bon de Beauvoir's possession. She let me read several dozen—those I asked to see, from periods I wanted to know more about.

My most precious insight into Sartre comes from the letters he wrote his Russian girlfriend, Lena Zonina, between 1962 and 1967. Lena's daughter, Macha Zonina, let me read the entire correspondence at my leisure—more than six hundred pages in Sartre's neat handwriting. In these letters, he writes a lot about the other women in his life.

The originals, in the Bibliothèque Nationale, have been placed under a forty-year embargo: no one has access to them. In the early 1980s, Lena Zonina wanted to publish these letters, but Arlette Elkaïm Sartre refused permission. After Lena's death, in February 1985, Macha Zonina, eager to keep the letters in France and knowing that her mother had wanted to make them public, sold the letters to the Bibliothèque Nationale. In light of the disparaging remarks they contain about his other women, including herself, Arlette Elkaïm Sartre has made them inaccessible to scholars for almost half a century.

The Beinecke Library at Yale is friendlier to the Sartre scholar. The Sartre collection includes thirty-one letters and postcards that Sartre wrote to Liliane Siegel and, more important, over two hundred hours of taped interviews that Sartre's biographer John Gerassi conducted between November 1970 and November 1973 with Sartre and members of his entourage, including Beauvoir, Olga and Wanda Kosakiewicz, Michelle Vian, Arlette Elkaïm Sartre, René Maheu, J.-B. Pontalis, André Gorz, Claude Lanzmann, and Jean Pouillon. It is wonderful to be able to hear these people's voices, and to attempt to decipher their hesitations, silences, and innuendoes. Interestingly, Olga, Wanda, and Arlette all give the impression that they did not feel able to say everything they wanted to say. Each one talked about Sartre with a degree of ambivalence. The fact is, Sartre was still alive; they did not want to be caught saying things behind his back to his biographer, and most of all, they were beholden to him.

In July 1985, Michel Rybalka taped more than twenty hours of interviews with Michelle Vian. His aim was primarily to find out more about the intellectual trajectories of Sartre and Boris Vian, but Michelle also made interesting comments about Sartre's character and her relationship with him. Rybalka let me listen to these interviews, which filled out and reinforced my own conversations with Michelle Vian.

At all times, I worked with the original French sources. Where they exist, I quote from the English translations, but if I did not find these accurate enough, I modified them, and indicated this in the endnotes. Otherwise, the translations from French are mine.

ACKNOWLEDGMENTS

My primary thanks are to Simone de Beauvoir, who has inspired me, throughout my adult life, to stretch my horizons, to dare, and to live each drop of life to the fullest. I first read her when I was studying French at the University of Adelaide. Stimulated by Peter Hambly's impassioned lectures on Sartre, Beauvoir, and the notion of "committed literature," I plunged into a doctoral thesis on existentialism. In November 1976, I had the privilege of interviewing Beauvoir. Looking back, although I did not begin it for another quarter of a century, this book had its origin at that time.

Tête-à-Tête has been a pleasure to write, partly because my main sources have been stimulating to talk to and extremely generous with their help, while also being fun, warm, and encouraging—in the best Sartre/Beauvoir tradition. I owe most of all to Sylvie Le Bon, Beauvoir's literary executrix, who shared her knowledge, memories, and archival material with abundant goodwill, and gave me permission to quote from Beauvoir's unpublished writings. Moreover, to encourage me and celebrate my progress, she introduced me to some of her and Beauvoir's favorite Montparnasse restaurants. She never asked to read my manuscript, and in every way respected my liberty to write the book as I saw fit.

I am beholden to the well-known Sartre scholars Michel Rybalka and Michel Contat, who were encouraging and helpful from start to end. My heart will forever be warmed by Michel and Maya Rybalka's kind and generous hospitality at their home in the Basque country, while Michel let me work through his Sartre library, files, and taped interviews. Michel Contat was full of helpful suggestions, references, and good stories, and liable to hand me a jazz CD on my way out of his apartment.

I am very grateful to Michelle Vian, who despite her physical fragility, gave up five afternoons for me, and answered my questions with honesty, thoughtfulness, and astoundingly youthful vitality. I am deeply indebted to Macha Zonina for her helpfulness, generosity, warmth, and admirable integrity. Liliane Siegel was encouraging and insightful.

I heartily thank all those people in France and the United States who granted me interviews: Barbara Aptekman, Sylvie Le Bon de Beauvoir, Lucia Cathala, Nadine Chauveau, Michel Contat, Gilbert Dagron, Marie-Chantal Dagron, Dominique Desanti, Boris Frezinsky, Robert Gallimard, John Gerassi, Geneviève Idt, Bianca Bienenfeld Lamblin, Claude Lanzmann, Jacques Lanzmann, Judith Magre, Jean Maheu, Robert Misrahi, Grégory Mouloudji, Patrick Nizan, Nikos Papatakis, J.-B. Pontalis, Serge Rezvani, Joshua Rubenstein, Michel Rybalka, Sally Swing Shelley, Liliane Siegel, Olivier Todd, Alexandre and Anahit Toptchian, Michelle Vian, Patrick Vian, Nicole Zand, and Macha Zonina.

I would like to thank Madame Mauricette Berne at the Bibliothèque Nationale; Stephen Jones at the Beinecke Library, Yale University; Elvira Griffith at Ohio State University; Madame Lili Phan, who manages the Gallimard archives; Laura Schmidt at the Bentley Historical Library, University of Michigan; Pascale Charles-Lavauzelle at the Mairie in Uzerche, Limousin; and the helpful staff at the Archives de Marseille.

I am deeply grateful to Denise Shannon, my literary agent, whose enthusiasm and helpfulness have set me on my feet in all sorts of ways. I feel privileged to have Terry Karten as my editor at HarperCollins, whose knowledge, passionate interest, and encouragement have bolstered me all the way along. I also thank Danny Mulligan, Jenna Dolan, and Kyran Cassidy.

Others to whom I am beholden for their support, stimulation, friendship, and help are John Baxter, Eliane Benisti, Elaine Bernard, Brian Boyd, Lynn Buchanan, Patrick Cazals, Frédéric Chaubin, James Cohen, Kathy Coit, Margaret Collins Weitz, Sandrine Dauphin,

Linda Dittmar, Madhu Dubey, Gerald Early, Emory Elliott, Louise Fuller, Inez Hedges, Odile Hellier, Ann Timoney Jenkin, Rosemary Jones, Sonia Kruks, Béatrice Lévy, Rosemary and Paul Lloyd, Herbert Lottman, Hilary Masters, Alex Miller, Edward and Claire Margolies, Toril Moi, Richard Munday, Sabina Murray, Douglas and Deborah Paterson, Yolanda Patterson, Louis Phillips, Dorothy Porter, Karen Sharpe, Dan Simon, Margaret Simons, Kathleen Spivack, Richard and Pamela Stanley, Ursula Tidd, Irene Tomaszewski, Beverly Tucker, Karina Veal, David Walker, Victor Wallis, Constance Webb, Asa Zatz, Howard and Roslyn Zinn.

Christine Levecq was with me when I thought up the topic in Chicago; Christina Thompson came up with the title over lattes in Harvard Square. I bashed around ideas with Pam Painter, and turned to her at various points for advice; I don't know where I'd be without her sparkling mind and generous spirit. In Paris and the surrounding forests, I had stimulating discussions with Emily Blake and Dominique Ridou, both of whom read the manuscript carefully, and astounded me by their thoroughness. Dominique helped me in numerous ways, and greatly enriched my stay in France. Jeannette Ambrose made me feel almost instantly at home in Paris; what warmth and vitality! Lincoln Siliakus and Frank Campbell were invaluable advisors and editors. Julie Wark is always there for me, in Barcelona. In the late stages of this book, I got to know that "naughty man," the Chicago photographer Art Shay, who seems to stop at nothing to help those he cares for. To these wonderful friends around the world, my deepest thanks.

My father was very ill in Australia during the writing of this book. It made the writing a particularly emotional experience. I was grateful to my mother for her strength and courage during this time. I relied heavily on my sister, Della, who is simply the best sister I could possibly imagine having. My brother, Martin, and my cousin Monica were marvelous—full of strength, and tenderness. Somehow, despite the great sadness, I felt blessed. Blessed to be in Paris, blessed by the many people who helped me in my research and writing, blessed to have a cozy study overlooking the Paris rooftops, and blessed by the loving support of friends and family. I feel a very lucky woman.

INDEX

Aden Arabie (Nizan), 6

Albi, France, 227

Algeria, 158–59, 192, 199, 201, 235, 244; FLN, 247, 259, 375n 36; "Manifesto of the 121," 258–59; Sartre and, 259–62; War, 237, 247, 248–49, 253, 255, 307

Algren, Nelson, xiv, 128, 175–77, 181–84, 185–86, 187–92, 198–99, 201–4, 214, 221, 223, 233, 234, 235, 239–40, 256, 257, 258, 262, 301–5, 321–22, 370n 25

American Dilemma (Myrdal), 371n 41

Amiens, France, 83, 84

Amsterdam, Netherlands, 226

anti-Semitism, 74, 121, 133, 136, 139, 143, 216, 217, 307; Russia, 264–65

Antoine Bloyé (Nizan), 55

Aptekman, Barbara, 377n 17

Aragon, Louis, 217

Arlen, Michael, 10

Aron, Raymond, 33, 55

Asabuki, Tomiko, 294–95, 312, 327, 378n 40

Astruc, Alexandre, 325

Audry, Colette, 50, 52, 56–57, 61, 119, 319, 358n 6, 379n 38

Bair, Deirdre, 47, 127, 298, 329, 350

Bal Nègre, Rue Blomet, 110, 114

Barbezat, Olga, 139, 142–43

Barnaby Rudge (Dickens), 102

Barrault, Jean-Louis, 135, 136

Barrès, Maurice, 16

Bataille, Georges, 141

Beauvoir, Georges de (father), 14, 29, 33, 73, 127, 361n 36

Beauvoir, Françoise de (mother), 127, 129, 138–39, 234, 278–79, 286

Beauvoir, Hélène de, "Poupette" (sister), 2–3, 14, 21, 23, 29, 37, 45, 89, 101, 129, 151, 244, 278–79, 305, 319, 348, 350–51, 352, 382n 52; boyfriend/husband, Lionel de Roulet, 119, 151, 350; girlfriend Gégé, 37

Beauvoir, Simone de: adoption of Sylvie Le Bon, 351; America, interest in, 147–48; American tour, 1947, 170–80; appearance, 1, 53, 74, 104, 155, 158, 178, 309, 363n 24; breast lump, 209; car accident, 1965, 288–89; cars owned by, 208, 240; Catholic girlhood, 185; death, funeral, and burial, 353; family's apartment, 10; family visits, 73, 120; finances and sharing of funds, 27, 61, 75, 98, 115, 151, 166, 193, 208, 229, 235, 342; lecturing in Tunis and Algiers, 1946, 158–59, 368n 31; mother's death, 278–79, 286; mythology and fame of, ix, xiii, 138, 153–56, 198–99, 219, 234, 243, 299; nickname, *le Castor* (Beaver), xiii, 8, 12, 73, 97, 126, 227, 241; pill taking and alcohol, 186, 204, 249, 255, 327, 341–42, 348; pneumonia, 1937, 67–68, 69; pneumonia, 1980, 349–50; restrictive society of, 17; sister, Hélène "Poupette" (*see* Beauvoir, Hélène "Poupette" [sister]); tête-à-têtes, as social habit, 73

Beauvoir, Simone de *(cont.)*:
CHARACTER AND PERSONALITY:
aging and, 209, 211, 247, 275–76, 310,
321–22; as bourgeoisie, 41, 56;
brilliance and intellectual diligence,
7–8, 13, 15, 19–20, 126, 220; children
and, 30, 174; conversation *à deux*,
preference for, 129–30; courage and
determination, xiii, 50, 75; death and
mortality, fears of, 220, 275–76, 323,
380n 2; emotionality and
vulnerability, xiv, 41, 50, 90, 93, 95,
117, 160, 163, 181, 184–86, 211, 220,
278–79, 344; friends and students as
acolytes, xii, 53, 61, 73, 219–20;
handwriting, 82, 125; hiking and
strenuous activities, 44–45, 71–72, 75,
80, 158, 168, 184–85, 247;
housekeeping and cooking, 129, 193;
loneliness, 17–18, 43, 44, 47, 52, 117,
157, 249; male values, xiii; music
preferred by, 208; obsessive behavior,
44–45; rebellion against convention,
xiv, 11–12, 16–18; seasickness, 41, 71;
self-image, 104; solitariness, 44, 45,
47; speaking voice and manner, 1,
309; work habits, 73, 125–26, 192–93,
212, 220, 238, 311, 325
EARLY YEARS AND EDUCATION:
Cours Adeline Désir, 13, 14; exams for
agrégation in philosophy, 1929, 1, 2, 7,
10, 14, 15–16, 19–20; father's loss of
wealth, 14, 33; friend Stépha, 9, 25, 29,
37; friend Zaza, 9, 13–15, 16, 28,
30–33, 37, 244, 357n 11; love for
cousin, Jacques, 8–9, 10, 21, 29, 37;
room at 91 Avenue Denfert-
Rochereau, 24–26; Sorbonne, 1, 14;
summers in Limousin, 20–23
JEAN-PAUL SARTRE AND: advice and
criticism of her writing, 84–85, 103,
107, 170, 208, 225–26, 243, 270, 325,
374n 13; Algeria, 1947, 192; American
trips of Sartre (and his liaison with
Vanetti), 1945–1946, 151–52, 160–63;
Brazil trip, 1960, 257–58; burial, joint
grave, ix, 353; China trip, 1955, 236;
consummation of relationship, 1929,
26–27; Cuba trip, 1960, 256, 257;
Czechoslovakia trip, 1968, 314; daily
schedule, 311; death and burial of
Sartre, 346–49; discontent of Sartre,

55–57; Easter vacation, Saint-Tropez,
1953, 220–21; Elkaïm's behavior
following Sartre's death and, 350;
family's disapproval of, 37, 361n 36; as
famous couple, 155–56, 161, 234, 244,
274, 299; first meetings, 1929, 1–3, 7,
11–13, 15–16; first summer in
Limousin, 1929, 20–23; games
between them, 64–65; health decline
of Sartre, 323–46; his love affairs and
her response, x, 52, 75–77, 79, 87,
88–89, 100, 101, 103–4, 107, 111–12,
115, 127, 153, 156, 160, 161, 174,
180–81, 184, 185, 204, 243–44, 280,
291–94, 298, 321, 338, 358n 10, 381n
34, 382n 54; Italy trips, 211, 224–26,,
330–31; Italy, yearly retreat in Rome,
1956 on, 241–42, 249, 251, 270,
277–78, 287–88, 320, 324, 327,
329–30; Japan, 1966, 294–95; letters
given to Bibliothèque Nationale, 352;
living arrangements, Paris, 1937–1939,
72–73; Middle East trip, 1967, 306–7;
military service of Sartre, 1929–1930,
relationship during, 33–41; Morocco
vacation, 1938, 79, 81–83; note from
1930, 34; "oneness," 98, 119; as open
relationship, xii–xiii; pact, 27–30, 43,
50, 97–98, 159, 164, 172, 220, 222,
301–2; passion for, xiv, 47, 100–101,
104, 121, 159, 180; physical
relationship, 26–27, 35–36, 104, 108,
127–28; in Rouen, 1932–1933, 50;
Russian trips, 236, 262, 263–65,
273–74, 276–77, 290–94, 295; Sahara
crossing together, 201; Saint-Lambert
sojourn, 1947, 184–85; Sartre's friends
and, 37–39; Sartre's interview, 1975,
and, 334–35; skiing in Mégève, 1945,
158; Spanish trip, 1931, 43–44;
summer vacations with, 70–71,
92–93, 167–68; 226–27, 240–41;
360n 5; "superiority" of Sartre, 34–35,
36, 37; tenth anniversary, 98; vacation,
1934, 54; visit in Berlin, 1933, 52;
Yugoslavia visits, 226, 240
LOVE AFFAIRS AND LIAISONS:
Arthur Koestler, 171, 233, 369n 53;
Bianca Bienenfeld, 74–75, 83, 86–89.
90, 91, 104, 105, 157, 366n 22; Claude
Lanzmann, 210–11, 213–25, 226–27,
230, 234, 235, 240–41, 247, 249, 251,

252–53, 288, 298, 320, 342, 372n 25; diaphragm and, 189; the Family, 66; formality, *vous* vs. *tu*, 9, 215; her love affairs and duplicity, x, xiii, xiv, 42, 80–81, 84, 90–91, 101, 103, 104–6, 113, 128, 156–58, 188–89, 192; Jacques-Laurent Bost, xiv, 70, 71–72, 75, 80–81, 82–84, 85, 89–91, 92–93, 101–2, 103, 104, 106, 108–10, 120–21, 128, 129, 132, 134, 138, 153, 158, 172, 185, 194, 209, 234, 363n 43; jealousy, 40, 50, 89, 90, 102, 107, 129, 159–60, 163–64, 358n 10; "Kos" factor, 89, 92–93; lesbianism, xiv, 45–46, 74, 86–89, 90, 91, 104–6, 131–33, 286–87, 310–11; Michel Vitold, 151; Nathalie Sorokine, 105–6, 120, 129, 130, 131–33, 141, 177–78, 365n 18; Nelson Algren, xiv, 128, 175–77, 181–84, 185–86, 187–92, 198–99, 201–4, 208, 214, 221, 233, 234, 235, 239–40, 256, 257, 258, 262, 301–5; Olga Kosakiewicz, 53–54, 57–69, 72, 81, 85–86, 100, 101, 114, 117, 120, 128, 131, 138, 171, 185, 234, 299; Pierre Guille, 41–42, 52–53; René Maheu, 1, 2, 7–13, 15, 20, 23–24, 28, 37, 40, 42, 43, 152, 368n 18; seductions and lies, xiii–xiv, 81, 83, 84, 86, 192, 221; sexuality of, xi, 26–27, 35–36, 81, 105–6, 108, 127–28, 183, 275, 372n 25; Sylvie Le Bon, 286–87, 300, 309–11, 319–20, 321, 326–29, 330, 341–42, 351, 352; trios, 60–61, 62–64, 74, 107, 138, 157, 327
PHILOSOPHY AND BELIEFS: on "the biographical illusion," xi; choice and responsibility, x–xi, 36, 103, 274; existentialism, x, 36, 159, 178, 179, 195, 276; feminism, 315, 318–19, 326, 327–28, 380n 48; freedom of the press, 315–16; on love, 17–18, 28, 36; on marriage, x, 17, 28–29, 43, 74; loss of belief in God, 15, 16; the "Other," 85, 194, 371n 41; politics and, 50, 208, 237, 243, 249, 252, 257, 258–59, 294, 307–9, 315–16, 379n 38; Sartre's volunteerism and, 41; on sex and sexuality, 29; "sincerity toward oneself," 17; treason accusations and violence against, 259–62; on women's status and rights, xiii, 28, 179–80, 194–96

PUBLISHED WORKS AND WRITINGS: *Adieux: A Farewell to Sartre*, ix, 323, 327, 337, 338, 351–52, 382n 54; *All Men Are Mortal*, 152, 156, 164, 167, 177; *All Said and Done*, 286–87, 297–98, 309–10, 325, 326, 377n 13; *America Day by Day*, ix, 178, 179, 185, 187, 301, 370n 15, 371n 56; attempts at novels, 52; *Les Belles Images*, 376n 2; *Blood of Others, The*, 119, 130, 152, 153, 365n 9; cafés as workplace, 120, 125–26, 158, 159, 192–93; characters, real-life people thinly disguised, 31–32, 59, 63–64, 85–86, 107, 127, 130, 138, 183, 231, 233, 239–40, 291–94, 301, 365n 9; collaboration with Sartre, 169; *Combat* articles, 151; *The Coming of Age*, 321–22; criticism and reviews, 137–38, 155–56, 179, 198, 233–34, 239, 302–5, 321–22, 368n 24, 382n 54; dedication, *All Said and Done*, 326; dedication, *The Blood of Others*, 130; dedication, *The Mandarins*, 233, 239; dedication, *The Second Sex*, 194; dedication, *She Came to Stay*, 64; dedication, *A Very Easy Death*, 279; *Force of Circumstance*, 192, 270–71, 274, 298, 299, 300, 301, 377n 13; "Jean-Paul Sartre: Strictly Confidential," 161–62; journals, 16, 37, 103, 106, 108, 162, 172, 249, 251; letters and journals, intent of publication, xiii, 352, 382n 52; *The Long March*, ix, 238–39, 243; love letters to Nelson Algren, xiv, 185–86, 191, 192, 193, 199, 201, 208; *The Mandarins*, ix, 171, 182, 183, 184, 204, 208, 212, 231, 233–34, 238, 239, 243, 301; as memoirist, ix, xi, 243–44, 249, 299–300; *Memoirs of a Dutiful Daughter*, 17, 31–33, 244, 249; "Merleau-Ponty and Pseudo-Sartrianism," 212; "Misunderstanding in Moscow," 291–94; novellas rejected by publishers, 83, 361n 31; novels and authors read, xi, 10, 11, 16–17, 45, 46–47, 69, 102, 120, 147, 205, 244; *Prime of Life, The*, 45, 260, 299, 301; Prix Goncourt award, 234, 235; *The Second Sex*, ix, xi, 28, 36, 170, 187, 194–96, 198, 208, 234, 243, 294; self-revelation in, 84–86, 171, 182, 183; *She Came to Stay (L'Invitée)*, ix, 59, 63–64, 85–86, 107, 120, 121, 127,

Beauvoir, Simone de (*cont.*): 137–39; *Les Temps modernes,* journal, 153, 156, 159, 169, 189, 229, 237, 315; *Useless Mouths,* 151, 153, 367n 16, 368n 24; *A Very Easy Death,* ix, 279, 382n 54; *The Woman Destroyed,* 310
TEACHING CAREER: Marseille, 43, 44–47, 358n 39; Paris, 66, 117; popularity and influence, xii, 74; Rouen, 48, 50, 52–55, 60–61; scandal of Sorokine and loss of position, 131–33, 138, 364n 64, 366n 22
WORLD WAR II: Bost called up, 1939, 93, 96, 363n 43; consciousness of history and, x, 96, 146; fears and, 93, 96, 97, 152, 153; flees Paris, June, 1940, 116–17; leaves of Bost and Sartre, 1940, 106–10; liberation of Paris and, 145; life in Paris during the Occupation, 120–46; meeting with Sartre, Brumath, 1939, 102–4; resistance efforts, 123–26, 365n 3; return to Occupied Paris, July, 1940, 117; Sartre called up, 1939, 93–95, 96–98; Sartre's return, 1941, 121–22; writing to Bost and Sartre, 101
Bechet, Sidney, 250
Being and Time (Heidegger), 119
Ben Gal, Eli, 339, 379n 20
Berlin, 51–52
Berriau, Simone, 206, 248, 252
Bienenfeld, Bianca, 74–75, 83, 86–89, 90, 91, 94, 104, 105, 109, 112–13, 116, 157, 223, 366n 22
Blin, Roger, 99
Bost, Jacques-Laurent "Little Bost," xiv, 57, 61, 64–65, 66–67, 74, 96, 97, 101–3, 113–17, 120–24, 131, 141–42, 144, 147, 152, 159, 192, 199, 202, 211, 230, 251, 259, 271, 307–8, 309, 315, 325, 330, 342, 344, 345, 347, 363n 43, 377n 17, 378n 11; affair with Dolores Vanetti, 153, 202, 368n 21; affair with Nathalie Sorokine, 130, 365n 18; affair with Sylvie Le Bon, 320, 380n 50; Beauvoir and, xiv, 70, 71–72, 75, 80–81, 82–84, 85, 89–91, 92–93, 101–2, 103, 104, 106, 108–10, 120–21, 128, 129, 132, 134, 138, 153, 158, 172, 185, 194, 209, 234, 363n 43; Olga Kosakiewicz and, 67, 81, 83–84, 89, 91, 92, 93, 101–3, 109–10,

113–14, 128, 129, 142, 143, 145, 158, 165, 171, 185, 194, 211, 271, 363n 45, 369n 54
Bost, Pierre, 360n 2
Boully, Monny de, 217, 218, 222, 373n 34
Boully, Paulette Lanzmann de, 216, 217–18
Bourla, Jean-Pierre, 133, 134, 141, 143, 366n 24
Brasseur, Pierre, 207
Brazil, 257–58
Breton, André, 150, 162, 259
Brioude, France, 216, 218, 223
Brodsky, Joseph, 285–86
Brumath, France, 102–4; Boeuf Noir, 104; Lion d'Or hotel, 102; Tavern du Cerf, 103
Brunschvicg, Leon, 8

Cahors, France, 226–27; Truffe Noire hotel, 226
Camus, Albert, 139–40, 141, 142, 143–44, 147, 156–57, 159, 171, 198, 233, 255–56, 281–82, 367n 8, 368n 29, 375n 36; break with Sartre, 212–13; death of, 255, 375n 28
Casarès, Maria, 144, 207
Castro, Fidel, 257
Cathala, Lucia, 378n 37
Cau, Jean, 165–67, 206, 210, 211, 216, 219, 227, 230, 246–47, 307–8, 369n 40
Claudel, Paul, 16, 17, 136
Chaveau, Nadine, 367n 17, 368n 18
Chicago, 175–77, 181–84, 186, 203–4, 208, 240, 370n 25; Hotel Alexandria, 182
China, 236
CNE (National Committee of Writers), 140, 145, 366n 31
Cocteau, Jean, 206, 217, 218
Cohen-Solal, Annie, 150
Cohn-Bendit, Daniel, 314
Collège de France, 31
Combat, 140, 145, 149, 151, 152, 153, 255, 367n 8, 367n 53
Commentaire (journal), 269–70
Communism, x, xiii; American denial of passports and, 239; Cold War and, 170–71, 210; Cuba, 257; French, 50, 168, 210, 212; Italian, 168; Maoism,

315–17, 333; Resistance in France, 124, 125, 140, 143, 216; Sartre, as "fellow traveler," 210, 212, 242, 257; Sartre's conversion, 210
Conspiration, La (Nizan), 73
Contat, Michel, xiv–xv, 325, 377n 10
Corsica, Beauvoir-Le Bon in, 287
Crucible, The (Miller), 237
Cuba, 256, 257, 262, 326
Cuzin, François, 125
Czechoslovakia: Sartre-Beauvoir trip, 1968, 314; Soviet invasion, 314

Dagron, Gilbert, 269
Daniel, Jean, 344
Daniel, Yuly, 290
Darkness at Noon (Koestler), 171
Dedijer, Vladimir, 309, 318
De Gaulle, Charles, 145, 248–49, 251, 252, 260, 375n 28
Deleuze, Gilles, 216, 218, 224
Deneuve, Catherine, 319
Dernier des Métiers, Le (Bost), 165
Desanti, Dominique, 124–25, 126, 137, 319, 365n 3
Desanti, Jean-Toussaint, 123, 124, 125
Devouassoux, Simone Debout, 365n 3
Discourse on Metaphysics (Leibniz), 11
Disgraceful Affair, A (Bienenfeld Lamblin), 87–88
Dorosh, Yefim, 270
Duchamp, Marcel, 150
Duclos, Jacques, 210
Dullin, Charles, 38–39, 92, 101, 120, 136–37, 139, 142, 360n 2, 366n 30
Duras, Marguerite, 209, 259, 319

L'Ecume des Jours (Vian), 154, 159, 368n 27
Egypt, Sartre-Beauvoir trip, 1967, 306
Ehrenburg, Ilya, 231, 263, 265, 267, 268, 285, 290, 376n 1, 377n 21
Elkaïm, Arlette, 244–46, 253–54, 272, 286, 289, 307, 309, 311–12, 313, 318, 319, 321, 324, 328, 330, 332, 334, 334, 335, 338, 339, 341, 342, 345–46, 348, 351, 352, 377n 18, 379n 20, 379n 33; adoption and literary executor for Sartre, 246, 280, 283, 284–85, 318, 350, 378n 31
Eluard, Paul, 217
d'Estaing, Giscard, 333, 347

L'Express magazine, 242, 251
existentialism, x, xiii, 36, 153, 154–56, 159, 178, 179, 195, 248

Fanon, Frantz, 261, 379n 22
Fest, Joachim, 331
Figaro, Le, 149, 151, 269, 347, 367n 8
Figaro Littéraire, 280
Flaubert, Gustave, 52, 233, 237–38, 272, 297, 317, 322, 326, 334
France Dimanche, 213, 219
France Soir, 284, 289, 313

Gallimard, Gaston, 360n 2
Gallimard, Michel, 375n 35
Gallimard, Robert, 140, 213, 279
Gallimard publishers, 67, 71, 83, 137, 166, 225, 234, 276, 284, 322, 360n 2, 368n 25, 371n 56, 381n 25
Genet, Jean, 199–200, 206, 233, 238
Gerassi, Fernando, 37, 43, 57, 70, 119
Gerassi, John, 70, 215, 228, 254, 298, 308, 338, 342
Gerassi, Stépha, 9, 25, 29, 37, 43, 70, 119, 189
Gide, André, 16, 73, 97, 124, 132
Gilbert, Colette, 76–77, 78, 110–11
"Goodbye Lilies, Hello Spring" (Algren), 304–5
Gorz, André, 315, 344
Grasset publishers, 83
Greco, Juliette, 197
Greece, 71–72, 336–37, 360n 5
Green Hat, The (Arlen), 10
Guérin, Daniel, 379n 38
Guevara, Che, 257
Guille, Pierre, 33, 37–38, 52–53, 55, 62, 65
Gulag Archipelago (Solzhenitsyn), 331
Guttoso, Renato, 242

Halimi, Gisèle, 247, 308, 309, 319
Hare, David, 162
Harper's Bazaar, 161
Harper's magazine, 301, 303
Heidegger, Martin, 51, 119, 124
Hermantier, Raymond, 207
Hitler, Adolf, 51, 93
Humanité Dimanche, 234
Hungary, 232, 242–43, 263
Husserl, Edmund, 51, 52
Huston, John, 253–54, 271, 377n 16

Idt, Geneviève, xiii
L'Inachevé (Puig), 377n 18
Ireland, 253–54
Israel, 211, 214, 307, 339; Sartre on, 189, 307, 339–40, 379n 22; Six-Day War, 307, 379n 22
Italy: Albergo Nazionale, Piazzo Montecitorio, Rome, 320, 324; Albergo del Sole, Rome, 320; Beauvoir-Algren trip, 1949, 199; Beauvoir-Le Bon trip, 1971, 324–25; Beauvoir-Sartre trips, 167–68, 211, 212, 224–26, 330–31; Beauvoir-Sartre, yearly retreat in Rome, 1956 on, 241–42, 249, 251, 270, 277–78, 287–88, 320, 324, 327, 329–30; Café Florian, Venice, 225; Café della Scala, Milan, 212; communist party in, 168; Hotel Luna, Venice, 224–25; Minerva Hotel, Rome, 169, 277, 278; Naples, 324; Piazza Navona, Rome, 241; Sartre-Kosakiewicz trips, 324, 328–29; Sartre's convalescence in, 1954, 232; Sartre's love for, 206

Jacob, Max, 133, 143, 217
Japan, 153. 294–95. *See also* Asabuki, Tomiko
Jeanson, Francis, 213, 259
Jollivet, Simone, 18–19, 38–40, 142, 359n 39
Juan-les-Pins, France, 93
Junas, France, 328

Khrushchev, Nikita, 263, 264, 277, 283, 377n 21
Koestler, Arthur, 140, 171, 233, 369n 53
Kosakiewicz, Marthe, 59, 60
Kosakiewicz, Olga, 74, 76, 81, 83, 84, 90, 91, 92, 93, 98, 100, 101–2, 106, 109–10, 113–14, 117, 120, 131, 141, 143, 158, 159, 198, 199, 256, 300, 330, 342; abortion of, 118–19, 319, 364n 56, 364n 57; acting career, 92, 101, 120, 135, 136–37, 138, 153, 165, 207, 366n 30, 368n 24; Beauvoir and, 53–54, 57–69, 72, 81, 85–86, 100, 101, 114, 117, 120, 128, 131, 138, 171, 185, 234; Bost and, 67, 81, 83–84, 89, 91, 92, 93, 101–3, 109–10, 113–14, 128, 142, 143, 145, 165, 171, 194, 211, 271, 363n 45, 369n 54; fictional portraits of, 59,

63–64, 85–86; Sartre and, 57–69, 70, 76, 92, 114, 131, 299; tuberculosis of, 165, 168, 171, 185, 207
Kosakiewicz, Victor, 58, 59, 132
Kosakiewicz, Wanda, 58, 61, 68–69, 89, 93, 101, 113, 114–15, 120, 127, 141, 142, 143–44, 145, 158, 166, 360 n 54, 378n 11, 380n 49; acting career, 139, 144, 188, 206–7, 229, 248, 253, 272, 287–88; Camus and, 140, 141, 143–44; Sartre and, 68–69, 70, 72, 74, 75–76, 78–79, 84, 91–92, 94, 98, 99–100, 103–4, 106, 107, 110–12, 126, 128, 130, 132, 138, 139–40, 144, 158, 167, 168, 206–7, 222, 228, 229, 230, 248, 249, 253, 272, 280, 284, 286, 299–300, 311, 312, 313, 319, 324, 328–29, 334, 335, 341, 346, 360n 5, 363n 45, 379n 33
Kreindlina, Irina, 378n 28

Lacan, Jacques, 157
La Cause du peuple newspaper, 315–16
Lacoin, Zaza, 9, 13–15, 16, 28, 30–33, 37, 244, 357n 11
Lagache, Daniel, 56
Laigle, Normandy, France, 58, 59, 76, 79, 94, 100, 117, 159, 342, 358n 14
Lalande, André, 19
Lamba, Jacqueline Breton, 150, 162, 368n 21
Lanzmann, Claude, 210–11, 212, 213–25, 226–27, 234, 235, 240–41, 247, 249, 251, 252–53, 259, 288, 296, 297, 298, 306, 307–8, 309, 313, 315, 320, 342, 344, 347, 348, 372n 25, 373n 36, 375n 28, 378n 10, 379n 22
Lanzmann, Evelyne/Evelyne Rey, 216, 218, 222–24, 227–29, 230, 243, 248, 251, 253, 272, 284, 287–88, 296–99, 305–6, 373n 52, 373n 55, 374n 64, 378n 2, 378n 5, 378n 8
Lanzmann, Jacques, 216, 217, 219, 222, 227, 228, 229, 372n 25, 378n 8
Laon, France, 66, 69
Lapouge, Gilles, 325
La Rochelle, France, 4, 32, 357n 11
Lassithiotakis, Hélène, 334, 335–36
Le Bon de Beauvoir, Sylvie, 286–87, 300, 309–11, 315, 319–20, 321, 324, 326–29, 330, 336, 341–42, 347, 348,

378n 11, 380n 49; adoption by
  Beauvoir, 351
Léger, Fernand, 150
Le Havre, France, 43, 44, 48–49, 56–57,
  146; Café de la Grande Poste, 49;
  Café Les Mouettes, 56; Guillaume
  Tell café, 49; Hotel Printania, 48;
  Lycée François, 49
Leibniz, Gottfried Wilhelm von, 11
Leiris, Michel, 138, 140–41, 259, 379n 38
Leiris, Zette, 140–41
Levi, Carlo, 168, 270
Lévi-Strauss, Claude, 138, 150
Lévy, Benny. *See* Victor, Pierre
Lévy, Bernard-Henri, xiv
Libération, 225, 239, 326, 347, 373n 56,
  380n 6; open letter by Arlette Elkaïm,
  352
Limousin, France, 20–23
Lone Pine, California, 178
Los Angeles, California, 177–78
Los Angeles Times, 321–22
Loursais, Claude, 378n 5
Lycées. *See city where located*
Lyon, France, 42, 134

Madame Bovary (Flaubert), 52, 237, 322
Magnani, Anna, 242
Magre, Judith, 219, 378n 10
Maheu, Inès, 9
Maheu, René, 1–2, 7–13, 15, 20, 23–24,
  28, 37, 40, 42, 43, 119, 152, 367n 17,
  368n 18
Malraux, André, 124
Mancy, Anne-Marie Schweitzer Sartre
  (mother), 4, 18, 37, 73, 106, 107, 152,
  158, 160, 206, 228, 229, 311; death of,
  311; Sartre lives with, 1946, 164–67
Mancy, Joseph (stepfather), 4, 37, 152
"Manifesto of the 343," 319, 380n 48,
  380n 49
Mansfield, Katherine, xi, 45, 46–47
Man with the Golden Arm (Algren), 199,
  239
Marr, Dora, 141
Marron, Germaine, 18, 357n 10
Marseille, France, 43, 44–47, 81, 83,
  92–93, 240–41, 358n 39; cafes and
  brasseries, 47; Lycée Montgrand,
  Marseille, 44, 358n 34; Tuffreau
  apartment, Avenue du Prado, 46
Marxism, 6, 123, 213, 248

Matín de París, Le, 347
Mauriac, François, 17, 82, 198
McCarthy, Mary, 179
Mégève, France, 156, 158
Menton, Côte d'Azur, France, 253
Meredith, George, 37
Merleau-Ponty, Maurice, 6, 13, 76, 123,
  169, 171, 212, 244, 357n 11, 369n 50;
  Zaza's death and vilification by
  Simone de Beauvoir, 30–33, 244
Mexico City, Mexico, 189, 190
Mezzrow, Mezz, 175
Michel, Georges, 350
Miller, Arthur, 237
Miracle of the Wolves, The (film), 38
Modern Times (film), 153
Moffat, Ivan, 177–78
Moi, Toril, 380n 2, 382n 54
Monde, Le, 223, 314, 373n 52, 379n 38
Monteil, Claudine, 319
Moreau, Jeanne, 319
Morel, Madame, 38, 42, 43, 48, 55,
  56, 65, 67, 93, 104, 116, 129, 199,
  366n 39
Morocco: Beauvoir-Algren trip, 199;
  Beauvoir-Sartre trip, 79, 81–83;
  Maheu teaching in Fez, 119
Mouloudji, Marcel, 110–11, 114, 130,
  138, 141, 142, 360 n 54, 365n 19
Myrdal, Gunnar, 371n 41

Nancy, France, 95
Nasser, Gamal Abdel, 306
Never Come Morning (Algren), 184, 199,
  204
New Philosophers, xiii, xiv, 313–14
New York City: Beauvoir in, 1947,
  172–75; Brevoort Hotel, 180, 184;
  French expatriates in, 150; Harlem,
  151; Jimmy Ryan's, 151; Nick's Bar, 151;
  Plaza Hotel, 148; Russian Tea Room,
  151; Sartre in, 1945–1946, 148–52,
  156, 160–63; Stépha and Fernando in,
  119; Tavern on the Green, 190; Times
  Square, 151
New Yorker, 175, 183
Nizan, Henriette, 12, 29, 37, 148–49,
  160
Nizan, Paul, 2, 5, 6–7, 8, 10, 12, 16, 19,
  29, 37, 55, 73, 93, 116, 148
Nouvelle Revue Française, 71, 73, 82
Nouvelles Littéraires, Les, 73

Nouvel Observateur, 245, 296, 309, 314, 319, 339; discussions of Sartre-Victor, 342–45
Novy Mír, 264, 376n 1, 377n 11, 377n 21

One Day in the Life of Ivan Denisovich (Solzhenitsyn), 264
Outsider, The (Camus), 140

Papatakis, Niko, 113–14, 118, 364n 48, 364n 56
Paris of Sartre and Beauvoir: Algerian conflict and, 235, 259–61; Anne-Marie Mancy/Sartre apartment, 42 Rue Bonaparte, 164–67, 187, 210, 228, 235, 260, 261, 353; Anne-Marie Mancy hotel, Boulevard Raspail, 260, 261, 289; L'Atelier drama school, 39, 92, 101, 110, 120, 136, 139; Bal Nègre, Rue Blomet, 110, 114; Beaujon Hospital, 165; Beauvoir apartment, Avenue Denfert-Rochereau, Montparnasse, 24–26, 119; Beauvoir apartment, Rue de la Bûcherie, 193–94, 211, 214, 227, 230, 231, 235; Beauvoir apartment, Rue Schoelcher, Montparnasse, xiii, 235–36, 256, 257, 278, 283–84, 288–89, 324, 330, 346, 380n 50; Beauvoir family apartment, Rue de Rennes, 10; Bibliothèque Nationale, 1, 170, 244, 352; bombing of, 143; Bost apartment, Boulevard Edgar Quinet, 342; Bost apartment, Rue de la Bûcherie, 194, 211, 230; Boulevard du Montparnasse, 72; Boully apartment, Rue Alexandre-Cabanel, 217–18; Café Coupole, Boulevard du Montparnasse, 68, 72, 73, 75, 235, 240, 311, 324, 327; Café Deux Magots, 164, 167, 168, 192, 224, 353; Café Dôme, 72, 73, 76, 94, 100, 107, 117, 120, 145, 235, 328; Café Dupont, Montmartre, 12; Café de Flore, Boulevard Saint-Germain, 114, 116, 125–26, 129–30, 133, 141, 143, 158, 167; Café Palette, Boulevard du Montparnasse, 311; Café Pont-Royal, 159, 197; Le Café Rouge, 68, 88; Cafe Sélect, 67, 72; Café des Trois Mousquetaires, Avenue du Maine, 72, 107–8, 121–22, 380n 50; Comédie Française, 145; Ecole Normale

Supérieure, 5–6, 20, 34, 37, 51, 56, 124, 125, 216, 244, 245, 286, 300, 356n 23; Elkaïm studio, Rue Delambre, 328, 330, 379n 33; Evelyne Lanzmann apartment, 26 Rue Jacob, 228; gardens of the Palais Royal, 8; Gare de l'Est, 94–95, 106–7, 108, 109; Gare Saint-Lazare, 48; Gestapo and arrests, 142, 143; Hôtel Aubusson, Rue Dauphine, 134, 366n 26; Hôtel Chaplain, Rue Jules-Chaplain, 120, 127, 139, 143–44, 145, 147; Hôtel du Danemark, Rue Vavin, 100, 116, 117, 120, 121; Hôtel La Louisiane, Rue de Seine, 141, 157, 180, 191, 193, 366n 44; Hôtel Lutétia, 152; Hôtel Mistral, Rue de Cels, 72, 74, 75, 76–77, 87, 90, 100, 106, 107, 123, 127, 129, 134, 353; Hôtel Oriental, Place Denfert-Rochereau, 109; Hôtel du Poirier, Emile Goudeau Square, 83, 120–21, 364n 65; Hôtel Royal Bretagne, Rue de la Gaîté, 66, 72; Israeli-Palestinian conference, 1979, 339–40; jazz clubs, Saint-Germain, 155, 164; the Jockey, 101; Le Bon apartment, Avenue du Maine, 327, 347; Leiris's apartment, Quai des Grands-Augustins, 140–41; Liberation, 144–46; Luxembourg Gardens, 1, 2; Lycée Condorcet, 125; Lycée Duruy, 117; Lycée Henry IV, Paris, 5; Lycée Louis-le-Grand, Paris, 5, 216; Lycée Molière, Paris, 66, 74; Lycée Pasteur, 73, 133; Madame Morel's apartment, Boulevard Raspail, 38, 49, 56; Méphisto club, 164; Montparnasse Cemetery, 235, 330, 346, 348–49, 353; Nox restaurant, 109; Occupation, 116–46; Place Saint-Germain (Place Sartre-Beauvoir), 353; Poupette's studio, Jardin des Plantes, 101, 129; Rue Delambre, 66, 68; St.-Anne's Hospital, 56, 336; Sally Swing's apartment, Rue Grenelle, 187; Sartre apartment, Boulevard Edgar Quinet, 330–31, 349; Sartre apartment, Boulevard Raspail, 261, 272; Sartre's childhood in, 3–4; Sartre's funeral procession, 348–49, 382n 49; Sorbonne, 1, 8, 14, 66, 87, 105; street market, Rue Daguerre, 315; student revolution, 1968, 314–18, 379n 38; tearoom on Rue de Médicis, 2; Théâtre Antoine, 188, 206–7, 248, 252; Théâtre de la Athénée, 223; Théâtre de la Cité, 136–37, 138; Théâtre du Vieux Colombier, 143; Wanda Kosakiewicz apartment, Rue du Dragon, 300, 379n 33l; wartime, 94–95; Zazou movement, 196–97

Pasternak, Boris, 269, 281, 283, 290

Peace Movement, 229, 242, 263, 268, 377n 10

Périer, François, 287

Pétain, Marshal, 117, 132

Petit Invité, Le (Mouloudji), 110

phenomenology, 51, 52, 86, 244

Picard, Yvonne, 125

Picasso, Pablo, 141

Pingaud, Bernard, 347, 380n 41

Politzer, Georges, 41

Pontalis, Jean Bertrand, 159–60, 259, 380n 41

Portugal, 119, 129, 151

Pouillon, Denise, 345

Pouillon, Jean, 124, 259, 260, 315, 325, 333, 344, 345

Proust, Marcel, 132

Provence, France, 42; Reine Jeanne, 42

Puig, André, 312, 331, 334, 338, 345, 377n 18

Queneau, Raymond, 138, 140, 141, 142, 159, 367n 48

Quimper, Brittany, 116

Racine, Jean, 185

Ramparts magazine, 302

Rassemblement Démocratique Révolutionnaire (RDR), 188

Rat d'Amérique, Le (Lanzmann), 229

Really the Blues (Mezzrow and Wolfe), 175

Rebel, The (Camus), 212–13

Reggiani, Serge, 253, 287

Reweliotty, André, 197, 201, 240, 250–51, 256, 272–73, 371n 43

Rey, Evelyne. *See* Lanzmann, Evelyne

Rezvani, Serge, 217–18, 222, 223, 224, 298–99, 373n 36, 373n 55

Robbe-Grillet, Alain, 259

Roosevelt, Franklin Delano, 150

Rosenberg, Ethel and Julius, 224–26

Rouen, France, 48, 50, 52–55, 79, 309; Brasserie de l'Opera, 79; Brasserie Paul, 50; Brasserie Victor, 53; Hôtel du Petit Mouton, 60, 65, 78–79; Hôtel La Rochefoucauld, 50, 309; Lycée Jeanne d'Arc, 44, 53, 309; Métropole, 309

Roulet, Lionel de, 119, 151, 350

Rousseau, Jean Jacques, 11

Roy, Claude, 239

Russell, Bertrand, 308, 332

Russell Tribunal, 308–9, 332

Russia (Soviet Union): Algren's criticism, 225–26; Beauvoir and Sartre's works in, 376n 2; Brodsky trial, 285–86; Czechoslovakia invasion, 314; Hungarian invasion, 232, 242–43; Leningrad, 264, 274; Moscow, 236–37, 262, 264, 273–74; Peking Hotel, Moscow, 264; *samizdat*, 290; Sartre-Beauvoir break from, 314, 326; Sartre-Beauvoir trips, 236, 262, 263–67, 273–74, 290–94, 295, 377n 13; Sartre's belief in desires for peace of, 209, 268, 377n 10; Sartre's writing and apologia for, 231–32, 268–70, 283, 285–86, 290, 374n 73; Soviet Writers Union, 229, 268, 269, 290, 378n 37; "thaw," 1962, 263, 376n 1; translation of Sartre's *Words*, 376n 2, 377n 11; Writers Club, Moscow, 264, 271. *See also* Zonina, Lena

Rybalka, Michel, 228, 374n 66

Sagan, Françoise, 341, 381n 41

Said, Edward, 340

Saint-Cyr, France, 30, 33; Soleil d'Or, brasserie, 33

Saint-Germain-les-Belles, France, 20, 21; Hôtel de la Boule d'Or, 21

Saint-Lambert, France, 184–85

Saint-Paul-de-Vence, France, 320–21

Saint-Raphael, France, 289

Saint-Symphorien, France, 33

Saint-Tropez, France, 220–21

Samedi Soir (tabloid), 156

Samman, Ali el, 306

Sarraute, Nathalie, 259

Sartre (film), 325

Sartre, Jean-Baptiste (father), 3

Sartre, Jean-Paul: adoption of Arlette Elkaïm and her behavior as executor,

Sartre, Jean-Paul *(cont.)*: 272, 280, 283, 284–85, 318, 350, 378n 31; American trips, 1945–1946, 147–52, 156; appearance, 2, 3, 5, 55, 58, 62, 77, 78, 140, 161, 313–14, 352–53; blindness, final years, 328–29, 330, 331–32, 341, 344; cigarettes, giving up, 336; death and burial, 346–49; detective stories, love of, 16, 75, 97, 205, 346; documentary, 1972, 325; fame of, ix, 153–56, 160–63, 219; finances and financial support of others, 27, 61, 75, 98, 115, 144, 166–67, 206, 207, 228–29, 230, 240, 243, 245, 279–80, 326, 328, 333, 334, 336, 376n 2, 379n 33, 381n 25; health problems and final decline, 229, 230–31, 252, 255, 323–25, 328–46; intellectual decline, 330–34, 381n 41; interview, 1975, 334–35; mother, Anne-Marie, relationship with, 3–4, 18, 37, 73, 107, 152, 158, 164–67, 206, 229, 311; nickname, "the Little Man," 8, 356n 11; pill taking and alcohol intake, problems with, 162, 171, 186, 204, 205–6, 229, 230, 233, 236–37, 247–48, 254–55, 272, 300, 305–6, 324, 327, 328, 336–37, 338, 341; secretary, André Puig, 331, 334, 338, 345, 377n 18; secretary, Claude Faux, 247; secretary, Jean Cau, 165–67, 206, 210, 211, 219, 227, 230, 246–47, 307–8, 369n 40; secretary, Pierre Victor, 331–32, 334, 338–40; self-image, as ugly, 4–5, 78; stepfather, Joseph Mancy, relationship with, 4, 37, 152; tête-à-têtes, as social habit, 73; weight and obesity, 55, 62, 97
CHARACTER AND PERSONALITY: ambitions and commitment to writing, x, 22, 29, 77–78; beauty in women, need for, 78, 361n 21; belief in his own superiority and genius, 5, 34–35, 130, 154; as bourgeoisie, 41, 56, 164, 280; children and, 30; coldness or indifference, 35, 76, 79, 249; communal living and, 51, 97; conversation *à deux*, preference for, 129–30; foods preferred by, 49, 51, 229; freedom and lack of attachment, 29–30, 35; friends encouraged to have affairs, 379n 20; friends and students

as acolytes, xii, 34–35, 37, 61, 73, 97, 106, 219–20; friends as physically attractive, 37–38, 57, 65, 317; handwriting, 125; irascibility, 72–73; as listener, 21; living quarters unkempt, 10–11, 337; melancholy and depressions, 4, 30, 55–57, 58, 99, 233, 330; music preferred by, 208; personal hygiene, 126; seduction of women, need for, xiii–xiv, 5, 28, 47, 51–52, 57–58, 76–78, 87–88, 92, 160, 187, 258, 295, 306, 341, 361n 18; self-analysis, 78; sexuality of, 127–28, 187, 189–90, 227, 337; temper, 72; temperament, 5–6; transformation to "new intellectual," 313–14; unconventionality, nonconformity, x, xiv, 21–22; work habits, 73, 125–26, 134, 165–67, 202, 205–6, 212, 311, 325
EARLY YEARS AND EDUCATION: death of father, 3; École Normale Supérieure, Paris, 5–6, 20, 34, 37, 51, 56, 124, 333, 356n 23; *agrégation* exams, 1, 2, 7, 10, 15–16, 18, 19, 20; the "little comrades," 8, 10, 11–12; living with grandparents in Paris, 3, 51; living in La Rochelle, 4; Lycée Henry IV, Paris, 5; Lycée Louis-le-Grand, Paris, 5; military service, 1929–1930, 27, 30, 33–37; nickname "Poulou," 3, 18; student residence, Cité Universitaire, 10–11
LOVE AFFAIRS AND LIAISONS: Arlette Elkaïm, 244–46, 253–54, 272, 280, 283, 284–85, 286, 289, 307, 309, 311–12, 313, 318, 319, 321, 324, 328, 330, 332, 334, 335, 338, 339, 341, 342, 345–46, 379n 33; attraction to "drowning women," 61, 223, 261–62, 336, 373n 55; Bianca Bienenfeld, 87–89, 94, 112–13, 157; coitus interruptus practiced by, 88, 199; Colette Audry, 50, 358n 6; Colette Gilbert, 76–77, 78, 110–11; convalescence in Italy, Austria, and Germany with Michelle Vian, 1954, 232; Dolores Vanetti, 149–53, 156, 160, 162–64, 167, 174, 180, 184, 186, 188, 191–92, 202, 204, 243, 299, 301, 371n 35; Dolores Vanetti, proposal and talk of marriage, 163, 184, 202; Evelyne Lanzmann, 223–24, 227–29,

230, 243, 248, 251, 253, 272, 284, 287–88, 296–99, 305–6, 373n 55, 374n 64; the Family, 66; Françoise Sagan, 341, 381n 41; Germaine Marron, 18, 357n 10; Hélène Lassithiotakis, 334, 335–36; his love affairs and duplicity, x, xiii–xiv, 52, 68, 75–77, 79, 87, 88–89, 94, 100, 103–4, 106, 107, 111–13, 115, 127, 128, 153, 156, 157, 160, 161, 163, 174, 180–81, 184, 204, 221, 227–28, 246, 289–94, 298, 311–13, 337–38, 374n 66, 381n 34; jealousy and, 39, 40, 65, 67, 70, 99–100, 110, 129, 250–51; Lena Zonina, 263–78, 280, 282–84, 285, 286, 289–94, 295, 297, 312–13, 314, 330, 376n 2, 376n 7, 376n 9, 377n 14, 378n 37; Liliane Siegel, 261–62, 284–85, 330, 331, 337, 341; Marie Ville, 52, 55; Michelle Vian, 196–97, 199–201, 207–8, 209, 220–21, 222, 228, 230, 232, 240–41, 243, 249–51, 253, 256, 272–73, 284, 289, 311, 312, 313, 317–18, 321, 334, 335, 336–37, 338, 345–46, 374n 66, 376n 41; Nathalie Sorokine, 130, 365n 18, 366n 23; Olga Kosakiewicz, 57–69, 70, 76, 92, 114, 131; Sally Swing, 187, 189–90; scandal of Nathalie Sorokine, 131–33, 364n 64, 366n 22; schedule, daily, later life, 311–12; Simone Jollivet, 18–19, 38–40, 359n 39; Tomiko Asabuki, 294–95, 312, 327, 378n 40; the trios, 60–61, 62–64, 74, 107, 157; Wanda Kosakiewicz, 68–69, 70, 74, 75–76, 78–79, 84, 91–92, 94, 98, 99–100, 103–4, 106, 107, 110–12, 126, 128, 130, 132, 138, 139–40, 144, 158, 167, 168, 206–7, 222, 228, 229, 230, 248, 249, 253, 272, 280, 284, 286, 287–88, 299–300, 311, 312, 313, 319, 324, 328–29, 334, 335, 341, 346, 360n 5, 363n 45, 379n 33. *See also* Simone de Beauvoir (*below*)

PHILOSOPHY AND BELIEFS: anticolonialism, xi, 259–62, 375n 36; "antipsychiatry" movement, 380n 41; "authenticity," xi, 61–62, 359n 39; on "the biographical illusion," xi; communism and, x, xiii, 124, 168, 171, 210, 212, 257; on emotions vs. will, 39–41; existentialism, x, 154–56, 179,

195, 237, 248, *see also Being and Nothingness* (below); existential psychoanalysis, 232, 245, 261–62, 284; on freedom, choice (volunteerism), and responsibility, x–xi, 40–41, 246; freedom of the press, 315–16; intellectual's commitment to truth, 212; Israel and, 189, 307, 339–40, 379n 22; Israeli-Palestinian conference, 1979, 339–40; literature as religion, 232; Maoism, 315–17; on marriage and monogamy, x, 7, 27, 28, 43; mescaline experiment, 56–57, 186; peace and, x, 209, 229, 242, 263, 268, 377n 10; phenomenology, 51, 52; politics and, 51, 188, 189, 205–6, 208, 224–25, 237, 242–43, 248–49, 251–52, 257, 258–59, 294, 307–9, 314–17, 326, 379n 38 (*see also* Russia); *Rassemblement Démocratique Révolutionnaire* (RDR), 188; relationships and conflict, 100; on romance and love, 18, 28–30, 62, 99–100, 154, 359n 40; Rosenberg executions and, 224–25; on sex, 18; *the situation,* 246; socialism and, x, 123; Soviet Union, articles and apologia for, 209, 231–32, 268–70, 283, 285–86, 374n 73; temporary morality, 246; theory of liberty and contingency, 22; on "transparency," xi–xii, 28, 352; USSR, Hungarian invasion and, 242–43, 263; USSR, trips to and politics, 229–31, 265–67

PUBLISHED WORKS AND WRITINGS: *The Age of Reason,* 63, 97, 119, 153, 359n 40, 360 n 55; American articles, 1945, 149; Antoine Roquentin, character, based on himself, x, 55; article on the Rosenberg executions, 225; articles on Cuba, 257; articles on de Gaulle for *L'Express,* 251; on Baudelaire, 238; *Being and Nothingness,* ix, 100, 119, 134, 137, 155, 161, 217, 244, 369n 40; biographical essays, ix; cafés as workplace, 125–26, 158; *The Chips Are Down,* 187; on colonialism and racism, xi, 150, 167–68, 237; *Combat* articles, 145, 149, 151, 367n 8, 367n 53; *The Communists and Peace,* 210, 212, 242; *The Condemned of Altona,* 248–49, 252, 253, 272, 287–88, 296; criticism and

Sartre, Jean-Paul (*cont.*): reviews, 73, 87, 155, 276; *The Critique of Dialectical Reason*, ix, 248; dedication of *Being and Nothingness*, 137; dedication of *Nausea*, 73; dedication of *No Exit*, 366n 39; dedication of *Roads to Freedom*, 127; dedication of *The Victors*, 167; dedication of *The Wall*, 87, 127, 361n 36; dedication of *Words*, 276, 376n 2; *The Devil and the Good Lord*, 206–7; *Dirty Hands*, 188; discussions of Sartre and Pierre Victor, 342–45; *Ethics*, 206; *The Family Idiot: Gustave Flaubert, 1821–1857*, ix, 233, 237–38, 272, 297, 317, 322, 325, 326, 334; fictional portraits of Olga Kosakiewicz, 63–64, 85–86; *Le Figaro* articles, 151, 367n 8; *The Flies*, 136, 138, 140, 207, 366n 30, 366n 31, 376n 2; foreword to Nizan's *Aden Arabie*, 6; "The Imagination," 56; Italy, book begun on (published posthumously), 206; journals, 72, 97, 100, 103; *Kean*, 229, 374n 68; letters to Beauvoir, published 1983, 110; letters and journals, intent of publication, xiii, 350, 382n 52; *Libération* newspaper, editing and contributions, 326, 380n 6; literary estate, 279–80, 284–85, 350, 378n 31; Mathieu Delarue, characters based on himself, 63; *Melancholia* (early version of *Nausea*), 67; *Nausea*, ix, x, 71, 73, 77, 244, 299, 322, 360n 2; Nobel Prize, ix, 233, 280–83, 290; *No Exit*, 139, 142–43, 151, 153, 160, 223, 296, 366n 39; "Paris Under the Occupation," 134–35, 142; plays of, ix, 135–37, 376n 2 (*see also specific titles*); *Portrait of an Anti-Semite*, 344; *Power and Liberty* (with Pierre Victor), 332–33; preface, Cartier-Bresson's China book, 229; preface, Frantz Fanon's *Wretched of the Earth*, 261, 379n 22; reading and influences, 97, 119, 147; rejections of early works, 55; *The Reprieve*, 153; *The Respectful Prostitute*, 167, 376n 2; *Roads to Freedom*, 127; Russia, articles and apologia for, 209, 231–32, 268–70, 283, 285–86, 374n 73; *Saint Genet*, ix, 199–200, 206, 233, 238; *The Salem Witches*, 237; *Search for a Method*, 248; *Situations*, 322; *Temps modernes*, journal, 153, 156, 167, 169, 210, 212, 237, 315, 368n 25; *The Victors*, 167; "The Wall," 73; *The Wall*, 87, 127, 361n 36, *Words*, ix, 3–4, 77, 227, 232, 233, 248, 268, 276, 279, 282, 284, 322, 331, 376n 2, 377n 11

SIMONE DE BEAUVOIR AND: advice on her writing, 84–85, 103, 107, 170, 208, 225–26, 243, 270, 325, 374n 13; Algerian trip, 1947, 192; American trip, 1945, and, 151–52; in Berlin and, 1933, 52; Brazil trip, 1960, 257–58; China trip, 1955, 236; consummation of relationship, 1929, 26–27; Cuba trip, 1960, 256, 257; Czechoslovakia trip, 1968, 314; daily schedule, later life, 311; declarations of love, 79–80, 335, 346; discontent and, 55; Easter vacation, Saint-Paul-de-Vence, 320–21; Easter vacation, Saint-Tropez, 1953, 220–21; as famous couple, 155–56, 161, 234, 244, 274, 299; first meetings of, 1929, 1–3, 11–13, 15–16; first summer in Limousin, 1929, 20–23; games between them, 64–65; her love affairs and his response, x, 42, 80–81, 84, 103, 104–6, 108–10, 156–58, 188–89; illness of Simone, 1937, 67–68; inequality of relationship, 34–35; interview, 1975, and, 334–35; Italy trips, 169, 211, 224–26, 330–31; Italy, yearly retreat in Rome, 1956 on, 241–42, 249, 270, 277–78, 287–88, 320, 324, 327, 329–30; Japan, 1966, 294–95; living arrangements, Paris, 1937–1939, 72–73; Mégève, 1945, letters to, 158; Middle East trip, 1967, 306–7; military service, 1929–1930, relationship during, 33–41, 43; Morocco trip, 1938, 79, 81–83; note from 1930, 34; "oneness," 98, 119; as open relationship, xii–xiii; pact, 27–30, 43, 50, 97–98, 159, 164, 172, 220, 222, 301–2; physical relationship, 26–27, 35–36, 104, 108, 127–28; reading and criticism by Beauvoir of his writing, 103, 107, 249, 251, 325, 342–45; in Rouen, 1932–1933, 50; Russian trips, 236, 262, 263–65, 273–74, 276–77, 290–94, 295; Sahara crossing with,

201; Saint-Lambert trip, 1947, 184–85; Spanish trip, 1931, 43–44; stepfather's disapproval, 37; summer vacations with, 70–71, 92–93, 167–68, 226–27, 240–41, 360n 5; tenth anniversary, 98; vacation, 1934, 54; Yugoslavia visits, 226, 240
TEACHING CAREER: fellowship at French Institute, Berlin, 51–52; influence and popularity, xii, 49; Laon, 66, 69; Le Havre, 43, 44, 48–49; Paris, 71, 73, 125, 133
WORLD WAR II: called up, 1939, 93–95, 96–98; impact on, x, 41, 146, 153; leaves, 1940, 106–8, 113; letters to Beauvoir, 102; liberation of Paris and, 145; meeting with Beauvoir, Brumath, 1939, 102–4; as prisoner of war, 118–19; as reservist, 96; resistance efforts, 122, 123–26, 365n 3; resistance group, CNE, 140, 145, 366n 31; return to Paris, March, 1941, 121–22
Sartre (Lévy), xiv
Satin Slipper, The (Claudel), 136
Schoenmann, Ralph, 332
Schwarzer, Alice, xii, 372n 28
Schweitzer, Albert, 3
Schweitzer, Charles, 3, 27
Scotland, 310
Shay, Art, 370n 25
Shoah (film), 315, 342
Sholokhov, Mikhail, 283, 290
Siegel, Liliane, 261–62, 284–85, 319, 330, 331, 334, 337, 341, 351
Signoret, Simone, 259, 319
Silone, Ignazio, 168
Simon, Pierre, 376n 41
Simon, René, 224
Simone de Beauvoir (film), 366n 45
Simonov, Konstantin, 229, 236–37
Sinyavsky, Andrei, 290
Social Contract (Rousseau), 11
Solzhenitsyn, Alexander, 264, 269, 290, 331
Sorbonne. *See* Paris
Sorokine (Moffat), Nathalie, 105–6, 117–18, 120, 124, 129, 130, 133, 134, 141, 143, 145, 157–58, 159, 177–78, 365n 18, 365n 19; scandal caused by, 131–33, 364n 64, 366n 22
Soupault, Philippe, 170

Spain, 202, 313
Spain Day by Day (Bost), 202, 371n 56
Stalin, Josef, and Stalinist Russia, xiii, 168, 171, 212, 374n 73
Stevens, George, 177, 178
structuralism, 332
Swing, Sally, 187, 189–90

Taverny, France, 117, 141–42
Temps modernes, Les, 153, 156, 159, 167, 169, 189, 196, 210, 212, 213, 219, 227, 229, 237, 247, 259, 260, 281, 289, 315, 333, 339, 347, 360n 5, 368n 25, 369n 50; "Everyday Sexism" column, 315
Testament amoureux, Le (Rezvani), 223, 373n 36
Thaw, The (Ehrenburg), 376n 1
Todd, Oliver, 219, 337–38, 381n 34
Tous les désespoirs sont permis (Papatakis), 114, 364n 48, 364n 56
Trieste, Italy, 226
Tuffreau, Suzanne, 45–46, 358n 34
Tunisia, 158–59, 199, 297, 368n 31

United States: *America Day by Day* published in, 179, 370n 15; Bay of Pigs and embargo of Cuba, 262; Beauvoir's American tour, 1947, 170–80; Beauvoir's return to Chicago, 1947 and 1950, 186, 370n 25; Cold War and, 170–71, 210; *The Coming of Age* published in, 321–22; fame of Sartre and Beauvoir in, 160–63; *Force of Circumstance* translated, 301; *The Mandarins* published in, 239–40; racism in, 149, 150, 167; Rosenberg executions, 224–26; Sartre's criticism of, 225–26, 243, 374n 13; Sartre's visits, 1945–1946, 147–52, 160–63; *The Second Sex* published in, 234; women's status in, 179–80

Valéry, Paul, 16
Vanetti, Dolores, 149–53, 160, 162–64, 174, 180, 184, 186, 188, 191–92, 202, 204, 243, 299, 301, 368n 21, 371n 35
Verstraeten, Pierre, 382n 49
Vian, Boris, 154–55, 159, 169, 196–97, 207, 208, 220, 368n 27, 379n 33
Vian, Michelle, 196–97, 198, 199–201, 207–8, 209, 220–21, 222, 228, 230, 234, 240–41, 249–51, 253, 256, 284,

Vian, Michelle *(cont.)*: 289, 311, 312, 313,
    317–18, 321, 334, 335, 336–37, 338,
    345–46, 351, 368n 27, 371n 43, 374n
    66, 376n 41, 378n 31, 379n 33;
    abortions of, 200–201, 256, 319;
    attempt to have Sartre's child, 256,
    376n 41
Vian, Patrick, 317
Vichy, France, 117
Victor, Pierre (Benny Lévy), 315, 316–17,
    331–34, 338–40, 346, 350, 351;
    discussions with Sartre, 342–45
Vietnam: Dien Bien Phu, 237; Russell
    Tribunal, 308–9, 332; U.S. war in,
    protesting, 294, 308–9
Ville, Jean-André, 52
Ville, Marie, 52, 55
Vitold, Michel, 151
Vittorini, Elio, 168
VVV magazine, 150

Weatherby, W. J., 305
Weill-Hallé, Lagroua, 256, 376n 41
Wolfe, Bernard, 175, 180
Women: abortion issue and the
    "Manifesto of the 343," 319, 380n 48,
    380n 49; Beauvoir on American,
    179–80; Beauvoir on, in *The Second
    Sex*, 194–96, 209; liberation groups,
    318–19
World War II: Auschwitz, 143; Bost
    called up, 1939, 93, 101, 363n 43; Bost
    return to Paris, 1940, 120; Bost
    wounded, 115–16, 117; Dachau, 152;
    death of Nizan, 6, 116; death of
    Politzer, 41; Drancy internment camp,
    143; France, Free Zone, 117, 124, 134;
    France surrenders, 116–17; French
    complicity with Jewish genocide, 216;
    French Resistance (communist), 124,

125, 140, 143, 216; Fresnes prison,
    France, 143; German invasion of
    Denmark and Norway, 113; German
    invasion of Holland, Belgium, and
    Luxembourg, 115; Germany
    surrenders, 152; Gestapo in Paris and
    arrests, 142, 143; impact on Beauvoir
    and Sartre's thinking, x; Japan
    surrenders, 153; Jewish persecution,
    121, 133, 136, 143; liberation of Paris,
    144–46; Maginot Line broken, 115;
    Paris occupied, 116–46; "Phony War,"
    97; Sartre and Beauvoir in resistance
    (Socialism and Liberty), 122, 123–26,
    365n 3; Sartre called up, 1939, 93–95,
    96, 101; Sartre in the CNE (National
    Committee of Writers), 140, 145,
    366n 31; Sartre as prisoner of war,
    118–19; Sartre return to Paris, 1941,
    121–22; "Under the Boot" resistance
    group, 123; Vichy government and
    French collaborators, 117, 133, 135, 138,
    139, 145–46, 179; Zazou movement,
    196–97
Wretched of the Earth, The (Fanon), 261,
    379n 22
Wright, Ellen and Richard, 174–75, 180,
    187

Yugoslavia, 226, 240

Zeitgeist magazine, 303
Zonin, Alexander, 264
Zonina, Lena, 263–78, 280, 282–84,
    285, 286, 289–94, 295, 297, 312–13,
    314, 330, 351, 376n 2, 376n 7, 376n 9,
    377n 14, 378n 37

Zuorro, Marc, 65, 66–67, 68

PERMISSIONS

Grateful acknowledgment is made to Éditions Gallimard for permission to quote from the following books:

Simone de Beauvoir: *Mémoires d'une jeune fille rangée, La Force de l'âge, La Force des choses, Tout compte fait, Le Sang des autres, Journal de guerre, Une mort très douce,* and *La Cérémonie des adieux.*

Jean-Paul Sartre: *Carnets de la drôle de guerre* and *Situations I* (1948), *Situations III* (1949), *Situations IV* (1964).

Simone de Beauvoir and Jacques-Laurent Bost: *Correspondance croisée (1937–1940).* Claude Francis and Fernande Gontier: *Les Écrits de Simone de Beauvoir.* Michel Leiris: *Journal (1922–1989).* Raymond Queneau: *Journaux (1914–1965)* and *Journal (1939–1940).* Françoise Sagan: *Avec mon meilleur souvenir.*

Grateful acknowledgment also is made to the following for permission to reprint previously published material:

Nelson Algren. Excerpts from *Ramparts, Zeitgeist,* and *Harper's Magazine.* Reprinted with the permission of the Estate of Nelson Algren.

Jacques-Pierre Arnette. Excerpt from "Simone de Beauvoir: Ces lettres qui ébranlent un mythe" in *Le Point.* Reprinted with permission.

Deirdre Bair. Excerpts from *Simone de Beauvoir.* Copyright © 1990 Deirdre Bair. Reprinted in the U.S. with the permission of Simon & Schuster Adult Publishing Group. Reprinted in the U.K. with the permission of The Random House Group Ltd.

Simone de Beauvoir. Excerpts from unpublished early journals, unpublished correspondence, and the short story, "Malentendu à Moscou." Reprinted with the permission of Sylvie Le Bon de Beauvoir. Excerpts from *Adieux: A Farewell to Sartre,* translated by Patrick O'Brian. Translation copyright © 1984 by Patrick O'Brian. Reprinted in the U.S. with the permission of Pantheon Books, a division of Random House, Inc.